# ECONOMIC PROBLEMS IN A NONLINEAR WORLD

## A COMPLEXITY ECONOMICS INQUIRY INTO INEQUALITY, INFLATION, DEBT, MARKETS, AND CRISIS

LAWRENCE R. KUNKEL

ISBN: 979-8-9953857-6-9 (Hardcover print)
ISBN: 979-8-9953857-7-6 (Softcover print)
ISBN: 979-8-9953857-8-3 (Digital)

First Edition.



The Economic Justice Press, New York City, printed and sent out
The design and typography were done by The Economic Justice Press.

# TABLE OF CONTENTS

# List of Figures

## Chapter 1

# Introduction: The End of Simple Economic Explanations

Modern economic life has become too complex for simple explanations. The great economic problems of our time no longer fit neatly into the familiar categories through which they are most often discussed. Inflation is not merely a problem of too much money. Inequality is not merely the result of differences in talent, effort, or education. Debt is not merely a question of fiscal irresponsibility. Housing scarcity is not merely a failure to build enough homes. Financial crises are not merely accidents of speculation. Supply chain breakdowns are not merely logistical failures. Labor market instability is not merely a mismatch between workers and jobs. Each of these problems is real, material, and measurable, but none can be understood adequately as a single-cause phenomenon.

This book begins from a simple but demanding proposition: the economy is not a machine. It is a complex adaptive system. It is composed of households, firms, banks, governments, investors, workers, technologies, institutions, expectations, narratives, rules, and power relations, all interacting with one another across time. These interactions generate outcomes that cannot be reduced to the intentions of individual actors or the isolated movement of a single variable. Economic life is recursive. Decisions today alter the conditions under which decisions are made tomorrow. Prices shape expectations; expectations shape behavior; behavior shapes institutions; and institutions shape prices. Wealth produces power, power shapes rules, rules influence markets, and markets distribute wealth. Debt enables expansion, expansion encourages leverage, leverage magnifies fragility, and fragility converts ordinary shocks into systemic crises.

In such a world, linear thinking becomes dangerous. Linear thinking assumes proportionality. If one unit of policy produces one unit of effect, then two units should produce two units. If a market is out of balance, a price adjustment should restore equilibrium. If unemployment rises, lower interest rates should stimulate demand. If inflation rises, higher interest rates should suppress it. If housing is scarce, more construction should solve the problem. If wages are too low, education should raise them. If banks are fragile, more capital should make them safe. These claims are not always wrong. Often they contain partial truths. The danger lies in treating partial truths as general laws.

Economic systems frequently respond in nonlinear ways. A small disturbance can be absorbed for years, then suddenly trigger a cascade. A policy that works under one set of conditions can fail under another. A market that appears efficient can become fragile precisely because it has optimized away redundancy. A debt burden that seems manageable can become destructive once interest rates, asset prices, or confidence cross a threshold. A housing market can remain strained for decades because scarcity, speculation, zoning, credit, local politics, and wealth inequality reinforce one another. A labor market can appear healthy while millions of workers experience insecurity, exhaustion, and declining bargaining power. Inflation can begin as a supply shock, become embedded in expectations, interact with market concentration, and produce social conflict over who will bear the cost of adjustment.

The central thesis of this book is that the most important economic problems of the twenty-first century are nonlinear problems. They are generated by feedback loops, thresholds, cumulative advantage, network effects, institutional constraints, adaptive behavior, delayed consequences, and emergent patterns. They cannot be solved by returning to the old comfort of equilibrium diagrams or by pretending that the economy is a self-correcting mechanism disturbed only by bad policy or irrational behavior. We need a different way of seeing.

Complexity economics offers a different way of seeing. It does not reject markets, prices, incentives, or rational calculation. Rather, it places them inside a broader framework. It asks how agents learn, adapt, imitate, compete, cooperate, panic, speculate, and coordinate under uncertainty. It asks how institutions shape behavior and how behavior reshapes institutions. It asks how local interactions generate macroeconomic patterns. It asks why economies can settle into inefficient, unjust, or fragile states. It asks why crises often appear sudden, even when their underlying causes have accumulated slowly. It asks why policy must be designed not only for efficiency, but also for resilience, fairness, legitimacy, and adaptive capacity.

The need for such a framework is not merely academic. The world economy has repeatedly demonstrated the inadequacy of simple explanations. The global financial crisis revealed that sophisticated financial markets could generate systemic ignorance. The instruments designed to spread risk actually concentrated it. The institutions designed to price risk often concealed it. The models designed to measure stability helped legitimate fragility. A housing downturn in one part of the financial system propagated through mortgage-backed securities, derivatives, banks, shadow banks, rating agencies, credit markets, and sovereign balance sheets. What appeared to many as a contained problem became a global crisis because the system was tightly coupled, highly leveraged, and deeply interdependent.

The pandemic economy exposed another dimension of the same problem. Supply chains celebrated for efficiency proved vulnerable to disruption. Labor markets reorganized in unpredictable ways. Demand shifted faster than production systems could adjust. Ports clogged, inventories vanished, prices moved unevenly, and governments discovered that resilience had been sacrificed in the name of lean optimization. The problem was not simply that firms made mistakes. It was that the global production system had been designed around an assumption of smooth continuity. Redundancy looked wasteful until the shock arrived. Local efficiency had produced systemic fragility.

Inflation after the pandemic further demonstrated the limits of linear explanation. Some described it as a monetary phenomenon, others as a supply shock, others as a wage problem, others as corporate opportunism, and others as the result of fiscal stimulus. Each explanation captured part of the story, but none captured the whole. Inflation emerged from the interaction of supply bottlenecks, energy prices, fiscal transfers, household balance sheets, shifting demand, labor market pressures, geopolitical conflict, monetary policy, pricing power, and expectations. It became not one thing, but a process. It moved through the economy unevenly, affecting food, energy, housing, durable goods, services, and wages in different ways. It also became political, because inflation is never merely a technical phenomenon. It is a struggle over income, security, and the distribution of pain.

Inequality reveals the same pattern over a longer time horizon. It is often discussed as if it were the natural result of individual differences in skill, effort, risk-taking, or productivity. These factors matter, but they do not explain the scale, persistence, and self-reinforcing structure of modern inequality. Inequality compounds. Wealth generates returns. Returns purchase assets. Assets appreciate. Appreciated assets provide collateral. Collateral enables borrowing. Borrowing enables further acquisition. Wealth also buys education, neighborhood advantage, political access, legal protection, tax planning, social networks, and influence over public policy. At the bottom of the distribution, the same process runs in reverse. Low income produces insecurity. Insecurity limits mobility. Limited mobility reduces opportunity. Reduced opportunity weakens bargaining power. Weak bargaining power reproduces low income.

This is not a simple distributional problem. It is a cumulative advantage machine. Once inequality becomes embedded in housing markets, education systems, health outcomes, political institutions, and financial markets, it becomes self-reinforcing. The system does not merely distribute unequal rewards. It generates unequal starting points, unequal risk exposure, unequal voice, unequal resilience, and unequal capacity to shape the future. Complexity economics helps us see inequality not as a static gap, but as a dynamic process.

Debt, too, must be understood dynamically. A certain amount of debt can support investment, consumption, and growth. But debt changes the structure of vulnerability. It links present decisions to future obligations. It makes households sensitive to job loss, firms sensitive to revenue declines, banks sensitive to asset prices, and governments sensitive to interest rates and political confidence. Debt is nonlinear because its consequences depend on context. The same level of debt may be manageable in a low-rate environment and destabilizing in a high-rate environment. It may be sustainable when growth is strong and destructive when growth slows. It may support productive investment or fuel speculative bubbles. It may expand opportunity or trap borrowers in dependency.

Debt becomes especially dangerous when it is combined with leverage, asset inflation, and optimistic expectations. Rising asset prices make borrowers and lenders feel safer. Greater perceived safety encourages more borrowing. More borrowing pushes asset prices higher. The feedback loop continues until confidence falters. Then the process reverses. Falling prices reduce collateral values. Reduced collateral triggers margin calls, defaults, or forced selling. Forced selling pushes prices lower. What looked like wealth creation becomes balance-sheet destruction. This is why financial crises often feel like sudden ruptures. The collapse appears sudden because the accumulation of fragility was gradual, hidden, and normalized.

Housing markets offer another example of nonlinear economic life. Conventional analysis often presents housing as a matter of supply and demand, and this is not wrong. Scarcity matters. Construction matters. Interest rates matter. Yet housing is also a positional good, an asset class, a credit instrument, a zoning problem, a political battlefield, and a mechanism for transmitting inequality across generations. A home is shelter, but it is also collateral, retirement security, school access, neighborhood membership, and speculative investment. Once housing becomes a primary vehicle of wealth accumulation, its social function becomes distorted. Existing owners benefit from rising prices, while new buyers and renters suffer. Local politics then reflects this conflict. Those who already own scarce assets often resist the changes that would reduce scarcity.

This creates a self-reinforcing trap. High housing prices increase the wealth of incumbents. Wealthy incumbents gain political influence. Political influence restricts supply or shapes development in ways that preserve scarcity. Scarcity raises prices further. Younger households, renters, lower-income families, and newcomers are pushed outward or downward. Labor markets suffer because workers cannot afford to live near opportunity. Family formation is delayed. Commutes lengthen. Public trust erodes. What begins as a housing problem becomes a social, political, and macroeconomic problem.

Labor markets are similarly misunderstood when reduced to a simple supply-and-demand framework. Workers are not interchangeable units of labor. Jobs are not merely wage offers. Labor markets are adaptive networks shaped by skills, credentials, geography, discrimination, family obligations, bargaining power, firm structure, technology, norms, unions, immigration, monopsony power, and social expectations. People do not simply move wherever wages are highest. They are embedded in families, communities, housing markets, care responsibilities, health constraints, and identity. Firms do not simply pay the market wage. They structure jobs, shape productivity, control information, influence policy, and exercise power.

In a nonlinear economy, labor market outcomes can diverge sharply from the predictions of simple models. A region can have job openings and still suffer from unemployment or underemployment. Wages can stagnate even when productivity rises. Low unemployment can coexist with insecurity. Technological change can increase aggregate output while weakening the bargaining position of large groups of workers. Labor markets can become segmented, with high-wage networks pulling away from low-wage networks. Once this segmentation occurs, mobility becomes harder. Those outside the high-opportunity networks face barriers that cannot be overcome by motivation alone.

Financial markets intensify the argument. Classical accounts often treat financial markets as information-processing mechanisms. Prices are said to reflect available information. Investors allocate capital based on risk and return. Speculation helps reveal value. Yet actual financial markets are also arenas of imitation, narrative contagion, leverage, panic, algorithmic amplification, regulatory arbitrage, and institutional herding. Investors do not merely process information independently. They watch one another. They infer meaning from price movements. They fear missing out. They fear being left holding losses. They respond to incentives shaped by quarterly performance, benchmarks, compensation structures, and reputational pressures.

The result is that financial markets can generate the very signals they then interpret as reality. Rising prices attract buyers. New buyers push prices higher. Higher prices validate the original optimism. Analysts revise narratives. Credit expands. Skeptics are punished for being early. Risk models incorporate recent calm and declare the system safer. The boom becomes self-confirming until it is not. Then falling prices produce the opposite feedback loop. Confidence evaporates, liquidity disappears, and institutions discover that what they treated as diversification was actually correlated exposure.

Technological change adds another layer of nonlinear disruption. New technologies do not simply increase productivity in a smooth and evenly distributed way. They reorganize industries, alter labor demand, create new monopolies, destroy old business models, reshape consumer behavior, and shift political power. Technology may begin as a tool, but it can become an infrastructure. Once it becomes infrastructure, it shapes the conditions under which other actors must operate. Digital platforms provide a clear example. Their value often increases with scale. More users attract more users. More data improves services. Better services attract more customers. More customers attract more sellers, advertisers, developers, or complementary businesses. These network effects can generate winner-take-most markets.

Such markets do not behave like the competitive markets described in introductory textbooks. They can produce rapid concentration, dependency, surveillance, behavioral manipulation, and new forms of economic extraction. The problem is not technology itself. The problem is that technological systems evolve within institutional environments. If the rules reward concentration, extraction, and opacity, then technology will amplify those tendencies. If the rules encourage openness, competition, accountability, and broad-based capability, then technology can support shared prosperity. The effect of technology is therefore not predetermined. It is emergent, shaped by feedback between innovation, markets, law, culture, and power.

The recurring theme is this: economic problems become harder to solve when we misunderstand their structure. Linear models encourage policymakers to search for single levers. Raise rates. Cut taxes. Increase spending. Deregulate. Regulate. Build more. Educate more. Save more. Consume less. These prescriptions may sometimes be necessary, but they are rarely sufficient. Complex systems require attention to interaction effects. A policy may work in isolation and fail in combination. A reform may help one part of the system while destabilizing another. A subsidy may relieve immediate pain while reinforcing long-term dependency. A rate hike may reduce inflation but trigger financial stress. A tax cut may stimulate investment or inflate assets. A housing policy may increase supply but accelerate displacement if not designed carefully. A labor reform may raise wages but fail if firms respond by automating, outsourcing, or misclassifying.

This does not mean that policy is futile. On the contrary, complexity makes policy more important, not less. But it changes what good policy requires. Policy must be adaptive rather than rigid, systemic rather than fragmented, precautionary rather than overconfident, and morally aware rather than merely technical. It must ask not only, "What is the immediate effect?" but also, "What feedback loops will this create?" It must ask not only, "Is this efficient?" but also, "Is this resilient?" It must ask not only, "Does this raise aggregate output?" but also, "Who gains power, who bears risk, and what happens when conditions change?"

The failure of simple economic explanations is partly a failure of metaphor. For generations, economic thought has been shaped by mechanical images. The economy has been imagined as a machine, a clock, a balancing mechanism, or a system of pipes and flows. These metaphors are not useless. They clarify certain relationships. They help organize thought. But they also conceal. Machines have parts with fixed functions. Complex economies have agents that learn and adapt. Machines can be repaired by replacing broken components. Economies change when interventions alter incentives, expectations, norms, and power. Machines do not interpret their repair manuals. Economic actors interpret policy, anticipate other actors, and change behavior accordingly.

The mechanical imagination also encourages the search for equilibrium. Equilibrium is a powerful concept, but it can become a trap. In many models, equilibrium represents a state in which plans are mutually consistent, markets clear, and no actor has reason to change behavior. But real economies often operate far from equilibrium. They are shaped by innovation, uncertainty, conflict, institutional change, financial cycles, technological disruption, ecological constraints, and political struggle. Even when temporary stability emerges, it may not be just, efficient, or durable. A society can settle into a bad equilibrium, such as persistent poverty, entrenched inequality, underinvestment, low trust, or political paralysis. Stability is not always success. Sometimes it is stagnation. Sometimes it is repression. Sometimes it is the calm before a crisis.

Complexity economics invites us to replace the ideal of equilibrium with the study of patterns, processes, and regimes. Instead of asking whether the system naturally returns to balance, we ask what kinds of feedback dominate. Are they stabilizing or destabilizing? Do they reduce inequality or amplify it? Do they disperse power or concentrate it? Do they absorb shocks or magnify them? Do they encourage learning or lock in failure? Do they produce resilience or fragility? Do they strengthen legitimacy or corrode it?

This shift is intellectually significant because it changes how we understand causation. In simple models, causation often moves in one direction. A change in money supply causes a change in prices. A change in tax rates causes a change in investment. A change in wages causes a change in employment. A change in interest rates affects borrowing. In complex systems, causation is circular. Prices affect wages, wages affect expectations, expectations affect prices, and policy affects all three. Asset prices affect credit, credit affects asset prices, and both affect confidence. Inequality affects politics, politics affects institutions, institutions affect markets, and markets affect inequality. Cause and effect become entangled through feedback.

This does not abolish responsibility. Complexity should not become an excuse for fatalism. It should not allow leaders to say, "The system is too complicated, so no one is accountable." Rather, it demands a deeper form of accountability. If policymakers, executives, investors, and institutions operate within complex systems, they have a responsibility to understand how their actions may amplify fragility, inequality, or instability. Ignorance of feedback is not innocence. A banker who profits from leverage while socializing losses participates in systemic risk. A corporation that uses market power to raise prices during scarcity participates in distributive conflict. A government that ignores housing scarcity for decades participates in the reproduction of inequality. A central bank that treats inflation only as aggregate demand may miss the institutional and sectoral dynamics that shape price formation. A political system that allows wealth to purchase influence participates in cumulative advantage.

The purpose of this book is therefore both analytical and moral. It is analytical because it seeks to explain economic problems more accurately. It is moral because explanation shapes responsibility. If inequality is understood as the natural result of merit, then society owes little to those left behind. If it is understood as a cumulative advantage process shaped by institutions, then justice requires institutional redesign. If inflation is understood only as excessive demand, then the burden of adjustment may fall primarily on workers through unemployment. If inflation is understood as a conflictual process involving supply chains, energy, market power, expectations, and distribution, then policy must be more nuanced. If debt crises are understood as the result of individual irresponsibility, then punishment appears appropriate. If they are understood as systemic outcomes of credit regimes, asset inflation, and insecurity, then prevention, restructuring, and regulation become central.

The end of simple explanations does not mean the end of explanation. It means the end of explanations that comfort us by making the world smaller than it is. Complexity does not tell us that everything is unknowable. It tells us that knowledge must be humble, relational, and adaptive. We can identify patterns. We can map feedback loops. We can study thresholds. We can build institutions that reduce fragility. We can design policies that distribute risk more fairly. We can create buffers, circuit breakers, automatic stabilizers, public options, countercyclical tools, and democratic mechanisms of correction. We can learn from failure. But we cannot govern wisely if we cling to models that deny the nature of the system we are governing.

The intellectual arc of this book follows from this premise. The next chapter introduces nonlinearity itself, the idea that economic relationships are often disproportional, context-dependent, and threshold-sensitive. Nonlinearity means that more can become different. A manageable debt load can become a crisis. A modest price increase can become an inflationary psychology. A local housing shortage can become a national affordability crisis. A small technological advantage can become market dominance. A temporary supply disruption can become a geopolitical vulnerability. Nonlinearity is the language of tipping points, cascades, increasing returns, and emergent order.

The chapter on inflation then examines price instability as a feedback process rather than a single monetary event. Inflation moves through expectations, contracts, wages, supply chains, energy systems, market structure, and political narratives. It is not simply a technical inconvenience. It is a social conflict over claims on real resources. Some groups can protect themselves from inflation, while others cannot. Some firms can pass along costs, while others cannot. Some households own appreciating assets, while others face rising rents, food bills, and debt costs. Inflation is therefore both macroeconomic and moral. It reveals the structure of power in the economy.

The chapter on debt, leverage, and systemic fragility explores how financial obligations bind the present to the future. Debt can be productive, but it can also create chains of vulnerability. The chapter examines households, corporations, banks, governments, and financial markets as connected balance sheets. It argues that fragility often accumulates during periods of apparent stability. When volatility is low, actors borrow more. When borrowing increases, the system becomes more sensitive to shocks. When shocks arrive, the adjustment is nonlinear. The problem is not debt alone. The problem is debt embedded in a system of leverage, asset dependence, and confidence.

The chapter on inequality treats unequal outcomes as the product of cumulative advantage. It examines how wealth, education, health, geography, political influence, and social networks reinforce one another.

It argues that inequality is not merely a distributional endpoint, but a generative process. Once inequality becomes embedded, it shapes the rules of the game. It determines who can take risks, who can recover from failure, who can access opportunity, and who can influence public decisions. Inequality is therefore not only an economic problem. It is a systemic threat to democracy, legitimacy, and social cohesion.

The chapter on housing examines scarcity as a dynamic system. Housing markets are shaped by construction costs, zoning, interest rates, speculation, credit, local control, demographic change, and wealth inequality. The chapter argues that housing is where macroeconomics enters daily life. It determines access to schools, jobs, safety, family stability, and intergenerational wealth. When housing becomes unaffordable, the effects ripple outward through labor markets, birth rates, migration, homelessness, public finance, and political resentment. Housing scarcity is therefore not a side issue. It is one of the central nonlinear systems of modern capitalism.

The chapter on labor markets challenges the idea that work can be understood through a simple wage-quantity diagram. Labor markets are networks of power, skill, identity, geography, care, institutional rules, and technological change. The chapter explores monopsony power, credential barriers, occupational sorting, unions, fissured workplaces, algorithmic management, and the decline of worker voice. It argues that labor markets do not merely allocate workers to jobs. They shape dignity, identity, family life, civic participation, and democratic stability. A society that treats labor as a commodity eventually destabilizes the human foundations of prosperity.

The chapter on supply chains examines the fragility of efficiency. For decades, firms were rewarded for minimizing inventories, outsourcing production, consolidating suppliers, and optimizing logistics. These strategies lowered costs, but they also reduced buffers. The result was a production system that appeared efficient under normal conditions but vulnerable under stress. The chapter argues that resilience must be treated as a form of economic value. Redundancy, geographic diversity, public capacity, and strategic reserves may look inefficient in the short run, but they are essential to systemic stability.

The chapter on financial markets studies herding, cascades, and the instability of expectations. It examines how investors imitate one another, how leverage magnifies movements, how algorithms accelerate reactions, and how narratives shape valuation. It argues that financial markets are not passive mirrors of economic reality. They help create the reality they claim to measure. This creative power makes them useful, but also dangerous. Without proper rules, financial systems can convert optimism into bubbles, uncertainty into panic, and private risk-taking into public loss.

The chapter on technological change examines disruptive feedback. Technology transforms productivity, but it also transforms power. It creates new capabilities, new dependencies, new monopolies, and new vulnerabilities. The chapter considers automation, artificial intelligence, digital platforms, data extraction, network effects, and the changing structure of work. It argues that technology policy cannot be separated from political economy. The question is not whether technology will advance. It will. The question is whether institutions will guide that advance toward broad-based human flourishing or allow it to intensify inequality, surveillance, and economic insecurity.

The chapter on public policy under conditions of complexity then turns from diagnosis to governance. If economies are nonlinear systems, policy must be designed differently. It must focus on resilience, feedback monitoring, adaptive regulation, institutional learning, distributive legitimacy, and democratic accountability. Policymakers must abandon the fantasy of perfect control, but they must also reject passivity. Complexity requires active stewardship. The goal is not to command the economy like a machine, but to cultivate conditions under which markets, institutions, and communities can adapt without collapsing into crisis or injustice.

The conclusion, "Economic Governance After Equilibrium," draws the argument together. It suggests that the old debate between the market and the state is too simplistic. The real question is how societies design systems of coordination, correction, resilience, and justice. Markets are powerful forms of discovery and allocation, but they are not morally self-sufficient. States are necessary institutions of stabilization and collective purpose, but they are not automatically wise. Civil society, law, democratic voice, public investment, and moral norms all matter. Economic governance after equilibrium means designing institutions for a world of uncertainty, feedback, and interdependence.

This book is written against the complacency of reduction. Reduction is tempting because it simplifies responsibility. If inflation has one cause, then one institution can fix it. If inequality has one cause, then one reform can solve it. If financial crises are caused by a few bad actors, then punishment can restore order. If housing scarcity is caused only by supply, then construction alone is enough. If labor market insecurity is caused only by inadequate skills, then training is the answer. But the world is more difficult than that. Economic problems are layered. They are historical. They are institutional. They are behavioral. They are political. They are moral.

To say this is not to make analysis vague. It is to make it more precise. A vague analysis says, "Everything is connected," and stops there. A complexity analysis asks how things are connected, which feedback loops matter, where thresholds lie, what patterns emerge, who benefits from the current structure, who bears risk, and what interventions might change the system's trajectory. Complexity is not a retreat from rigor. It is a demand for better rigor.

The old economic imagination sought elegance through simplification. The new economic imagination must seek understanding through relationship. It must study how wage systems interact with housing systems, how debt interacts with asset prices, how inequality interacts with politics, how financial markets interact with expectations, how supply chains interact with geopolitical risk, how technology interacts with labor power, and how public policy interacts with legitimacy. It must treat the economy not as a set of isolated markets, but as an evolving ecology of institutions, incentives, behaviors, and moral choices.

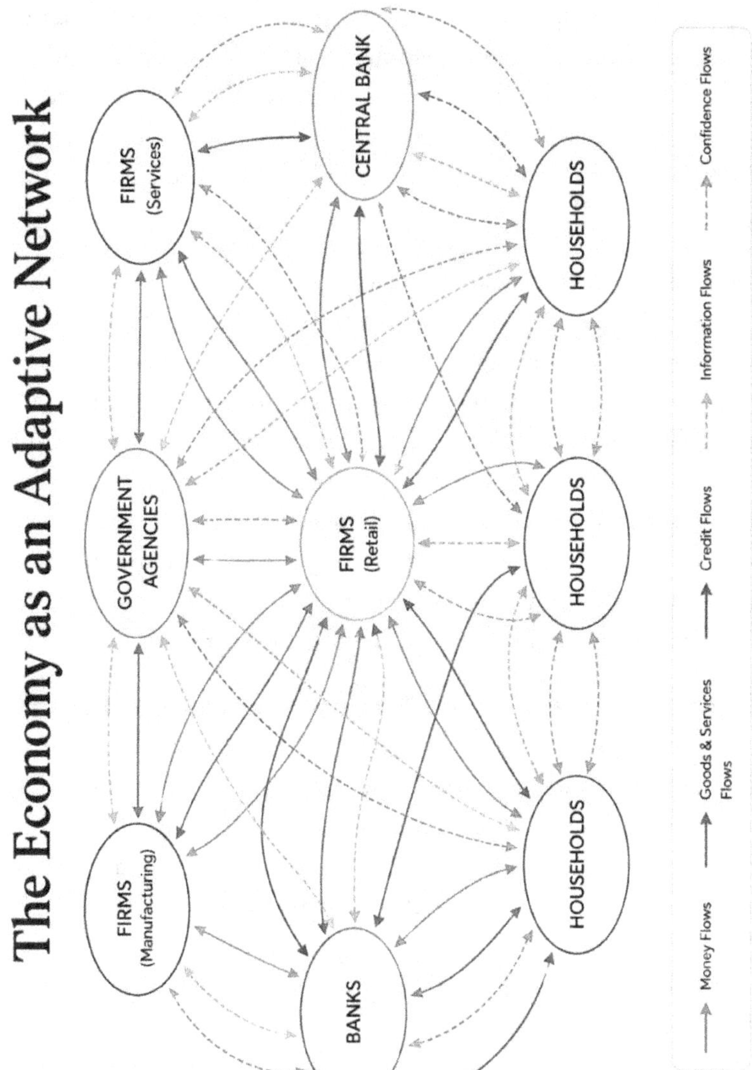


*Figure 1.0 – The Economy as an Adaptive Network*

The term "ecology" is important. An ecology is not a machine. It is a living system of interdependence. Remove one species, and the consequences may move through the system in unexpected ways. Introduce a new predator, and the balance changes. Reduce diversity, and resilience declines. Stress the system long enough, and it may cross a threshold into a new regime. Economies are not biological ecosystems, but the analogy is useful because it emphasizes adaptation, interaction, and fragility. A healthy economy, like a healthy ecology, requires diversity, redundancy, balance, renewal, and limits. It cannot be judged solely by output. It must be judged by whether it can sustain life, dignity, opportunity, and stability over time.

This ecological perspective also clarifies why economic policy cannot be morally neutral. Every economic system distributes security and insecurity. Every market order assigns bargaining power. Every tax code rewards some activities more than others. Every monetary regime protects certain claims and exposes others. Every housing policy shapes who belongs where. Every labor law defines the practical meaning of dignity at work. Every financial regulation determines how much private risk can be imposed on the public. There is no purely technical economy outside moral judgment. The denial of moral choice is itself a moral choice, usually one that protects the existing distribution of power.

Simple explanations often survive because they serve interests. They make inequality appear deserved, fragility appear accidental, concentration appear efficient, and insecurity appear personal. They turn systemic outcomes into individual failures. They ask indebted households why they borrowed, but not why wages stagnated, housing costs soared, healthcare became unaffordable, and credit filled the gap. They ask workers why they lack skills, but not why firms degraded jobs, weakened unions, outsourced risk, and captured productivity gains. They ask renters why they cannot buy homes, but not why housing became an asset strategy for the already wealthy. They ask citizens why they distrust institutions, but not why institutions repeatedly failed to protect them from predation, crisis, and abandonment.

Complexity economics disrupts these stories. It does not eliminate individual agency, but it refuses to isolate agency from structure. People make choices, but they make choices within systems that shape incentives, constraints, information, and risk. A household's financial behavior cannot be separated from wages, rents, healthcare costs, credit markets, and social expectations. A firm's pricing behavior cannot be separated from market concentration, supply conditions, shareholder pressure, and consumer dependency. A government's fiscal choices cannot be separated from political coalitions, institutional capacity, bond markets, demographic change, and social needs. A worker's career cannot be separated from education, geography, discrimination, technology, and bargaining power.

The great danger of simple economic explanations is that they encourage cruel policy. If poverty is simple, then the poor are at fault. If unemployment is simple, then the unemployed lack effort. If debt is simple, then borrowers lack discipline. If inflation is simple, then workers must accept unemployment to restore price stability. If housing is simple, then displacement is merely the cost of growth. If markets are simple, then regulation is interference. If crises are simple, then rescue can be temporary while the deeper structure remains unchanged.

A nonlinear world demands a more humane economics because it reveals shared vulnerability. In complex systems, no group is fully insulated from systemic failure. Inequality may benefit elites for a time, but extreme inequality corrodes demand, legitimacy, trust, and democratic stability. Financial deregulation may enrich insiders, but systemic crisis spreads outward. Housing scarcity may enrich property owners, but it weakens labor mobility, family formation, and social cohesion. Underinvestment in public health may save money in the short run, but it magnifies collective vulnerability. Climate neglect may benefit current incumbents, but it destabilizes insurance, agriculture, migration, infrastructure, and public finance. The fantasy of separation is one of the deepest errors of modern political economy.

Interdependence does not mean sameness. Different groups experience the economy differently. The wealthy experience inflation differently from the poor. Homeowners experience housing inflation differently from renters. Creditors experience debt differently from debtors. Asset owners experience monetary policy differently from wage earners. Platform owners experience technological change differently from workers subject to algorithmic control. Complexity economics helps explain these differences because it pays attention to position within the system. Where one stands in the network determines what one sees, what risks one bears, what options one has, and what forms of adaptation are available.

This positional insight is crucial for democracy. Democracies fail when large groups come to believe that institutions no longer see them, hear them, or protect them. Economic complexity can either be acknowledged democratically or exploited demagogically. When leaders refuse to explain systemic problems honestly, citizens search for simpler stories. They may blame immigrants, foreign competitors, urban elites, rural voters, central banks, corporations, welfare recipients, or cultural enemies. Some of these criticisms may contain fragments of truth, but demagoguery turns fragments into total explanations. It offers emotional clarity at the price of analytical falsehood.

A democratic economics for a nonlinear world must therefore do more than design better models. It must cultivate better public understanding. Citizens do not need to become technical economists, but they do need a language for feedback, interdependence, power, fragility, and cumulative advantage. They need to understand why a policy may have delayed effects, why a crisis may have many causes, why markets may fail without villains, why villains may hide behind markets, and why justice is not separate from stability. Public explanation is part of public governance. A democracy that cannot explain its economy cannot govern it well.

The intellectual humility required by complexity should not be mistaken for indecision. Humility means recognizing uncertainty, not surrendering to it. It means designing policies that can learn. It means monitoring outcomes, correcting mistakes, and building institutions that can adapt. It means avoiding overconfidence in elegant theories that ignore lived reality. It means respecting evidence while recognizing that evidence is always interpreted within models. It means acknowledging that economic policy is not engineering in the narrow sense. It is institutional design under uncertainty.

Good institutional design begins by asking what kinds of failure are likely. Where can shocks enter the system? Which actors are overleveraged? Which households lack buffers? Which markets are too concentrated? Which supply chains lack redundancy? Which communities are exposed to environmental risk? Which public institutions lack capacity? Which narratives could trigger panic or resentment? Which incentives reward short-term extraction over long-term resilience? Which groups can externalize risk onto others? These questions move policy beyond the fantasy of equilibrium and toward the discipline of systemic care.

Systemic care is not sentimental. It is practical. A society that allows millions of households to live one emergency away from ruin is not efficient. It is fragile. A society that permits financial institutions to privatize gains and socialize losses is not innovative. It is reckless. A society that treats housing primarily as an asset class is not prosperous. It is cannibalizing the foundations of family and community life. A society that concentrates technological power without accountability is not future-oriented. It is creating new dependencies. A society that celebrates cheap goods while ignoring brittle supply chains is not well managed. It is mistaking low prices for real security.

The end of simple explanations also requires rethinking the meaning of prosperity. If prosperity is defined only as gross domestic product, asset values, or aggregate consumption, then the deeper conditions of stability disappear from view. A nation can grow while becoming more unequal. It can innovate while making work more precarious. It can increase asset wealth while making housing unattainable. It can lower consumer prices while weakening domestic capacity. It can expand credit while increasing fragility. It can produce billionaires while producing despair. Aggregate measures can rise while the system becomes morally and structurally unstable.

A complexity approach asks whether prosperity is broadly distributed, institutionally resilient, socially legitimate, and ecologically sustainable. It asks whether households have buffers, whether workers have voice, whether communities have investment, whether markets remain competitive, whether finance serves production, whether technology serves human development, and whether democratic institutions can correct failure. Prosperity is not merely the output of an economy. It is the quality of the system that produces and distributes economic life.

This book does not claim to offer a final theory of everything. No serious complexity approach could make such a claim. Rather, it offers a framework for better questions. It asks readers to look at familiar problems with new eyes. Inflation is not simply a price problem. Debt is not simply a budget problem. Inequality is not simply a fairness problem. Housing is not simply a construction problem. Labor is not simply a market-clearing problem. Supply chains are not simply logistics. Finance is not simply capital allocation. Technology is not simply progress. Policy is not simply intervention. Each is a complex system embedded in other systems.

To see this clearly is to understand why our politics so often disappoints. Political debate rewards simplicity. Campaigns require slogans. Media systems favor conflict. Interest groups prefer explanations that protect their advantages. Bureaucracies divide problems into departments. Academic disciplines divide reality into specialties. Markets reward short-term gains. Citizens overwhelmed by complexity often seek clarity wherever they can find it. The result is a public sphere in which the problems are systemic but the explanations are fragmented.

This fragmentation has consequences. Inflation policy becomes separated from competition policy, energy policy, labor policy, and supply chain policy. Housing policy becomes separated from transportation, education, finance, and climate policy. Labor policy becomes separated from antitrust, trade, immigration, care work, and technological policy. Financial regulation becomes separated from inequality, housing, corporate governance, and public debt. Climate policy becomes separated from industrial policy, insurance markets, migration, and fiscal stability. Each domain is governed as if it were separate, even though the economy experiences them together.

The task, then, is integration. Not simplification, but integration. The chapters that follow seek to integrate economic analysis across systems. They do not abandon the insights of traditional economics. Prices matter. Incentives matter. Scarcity matters. Tradeoffs matter. But these concepts must be placed within a richer understanding of feedback, power, adaptation, and institutional context. The question is not whether economics should be mathematical or moral, technical or political, empirical or philosophical. It must be all of these, because the economy is all of these.

A nonlinear world does not forgive intellectual laziness. It punishes delay, denial, and overconfidence. Fragility accumulates quietly. Inequality compounds silently. Debt expands during optimism. Supply chains become brittle during calm. Financial bubbles inflate while skepticism is mocked. Housing crises deepen one local decision at a time. Institutional trust erodes gradually, then suddenly. By the time crisis becomes visible, the system has often been moving toward it for years.

This is why early warning matters. Complexity economics pays attention to stress indicators, not only breakdowns. Rising household debt, widening wealth gaps, declining trust, increasing market concentration, falling labor share, housing cost burdens, fragile supply chains, speculative asset inflation, ecological stress, and political polarization should not be treated as separate issues. They are signals. They tell us something about the system's trajectory. A wise society does not wait until signals become collapse.

The old language of economic management is insufficient for this task. We need a language of resilience, adaptation, buffers, networks, tipping points, feedback, legitimacy, and moral architecture. We need to ask how systems fail, how they recover, and how they can be redesigned to fail less catastrophically. We need to recognize that efficiency without resilience is brittle, growth without fairness is unstable, innovation without governance is dangerous, and markets without morality are incomplete.

The end of simple economic explanations is therefore not a loss. It is an intellectual liberation. It frees us from false choices. We do not have to choose between markets and morals, efficiency and justice, growth and resilience, individual agency and structural analysis, technical policy and democratic legitimacy. A complexity framework allows us to see that these are not separate categories. They interact. A more just economy may be more stable. A more resilient economy may be more productive over time. A more democratic economy may produce better information. A more inclusive economy may generate broader innovation. A better-regulated financial system may support healthier markets. A less unequal society may sustain stronger demand, higher trust, and more legitimate governance.

The simplicity we must abandon is not clarity. Clarity remains essential. The simplicity we must abandon is false reduction. We need explanations clear enough to guide action, but complex enough to be true. That is the standard this book attempts to meet.

*Economic Problems in a Nonlinear World* is written for readers who sense that the old explanations no longer fit the facts. It is written for those who see that crises are not isolated accidents, that inequality is not merely a distributional statistic, that markets are not self-contained moral machines, and that policy cannot succeed by pulling one lever at a time. It is written for those who believe that economics must recover its ambition as a study of human systems, not merely formal models. It is written for those who want to understand why modern economies generate both abundance and anxiety, innovation and insecurity, wealth and fragility.

The chapters that follow will return again and again to one central claim: economic outcomes emerge from systems. They emerge from relationships among people, institutions, technologies, markets, laws, narratives, and power. To change outcomes, we must change systems. To change systems, we must understand feedback. To understand feedback, we must give up the comfort of simple explanations.

The end of simple economic explanations is the beginning of economic realism. It is the beginning of an economics adequate to crisis, inequality, inflation, debt, markets, technology, and democratic survival. It is the beginning of an economics that recognizes the economy as a living, adaptive, morally consequential order. It is the beginning of an economics for a nonlinear world.

## Chapter 2

# THE FAILURE OF EQUILIBRIUM THINKING

MODERN ECONOMICS HAS long been organized around the image of equilibrium. The term carries an aura of elegance, discipline, and scientific authority. It suggests a world in which opposing forces balance, prices adjust, markets clear, and rational actors coordinate their plans based on the information in supply and demand. In this image, disorder is temporary. Imbalances invite correction. Excess demand raises prices. Excess supply lowers them. Unemployment reflects a market not yet adjusted. Inflation reflects a monetary or demand imbalance. Financial crises reflect distortions, shocks, or irrational departures from normal market functioning. The deep structure of the economy is assumed to be self-stabilizing, provided that interference does not prevent adjustment.

This way of thinking has shaped economics for generations. It has influenced textbooks, policy debates, central banking, fiscal policy, financial regulation, trade theory, labor economics, welfare analysis, and the public imagination. Its appeal is obvious. Equilibrium thinking gives economic life a comprehensible order. It turns the apparent chaos of millions of decisions into a coordinated pattern. It explains how decentralized markets can allocate resources without central direction. It provides mathematical tools, conceptual clarity, and policy discipline. It teaches that prices convey information, incentives matter, tradeoffs are unavoidable, and scarcity cannot be wished away. These are not trivial insights. Any serious economic theory must preserve them.

Yet the power of equilibrium thinking is also its danger. It simplifies a world that is not always simple. It often treats instability as an exception rather than a central feature of economic life. It assumes that systems tend toward balance even when history shows that economies can drift toward fragility, lock into inequality, amplify shocks, and generate crises from within. It imagines that markets clear even when labor markets are segmented, housing markets are politically constrained, financial markets are driven by leverage and herding, and technological markets are shaped by increasing returns. It treats deviations from equilibrium as temporary disturbances, even though many of the most important economic problems are persistent, self-reinforcing, and path-dependent.

The failure of equilibrium thinking is not that it is always wrong. It is incomplete precisely in the areas where modern economic life has become most dangerous. Equilibrium thinking works best when relationships are stable, actors are numerous and relatively powerless, information is widely available, adjustment is smooth, institutions are given, externalities are limited, and feedback loops are weak. But many of the defining problems of the twenty-first century violate these assumptions. Inequality compounds across generations. Financial markets generate bubbles and crashes. Debt transforms confidence into fragility. Housing scarcity persists through political feedback. Inflation travels through expectations, supply chains, market power, and distributive conflict. Labor markets reflect unequal bargaining power and network advantage. Technology produces winner-take-most dynamics. Climate change introduces thresholds, irreversibility, and systemic risk.

In such a world, equilibrium is not the natural destination of economic life. Sometimes it is not even the right question. The more urgent questions are different. What kinds of feedback are operating? Are they stabilizing or destabilizing? Which actors gain power as the system evolves? Where are thresholds accumulating? What forms of fragility are hidden during apparent calm? What patterns become locked in by past choices? How do expectations shape reality? How do institutions distribute risk? How do local decisions generate systemic outcomes? These questions move us beyond equilibrium thinking and into the domain of complexity economics.

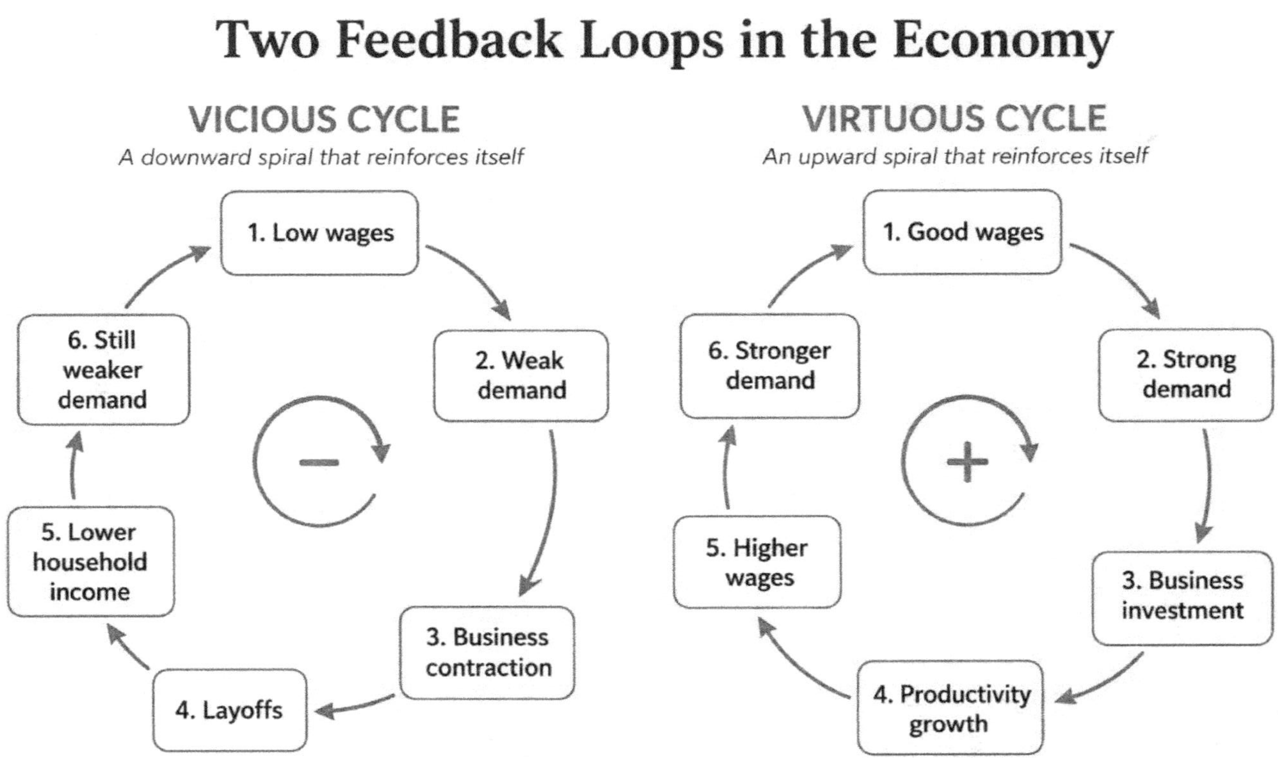


*Figure 2.0 – Feedback Loops in Economic Life*

Equilibrium thinking begins from a noble ambition: to explain order without command. Adam Smith's invisible hand remains one of the most profound metaphors in the history of social thought. It suggested that individuals pursuing their own purposes in markets could generate social coordination that no single mind could design. This was a revolutionary insight. It challenged the idea that prosperity required centralized control. It showed how prices could coordinate dispersed knowledge, how specialization could increase productivity, and how exchange could align private interest with mutual gain. In its best form, equilibrium economics preserves this insight by demonstrating how decentralized choices can become mutually consistent.

But the invisible hand was never a complete theory of society. Smith himself understood that markets depend on moral norms, legal institutions, trust, restraint, and public goods. Later economic theory often abstracted from these foundations. It transformed the market into a formal mechanism and treated the institutional and moral environment as background. Once that move was made, equilibrium became not merely a useful analytical device, but a governing metaphor. The economy came to be imagined as a system that, if left to its own logic, would tend toward efficient coordination.

The textbook supply-and-demand diagram is the purest expression of this metaphor. A downward-sloping demand curve meets an upward-sloping supply curve. The point of intersection represents the equilibrium price and quantity. If the price is too high, surplus emerges, and sellers lower prices. If the price is too low, a shortage emerges, and buyers bid the price up. The model is elegant because it captures a real mechanism. Prices do adjust. Scarcity does matter. Incentives do shape behavior. Yet the diagram also trains the mind to expect smooth adjustment. It implies that disequilibrium carries within itself the forces of correction.

Many economic problems do not behave this way. Housing shortages can persist for decades because prices do not automatically produce adequate supply when zoning, land scarcity, financing constraints, construction bottlenecks, neighborhood opposition, and political incentives block adjustment. Labor shortages do not always produce rapid wage growth when workers lack mobility, firms possess monopsony power, credentials restrict entry, or care responsibilities bind people to place. Financial markets do not always correct mispricing when rising prices attract more buyers precisely because prices are rising. Healthcare prices do not behave like ordinary market prices when buyers are vulnerable, information is unequal, insurance obscures cost, and providers possess market power. Education markets do not clear in a simple way because credentials are positional, opportunity is cumulative, and debt reshapes life chances.

The equilibrium model remains useful as a beginning, but it becomes misleading when treated as a destination. It teaches us to expect correction where we should look for reinforcement. It teaches us to expect proportionality where we should look for thresholds. It teaches us to expect representative agents where we should look for unequal positions within networks. It teaches us to expect stable preferences where we should look for adaptive desires shaped by advertising, status, insecurity, and imitation. It teaches us to expect efficient outcomes by looking for power, lock-in, and institutional design.

The deepest failure of equilibrium thinking is its tendency to erase time. In many formal models, time appears as a sequence of periods, but history itself has little weight. The past matters mainly through variables carried into the present. The system's underlying structure remains stable. Yet real economies are historical systems. They remember. They accumulate. They become what they have been. Past investments shape present geography. Past discrimination shapes present wealth. Past zoning choices shape present housing supply. Past union decline shapes present bargaining power. Past deregulation shapes the present financial structure. Past technological standards shape present market dominance. Past crises shape present expectations. Institutions are sedimented history.

Path dependence is therefore central to economic life. Once a system moves down one path, it may become increasingly costly to change direction. Early advantages can become durable dominance. A firm that gains an initial platform lead can attract users, developers, advertisers, data, and capital, which then reinforce its lead. A neighborhood with high property values can fund better schools, attract wealthier residents, and resist development that would dilute scarcity. A wealthy family can purchase education, housing, social networks, and risk protection for the next generation. A region that loses industrial employment can suffer declining tax bases, outmigration, weakened institutions, and reduced attractiveness to future investment. These outcomes are not equilibrium adjustments in the simple sense. They are historical trajectories.

Equilibrium thinking often treats the economy as if it can return to a prior state after a disturbance. Complexity thinking asks whether the disturbance has changed the system itself. A recession can permanently damage workers' earnings trajectories. A wave of foreclosures can destroy family wealth for generations. A financial crisis can alter trust, regulation, and political legitimacy. A pandemic can reorganize work habits, supply chains, migration patterns, and household expectations. An inflationary episode can change wage bargaining, pricing behavior, political attitudes, and central bank credibility. Shocks are not merely deviations from trend. They can reshape the trend.

This matters profoundly for policy. If policymakers believe that economies naturally return to equilibrium, they may underestimate the cost of inaction. They may tolerate unemployment because they expect labor markets to heal. They may accept austerity because they expect confidence to restore growth. They may allow foreclosures because they expect housing markets to clear. They may permit deindustrialization because they expect workers to move to new opportunities. They may ignore inequality because they expect education and mobility to correct it. But if economic systems are path dependent, delay can become destiny. What is allowed to deteriorate may not automatically recover.

The global financial crisis illustrated this failure with painful clarity. Before the crisis, many models treated financial markets as broadly efficient and self-correcting. Risk was assumed to be priced, dispersed, and managed. Innovation in financial instruments was widely interpreted as improving allocation and spreading exposure. Housing prices were not supposed to fall nationally in a catastrophic way. Market participants were presumed to have incentives to monitor risk because they bore the consequences of failure. Equilibrium thinking encouraged confidence that deviations would be contained.

But the system was not self-stabilizing. It was self-amplifying. Rising housing prices encouraged lending. Easier lending raised housing prices. Mortgage originators passed loans to securitizers. Securitizers packaged them into instruments rated as safe. Investors demanded more yield. Rating agencies legitimized risk. Shadow banks increased leverage. Derivatives connected institutions in opaque ways. The appearance of stability encouraged greater fragility. Low volatility was interpreted as safety, when it was partly the result of a boom that concealed vulnerability. The system did not move toward equilibrium. It moved toward a cliff.

When the reversal came, the feedback changed direction. Falling home prices increased defaults. Defaults damaged mortgage securities. Falling security values weakened financial institutions. Weakened institutions reduced lending. Reduced lending deepened economic contraction. Contraction produced more defaults. Trust evaporated. Liquidity disappeared. The crisis was nonlinear because the relationship between initial losses and systemic consequences was not proportional. A problem in one sector became a global financial emergency because the system was leveraged, interconnected, and dependent on confidence.

Equilibrium thinking failed not only analytically, but morally. It permitted policymakers and market participants to mistake private profit for systemic value. It obscured the distribution of risk. It ignored how gains were privatized during the boom while losses were socialized during the collapse. It treated financial innovation as efficiency without asking whether complexity was being used to hide fragility. It treated market prices as information without asking whether those prices were being generated by the very bubble they appeared to validate.

The same failure appears in discussions of inequality. In equilibrium models, income differences often reflect differences in productivity, skill, effort, or preferences. Labor earns its marginal product. Capital earns its return. Markets allocate rewards according to contribution. In this framework, inequality may be unfortunate, but it is not necessarily evidence of systemic failure. It may even be interpreted as necessary for incentives, investment, and innovation.

But modern inequality cannot be understood adequately as an equilibrium distribution of rewards. It is a dynamic process shaped by cumulative advantage, institutional power, asset ownership, inheritance, education, geography, health, political influence, and bargaining structures. Wealth does not simply reward past productivity. It changes future opportunity. It buys access to neighborhoods, schools, legal advice, tax strategies, business networks, political influence, and resilience against failure. It allows some people to take risks because they have buffers, while others avoid risks because one mistake could be catastrophic. It compounds not only financially, but socially and institutionally.

Equilibrium thinking often asks whether inequality reflects market outcomes. Complexity thinking asks how market outcomes are produced and reproduced. It asks how property rights are designed, how labor power is structured, how tax systems treat capital and work, how education is funded, how housing markets sort families, how campaign finance shapes policy, and how corporate governance allocates gains. It recognizes that inequality is not simply the result of millions of independent transactions. It is the result of a system whose rules generate cumulative divergence.

This divergence can become politically destabilizing. Extreme inequality does not merely change consumption patterns. It changes power. Wealth becomes influence. Influence shapes law. Law shapes markets. Markets generate further wealth. This feedback loop can produce a political economy in which formal democracy survives while substantive equality of voice erodes. Equilibrium thinking struggles to capture this because it often separates economics from politics. Complexity economics places them back together. It recognizes that markets are embedded in institutions and that institutions are shaped by those who gain power within markets.

Inflation provides another example. In simple equilibrium terms, inflation is often framed as excess aggregate demand relative to supply, or as excessive growth in the money supply. These explanations can be important, but they become inadequate when treated as exhaustive. Inflation is a process that moves through sectors, expectations, contracts, institutions, and power relations. It may begin with energy shocks, supply bottlenecks, exchange rates, fiscal transfers, labor shortages, or market concentration. Once it begins, it can change behavior. Firms may raise prices not only because costs rise but also because competitors raise prices or because customers expect price increases. Workers may demand higher wages because prices have risen. Landlords may raise rents because market conditions allow it. Central banks may tighten policy, altering debt burdens and investment decisions. Politicians may turn inflation into a narrative of blame.

The equilibrium approach seeks the price level at which demand and supply balance. The complexity approach asks how inflationary dynamics propagate. Which sectors lead? Which actors have pricing power? Which households are most exposed? Which contracts adjust automatically? Which expectations are adaptive? Which institutions mediate conflict over real income? Which policies reduce inflation by destroying demand, and which reduce it by easing bottlenecks or limiting market power? These questions matter because anti-inflation policy is distributive. It decides who will bear the cost of restoring stability.

The equilibrium imagination often treats central banking as a technical adjustment mechanism. Inflation rises, interest rates increase. Demand cools, inflation falls. Again, there is truth here. But the relationship is neither simple nor morally neutral. Higher interest rates affect homeowners, renters, small businesses, banks, governments, investors, and workers differently. They may reduce demand, but they may also increase debt burdens, slow construction, weaken employment, and generate financial stress. If inflation is driven partly by supply constraints or market power, rate hikes may work only by imposing broad pain rather than addressing the source. A complexity approach does not deny the role of monetary policy. It asks monetary policy to understand the system it is acting upon.

Equilibrium thinking also struggles with financial markets because it overstates the independence of judgment. Many models assume that investors respond to information and prices efficiently incorporate available knowledge. But actual markets are social systems. Investors watch other investors. They follow trends, narratives, benchmarks, and institutional incentives. Professional investors may buy assets they privately doubt because underperforming peers is more dangerous than being wrong with the crowd. Algorithms respond to signals generated by other algorithms. Risk models use historical data that may become least reliable when conditions change. Liquidity appears abundant until everyone wants it at once.

Markets can therefore become reflexive. Prices do not merely reflect beliefs. They shape beliefs. A rising stock price can make a company appear more promising, attract media attention, lower its cost of capital, enrich employees with stock compensation, and support further growth. A falling price can damage confidence, raise financing costs, trigger downgrades, and weaken the company's actual prospects. Expectations become causal. The market is not a passive mirror. It is an active force.

This reflexivity undermines simple equilibrium thinking. If prices shape fundamentals, then markets may not simply move toward correct valuation. They may create self-fulfilling booms and self-fulfilling collapses. The question becomes not only, "What is the asset worth?" but also, "What dynamics are being produced by the process of valuation itself?" This is why bubbles are so difficult to stop. During the boom, participants can point to rising prices as evidence that optimism is justified. Those who warn of danger may be dismissed as pessimists until the reversal begins. Once the reversal begins, pessimism becomes self-confirming.

Technological markets reveal another limitation of equilibrium thinking: the assumption of diminishing returns. In many traditional models, competition erodes excess profit. High returns attract entry. Entry increases supply. Prices fall. Profits normalize. This logic works in many settings, but it fails in markets characterized by increasing returns, network effects, data advantages, platform dependency, and scale economies. In such markets, success can generate more success. The more users a platform has, the more valuable it becomes. The more data it collects, the better it can refine services. The more sellers it attracts, the more buyers arrive. The more developers build around it, the harder it becomes to leave.

These dynamics can produce concentration without requiring superior merit at every stage. Early advantage, capital access, strategic behavior, and network effects can lock in dominance. Equilibrium thinking may interpret market concentration as the reward for efficiency. Complexity thinking asks whether the system has entered a winner-take-most regime in which competition cannot easily reemerge. It asks whether users are locked in, whether rivals can access essential infrastructure, whether data advantages are self-reinforcing, and whether private control over platforms has become a form of public power.

Labor markets, too, are not equilibrium machines. Workers are human beings embedded in place, family, identity, health, debt, care obligations, and community. They cannot instantly move to where wages are higher. They may not know where opportunities exist. They may lack credentials, transportation, childcare, or savings. Employers may have wage-setting power, especially in regions or sectors with limited competition. Firms may use scheduling practices, noncompete agreements, subcontracting, franchising, surveillance, and algorithmic management to reduce worker bargaining power. Labor markets are also shaped by norms of fairness, dignity, and status.

Equilibrium thinking often predicts that low wages will eventually attract fewer workers and force employers to raise pay. Sometimes this happens. But low-wage labor markets can persist because workers are constrained. Poverty reduces exit options. Debt disciplines behavior. Weak unions reduce collective bargaining. Public benefits may subsidize low wages. Immigration status may limit worker voice. Monopsony power may suppress pay. In such cases, the market does not clear in a morally meaningful way. It reproduces dependency.

This point is essential: equilibrium can exist alongside injustice. A labor market can reach a stable pattern in which workers remain poor, firms remain profitable, and consumers enjoy low prices. A housing market can reach a stable pattern in which owners accumulate wealth and renters face permanent insecurity. A political economy can reach a stable pattern in which the wealthy shape policy and the majority loses trust. A financial system can reach a stable pattern in which periodic crises are treated as acceptable costs. The presence of stability does not prove the presence of justice. Equilibrium is not a moral achievement.

Nor does equilibrium imply resilience. A system can be balanced and brittle. A supply chain optimized for low cost may function smoothly under ordinary conditions and fail catastrophically under stress. A bank may satisfy regulatory ratios and still be vulnerable to a rapid loss of confidence. A household may manage monthly payments and still be one illness away from insolvency. A government may finance itself easily while interest rates are low and face crisis when conditions shift. An ecosystem may appear stable until a threshold is crossed. Stability observed under normal conditions may conceal fragility under stress.

This is one of the most important lessons of complexity economics: calm is not the same as safety. Indeed, calm can produce danger by encouraging risk-taking. When markets are stable, actors borrow more, reduce buffers, stretch maturities, lower lending standards, and assume that recent patterns will continue. This is the paradox of stability. The longer stability persists, the more people behave as if instability has disappeared. Their behavior then creates the conditions for instability. Equilibrium thinking often misses this because it treats stability as evidence that the system is near its natural state. Complexity thinking asks what hidden fragilities stability may be producing.

The failure of equilibrium thinking also appears in the treatment of externalities. Traditional economics recognizes externalities as cases where private decisions impose costs or benefits not reflected in prices. Pollution is the classic example. The standard solution is to internalize the externality through taxes, regulation, or property rights. This framework is useful, but it understates the systemic nature of many externalities. Climate change is not merely an unpriced cost. It is a planetary-scale nonlinear process involving thresholds, feedback loops, irreversibility, migration, insurance markets, food systems, infrastructure, finance, public health, and geopolitical instability.

Once ecological systems enter the analysis, equilibrium thinking becomes even less adequate. Climate risk is not a marginal adjustment problem. It involves tipping points, cumulative emissions, delayed effects, uncertain thresholds, and unequal exposure. Markets are not well equipped to price risks that unfold over generations, cross borders, interact with political systems, and threaten the basic conditions of economic life. A carbon price may be necessary, but it is not sufficient. The problem requires industrial policy, public investment, adaptation planning, financial regulation, infrastructure redesign, and democratic legitimacy. It is not a single market failure. It is a systemic coordination failure.

Equilibrium thinking is especially weak when confronting power. In many models, power is absent or reduced to market imperfections. Yet power is central to economic life. Firms have power over workers, suppliers, consumers, and regulators. Wealthy actors have power over politics. Creditors have power over debtors. Landlords have power over tenants. Platforms have power over users and dependent businesses. Central banks have power over employment and asset prices. Governments have power to define property, enforce contracts, tax income, regulate markets, and provide public goods. Power determines who can wait, who can exit, who can impose costs, who can shape rules, and who can survive shocks.

Equilibrium analysis often abstracts from power in order to achieve mathematical clarity. But an economy without power is an economy without politics, history, or moral conflict. It is a world of voluntary exchange among formally equal agents. Real markets are never only that. Formal freedom can coexist with material compulsion. A worker may be legally free to quit and economically unable to do so. A tenant may be legally free to move and practically trapped by rents, schools, jobs, and savings. A borrower may sign a contract voluntarily under conditions of desperation. A small supplier may accept unfavorable terms because a dominant buyer controls access to the market. A consumer may agree to digital surveillance because the platform has become socially indispensable.

A complexity economics inquiry must therefore place power at the center. Power shapes feedback loops. It determines who benefits from increasing returns, who can externalize risk, who can influence policy, and who can define the narrative of crisis. During inflation, firms with pricing power can protect margins, while workers without bargaining power fall behind. During financial crises, large institutions may receive rescue, while households face foreclosure. During technological change, platform owners may capture gains, while workers experience insecurity. During housing scarcity, owners gain wealth, while renters face rising burdens. These are not incidental outcomes. They are systemic patterns.

The equilibrium imagination also tends to separate efficiency from distribution. It asks first how to maximize output or welfare, then how to redistribute if society dislikes the result. This sequence appears reasonable, but it can be misleading. Distribution affects efficiency. Inequality shapes education, health, trust, demand, entrepreneurship, political stability, and social cooperation. A highly unequal society may waste human potential, underinvest in public goods, encourage rent-seeking, and produce political backlash. A society with broad security may generate more risk-taking, innovation, and participation. Distribution is not merely what happens after markets operate. It shapes how markets operate.

Similarly, resilience cannot be added after efficiency has been maximized. If firms design supply chains solely for cost minimization, resilience disappears from the system. If households are expected to rely on private savings but wages are insufficient, resilience becomes class privilege. If financial institutions are rewarded for leverage during booms, regulation cannot simply assume that risk will remain contained. If public institutions are weakened in the name of fiscal efficiency, they may fail when crisis arrives. Efficiency measured too narrowly can destroy the capacities needed for long-term prosperity.

This is why equilibrium thinking became so attractive to certain forms of political ideology. It offered a language in which markets appeared natural, intervention appeared distortionary, inequality appeared earned, and crises appeared exceptional. If the economy tends toward equilibrium, then policy should often step back. If markets efficiently process information, then regulation is suspect. If wages reflect productivity, then labor power is unnecessary. If capital markets allocate resources efficiently, then financial innovation should be encouraged. If inequality reflects contribution, then redistribution threatens incentives. This does not mean that all equilibrium economics is ideological. But it does mean that equilibrium thinking can be used ideologically.

A complexity perspective unsettles this comfort. It shows that markets can generate order, but also disorder. They can allocate resources, but also amplify inequality. They can process information, but also produce misinformation through bubbles and panics. They can reward innovation, but also entrench monopoly. They can discipline waste, but also underprovide resilience. They can create wealth, but also corrode the social foundations on which wealth depends. The question is not whether markets are good or bad. The question is how markets behave within particular institutional ecologies.

This brings us to the concept of multiple equilibria. Even within formal economics, there is recognition that systems may settle into more than one possible state. A society may have high trust or low trust. A region may have high investment or low investment. A labor market may have strong worker voice or weak worker voice. A financial system may be conservative or speculative. A country may have inclusive growth or extractive concentration. The outcome depends on expectations, institutions, coordination, and history. This insight weakens the older assumption that there is one natural equilibrium toward which the economy tends.

Multiple equilibria are important, but complexity economics pushes further. It asks how systems move among regimes, how they become locked into bad patterns, and how they cross thresholds. A low-trust society may remain low trust because people behave defensively, and defensive behavior confirms the expectation that others cannot be trusted. A corrupt political economy may remain corrupt because honest actors are punished and corrupt actors are rewarded. A segregated housing system may persist because past exclusion shaped wealth, schools, and political boundaries. A low-wage labor system may persist because workers lack the power to coordinate. A fossil-fuel economy may persist because infrastructure, subsidies, habits, and political influence reinforce one another.

In such cases, policy must do more than correct marginal incentives. It must change the regime. That may require coordinated intervention, public investment, legal reform, institutional redesign, and shifts in expectations. A society trapped in a bad equilibrium cannot always escape through small adjustments. It may need a deliberate transition strategy. This is why complexity economics is not a counsel of passivity. It is a theory of strategic intervention.

The distinction between marginal change and regime change is crucial. Equilibrium thinking is most comfortable at the margin. What happens if the tax rate changes slightly? What happens if the interest rate rises by one percentage point? What happens if a regulation increases cost?

Marginal analysis is useful, but many historical transformations are not marginal. The rise of mass production, the New Deal, the postwar welfare state, the neoliberal turn, globalization, financialization, digitization, and decarbonization are regime shifts. They change institutions, expectations, power, and social organization. Their consequences unfold through time in ways that cannot be fully captured by small variations around a stable equilibrium.

Modern capitalism is now in a period of regime stress. The old settlement that promised growth, globalization, low inflation, cheap goods, rising asset values, flexible labor, and technocratic management has become unstable. Inequality has widened. Housing has become unaffordable in many regions. Debt burdens households, corporations, and states. Supply chains have revealed vulnerability. Financial markets remain prone to excess. Climate change is no longer distant. Technology is concentrating power faster than institutions can respond. Political trust is eroding. These are not separate deviations from equilibrium. They are symptoms of a system whose governing assumptions have become inadequate.

Equilibrium thinking encourages us to treat each symptom separately. Inflation belongs to central banks. Housing belongs to local zoning boards. Labor insecurity belongs to education and training. Financial instability belongs to regulators. Inequality belongs to tax policy. Supply chains belong to corporate logistics. Technology belongs to innovation policy. Climate belongs to environmental agencies. But the economy does not experience these problems separately. They interact. Housing costs affect wages. Wages affect inflation. Inflation affects interest rates. Interest rates affect housing supply, debt service, and financial stability. Inequality affects political power. Political power affects regulation. Regulation affects market concentration. Market concentration affects prices, wages, and innovation. Technology affects labor power, inequality, and market structure. Climate affects insurance, migration, public budgets, and supply chains.

The failure of equilibrium thinking is therefore also a failure of institutional imagination. Our policy institutions are organized into domains, but the problems are systemic. Each institution sees part of the elephant and mistakes it for the whole. Central banks see aggregate demand and inflation expectations. Housing agencies see affordability and supply. Labor departments see employment and wages. Financial regulators see bank balance sheets. Antitrust authorities see competition. Environmental agencies see emissions. But complexity requires a capacity to see across domains. Without such integration, policy may solve one problem by worsening another.

This is especially true of austerity. Equilibrium thinking has often supported the view that governments should reduce deficits to restore confidence, lower interest rates, and permit private investment to flourish. There are circumstances in which fiscal discipline matters. No government can ignore debt dynamics forever. But austerity imposed under conditions of weak demand, fragile households, underinvestment, and social stress can be self-defeating. Cuts reduce income. Reduced income weakens demand. Weak demand lowers growth. Lower growth worsens debt ratios. Public services deteriorate. Trust declines. Political backlash intensifies. What appears responsible in accounting terms may be destructive in systemic terms.

The same is true of deregulation. If one assumes markets naturally move toward efficient equilibrium, regulation appears as a cost unless a specific market failure can be proven. But in complex systems, rules are not external burdens. They are part of the system's architecture. Financial regulations shape risk-taking. Labor laws shape bargaining power. Antitrust rules shape market structure. Zoning rules shape housing supply. Environmental rules shape investment direction. Corporate governance rules shape time horizons. Tax rules shape incentives and power. The question is not whether to regulate or not regulate. Every market is governed by rules. The question is what kind of rules create resilience, fairness, innovation, and legitimacy.

Equilibrium thinking often treats institutions as constraints on markets. Complexity thinking treats institutions as constitutive of markets. There is no market without law, property, contract, enforcement, money, trust, information, and dispute resolution. Markets are not found in nature. They are built. Different institutional designs produce different market behaviors. A labor market with strong unions behaves differently from one without them. A financial market with strict leverage limits behaves differently from one built around shadow banking. A housing market with abundant public housing behaves differently from one dominated by speculative private ownership. A platform market with interoperability rules behaves differently from one controlled by proprietary ecosystems. Institutional design is not secondary. It is central.

This insight changes how we understand freedom. Equilibrium ideology often equates freedom with noninterference. The freer the market, the less the state interferes. But if markets are institutional systems, then freedom depends on how those systems are designed. A worker with no bargaining power is not meaningfully free simply because no law prevents quitting. A tenant facing unaffordable rents is not meaningfully free because the lease was voluntary. A small business dependent on a dominant platform is not meaningfully free because it clicked "agree." A household crushed by medical debt is not meaningfully free because credit was available. Freedom requires capacities, protections, options, and voice.

This does not mean that markets should be replaced by bureaucracy. It means that markets must be governed as human institutions. The goal is not to suppress price signals, competition, or entrepreneurship. The goal is to embed them in a moral and institutional order that prevents domination, reduces fragility, and distributes opportunity. Complexity economics helps clarify this because it reveals that individual outcomes depend on system design. A society can design markets that generate broad capability or markets that generate dependency and extraction.

Equilibrium thinking also fails to capture the role of narratives. Economic actors do not respond only to prices. They respond to stories about the future. A boom persists because people believe prices will keep rising. A bank run begins because people believe others will withdraw. Inflation accelerates when firms and households believe future prices will rise. A recession deepens when fear causes households to save and firms to delay investment. A technology bubble grows when investors believe a new era has arrived. Narratives coordinate expectations, and expectations shape outcomes.

This narrative dimension is not irrational noise. It is part of economic reality. Humans make decisions under uncertainty, and uncertainty cannot be eliminated by calculation. Stories help people interpret ambiguous signals. They tell firms whether to invest, households whether to buy, workers whether to demand higher wages, banks whether to lend, and governments whether to spend. Competing narratives can move markets, elections, and institutions. A complexity approach treats narratives as causal forces within the system.

Equilibrium thinking tends to assume that expectations converge toward rational forecasts. But expectations can be adaptive, social, emotional, and political. People learn from recent experience, imitate peers, trust familiar authorities, and respond to fear or hope. They may be wrong together. They may remain wrong for a long time. They may become right because their shared belief changes behavior. A society convinced that government is incompetent may underfund public institutions, producing incompetence. A market convinced that housing only rises may borrow and lend in ways that make housing rise until the bubble bursts. A political movement convinced that elites have rigged the economy may destabilize institutions, making governance worse. Expectations are not merely forecasts. They are ingredients of the future.

The failure of equilibrium thinking is therefore inseparable from the failure of technocracy. Technocracy assumes that expert management can adjust policy instruments to maintain stability. It is not wrong to value expertise. Modern economies require technical competence. But technocracy becomes dangerous when it ignores legitimacy, distribution, and complexity. A central bank can raise rates, but it cannot by itself restore trust. A finance ministry can reduce deficits, but it cannot by itself rebuild social cohesion. A regulatory agency can issue rules, but it cannot by itself overcome political capture. Experts can measure many things, but they cannot remove moral conflict from economic life.

Equilibrium thinking often dreams of depoliticized economics. Complexity economics shows why that dream is impossible. Economic systems distribute gains and losses. They create winners and losers. They allocate risk, voice, opportunity, and security. Every major economic policy has moral consequences. Even doing nothing preserves an existing structure of advantage. The question is not whether economics will be political. It will be. The question is whether politics will be honest about the systems it is shaping.

This honesty requires abandoning the myth that markets naturally reward virtue. Markets reward what the system is designed to reward. Sometimes they reward innovation, effort, service, and risk-taking. Sometimes they reward monopoly, extraction, speculation, arbitrage, manipulation, and inherited advantage. The difference depends on institutions. Equilibrium thinking often blurs this distinction by treating market outcomes as presumptively efficient. Complexity thinking asks whether the feedback loops of the system reward socially useful behavior or socially harmful behavior.

Consider corporate behavior. If financial markets reward quarterly earnings, firms may cut labor costs, reduce investment, engage in buybacks, raise prices where possible, and consolidate market power. If executive compensation is tied to stock prices, executives may prioritize short-term valuation over long-term resilience. If antitrust enforcement is weak, mergers may reduce competition. If labor law is weak, firms may suppress wages. If tax law favors debt, firms may increase leverage. None of these outcomes is simply the result of "the market." They are the result of a rule-bound system that channels behavior.

The same applies to households. If education, healthcare, housing, and retirement security are increasingly privatized, households may take on debt not because they are irresponsible, but because the system requires private borrowing to access basic life goods. If wages stagnate while social expectations remain high, credit fills the gap. If housing becomes the main path to middle-class wealth, families stretch to buy. If public support is weak, households self-insure through savings they may not be able to accumulate. Equilibrium thinking may interpret debt as a choice. Complexity thinking asks what system of necessity produced that choice.

A central theme of this book is that many economic problems are not failures to reach equilibrium. They are failures of system design. Inflation may reflect an economy whose supply chains, energy systems, market structures, and distributive institutions cannot absorb shocks without conflict. Debt crises may reflect a growth model dependent on leverage. Inequality may reflect institutionalized cumulative advantage. Housing scarcity may reflect the conversion of shelter into a speculative asset regime. Labor insecurity may reflect the weakening of worker power and the fragmentation of employment. Financial crises may reflect reward systems that encourage risk until the public must rescue the system. Technological disruption may reflect private control over infrastructures that society depends upon.

If these are design failures, then equilibrium cannot be the only standard of analysis. We need standards of resilience, justice, adaptability, and legitimacy. Does the system absorb shocks without mass suffering? Does it distribute opportunity widely? Does it prevent the concentration of power? Does it allow democratic correction? Does it reward productive activity over extraction? Does it maintain public trust? Does it protect the vulnerable? Does it preserve ecological foundations? These questions belong at the center of political economy.

The transition from equilibrium thinking to complexity thinking does not require rejecting all traditional economics. It requires reordering it. Supply and demand remain useful, but they must be placed within institutional context. Incentives matter, but incentives are designed and interpreted. Prices matter, but prices can be shaped by power, expectations, and scarcity regimes. Markets matter, but markets are embedded in law and culture. Efficiency matters, but it must be balanced with resilience. Growth matters, but it must be judged by distribution and sustainability. Individual choice matters, but choice is structured by systems.

The failure of equilibrium thinking is ultimately a failure to understand the economy as a living order. Living orders do not simply balance. They adapt, mutate, learn, decay, regenerate, and sometimes collapse. They contain conflict and cooperation. They depend on diversity and redundancy. They are shaped by history. They can become trapped in destructive patterns. They can also be redesigned. The economy is not alive in the biological sense, but it shares enough features with complex adaptive systems that mechanical metaphors mislead us. It is an evolving ecology of human coordination.

This ecological perspective changes the meaning of crisis. In equilibrium thinking, crisis is often an interruption of normal functioning. In complexity thinking, crisis may reveal normal functioning. The financial crisis revealed how financial profits had been generated. The housing crisis reveals how scarcity creates wealth for some by imposing insecurity on others. Inflation reveals which actors can defend income and which cannot. Supply chain breakdowns reveal the hidden cost of efficiency. Labor unrest reveals the limits of treating workers as inputs. Political backlash reveals the social consequences of economic abandonment. Crisis is not merely a breakdown. It is a disclosure.

What crisis discloses is often uncomfortable. It shows that the economy's apparent success may depend on hidden fragilities. Cheap goods may depend on vulnerable labor and brittle logistics. Low inflation may depend on global labor arbitrage and suppressed wages. Rising asset wealth may depend on debt, scarcity, and monetary conditions. Technological convenience may depend on surveillance and market concentration. Fiscal stability may depend on underinvestment. Corporate profitability may depend on weakened worker power. These are not arguments against prosperity. They are arguments for a more honest definition of prosperity.

Equilibrium thinking fails because it too often mistakes order for health. A society can have orderly markets and disordered lives. It can have full shelves and empty communities. It can have rising asset values and declining trust. It can have low unemployment and widespread insecurity. It can have technological progress and social regression. It can have balanced budgets and broken public institutions. It can have efficient firms and fragile systems. Health requires more than coordination. It requires the capacity of the whole system to sustain human flourishing over time.

This is why the chapters that follow do not treat economic problems as isolated deviations from an otherwise healthy equilibrium. They treat them as expressions of systemic dynamics. Inflation, debt, inequality, housing, labor markets, supply chains, financial markets, technology, and public policy are not separate problems stacked side by side. They are interacting components of one evolving political economy. Understanding them requires moving from equilibrium to complexity, from static balance to dynamic process, from isolated markets to institutional ecologies, from representative agents to unequal positions, from efficiency alone to resilience and justice.

The end of equilibrium thinking does not mean the end of economics. It means the renewal of economics. It means recovering the discipline's original breadth as a form of moral and social inquiry. Political economy was never merely about prices. It was about how societies organize production, distribute wealth, allocate power, sustain legitimacy, and define the conditions of human life. The technical achievements of modern economics are valuable, but they must be placed within this larger purpose. A model that is elegant but blind to crisis, power, and history is not rigorous enough for the world we inhabit.

The failure of equilibrium thinking is therefore an invitation. It invites us to build an economics that can understand instability without treating it as an anomaly. It invites us to understand inequality as a process rather than a snapshot. It invites us to analyze inflation as feedback rather than a single cause. It invites us to see debt as a structure of vulnerability. It invites us to examine housing as a scarcity system. It invites us to understand labor as human life embedded in networks of power and care. It invites us to treat supply chains as systems requiring resilience. It invites us to see financial markets as reflexive arenas of belief and leverage. It invites us to understand technology as institutional disruption, not automatic progress. It invites us to design public policy for uncertainty, adaptation, and moral responsibility.

Equilibrium thinking gave economics a language of balance. Complexity economics gives it a language of becoming. The economy is never simply at rest. It is always forming, deforming, adapting, concentrating, dispersing, stabilizing, destabilizing, learning, forgetting, including, excluding, creating, and destroying. The question is not whether it will change. It will. The question is whether change will be governed by institutions capable of protecting human dignity, democratic legitimacy, and systemic resilience.

The failure of equilibrium thinking is not a technical footnote. It is the central intellectual crisis of modern economics. A world of climate shocks, financial cascades, artificial intelligence, geopolitical fragmentation, aging societies, debt overhangs, housing scarcity, and democratic instability cannot be governed by an imagination built for smooth adjustment. We need models that can see turbulence before it becomes collapse. We need policies that can build buffers before crisis arrives. We need institutions that can learn before failure hardens into despair. We need a moral economics capable of recognizing that stability without justice is temporary, efficiency without resilience is dangerous, and markets without democratic governance are incomplete.

To move beyond equilibrium is to accept that economic life is more uncertain, more interconnected, and more morally consequential than simple models admit. It is also to accept that better futures remain possible. Systems can be redesigned. Feedback loops can be altered. Fragility can be reduced. Power can be dispersed. Opportunity can be broadened. Resilience can be built. The economy is not a machine with a natural resting point. It is a human creation, and because it is a human creation, it can be changed.

The chapters that follow begin that work of reinterpretation. They ask what happens when we stop asking how the economy returns to equilibrium and begin asking how economic systems actually evolve. They ask how problems grow, how crises cascade, how advantages compound, how institutions fail, and how governance might become wiser. They begin from the recognition that equilibrium thinking has reached its limit. In a nonlinear world, balance is not enough. We must learn to understand emergence.

## Chapter 3

# Nonlinearity: When More Becomes Different

The most important word in this book is not crisis, inequality, inflation, debt, markets, or policy. It is nonlinearity. The word may sound technical, but the idea is simple and profound: in many systems, effects are not proportional to causes. A small change can have a large consequence. A large intervention can have little effect. A process can appear stable for a long time, then suddenly transform. A trend can accelerate after passing a threshold. A system can absorb pressure until it cannot. More does not always mean more of the same. Sometimes, more becomes different.

This is the central insight needed to understand modern economic life. We are accustomed to thinking in straight lines. If demand rises, prices rise. If interest rates rise, borrowing falls. If wages rise, employment falls. If education increases, incomes rise. If housing supply expands, prices fall. If debt increases, risk increases. If public spending increases, output increases. These statements may contain partial truths, but they become misleading when treated as universal laws. Real economies do not always respond in smooth, proportional, predictable ways. They respond through interaction, adaptation, feedback, delay, expectation, power, and institutional constraint.

A linear relationship is easy to imagine. Turn the dial slightly, and the effect changes slightly. Push the accelerator, and the car moves faster. Add one more unit of input, and receive one more unit of output. This kind of reasoning is powerful because many aspects of daily life seem to work this way. If a family saves a little more each month, its savings rise. If a firm hires one more worker, it may produce more output. If a household buys more gasoline, it can drive more miles. But even here, linearity has limits. The family may reach a point where savings allow it to purchase a home, altering its entire economic trajectory. The firm may reach a scale at which coordination problems overwhelm productivity. The car may run smoothly until a small mechanical failure causes total breakdown.

Nonlinearity describes the world beyond simple proportionality. It appears when relationships change as scale changes, when thresholds matter, when feedback loops amplify or dampen outcomes, when networks transmit shocks, when expectations alter behavior, and when systems shift from one regime to another. In economic life, nonlinearity is not rare. It is everywhere. Inflation can move from a manageable price adjustment into a self-reinforcing process. Debt can move from useful financing into systemic fragility. Inequality can move from unequal rewards into entrenched class reproduction. Housing scarcity can move from inconvenience into social crisis. Financial optimism can move from investment into mania. Technological adoption can move from innovation into monopoly. Political dissatisfaction can move from frustration into institutional breakdown.

The failure to understand nonlinearity is one reason societies are repeatedly surprised by crises. Warnings are dismissed because the system appears stable. Debt levels rise, but defaults remain low. Asset prices rise, but volatility remains subdued. Housing prices rise, but homeowners feel wealthier. Inequality rises, but consumption continues through credit. Supply chains become leaner, but goods arrive on time. Trust erodes, but institutions continue functioning. Then conditions shift. A shock arrives. The system crosses a threshold. What looked manageable becomes explosive. Observers ask why no one saw it coming, but the problem was often visible in the wrong language. The danger was not always in the immediate data. It was in the structure of the system.

Linear thinking encourages societies to treat problems as continuous. If a little debt is manageable, a little more must be only slightly less manageable. If inequality has risen without collapse, more inequality must be tolerable. If a supply chain has worked for years, it must be robust. If housing prices have risen for decades, they must be sustainable. If financial markets are calm, risk must be low. The nonlinear view asks a different question: what happens when the system reaches a point at which its behavior changes? This point may not be visible from ordinary experience. It may be hidden inside balance sheets, expectations, networks, institutional weaknesses, or political resentment. Yet once crossed, it changes everything.

The phrase "when more becomes different" captures this transformation. More debt is not simply more debt if it changes incentives, raises fragility, and makes borrowers vulnerable to small interest-rate changes. More inequality is not simply a larger gap if it alters political power, undermines trust, and locks families into different worlds of opportunity. More market concentration is not simply fewer firms if it changes pricing power, wages, innovation, and democratic influence. More data is not simply more information if it creates surveillance capacity, behavioral manipulation, and platform dominance. More efficiency is not simply lower cost if it removes the buffers that allow systems to survive disruption.

Nonlinearity is difficult because it forces us to abandon the comfort of averages. Much economic analysis depends on aggregate measures: inflation rates, unemployment rates, gross domestic product, median income, debt-to-GDP ratios, productivity growth, housing starts, and stock market indexes. These measures are useful, but they can conceal the distribution of stress within a system. An economy can show moderate inflation while food, energy, rent, and insurance crush particular households. Unemployment can be low while workers experience insecurity, unpredictable schedules, or weak bargaining power. Debt-to-GDP can appear manageable while certain sectors are overleveraged. Average housing prices can hide regional crises. Gross domestic product can rise while trust, health, and social mobility decline.

Nonlinearity often begins in these hidden distributions. Crises do not always emerge from the average. They often emerge from vulnerable nodes, concentrated exposures, or stressed populations. A financial system can appear well capitalized on average while certain institutions rely on unstable funding. A labor market can appear strong on average while care workers, gig workers, and low-wage workers face burnout. A city can appear prosperous while young families, renters, and essential workers are priced out. A nation can appear wealthy while its public health system, infrastructure, schools, and social cohesion weaken. The average may remain calm while the margins approach rupture.

This is why complexity economics pays attention to structure. It asks where risk is located, how actors are connected, how stress travels, who has buffers, who lacks them, and which feedback loops are likely to activate under pressure. The same shock can have radically different effects depending on system structure. A rise in interest rates affects a low-debt economy differently from a highly leveraged one. An energy price shock affects a diversified economy differently from one dependent on imported fuel. A pandemic affects a society with strong public health capacity differently from one with fragmented healthcare and insecure workers. A housing shortage affects a society with social housing differently from one that treats shelter primarily as a speculative asset. The shock matters, but the system matters more.

The simplest form of nonlinearity is the threshold. A threshold is a point beyond which the system behaves differently. Below the threshold, change may be gradual. Above it, change may accelerate or transform. A household can manage debt as long as income, interest rates, and expenses remain within certain bounds. But after a job loss, medical bill, rent increase, or rate reset, the household may enter a spiral of late fees, damaged credit, higher borrowing costs, and reduced options. The movement from stability to instability is not smooth. It is a regime change.

The same is true for firms. A company may carry debt comfortably when sales are strong and credit is available. But if revenue falls below a certain level, debt service consumes cash flow, lenders tighten terms, suppliers demand faster payment, employees leave, and customers lose confidence. The firm is not simply less profitable. It becomes fragile. It enters a different state. Financial distress has its own dynamics, and those dynamics can make recovery harder precisely when recovery is most needed.

Governments face thresholds as well. Public debt may be sustainable for long periods, especially when growth exceeds interest costs and investors trust institutions. But if interest rates rise, growth slows, political conflict intensifies, or currency credibility weakens, the same debt stock can become destabilizing. The threshold is not purely mathematical. It depends on institutions, currency sovereignty, investor expectations, central bank credibility, external financing needs, and political legitimacy. This is why countries with similar debt ratios can face different market reactions. Debt sustainability is nonlinear because confidence is nonlinear.

Thresholds also govern social life. A society can tolerate inequality for some time if mobility remains plausible, public goods remain functional, and institutions retain legitimacy. But when large groups conclude that the system is rigged, that effort no longer leads to security, and that elites are insulated from consequence, inequality becomes politically explosive. The gap is no longer merely economic. It becomes moral and institutional. It reshapes how citizens interpret law, taxes, elections, expertise, and one another. A society can remain formally stable while legitimacy drains away, then experience sudden political upheaval. The threshold is crossed not only in income statistics, but in collective belief.

Feedback loops are another core form of nonlinearity. A feedback loop occurs when the output of a process becomes an input into the same process. Feedback can stabilize or destabilize. Stabilizing feedback pushes a system back toward balance. If prices rise, consumers may buy less, reducing demand and moderating prices. If unemployment rises, wages may soften, encouraging hiring. These are the feedback loops most familiar to equilibrium thinking. But destabilizing feedback does the opposite. It amplifies movement. Rising prices may lead consumers to buy before prices rise further, increasing demand and pushing prices higher. Rising asset values may encourage borrowing, which fuels more asset purchases and raises prices further. Rising inequality may increase political influence among the wealthy, producing rules that increase inequality further.

Feedback is the engine of cumulative change. It is why small differences can become large differences. It is why early advantage matters. It is why instability can appear to grow out of stability. Feedback transforms events into processes. An increase in home prices is an event. If it encourages speculative buying, larger mortgages, looser lending, and political resistance to new supply, it becomes a process. A price increase in energy is an event. If it raises production costs, alters expectations, changes wage demands, and reshapes monetary policy, it becomes a process. A firm's market success is an event. If it generates data, network effects, capital access, and regulatory influence that make future success easier, it becomes a process.

Positive feedback is especially important in understanding inequality. Wealth produces opportunities to acquire more wealth. A family with assets can buy in a neighborhood with strong schools. Strong schools improve college prospects. College prospects improve earnings. Higher earnings enable homeownership and savings. Homeownership produces appreciation and collateral. Collateral supports business formation or further investment. The next generation begins at a higher point. This is not merely inheritance in the narrow sense. It is the compounding of social advantage.

The same logic operates in reverse for disadvantage. A family without wealth may rent in an underfunded school district. Lower school quality reduces future opportunity. Limited opportunity reduces earnings. Low earnings prevent savings. Lack of savings makes emergencies costly. Emergencies produce debt. Debt damages credit. Damaged credit raises the cost of borrowing. Higher costs reduce mobility. The next generation begins under constraint. The system tells a story of individual effort, but the structure is one of cumulative divergence.

This does not mean individual choices are irrelevant. It means individual choices occur within feedback systems that make some paths easier and others harder. Complexity economics does not deny agency. It contextualizes agency. A person can work hard, study, save, and make wise decisions, but the return to those decisions depends on the system in which they are made. One person's risk is cushioned by family wealth; another person's risk is punished by poverty. One person's failure becomes a lesson; another person's failure becomes a trap. Nonlinearity is not only mathematical. It is moral.

Debt provides another example of feedback. Borrowing can be productive when it finances education, business investment, housing, infrastructure, or innovation. But debt also creates fixed obligations. When income falls, debt becomes heavier. When debt becomes heavier, consumption falls. When consumption falls, business revenue may decline. When revenue declines, layoffs may follow. Layoffs reduce income further. What begins as a balance-sheet issue becomes a macroeconomic feedback loop. In highly indebted economies, downturns can be amplified because households, firms, and governments all attempt to repair balance sheets at the same time.

This is one reason debt crises can become self-reinforcing. Creditors demand higher rates because borrowers appear risky. Higher rates make borrowers riskier. Investors withdraw because they fear default. Withdrawal increases the probability of default. Governments cut spending to restore confidence. Cuts reduce growth and tax revenue, worsening debt ratios. Households reduce consumption to pay debt. Reduced consumption weakens firms, leading to layoffs. The attempt to become safer can make the system more dangerous. In nonlinear systems, rational behavior at the individual level can produce irrational outcomes at the collective level.

This is the paradox of composition. What is wise for one actor may be harmful when everyone does it simultaneously. One household saving more during uncertainty is prudent. If all households cut spending at once, demand collapses. One firm cutting costs may improve profitability. If all firms cut wages or employment, purchasing power declines. One bank reducing lending may protect its balance sheet. If all banks reduce lending, the economy contracts and loan quality deteriorates. One country pursuing export-led growth may succeed. If all countries try to run surpluses, global demand becomes inadequate. Linear thinking often aggregates individual logic. Nonlinear thinking asks what happens when individual actions interact.

The paradox of composition is central to macroeconomics, but its implications extend beyond recessions. In housing, one homeowner's desire to protect neighborhood character may be understandable. If many homeowners block new construction, regional affordability collapses. In finance, one investor's use of leverage may increase returns. If leverage becomes widespread, the system becomes fragile. In supply chains, one firm's inventory minimization may reduce costs. If all firms minimize inventory, the entire production network loses resilience. In labor markets, one firm's use of subcontracting may increase flexibility. If fissured employment becomes widespread, worker security and bargaining power decline. The collective outcome is not simply the sum of individual choices.

Networks intensify nonlinearity. In a networked economy, actors are connected through trade, finance, information, labor, technology, logistics, and institutions. A shock does not remain where it begins. It travels. A factory closure affects suppliers, workers, local businesses, tax revenue, schools, and housing markets. A bank failure affects depositors, borrowers, counterparties, investors, regulators, and public confidence. A port disruption affects manufacturers, retailers, consumers, and inflation. A cyberattack affects hospitals, firms, insurers, and public services. The structure of connections determines whether shocks are absorbed or amplified.

Network effects help explain why modern economies can be both efficient and fragile. Dense connections allow specialization, speed, and scale. They also transmit distress. A tightly integrated supply chain can reduce cost under normal conditions, but disruptions can cascade when substitutes are unavailable. A financial network can spread risk, but it can also spread panic. A digital platform can connect buyers and sellers, but it can also concentrate dependency. The same connections that create value can transmit vulnerability.

The nonlinear character of networks depends on concentration. If a network has many redundant pathways, shocks may be rerouted. If it depends on a few central nodes, failure at those nodes can produce disproportionate consequences. A single supplier of critical components, a dominant cloud provider, a major payment network, a systemically important bank, a key shipping lane, or a major energy producer can become a point of vulnerability. The problem is not merely size. It is centrality. A small node in the right position can matter more than a large node at the margins.

This insight challenges simplistic views of efficiency. Efficiency often rewards concentration, standardization, and reduced slack. Firms consolidate suppliers to gain bargaining power. They reduce inventories to lower carrying costs. They outsource functions to specialists. They rely on just-in-time logistics. These practices can increase productivity and lower consumer prices. But they also reduce redundancy. They make the system dependent on smooth coordination. When disruption occurs, the lack of slack becomes costly. What looked inefficient in normal times, inventory, spare capacity, domestic capability, public reserves, may prove essential in crisis.

The nonlinear world therefore forces us to reconsider the value of buffers. A buffer is unused capacity under ordinary conditions. It looks wasteful until the shock arrives. Household savings, unemployment insurance, public health capacity, bank capital, inventory reserves, diversified suppliers, local food systems, spare hospital beds, and resilient infrastructure are all buffers. They reduce the probability that stress becomes collapse. Linear efficiency often treats buffers as costs. Complexity economics treats them as investments in survival.

There is a deep moral dimension here. In unequal societies, buffers become class privileges. Wealthy households can absorb inflation, job loss, medical bills, and housing shocks. Poor households cannot. Large firms can access credit, legal advice, and political support. Small firms often cannot. Wealthy neighborhoods can resist shocks through private resources. Poor neighborhoods depend on public systems that are frequently underfunded. When shocks arrive, inequality determines who bends and who breaks. Resilience is distributed.

Nonlinearity also appears in expectations. Human beings do not simply observe the economy. They interpret it. Their interpretations alter their behavior, and their behavior alters the economy. If households expect prices to rise, they may buy sooner, demand higher wages, or accept price increases as normal. If firms expect competitors to raise prices, they may raise prices too. If investors expect an asset to appreciate, they may buy it, causing appreciation. If depositors expect a bank to fail, they may withdraw funds, making failure more likely. If voters expect government to fail, they may support leaders who weaken government, confirming the expectation.

Expectations make economics reflexive. A reflexive system is one in which beliefs about reality help create reality. This is why confidence is such a powerful economic force. Confidence can support investment, lending, hiring, and consumption. Loss of confidence can freeze credit, delay spending, and trigger contraction. Confidence is not irrational fluff. It is a form of coordination. But it is unstable because it depends on collective belief. People often act not only on what they believe, but on what they believe others believe.

This creates second-order uncertainty. A bank depositor may believe the bank is solvent, but if the depositor believes others will withdraw, withdrawal becomes rational. An investor may believe an asset is overvalued, but if the investor believes others will keep buying, holding the asset may be profitable. A firm may believe price increases will hurt customers, but if competitors raise prices, it may follow. A worker may desire higher wages, but if coworkers cannot coordinate, bargaining fails. Economic life is filled with such recursive expectations. Equilibrium thinking often simplifies them. Nonlinear thinking places them at the center.

The role of expectations explains why crises can appear sudden. The material conditions for crisis may build slowly, but the shift in belief can occur rapidly. A financial system can appear calm until investors question collateral values. A currency can remain stable until traders doubt the government's capacity to defend it. A political system can appear legitimate until citizens conclude that institutions no longer represent them. A housing market can rise for years until buyers believe prices have peaked. A technology bubble can grow until investors question the path to profits. The reversal is often abrupt because expectations are socially contagious.

Contagion is a nonlinear process. Ideas, fears, behaviors, and strategies spread through networks. Sometimes contagion is productive. Innovations diffuse, best practices spread, social movements grow, and new technologies become useful because others adopt them. Sometimes contagion is destructive. Panic spreads, misinformation spreads, speculative mania spreads, and scapegoating spreads. The speed of contagion depends on trust, communication channels, network structure, emotional intensity, and institutional credibility. Digital media has accelerated many forms of contagion, allowing narratives to move faster than institutions can respond.

Economic narratives are especially contagious when they simplify anxiety. In times of inflation, citizens seek explanations for rising prices. In times of inequality, they seek explanations for unfairness. In times of unemployment or displacement, they seek explanations for insecurity. Simple narratives can become politically powerful even when analytically weak. They identify villains, assign blame, and offer emotional clarity. Complexity economics cannot compete by becoming obscure. It must offer clarity without false reduction. It must explain feedback in language citizens can understand.

This is one of the purposes of this book: to make nonlinear economic thinking accessible. Complexity should not be used as a shield for technocratic authority. It should be a democratic language of realism. Citizens deserve to understand why economic problems do not yield to slogans. They deserve to know why inflation may involve supply chains, energy, market power, expectations, and policy. They deserve to know why housing scarcity involves zoning, finance, speculation, inequality, and local democracy. They deserve to know why debt can support growth and create fragility at the same time. They deserve to know why inequality compounds and why opportunity is not merely individual effort. A democratic society cannot govern nonlinear systems if public explanation remains linear.

Another key concept in nonlinearity is emergence. Emergence occurs when the behavior of the whole cannot be understood simply by examining the parts in isolation. Traffic jams emerge from the interaction of drivers, road design, timing, accidents, weather, and expectations. No single driver intends to create gridlock, but gridlock emerges. Financial bubbles emerge from the interaction of investors, lenders, media, models, incentives, and expectations. No single buyer creates the bubble, but the bubble emerges. Labor market norms emerge from firms, workers, laws, unions, culture, technology, and power. No single actor designs the whole pattern, but the pattern shapes everyone.

Emergence challenges individualistic explanations. An economy is made of individuals, but it is not reducible to individuals. The structure of interaction matters. A crowd behaves differently from isolated persons. A market behaves differently from isolated trades. A financial system behaves differently from isolated balance sheets. A city behaves differently from isolated buildings. A class structure behaves differently from isolated households. To understand emergent outcomes, we must study relations, not merely units.

This is particularly important for markets. A market is not a collection of independent transactions floating in empty space. It is an institutionally structured field of interaction. It has rules, norms, information channels, enforcement mechanisms, power asymmetries, entry barriers, and histories. The behavior of the market emerges from these features. Two markets for the same good can behave differently under different institutional conditions. A housing market with tenant protections, social housing, and abundant supply behaves differently from one dominated by speculation and exclusionary zoning. A labor market with strong unions and sectoral bargaining behaves differently from one characterized by fissured employment and monopsony power. A financial market with leverage limits behaves differently from one that rewards opacity and risk transfer.

The study of emergence also clarifies why policy interventions can have unintended consequences. A policy changes one part of the system, but actors adapt. Rent control may protect existing tenants, but if poorly designed, it may discourage maintenance or new supply. Deregulation may lower costs in one sector, but it may encourage risk-taking elsewhere. Interest-rate cuts may stimulate demand, but they may also inflate asset prices. Student loans may expand access to education, but they may also allow tuition to rise and burden young adults with debt. Subsidies may support households, but they may also be captured by firms with pricing power. The point is not that intervention fails. The point is that intervention must anticipate adaptation.

Adaptive behavior is central to nonlinearity. Economic actors are not passive. They learn, imitate, exploit, resist, evade, innovate, and reinterpret rules. A tax rule creates incentives for avoidance. A regulation creates incentives for compliance, lobbying, or circumvention. A subsidy creates incentives for entry, price adjustment, or dependency. A central bank signal changes market behavior before any formal policy takes effect. A labor law changes bargaining strategies. A platform rule changes seller behavior. Because actors adapt, policy is never a simple mechanical input. It is a move in an evolving game.

This does not make policy impossible. It makes policy strategic. Good policy must ask how actors will respond, how responses will interact, and how the system can be monitored and adjusted. It must include feedback mechanisms. It must be capable of learning. Static policy is vulnerable in adaptive systems. Rules designed for one environment may fail when actors discover loopholes or when technology changes. Financial regulation before the global financial crisis failed partly because risk moved into shadow banking and complex instruments. Labor protections designed for traditional employment can fail when firms classify workers as independent contractors. Antitrust designed for price effects can fail when digital platforms offer low prices while extracting data and controlling access.

Adaptive systems require adaptive governance. This means institutions must collect information, revise rules, coordinate across domains, and respond before crisis becomes catastrophic. It also means governance must include democratic accountability. Adaptation without accountability can become technocratic improvisation. Accountability without adaptability can become rigid failure. The challenge is to build institutions that are both capable and legitimate.

Nonlinearity also introduces the concept of regime change. A regime is a relatively stable pattern of behavior, rules, expectations, and outcomes. An economy can operate in a low-inflation regime, a high-inflation regime, a high-trust regime, a low-trust regime, a competitive regime, a monopolistic regime, a high-mobility regime, or a low-mobility regime. Regimes are not permanent, but they can be durable because feedback loops reinforce them. Moving from one regime to another may require more than small policy adjustments.

For example, a low-wage labor regime persists when workers lack bargaining power, firms compete on labor cost, public benefits subsidize low wages, unions are weak, and consumers expect cheap services. Raising the minimum wage may help, but if enforcement is weak, firms misclassify workers, or housing and healthcare costs continue rising, the regime may adapt without transforming. A more substantial shift may require labor law reform, sectoral bargaining, childcare support, immigration protection, antitrust enforcement, public procurement standards, and a changed cultural understanding of dignity at work. The problem is systemic, so the response must be systemic.

A housing scarcity regime persists when homeowners benefit from appreciation, local governments depend on property values, zoning restricts density, developers target luxury markets, investors treat housing as an asset, and renters lack political power. Increasing supply is essential, but the regime may persist if new construction is captured by high-income demand or if displacement accelerates. A transformation may require zoning reform, social housing, tenant protection, anti-speculation measures, infrastructure investment, public land use, transit planning, and regional governance. Housing cannot be solved by a single lever because housing is not a single-lever system.

An inequality regime persists when wealth buys political influence, tax systems favor capital, education is locally unequal, housing segregates opportunity, healthcare insecurity disciplines workers, and campaign finance amplifies elite voice. A small tax change may help, but cumulative advantage will adapt unless institutions are redesigned. Breaking the regime requires attention to wealth taxation, labor power, public education, housing access, healthcare security, campaign finance, antitrust, inheritance, and public investment. Complexity does not make reform vague. It makes reform comprehensive.

The nonlinear nature of regimes explains why some reforms disappoint. Policymakers often intervene at a surface level while leaving the underlying feedback loops intact. They subsidize demand in a market with constrained supply, so prices rise. They offer training in a labor market with weak demand or monopsony power, so credentials do not produce dignity. They provide credit in a society with stagnant wages, so debt rises. They regulate banks while risk migrates to nonbanks. They encourage innovation while allowing monopolies to acquire competitors. They provide tax incentives for investment without addressing aggregate demand, infrastructure, or market concentration. The system absorbs the reform and continues its trajectory.

This is not an argument against incrementalism. Incremental reforms can matter greatly. But incrementalism must be guided by a systemic understanding. A small intervention can have large effects if it targets a critical feedback loop. Conversely, a large intervention can fail if it does not alter the feedback structure. The scale of policy spending is not the same as the scale of systemic effect. A well-designed automatic stabilizer can prevent a recession from deepening. A modest change in bank capital requirements can reduce systemic risk. A targeted child allowance can alter family stress and child development trajectories. A zoning reform in a high-opportunity region can change labor mobility and wealth formation. The question is not only how much policy does, but where it acts in the system.

This brings us to leverage points. A leverage point is a place in a system where intervention can produce disproportionate effects. In mechanical systems, leverage is physical. In economic systems, leverage is institutional, informational, relational, or moral. Changing default rules in retirement savings can alter behavior more effectively than exhortation. Providing automatic unemployment insurance can stabilize demand faster than discretionary legislation. Creating public banking or credit facilities can prevent panic. Enforcing antitrust can alter pricing, wages, innovation, and political power. Strengthening unions can reshape income distribution, workplace dignity, and democratic participation. Building social housing can affect rents, family stability, segregation, and labor mobility.

Leverage points are not always obvious. They often lie in rules that appear technical. Bankruptcy law shapes risk-taking and failure. Corporate governance shapes time horizons. Accounting rules shape behavior. Zoning maps shape opportunity. Procurement rules shape labor standards. Patent law shapes innovation. Data rights shape platform power. Campaign finance rules shape economic policy. Central bank mandates shape employment and inflation tradeoffs. These institutional details are the hidden architecture of economic life. They are where nonlinearity becomes governance.

Because nonlinearity involves uncertainty, it also requires humility. No policymaker can fully predict every consequence of intervention. No model can capture all interactions. No expert can eliminate surprise. But humility is not paralysis. It is a discipline. It means designing policies with monitoring, adjustment, redundancy, and safeguards. It means avoiding irreversible damage where uncertainty is high. It means recognizing early warning signals. It means learning from local knowledge. It means allowing experimentation while preventing catastrophic harm. It means protecting those most vulnerable to policy error.

Humility also requires abandoning the fantasy that markets automatically perform this learning function in socially beneficial ways. Markets do learn, but they learn through profit and loss. Sometimes that is powerful. Sometimes it is brutal. A market may discover that a financial product is dangerous only after millions lose homes. It may discover that a supply chain is fragile only after shortages occur. It may discover that a platform is monopolistic only after competitors disappear. It may discover that climate risk is real only after disasters destroy communities. Social learning through catastrophe is not wisdom. Public policy exists partly to learn before collapse.

Nonlinearity helps explain why prevention is undervalued. The benefits of prevention are often invisible. If a banking rule prevents a crisis, no one sees the crisis that did not happen. If public health capacity prevents a pandemic surge, the avoided catastrophe has no constituency. If housing policy prevents displacement, the preserved community is taken for granted. If climate adaptation prevents flood damage, the success appears uneventful. Linear accounting often values what happens, not what is prevented. Complexity economics values avoided cascades.

This has implications for public budgets. Societies often treat prevention as spending and crisis response as necessity. They underinvest in infrastructure, health, education, housing, regulation, and climate adaptation, then spend enormously after failure. This is backward. In nonlinear systems, small investments in resilience can prevent large losses. The difficulty is political. Prevention requires imagination. It asks citizens to pay for a future harm that may not occur precisely because they paid. This is why trust matters. Low-trust societies struggle to invest in prevention because people doubt institutions will use resources well or distribute benefits fairly. Trust itself becomes a resilience asset.

Trust is nonlinear. It accumulates slowly and collapses quickly. Institutions can build trust through competence, fairness, transparency, accountability, and responsiveness. But a series of failures, scandals, or betrayals can produce sudden distrust. Once distrust spreads, policy becomes harder. Citizens resist public health guidance, monetary policy, taxation, regulation, climate action, and democratic compromise. Low trust increases the cost of governance. It also makes societies vulnerable to demagogic simplification. In this sense, trust is not merely a cultural virtue. It is economic infrastructure.

Legitimacy operates similarly. A society may tolerate hardship if citizens believe burdens are shared fairly and institutions act honestly. But if hardship is seen as imposed by insulated elites, legitimacy erodes. Inflation becomes more than rising prices. It becomes a symbol of unfairness. Austerity becomes more than budget discipline. It becomes abandonment. Bailouts become more than stabilization. They become evidence of unequal citizenship. Trade disruption becomes more than adjustment. It becomes betrayal. Nonlinear politics emerges when material stress interacts with moral interpretation.

This is why economic policy cannot be separated from democratic stability. A policy that is technically efficient but perceived as unfair may fail politically. A policy that reduces inflation by producing unemployment may restore price stability while destroying trust among workers. A policy that rescues banks without rescuing households may stabilize finance while delegitimizing the state. A policy that promotes growth while concentrating gains may improve aggregates while feeding resentment. A nonlinear world requires attention to both material outcomes and moral meaning.

The relationship between economics and politics is itself a feedback loop. Economic insecurity increases political distrust. Political distrust weakens capacity for policy. Weakened policy allows insecurity to worsen. Inequality increases elite influence. Elite influence shapes rules. Rules increase inequality. Regional decline produces resentment. Resentment supports disruptive politics. Disruptive politics discourages investment and reduces institutional performance. These loops can push democracies toward instability. Economic problems become constitutional problems when citizens lose faith that the system can correct itself.

Nonlinearity also changes how we think about responsibility. In a linear world, responsibility is easy to assign. One cause produces one effect. One actor is at fault. In complex systems, responsibility is distributed, but it does not disappear. A crisis may be produced by many actors responding to incentives. Yet those incentives were designed, defended, tolerated, or ignored. Banks may take excessive risk because regulation permits it. Firms may suppress wages because labor law allows it. Landlords may exploit scarcity because housing policy creates it. Platforms may extract data because legal frameworks fail to limit it. Politicians may serve donors because campaign finance systems reward it. Complexity reveals shared causation, but shared causation does not mean moral innocence.

Indeed, complexity may deepen responsibility. If leaders know that systems can amplify harm, they have a duty to design safeguards. If regulators know that financial stability breeds risk-taking, they must act before crisis. If policymakers know that inequality compounds, they must intervene early. If governments know that housing scarcity destabilizes families, they must treat shelter as infrastructure. If societies know that climate risk is nonlinear, they must act before thresholds are crossed. Responsibility in a nonlinear world is responsibility for foreseeable dynamics, not merely immediate intentions.

This is especially important because nonlinear harm often falls hardest on those least responsible for creating it. Low-income households did not design inflationary supply chains, concentrated markets, or monetary regimes, but they suffer from price increases. Workers did not design financialization, but they lose jobs in crises. Renters did not design zoning scarcity, but they pay the cost. Young people did not design student debt systems or housing inflation, but their life choices are constrained. Future generations did not emit past carbon, but they inherit climate instability. Complexity economics must therefore be an ethics of exposure. It must ask who is exposed to risks created elsewhere.

The idea of exposure is central to understanding crisis. Not everyone experiences the same shock in the same way. A rise in food prices is inconvenient for the affluent and devastating for the poor. A rise in interest rates benefits some savers and harms indebted households, homebuyers, governments, and firms. A stock market decline affects asset owners more directly than nonowners, but it can affect workers through investment, pensions, and business confidence. A supply disruption affects firms differently depending on inventory, supplier diversity, and pricing power. A heat wave affects neighborhoods differently depending on trees, housing quality, healthcare, and work conditions. Nonlinearity is always positional.

This means that aggregate policy must be distributionally aware. A central bank cannot assume that rate hikes move smoothly through a representative economy. A fiscal authority cannot assume that spending cuts affect all citizens equally. A housing policy cannot assume that supply additions automatically reach those most burdened. A technology policy cannot assume that productivity gains translate into shared income. A climate policy cannot assume that carbon prices are fair without redistribution. In nonlinear systems, distribution shapes dynamics. The exposed are often where cascades begin.

The phrase "more becomes different" applies powerfully to scale. When a small firm grows, it may become more efficient. When it becomes dominant, it may become a gatekeeper. When a city grows, it may become more productive through agglomeration. When housing supply fails to match growth, the city may become exclusionary. When a financial sector grows, it may improve capital allocation. When it becomes too large and politically powerful, it may extract rents and create systemic risk. When government debt rises to fund productive investment, it may support prosperity. When debt rises to compensate for stagnant wages, tax avoidance, or recurring crisis, it may signal structural failure.

Scale changes function. A technology platform with a few thousand users is a service. With billions of users, it becomes infrastructure. A landlord with one property is an owner. Large-scale institutional ownership of housing can become a market-shaping force. A hedge fund is one investor among many until its strategies are widely imitated or its positions become systemically relevant. A corporation is one legal entity until its supply chains, lobbying, labor practices, and data systems shape public life. At scale, private decisions acquire public consequences. Nonlinearity is the moment when private power becomes systemic power.

This has important implications for law and regulation. Rules appropriate for small actors may be inadequate for systemically important actors. A local bank and a global bank do not pose the same risks. A small online forum and a dominant platform do not have the same social role. A family landlord and a large institutional housing owner do not affect markets in the same way. A small employer and a dominant regional employer do not have the same labor power. Scale should alter public obligations. Complexity economics supports a principle of systemic responsibility: the greater an actor's capacity to affect the system, the greater its obligation to the public order on which it depends.

Nonlinearity also helps us understand why economic categories blur. Inflation is not only monetary. It is also supply-chain, energy-related, institutional, behavioral, and political. Debt is not only financial. It is psychological, social, and macroeconomic. Inequality is not only distributive. It is educational, spatial, political, and intergenerational. Housing is not only shelter. It is finance, wealth, geography, and citizenship. Labor is not only production. It is dignity, identity, care, and power. Technology is not only innovation. It is market structure, surveillance, labor displacement, and institutional transformation. The categories are analytically useful, but the reality is interconnected.

This interconnectedness means that policy failure often arises from category error. Treat housing only as a private market, and its role in education, labor mobility, family stability, and wealth inequality is missed. Treat labor only as a cost, and its role in demand, dignity, productivity, and democracy is missed. Treat finance only as capital allocation, and its role in crisis, inequality, and political power is missed. Treat technology only as productivity, and its role in monopoly, surveillance, and worker control is missed. Treat inflation only as aggregate demand, and its sectoral and distributive dynamics are missed. Nonlinearity punishes narrow categories.

The challenge is to think systemically without becoming vague. Systemic thinking must be disciplined. It must identify specific mechanisms. Feedback is a mechanism. Thresholds are mechanisms. Network centrality is a mechanism. Increasing returns are mechanisms. Path dependence is a mechanism. Expectations are mechanisms. Power is a mechanism. Institutional design is a mechanism. A complexity approach does not say, "Everything affects everything," as if that were enough. It asks which connections matter most, under what conditions, with what delays, and for whom.

Delay is another feature of nonlinearity. Effects do not always appear immediately. A policy can seem successful in the short run while creating long-term fragility. Financial deregulation can increase credit and profits before increasing crisis risk. Underinvestment in infrastructure can save money before producing breakdown. Weak labor protections can lower prices before weakening families, demand, and trust. Carbon emissions can support growth before producing climate damage. Housing restrictions can enrich current owners before excluding future generations. Delay makes nonlinear systems politically difficult because benefits and costs appear at different times.

Short-termism thrives in the presence of delay. Politicians seek reelection. Executives seek quarterly results. Investors seek annual returns. Households under pressure seek immediate survival. Delayed harms are discounted, ignored, or denied. Yet nonlinear systems accumulate consequences. The future is not separate from the present. It is being built through feedback, investment, neglect, and institutional choice. A society that cannot value delayed effects will repeatedly convert preventable risks into emergencies.

This is why nonlinear governance must include time horizons. Good policy asks how today's choices alter tomorrow's options. Does current growth depend on depleting trust, health, infrastructure, climate stability, or household balance sheets? Does current profitability depend on suppressing wages, evading taxes, weakening suppliers, or increasing systemic risk? Does current fiscal discipline depend on underinvesting in children, science, housing, and resilience? Does current technological convenience depend on building monopolies that will later control markets? The nonlinear question is always temporal: what trajectory are we creating?

Trajectories matter because systems can develop momentum. Momentum is not destiny, but it is real. Once an economy becomes dependent on debt-fueled consumption, shifting toward wage-led growth becomes difficult. Once housing wealth becomes central to household balance sheets, reducing housing prices becomes politically painful. Once firms depend on global labor arbitrage, rebuilding domestic capacity requires time. Once platforms dominate markets, restoring competition requires structural reform. Once inequality shapes politics, redistributive policy becomes harder to enact. The longer a system travels in one direction, the more costly reversal can become.

This is why early intervention matters. In nonlinear systems, waiting until harm is obvious often means waiting too long. Preventing a bubble is easier than cleaning up after a crash. Preserving affordable housing is easier than rebuilding it after displacement. Maintaining public trust is easier than restoring it after betrayal. Reducing emissions early is easier than adapting after climate damage accelerates. Keeping debt manageable is easier than restructuring under crisis. Protecting competition is easier than breaking entrenched monopoly. Nonlinearity rewards foresight and punishes complacency.

Yet foresight is politically difficult because nonlinear risks are often uncertain. Opponents of action can always say that crisis is not certain. They can point to years of stability as evidence that warnings are exaggerated. They can accuse reformers of alarmism. This happened before financial crises, climate disasters, supply chain disruptions, and democratic breakdowns. But uncertainty cuts both ways. The fact that collapse is uncertain does not justify ignoring risk. In nonlinear systems, uncertainty may strengthen the case for precaution because the cost of being wrong can be catastrophic.

Precaution is not fearfulness. It is rational humility under conditions of irreversible or systemic harm. A society does not need certainty of bank failure to require capital buffers. It does not need certainty of pandemic to maintain public health capacity. It does not need certainty of flood to strengthen infrastructure. It does not need certainty of monopoly abuse to enforce competition. It does not need certainty of political unrest to reduce inequality. Precaution recognizes that some failures are too costly to learn from after the fact.

Nonlinearity also changes how we interpret success. A policy may appear successful because nothing bad happens. But perhaps nothing bad happened because the system was resilient. Or perhaps nothing bad happened because risk had not yet matured. Low inflation may reflect good policy, but it may also reflect suppressed labor power, cheap imports, global slack, or temporary energy conditions. High asset prices may reflect innovation, but they may also reflect low rates and speculative expectations. Low unemployment may reflect labor market strength, but it may coexist with poor job quality. Budget surpluses may reflect prudence, but they may also reflect underinvestment. Complexity asks us to examine the foundations of apparent success.

The same applies to failure. Failure may not mean a policy was wrong. It may mean the policy was too small, poorly timed, badly targeted, or overwhelmed by other feedback loops. A housing subsidy that raises rents in a constrained market does not prove that housing assistance is foolish. It proves that demand support without supply reform and anti-speculation measures can be captured. A job training program that fails in a weak labor market does not prove that workers cannot learn. It proves that skills policy cannot substitute for job creation, bargaining power, and regional investment. A stimulus that produces inflation under supply constraints does not prove that fiscal policy is always inflationary. It proves that demand support must consider productive capacity and bottlenecks.

Nonlinear thinking therefore improves judgment. It resists simplistic success stories and simplistic failure stories. It asks what else was happening, what mechanisms were activated, how actors adapted, and what conditions shaped outcomes. It does not excuse poor policy. It demands better policy.

The chapters that follow apply these ideas to specific economic problems. Inflation will be examined as a feedback process, not merely a monetary aggregate. Debt will be examined as a structure of leverage and fragility, not merely a number. Inequality will be examined as cumulative advantage, not merely dispersion. Housing will be examined as a scarcity regime, not merely a supply curve. Labor markets will be examined as adaptive networks, not merely exchanges of wages for work. Supply chains will be examined as systems balancing efficiency and resilience. Financial markets will be examined as reflexive arenas of herding, leverage, and cascades. Technology will be examined as disruptive feedback, not automatic progress. Public policy will be examined as adaptive governance under uncertainty.

The purpose of this chapter has been to provide the conceptual grammar for that inquiry. Nonlinearity is the grammar of modern economic realism. It teaches that proportionality cannot be assumed, that thresholds matter, that feedback loops shape outcomes, that networks transmit shocks, that expectations create realities, that power changes dynamics, that history constrains possibility, and that systems can shift regimes. It teaches that economic life is not a sequence of isolated problems, but an evolving web of interactions.

This grammar is not only analytical. It is ethical. If more can become different, then societies must pay attention before difference becomes disaster. If inequality compounds, justice cannot wait. If debt fragility accumulates in calm periods, regulation cannot wait for panic. If housing scarcity becomes a trap, reform cannot wait for homelessness to become normalized. If climate risk crosses thresholds, delay is not neutrality. If technological platforms become infrastructure, governance cannot wait until dependency is complete. If trust collapses quickly, institutions must earn it continuously.

Nonlinearity makes complacency dangerous. It also makes hope realistic. If systems can spiral downward, they can also be redirected. Positive feedback can be used for inclusion, not only exclusion. Early childhood investment can compound through education, health, earnings, and civic participation. Affordable housing can support family stability, labor mobility, and community resilience. Strong labor institutions can raise wages, reduce inequality, and strengthen demand. Public investment can crowd in private innovation. Trustworthy institutions can increase compliance, cooperation, and legitimacy. Climate investment can create industries, jobs, and resilience. System design matters because feedback can be changed.

This is the constructive side of complexity economics. It does not merely warn that systems can fail. It shows that systems can be built differently. The economy is not governed by immutable laws that condemn societies to inequality, crisis, and fragility. It is shaped by rules, norms, institutions, technologies, and choices. Those choices operate in nonlinear ways, which means they can produce harm when badly designed, but also transformation when wisely designed.

The end of simple economic explanations begins with the recognition that more is not always more of the same. At certain points, more debt becomes fragility. More inequality becomes domination. More efficiency becomes brittleness. More concentration becomes power. More data becomes surveillance. More speculation becomes crisis. More insecurity becomes political instability. But the reverse can also be true. More trust can become cooperation. More security can become entrepreneurship. More fairness can become legitimacy. More resilience can become stability. More voice can become democracy. More public capacity can become freedom.

The task of economic thought is to understand these transformations. The task of economic policy is to guide them. In a nonlinear world, the question is never only how much. It is how, where, when, for whom, under what conditions, and through what feedback loops. Until we learn to ask these questions, we will continue to be surprised by crises that were long in preparation. Once we learn to ask them, economics can become what it must now become: a discipline of systemic understanding, moral responsibility, and democratic design.

## Chapter 4

# Feedback Loops, Tipping Points, and Economic Cascades

ECONOMIC SYSTEMS DO not merely move. They react to their own movement. A price change alters expectations. Expectations alter behavior. Behavior alters demand, supply, investment, credit, and politics. Those changes then reshape prices again. A debt boom raises asset values. Rising asset values encourage more borrowing. More borrowing raises asset values further. A housing shortage raises rents. Rising rents increase the wealth of owners, strengthen political resistance to new supply, and push workers farther from opportunity. Scarcity then deepens. A financial panic begins with fear. Fear causes selling, withdrawal, and defensive behavior. That behavior makes the feared outcome more likely.

This is the world of feedback loops. To understand modern economic problems, one must understand not only causes, but returning causes. A feedback loop exists when the result of a process becomes part of the process that produced it. Feedback gives economic life its recursive character. The economy does not simply receive shocks from outside and adjust. It produces reactions to shocks, and those reactions become new forces. The original cause may disappear while the process it triggered continues. This is why economic crises can outgrow their origins. A small disturbance in mortgage lending can become a global financial crisis. A temporary supply disruption can become persistent inflation. A local housing shortage can become a generational wealth divide. A short

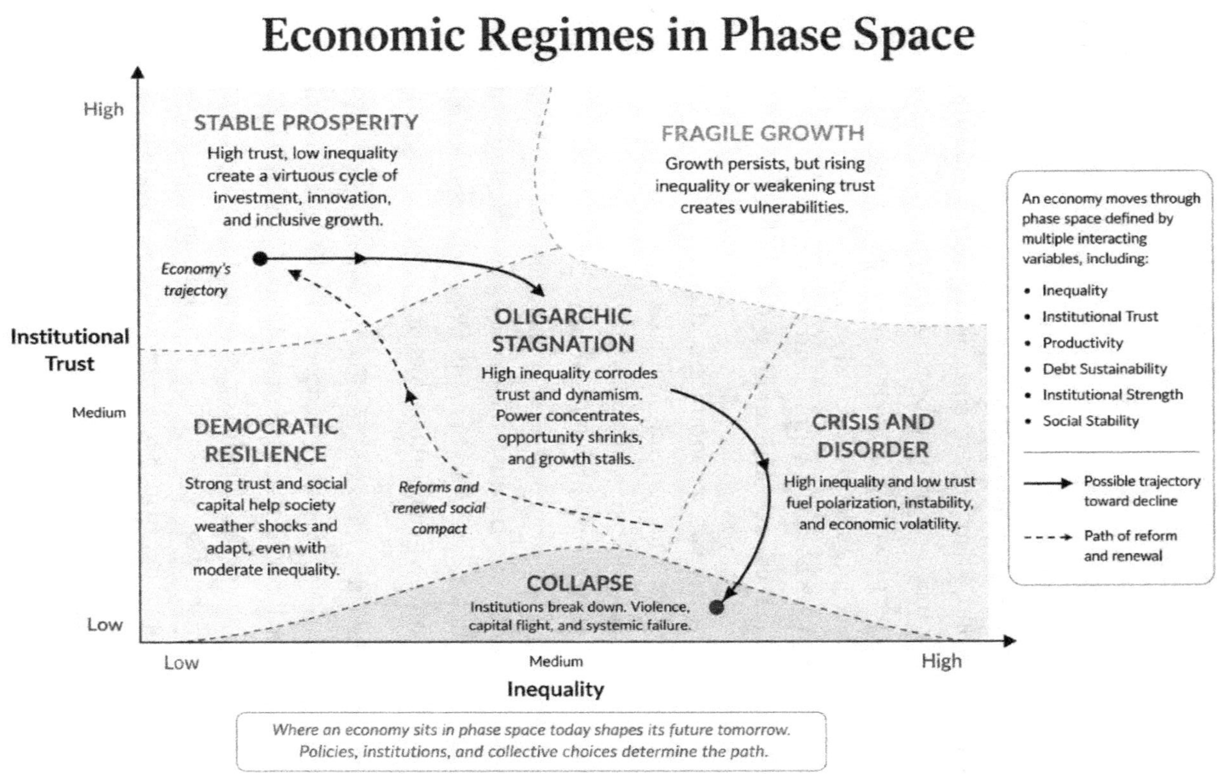


*Figure 3.0 – Economic Regions in Phase Space*

recession can become long-term labor market damage. A moment of distrust can become a self-fulfilling collapse.

Feedback loops are the machinery of nonlinearity. They explain why economic outcomes are often disproportionate to their apparent causes. They explain why stability can become fragility, why inequality compounds, why financial markets overshoot, why inflation becomes political, why technological advantage becomes dominance, and why public mistrust can become institutional paralysis. Feedback loops also explain why reform is difficult. Policies do not enter a passive world. They enter systems that respond, adapt, resist, and reinterpret. A subsidy may relieve hardship, or it may be captured by landlords, universities, hospitals, or firms with pricing power. A regulation may reduce risk, or risk may migrate elsewhere. A rate increase may slow inflation, or it may trigger financial stress, reduce housing supply, and deepen inequality. A policy becomes part of the feedback structure it seeks to change.

The first task of complexity economics is therefore to map feedback. Which loops stabilize the system? Which loops amplify instability? Which actors gain from the loop? Which actors are trapped by it? Where are delays hidden? Where are thresholds accumulating? What happens if the loop reverses? What begins as a technical question quickly becomes a moral and political one, because feedback loops distribute advantage and danger. They determine who benefits from self-reinforcing growth and who suffers from self-reinforcing decline.

There are two broad types of feedback: balancing feedback and reinforcing feedback. Balancing feedback works against change. It pushes a system back toward a range of stability. If the price of a good rises, consumers may reduce purchases, slowing further price increases. If unemployment rises, wages may moderate, encouraging firms to hire. If inventories accumulate, firms reduce production. Balancing feedback is the kind of feedback that makes equilibrium thinking plausible. It is the source of adjustment, moderation, and correction. It is real, and it matters.

But economies also contain reinforcing feedback. Reinforcing feedback amplifies change. It pushes the system farther in the direction it is already moving. Rising prices can lead consumers to buy sooner, raising demand and pushing prices still higher. Rising asset prices can increase collateral values, encouraging more borrowing and further asset appreciation. Rising market share can produce scale economies, data advantages, network effects, and capital access that increase market share further. Rising inequality can produce political influence that protects and increases inequality. Declining trust can produce defensive behavior that causes further decline in trust.

Equilibrium thinking tends to emphasize balancing feedback. Complexity economics insists that reinforcing feedback is equally central, especially in crisis, inequality, finance, housing, technology, and politics. A system dominated by balancing feedback may return to a familiar range after disturbance. A system dominated by reinforcing feedback may move toward extremes. The deepest question is not whether markets adjust, but what kind of feedback governs the adjustment. Sometimes price changes correct imbalance. Sometimes they amplify it. Sometimes profit attracts competition. Sometimes it entrenches monopoly. Sometimes credit supports investment. Sometimes it fuels speculative acceleration. Sometimes social stress produces reform. Sometimes it produces resentment, scapegoating, and institutional decay.

The difference matters because reinforcing feedback can create tipping points. A tipping point is a threshold at which a system's behavior changes qualitatively. Before the threshold, pressure may accumulate without dramatic visible consequences. After the threshold, change accelerates. The system enters a new regime. A bank can appear safe until depositors believe other depositors will withdraw. A currency can appear stable until investors believe the government cannot defend it. A housing market can appear merely expensive until workers, families, and employers begin reorganizing around unaffordability. A democracy can appear stable until enough citizens conclude that institutions no longer deserve legitimacy. An inflationary episode can appear temporary until firms and households change expectations.

Tipping points are difficult to identify in advance because they are often psychological, institutional, and relational, not merely numerical. There is no universal debt-to-income ratio at which every household collapses. There is no single inflation rate at which all societies lose confidence.

There is no exact inequality measure at which democracy becomes unstable. There is no fixed housing cost burden at which a city becomes socially unsustainable. Thresholds depend on context: buffers, institutions, narratives, trust, distribution, and power. The same economic pressure can be absorbed in one society and destabilizing in another.

This is why averages mislead. A society may have manageable average debt, but if debt is concentrated among households without savings, the system is vulnerable. Inflation may be moderate on average, but if essential goods rise sharply, political anger can surge. Housing prices may seem rational relative to regional income averages, but if essential workers, young families, and renters are excluded, the social threshold may already have been crossed. A banking system may appear capitalized in aggregate, but if confidence rests on a few fragile institutions or opaque assets, a cascade may be near. The tipping point often appears first at the margins, not in the mean.

A cascade occurs when a disturbance spreads through connected parts of a system, triggering additional disturbances as it moves. Cascades are the visible expression of hidden interdependence. A mortgage default damages a lender. The lender sells assets. Asset prices fall. Falling prices weaken other institutions. Weak institutions restrict credit. Restricted credit harms firms and households. The broader economy slows. More borrowers default. What began as a local problem becomes systemic. Cascades are not accidents in highly connected systems. They are possibilities built into the structure of connection.

Economic cascades are especially dangerous when networks are tightly coupled. A tightly coupled system is one in which parts depend on one another with little time, slack, or redundancy. Modern finance is tightly coupled through leverage, collateral, derivatives, payment systems, and confidence. Supply chains are tightly coupled through just-in-time logistics, specialized inputs, shipping routes, and vendor dependencies. Housing markets are tightly coupled to credit markets, labor mobility, municipal finance, family formation, and wealth accumulation. Digital economies are tightly coupled through platforms, cloud infrastructure, payment networks, and data systems. Tight coupling increases speed and efficiency, but it also accelerates contagion.

In a loosely coupled system, failure can be contained. If one supplier fails, another can replace it. If one bank weakens, others remain trusted. If one region experiences a shock, other regions compensate. If one household loses income, public systems stabilize consumption. In a tightly coupled system without buffers, failure travels. The speed of the cascade can exceed the speed of governance. By the time policymakers understand one failure, the system has already transmitted it elsewhere.

The global financial crisis remains a powerful example of feedback, tipping points, and cascades. The crisis did not arise from one bad loan, one reckless bank, or one mistaken forecast. It arose from reinforcing loops embedded in housing, credit, securitization, leverage, rating systems, and expectations. Rising home prices made mortgage lending appear safe. The appearance of safety encouraged looser lending. Looser lending brought more buyers into the housing market. More buyers pushed prices higher. Rising prices validated the belief that housing was safe collateral. Mortgage originators produced more loans. Securitizers packaged them. Rating agencies blessed them. Investors bought them. Financial institutions used leverage to increase returns. The loop reinforced itself.

The system crossed a tipping point when confidence in housing prices, mortgage securities, and institutional solvency began to break. Once confidence faltered, the cascade reversed the boom's logic. Falling home prices increased defaults. Defaults damaged mortgage securities. Securities lost value. Institutions holding those securities weakened. Weak institutions sold assets. Asset sales depressed prices. Interbank lending froze. Credit contracted. The real economy suffered. Workers lost jobs. Job losses increased defaults. The crisis became self-reinforcing.

The striking feature of such crises is that the same network that produces expansion produces collapse. During the boom, interconnection appears to spread opportunity and risk. During the bust, it spreads fear and loss. During the boom, leverage increases purchasing power. During the bust, leverage forces liquidation. During the boom, rising prices produce confidence. During the bust, falling prices produce panic. The feedback loop does not disappear. It changes direction.

This is why crisis prevention cannot rely on observing calm. Calm may be the product of the very feedback loop that is generating danger. Low defaults during a credit boom do not prove safety if rising asset prices are temporarily concealing borrower weakness. Low market volatility does not prove stability if it encourages leverage. Rising tax revenue during an asset boom does not prove fiscal strength if revenue depends on unsustainable prices. High corporate profits do not prove productive health if profits depend on monopoly power, cost cutting, financial engineering, or fragile global supply chains. In nonlinear systems, apparent success may be crisis in preparation.

Inflation also operates through feedback loops. At first, inflation may begin with a particular shock: energy prices, supply bottlenecks, currency depreciation, fiscal stimulus, labor shortages, geopolitical conflict, or food scarcity. But whether inflation persists depends on how the system responds. Firms may raise prices because costs rise. Workers may demand higher wages to protect purchasing power. Firms may then raise prices again to protect margins. Consumers may accelerate purchases because they expect future prices to be higher. Landlords may raise rents because market conditions permit it. Lenders may demand higher interest rates. Central banks may tighten policy. Governments may provide relief. Relief may support demand. The process becomes circular.

Inflation is not merely a number. It is a feedback process involving expectations, distribution, power, and trust. If citizens trust that inflation will be contained, temporary shocks may not become embedded. If workers have bargaining power, they may protect real wages. If firms have market power, they may protect margins. If households lack savings, they may turn to debt. If public institutions lack credibility, inflation can become a political crisis. The same price shock can produce different outcomes depending on the feedback structure of the economy.

This explains why inflation is also a conflict over real income. When prices rise, someone must absorb the loss unless income rises equally. Workers seek wage gains. Firms seek price increases. Landlords seek rent increases. Creditors seek higher rates. Governments seek to protect vulnerable households, or to protect budgets. Central banks seek to reduce demand. These responses interact. Inflation becomes not only a macroeconomic imbalance, but a struggle over who has the power to pass costs on and who is forced to bear them.

A society with strong institutions may contain this conflict through negotiated wage-setting, credible monetary policy, targeted fiscal support, competition policy, and supply-side repair. A society with weak institutions may allow the conflict to become chaotic. Firms raise prices opportunistically. Workers fall behind. Central banks overcorrect. Politicians blame convenient enemies. Public trust erodes. A temporary shock becomes a legitimacy crisis. The tipping point is not only economic. It is institutional.

Debt is another feedback system. Debt allows present spending against future income. Used wisely, it finances investment, homes, education, infrastructure, and business formation. But debt changes behavior because it creates fixed obligations. When income is stable and asset values rise, debt can appear harmless. When conditions shift, debt magnifies vulnerability. A household with debt responds to job loss differently from a household without debt. A firm with debt responds to declining revenue differently from a firm with cash reserves. A government with high refinancing needs responds to interest-rate changes differently from one with long-term stable financing. Debt turns shocks into obligations.

The debt feedback loop often begins benignly. Low interest rates encourage borrowing. Borrowing supports spending and asset purchases. Asset purchases raise prices. Rising prices increase collateral values. Higher collateral values support more borrowing. Rising asset prices make balance sheets look stronger, which encourages lenders to extend credit. The loop produces prosperity, or the appearance of it. But when rates rise, income falls, or asset prices decline, the loop reverses. Borrowers reduce spending to service debt. Asset sales depress prices. Falling prices weaken collateral. Lenders tighten credit. Tight credit reduces spending and investment. Reduced spending weakens income. Debt becomes harder to service.

The danger is that debt problems can become collective even when borrowing decisions were individual. One household cutting consumption to pay debt is prudent. Millions doing so reduce aggregate demand. One bank tightening credit is cautious. Many banks doing so produce contraction. One investor selling assets is rational. Many investors selling at once cause a crash. Debt creates synchronization under stress because obligations force similar behavior. The system becomes less diverse precisely when diversity is needed.

Inequality contains some of the most powerful feedback loops in modern capitalism. Wealth produces more wealth through returns, collateral, investment opportunities, tax advantages, inheritance, political influence, and social networks. Poverty produces further disadvantage through insecurity, debt, health stress, educational inequality, neighborhood disadvantage, and reduced bargaining power. These loops are not symmetrical in moral meaning, but they are structurally related. Advantage compounds. Disadvantage compounds.

One of the most important inequality loops runs through housing. Families with wealth can buy homes in high-opportunity neighborhoods. Homeownership provides stability, tax advantages, and asset appreciation. High property values support local schools and public services. Strong schools increase future income prospects. Rising values allow refinancing, intergenerational transfers, and political influence. Families without wealth rent in less advantaged areas, face instability, have limited access to high-performing schools, and miss asset appreciation. Over time, housing becomes not merely a reflection of inequality, but a generator of inequality.

Another loop runs through politics. Wealthy individuals and corporations can influence policy through campaign finance, lobbying, think tanks, media, philanthropy, litigation, and regulatory participation. Policy then shapes taxation, labor law, antitrust, financial regulation, corporate governance, housing rules, and public investment. These rules influence the future distribution of wealth. As wealth concentrates, influence concentrates. As influence concentrates, policy becomes less responsive to those without wealth. Democracy remains formally equal, but substantively unequal. Inequality becomes a feedback loop between markets and the state.

This loop is especially dangerous because it can undermine its own correction mechanisms. In a healthy democracy, rising inequality should produce political pressure for reform. But if inequality itself gives the wealthy greater power to shape politics, then the system's corrective feedback weakens. What should have been a balancing loop becomes a reinforcing loop. Citizens may recognize unfairness, but institutions fail to respond. Over time, frustration turns into cynicism, cynicism into distrust, and distrust into democratic instability.

Housing markets illustrate feedback with unusual clarity because they connect economics, politics, geography, and emotion. Rising home prices benefit existing owners. Owners then have incentives to protect scarcity through zoning restrictions, opposition to density, preservation of neighborhood exclusivity, and political pressure. Restricted supply supports further price increases. Higher prices increase owner wealth and political confidence. Renters, younger households, and newcomers are dispersed, delayed, or excluded, reducing their political power in the places where decisions are made. The loop reinforces itself.

This is why housing scarcity cannot be understood only as a technical failure to build. It is a political economy of incumbency. Those who own scarce assets often gain from scarcity. Those harmed by scarcity are often less organized, less wealthy, younger, more mobile, or excluded from local decision-making. The feedback loop protects itself. The result is a system in which private wealth accumulation conflicts with the public need for shelter, mobility, and family formation.

Housing also produces cascades. High rents reduce household savings. Low savings delay homeownership. Delayed homeownership reduces wealth accumulation. High housing costs force longer commutes. Long commutes reduce family time, health, and productivity. Employers struggle to attract workers. Regional inequality rises. Homelessness increases. Public budgets strain. Political resentment grows. A housing shortage becomes a labor problem, a family problem, a fiscal problem, a health problem, and a democratic problem. Cascades reveal that shelter is not a commodity like any other. It is foundational infrastructure for social life.

Labor markets contain feedback loops that determine whether work becomes a pathway to dignity or a mechanism of insecurity. Strong worker bargaining power can raise wages, support demand, reduce turnover, increase productivity, and strengthen communities. Higher wages can improve health, education, family stability, and civic participation. These improvements can reinforce productivity and social trust. This is a virtuous loop.

But weak bargaining power can create a vicious loop. Low wages reduce savings. Lack of savings reduces exit options. Reduced exit options weaken bargaining power. Weak bargaining power permits unstable schedules, poor benefits, and unsafe conditions. Instability reduces education, mobility, and political participation. Reduced voice allows further weakening of labor protections. The system then interprets worker insecurity as a personal failure rather than a structural outcome.

The decline of unions in many sectors demonstrates how feedback can alter the moral structure of labor markets. Unions do not only bargain wages. They create worker voice, establish norms, reduce arbitrary power, transmit information, train leaders, and connect workplaces to democratic politics. When unions weaken, wages may stagnate, but other feedback loops weaken as well. Workers lose institutional representation. Firms gain discretion. Political support for labor standards declines. Inequality rises. Rising inequality increases corporate influence. Corporate influence weakens labor protections further. A change in one institution becomes a broader transformation of political economy.

Supply chains are feedback systems organized around cost, speed, trust, and dependency. For decades, firms were rewarded for reducing inventory, outsourcing production, consolidating suppliers, and optimizing logistics. These practices lowered costs and raised profits. Lower costs reinforced the strategy. Investors rewarded firms for efficiency. Competitors imitated. Suppliers reorganized around global networks. Consumers became accustomed to low prices and rapid delivery. The loop intensified.

But this efficiency loop carried hidden fragility. Reduced inventory meant less buffer. Supplier consolidation meant fewer alternatives. Geographic concentration meant exposure to local shocks. Long-distance logistics meant vulnerability to ports, shipping lanes, fuel prices, labor disputes, and geopolitical conflict. The system looked efficient because normal conditions persisted long enough for fragility to be forgotten. When disruptions arrived, the cascade moved quickly: factory closures, shipping delays, input shortages, production stoppages, price increases, and political pressure.

The lesson is not that global trade is bad or that efficiency has no value. The lesson is that efficiency without resilience becomes brittle. A society that measures only cost reduction will underinvest in redundancy. A firm that measures only quarterly profitability will underinvest in shock absorption. A government that assumes private optimization will produce public resilience will be disappointed. Resilience must be designed. It does not automatically emerge from the pursuit of lowest cost.

Financial markets are perhaps the most feedback-sensitive institutions in the economy. They are built on expectations about expectations. Investors care not only about what an asset is worth, but about what others will believe it is worth. This creates herding. If enough investors move in one direction, price movements themselves become information. Rising prices suggest opportunity. Falling prices suggest danger. A market can become self-referential, interpreting its own movements as evidence.

This reflexivity explains bubbles. An asset rises in price. Rising price attracts attention. Attention attracts buyers. Buyers push the price higher. Higher price validates bullish narratives. Credit expands. Skeptics are dismissed. Media amplify the story. New financial products appear. More participants enter. The bubble becomes a social phenomenon, not merely a pricing error. It is sustained by stories, incentives, leverage, and imitation.

The crash is also reflexive. Price declines produce doubt. Doubt produces selling. Selling produces further declines. Declines trigger margin calls, redemptions, downgrades, and forced liquidation. Liquidity disappears. The same investors who claimed long-term conviction discover short-term constraints. Fundamentals may matter less than balance-sheet pressure. The cascade continues until a new stabilizing force enters: central bank action, fiscal support, lender-of-last-resort facilities, coordinated restructuring, or exhaustion of selling.

Technological change creates feedback loops through adoption, scale, data, and dependency. A digital platform becomes more valuable as more users join. More users attract more sellers, advertisers, developers, or creators. Their participation makes the platform more valuable to users. The platform gathers more data. More data improves targeting, prediction, and service quality. Better service attracts more users. Investors provide capital because growth appears self-reinforcing. Competitors struggle because they lack the user base, data, and ecosystem. The loop produces concentration.

This dynamic challenges the older belief that high profits naturally attract competition until returns normalize. In network markets, success can protect itself. Dominance may become a barrier to entry. Users remain because others remain. Sellers remain because buyers remain. Developers remain because users remain. Advertisers remain because attention remains. The system locks in. What began as innovation can become infrastructure. What began as service can become dependency. What began as market success can become private governance.

Technological feedback also affects labor. Automation can reduce demand for certain tasks. Reduced demand weakens worker bargaining power. Weaker bargaining power makes labor cheaper in some sectors, but also encourages firms to reorganize work around surveillance, scheduling algorithms, subcontracting, or gig arrangements. Workers facing insecurity may accept worse conditions. Firms then treat this acceptance as evidence of market preference. The labor market adapts to inequality by normalizing it.

At the same time, technology can produce positive feedback for human capability if institutions guide it differently. Public investment, education, worker voice, open standards, competition policy, and shared access can spread technological gains. The same nonlinearity that produces monopoly can produce broad-based innovation if feedback loops are designed around inclusion rather than extraction. Technology does not have one destiny. It follows institutional pathways.

Feedback loops also operate at the level of public trust. Trust supports cooperation. Cooperation improves institutional performance. Good performance strengthens trust. This is a virtuous loop. When citizens trust public institutions, they are more likely to comply with rules, pay taxes, accept temporary sacrifices, participate in civic life, and believe that burdens will be shared. This makes policy more effective. Effective policy reinforces trust.

Distrust creates the opposite loop. Citizens doubt institutions. They resist guidance, evade taxes, reject expertise, and interpret policy as manipulation. Policy becomes harder to implement. Poor implementation confirms distrust. Politicians exploit suspicion. Institutions become more defensive, opaque, or captured. Citizens withdraw further. The system becomes difficult to govern. Low trust is not merely an attitude. It is a structural condition that changes the effectiveness of policy.

Economic inequality, crisis, and institutional failure can all feed distrust. When banks are rescued but households are abandoned, trust falls. When workers are told the economy is strong but cannot afford housing, trust falls. When inflation erodes purchasing power while corporations report strong profits, trust falls. When experts minimize risks that later become crises, trust falls. When political leaders promise simple solutions to complex problems and fail, trust falls. A society can lose trust gradually, then suddenly. Once lost, trust is hard to rebuild because every reform is interpreted through suspicion.

Tipping points in trust are particularly dangerous for democracy. Democratic institutions depend on losers accepting losses, citizens accepting procedures, and groups believing that peaceful correction remains possible. If citizens conclude that institutions are permanently rigged, they may abandon democratic norms. Economic stress does not automatically produce authoritarian politics, but it can create fertile ground for demagogues who offer simple stories of betrayal, enemies, and restoration. Economic feedback becomes political cascade.

This connection between economic and political feedback is one of the central themes of this book. Economies do not fail only in markets. They fail in legitimacy. A housing crisis becomes a generational betrayal. A debt crisis becomes a moral judgment. Inflation becomes an accusation. Inequality becomes evidence that the social contract is broken. Financial rescue becomes proof of unequal citizenship. Labor insecurity becomes humiliation. These meanings matter because people do not experience the economy as data. They experience it as life.

A complexity economics inquiry must therefore take narratives seriously. Narratives are feedback carriers. They transmit interpretation through media, politics, markets, workplaces, families, and communities. A narrative can stabilize a system by creating shared understanding and patience. It can destabilize a system by spreading panic or resentment. A credible anti-inflation narrative can anchor expectations. A credible reform narrative can mobilize sacrifice. A false narrative can direct anger toward scapegoats and away from structural causes. A cynical narrative can persuade citizens that no reform is possible.

Narratives can also become self-fulfilling. If enough people believe a bank is unsafe, it becomes unsafe. If enough investors believe an asset will rise, it may rise for a time. If enough citizens believe government cannot work, they may elect leaders who ensure it does not. If enough workers believe collective action is futile, employer power increases. If enough renters believe homeownership is impossible, family decisions, savings behavior, and political expectations change. Belief is not separate from the economy. It is one of its inputs.

Because feedback loops, tipping points, and cascades are so powerful, governance must be designed around early warning and intervention. A linear model waits for the problem to become visible in aggregate data. A complexity model watches for stress patterns, concentration, leverage, fragility, and legitimacy erosion. It asks not only whether the system is currently functioning, but whether it is becoming more vulnerable. It does not ask only, "What is the inflation rate?" It asks, "Where are price pressures propagating, and how are expectations changing?" It does not ask only, "What is the debt ratio?" It asks, "Who owes, who holds, at what maturity, under what rate conditions, and with what buffers?" It does not ask only, "How many homes were built?" It asks, "Who can afford them, where are they located, and what political feedback does the housing system create?"

Early warning is especially important because cascades are easier to prevent than stop. Once a financial panic begins, authorities may need extraordinary measures. Once housing scarcity becomes entrenched, reform faces incumbent resistance. Once inequality captures politics, redistribution becomes harder. Once inflation expectations shift, restoring credibility can require pain. Once public trust collapses, competent policy may no longer be believed. Prevention is less dramatic than rescue, but it is far more humane.

Yet prevention is politically difficult because its success is invisible. A crisis avoided does not produce a photograph. A bank that does not fail, a family that does not become homeless, a supply chain that does not break, a child whose life improves because of early support, a democracy that does not collapse into resentment, these are real achievements, but they rarely receive the recognition given to emergency response. Democratic politics must learn to value avoided harm. Complexity economics can help by naming prevention as a central form of prosperity.

One of the practical implications of feedback analysis is that public policy must identify whether it is acting on symptoms or loops. A symptom is a visible outcome: high rents, rising prices, defaults, unemployment, shortages, market concentration, distrust. A loop is the process that reproduces the symptom. Treating symptoms may be necessary, but it is not sufficient. Rent relief helps households, but without supply reform, anti-speculation policy, and tenant protections, scarcity persists. Interest-rate hikes may slow inflation, but without supply repair and competition policy, price pressures may return or adjustment may fall unfairly on workers. Debt relief may prevent collapse, but without wage growth, healthcare security, and fair credit systems, debt dependence returns. Antitrust action may challenge monopoly, but without rules governing data, interoperability, mergers, and platform conduct, concentration may reappear.

Policy must therefore seek feedback redesign. It must ask how to turn vicious loops into virtuous ones. In inequality, this means interrupting cumulative disadvantage and expanding cumulative advantage for those historically excluded. Early childhood investment, universal healthcare, affordable housing, labor power, progressive taxation, public education, and wealth-building policies can create positive feedback for broad capability. In finance, this means designing rules that lean against leverage during booms rather than rescuing collapse during busts. In housing, this means aligning local incentives with regional affordability and treating shelter as social infrastructure. In technology, this means preventing network effects from becoming unaccountable domination. In labor markets, this means creating institutions that allow productivity gains to circulate through wages, dignity, and voice.

Feedback redesign also requires attention to timing. Intervening early can be more effective than intervening late. A child allowance early in life can alter health, stress, education, and future earnings. Capital requirements before a boom can reduce crisis risk. Housing construction before scarcity becomes extreme can prevent displacement and political backlash. Climate investment before disasters multiply can reduce costs and save lives. Competition enforcement before monopoly dominance can preserve market openness. Once a system has passed a tipping point, intervention becomes more expensive, more disruptive, and less certain.

This is why delayed action is not neutral. To delay is to allow existing feedback loops to operate. If inequality is compounding, delay increases inequality. If housing scarcity is enriching incumbents, delay strengthens incumbency. If financial leverage is rising, delay increases fragility. If climate risks are accumulating, delay raises the probability of irreversible harm. If public trust is eroding, delay allows cynicism to harden. In nonlinear systems, time is not empty. It is causal.

Another implication is that policy must be robust under uncertainty. Because tipping points are difficult to predict exactly, policy should not depend on precise forecasts. Bank capital rules do not require perfect prediction of the next crisis. Social insurance does not require knowing which household will suffer job loss. Public health capacity does not require knowing the next pathogen. Climate resilience does not require knowing the exact date of the next flood. Robust policy acknowledges uncertainty and builds capacity to absorb surprise.

Robustness may appear inefficient under ordinary conditions. Capital buffers reduce bank returns. Inventory reserves increase costs. Public housing requires investment. Social insurance requires taxation. Climate adaptation requires upfront spending. Redundancy may look wasteful until the shock arrives. The linear accountant sees unused capacity. The complexity economist sees prevented cascade. A humane society must learn to budget for resilience.

This does not mean every buffer is wise or every precaution justified. Resources are limited. Tradeoffs are real. Complexity does not abolish discipline. It changes the discipline. The question is not simply, "What is the cheapest system under normal conditions?" The question is, "What system performs acceptably under stress, distributes risk fairly, and prevents ordinary shocks from becoming social disasters?" A system that is cheap until it collapses is not truly cheap. It has merely hidden its costs in the future.

Feedback analysis also helps explain why some societies recover from shocks better than others. Recovery depends on buffers, trust, institutional competence, social solidarity, fiscal capacity, and adaptive learning. A society with strong automatic stabilizers can support demand quickly. A society with universal healthcare can reduce fear and financial distress. A society with affordable housing can preserve mobility. A society with strong labor institutions can coordinate wage adjustment. A society with trusted public agencies can implement emergency measures. A society with less inequality can share burdens more plausibly. Resilience is not an accident. It is the accumulated result of institutional design.

The moral lesson is clear. Economic systems should be judged not only by what they produce in good times, but by whom they protect in bad times. A system that generates high returns for asset owners while exposing workers, renters, debtors, and future generations to cascading harm is not successful in any deep sense. It is unstable prosperity. A system that distributes buffers broadly, limits destructive feedback, and allows democratic correction is more humane and more durable.

Feedback loops also teach that no economic actor is entirely separate from the system. The wealthy may believe they can insulate themselves from inequality, but inequality can erode trust, demand, safety, legitimacy, and democracy. Firms may believe they benefit from weak labor, but weak labor can reduce purchasing power, productivity, and social cohesion. Homeowners may benefit from scarcity, but scarcity can damage regional economies, family formation, and political stability. Financial institutions may profit from leverage, but systemic crisis can destroy markets and require public rescue. Nations may benefit from cheap imports, but excessive dependency can create strategic vulnerability. In complex systems, private advantage can become public danger, and public danger eventually returns to private life.

This interdependence is the basis for a renewed political economy. It rejects both naive market optimism and naive command-and-control confidence. It recognizes that decentralized markets can generate innovation, information, and adaptation. It also recognizes that markets generate feedback loops that may require public rules, social norms, and democratic correction. The question is not whether to have markets or government. The question is how to design institutions that channel feedback toward resilience, inclusion, and legitimate prosperity.

The end of simple economic explanations requires us to stop asking only what caused a problem and begin asking what sustains it. What sustains inflation once it begins? What sustains inequality across generations? What sustains housing scarcity despite visible suffering? What sustains financial risk-taking despite repeated crises? What sustains low wages despite productivity? What sustains political distrust despite democratic procedures? What sustains market concentration despite innovation? These are feedback questions. They lead us away from isolated causes and toward system dynamics.

They also lead us toward responsibility. If a problem is sustained by a loop, then reform must alter the loop. It is not enough to express concern about inequality while preserving the tax, labor, housing, education, and political systems that compound it. It is not enough to condemn financial crises while preserving incentives for leverage and rescue. It is not enough to lament housing unaffordability while allowing local vetoes and asset speculation to dominate shelter. It is not enough to celebrate technology while ignoring network dominance and data extraction. Moral seriousness requires structural seriousness.

Feedback loops, tipping points, and cascades are not abstractions. They are the hidden grammar of economic history. They explain why civilizations can rise through virtuous loops of trust, investment, innovation, and shared prosperity. They explain why societies can decline through vicious loops of inequality, extraction, distrust, underinvestment, and crisis. They explain why reforms sometimes transform systems and sometimes vanish into them. They explain why the same policy can succeed in one context and fail in another. They explain why the future is neither predetermined nor easily controlled.

The chapters that follow will apply this grammar to the major economic problems of our time. Inflation will be studied as a feedback process among prices, wages, expectations, supply, power, and policy. Debt will be studied as a system of obligations that can turn confidence into fragility. Inequality will be studied as cumulative advantage, a loop connecting wealth, opportunity, institutions, and political power. Housing will be studied as a scarcity system that cascades into labor, family, wealth, and democracy. Labor markets will be studied as adaptive networks shaped by power and voice. Supply chains will be studied as systems in which efficiency can eliminate the very buffers needed for survival. Financial markets will be studied as arenas where belief, leverage, and imitation produce cascades. Technology will be studied as disruptive feedback that can either broaden capability or concentrate control. Public policy will be studied as the art of governing loops under uncertainty.

The central claim is that economic governance must become feedback governance. It must identify the loops that generate harm, strengthen the loops that produce resilience, and intervene before tipping points become cascades. It must understand that policy failure often comes from acting too late, too narrowly, or too mechanically. It must recognize that legitimacy, trust, fairness, and public capacity are not soft concerns. They are stabilizing structures.

In a nonlinear world, crisis is rarely as sudden as it appears. It is prepared by feedback. Debt accumulates. Inequality compounds. Trust erodes. Housing scarcity hardens. Supply chains thin. Financial leverage grows. Market concentration deepens. Institutions weaken. Then a shock arrives, and the system reveals what it has become. The shock may be immediate, but the vulnerability is historical.

This recognition should make us neither fatalistic nor complacent. It should make us attentive. Systems can be redesigned. Feedback loops can be interrupted. Thresholds can be avoided. Cascades can be contained. Virtuous loops can be cultivated. The economy is not a machine returning naturally to balance. It is a living order of interaction, interpretation, power, and choice. Its future depends on the loops we allow, the thresholds we ignore, and the cascades we prepare for or fail to see.

The task of economic thought is to make these dynamics visible. The task of democratic politics is to govern them wisely. The task of moral political economy is to ask not only whether the system grows, but whether its growth strengthens or weakens the conditions of human flourishing. Feedback loops are not merely technical mechanisms. They are the pathways through which societies become more just or more unequal, more resilient or more fragile, more trusting or more suspicious, more democratic or more authoritarian.

To understand feedback is to understand that the economy is always teaching itself how to behave. The question is what lessons our institutions reward. If they reward extraction, extraction will compound. If they reward speculation, speculation will spread. If they reward monopoly, concentration will deepen. If they reward wage suppression, insecurity will grow. If they reward short-term efficiency without resilience, fragility will accumulate. But if they reward investment, care, fairness, competition, sustainability, voice, and public responsibility, those too can compound.

A nonlinear economy is therefore not merely a danger. It is a possibility. The same dynamics that produce crises can produce renewal. The same cascading structure that spreads panic can spread confidence. The same cumulative logic that entrenches privilege can expand opportunity. The same network effects that produce monopoly can support shared innovation if governed openly. The same feedback between trust and performance that destroys legitimacy can rebuild it when institutions act competently and fairly.

This is why the end of simple economic explanations is also the beginning of economic responsibility. We cannot say we did not know that systems amplify. We cannot say we did not know that thresholds exist. We cannot say we did not know that cascades happen. We have seen them in finance, housing, supply chains, public health, politics, technology, and climate. The question now is whether our economic imagination can become equal to the world it seeks to govern.

A society that understands feedback will not wait for collapse before acting. It will not mistake calm for safety. It will not confuse efficiency with resilience. It will not allow inequality to compound while hoping mobility will rescue legitimacy. It will not permit housing scarcity to enrich some while destabilizing the young. It will not allow finance to create private profit from public risk. It will not treat trust as expendable. It will not pretend that the future is separate from the present.

Feedback loops, tipping points, and cascades are the architecture of nonlinear economic life. They are the forces that turn more into different. They are the hidden pathways from policy to consequence, from market behavior to social order, from private decision to public destiny. To govern a nonlinear economy, we must learn to see them, name them, and redesign them. Only then can economics become not merely a study of allocation, but a discipline of foresight, resilience, justice, and democratic survival.

## Chapter 5

# Inflation as a Feedback Process

Inflation is one of the most misunderstood phenomena in economic life because it appears simple at the surface. Prices rise. Money buys less. Households feel poorer. Workers demand higher wages. Central banks raise interest rates. Politicians blame one another. Citizens become angry, anxious, and suspicious. The problem seems visible because everyone can see it at the grocery store, the gas station, the rent bill, the insurance premium, the utility statement, and the restaurant menu. Inflation is personal before it is theoretical. It enters daily life as irritation, fear, and moral accusation.

Yet beneath this immediate experience lies a complex and recursive process. Inflation is not merely a statistic. It is not merely a monetary event. It is not merely too much demand or too little supply. It is not merely the result of government spending, corporate greed, wage pressure, oil prices, supply chains, or central bank error, although each of these can matter. Inflation is a feedback process. It emerges from the interaction of costs, prices, wages, expectations, market power, credit conditions, supply constraints, public policy, institutional credibility, and distributive conflict. It begins in one place and moves through many others. It changes behavior, and changed behavior changes inflation itself.

This is why inflation cannot be understood adequately through simple economic explanations. A single-cause theory may capture one part of a particular inflationary episode, but inflation in the real world is almost always a process of propagation. An energy shock raises transportation and production costs. Firms raise prices. Households reduce real consumption or demand higher wages. Workers seek compensation for lost purchasing power. Firms facing higher wage bills raise prices again, if they have the power to do so. Consumers, expecting future increases, buy earlier or accept higher prices as unavoidable. Landlords raise rents because the market permits it. Financial markets anticipate central bank tightening. Interest rates rise. Debt burdens change. Governments consider relief measures. Relief may support demand. Political narratives harden. Trust in institutions becomes part of the inflation process.

Inflation is therefore not only about prices. It is about the social organization of price adjustment. When prices rise, society must decide who absorbs the loss. Workers, firms, creditors, debtors, renters, landlords, taxpayers, consumers, and governments all seek to defend their positions. Inflation exposes the power structure of the economy because not all actors can pass costs forward. Some can raise prices. Some can demand wages. Some can index contracts. Some can refinance. Some can hedge. Some can move capital. Others simply pay more and fall behind. Inflation is a macroeconomic phenomenon, but it is also a moral event.

The traditional language of inflation often obscures this. In many discussions, inflation is treated as a technical imbalance between money and goods, aggregate demand and aggregate supply, or expectations and credibility. These concepts are useful, but they are incomplete. They can make inflation appear as if it happens above society, in the realm of aggregates, rather than within society, through relationships of power, dependency, and adjustment. A complexity economics approach does not deny money, demand, or expectations. It places them within a wider system. It asks how inflation begins, how it spreads, who transmits it, who resists it, who benefits from it, who suffers from it, and what feedback loops allow it to persist.

At the most basic level, inflation is a decline in the purchasing power of money. But that definition tells us little about the process. It is like defining a fever as elevated body temperature. The definition is accurate, but it does not explain whether the cause is infection, inflammation, heat exposure, immune response, or something else. Similarly, inflation may reflect monetary expansion, supply disruption, energy shocks, fiscal stimulus, wage dynamics, exchange-rate movements, monopoly pricing, war, climate events, housing shortages, or shifting expectations. The same symptom can arise from different systems under stress.

A nonlinear account begins by rejecting the idea that inflation has one timeless structure. Inflationary episodes differ. Wartime inflation differs from wage-price inflation. Asset inflation differs from consumer price inflation. Supply-shock inflation differs from demand-driven overheating. Imported inflation differs from domestic service-sector inflation. Hyperinflation differs from moderate inflation. Housing inflation differs from commodity inflation. Medical inflation differs from energy inflation. A good theory must be flexible enough to distinguish among them while also identifying the feedback mechanisms they share.

The first feedback mechanism is the cost-price loop. A firm faces rising costs for labor, energy, materials, rent, financing, transportation, or imported inputs. It then decides whether to absorb those costs through lower margins or pass them on through higher prices. That decision depends on competition, demand conditions, customer loyalty, contracts, inventories, expectations, and market power. In highly competitive markets, firms may be unable to pass on costs fully. In concentrated markets, firms may protect or even expand margins. If many firms raise prices, the general price level rises. Those higher prices become costs for other firms and households, feeding the loop.

The cost-price loop is especially visible when energy prices rise. Energy is not one commodity among many. It is an input into transportation, manufacturing, heating, agriculture, logistics, and daily life. A rise in fuel prices raises shipping costs. Higher shipping costs affect food, retail goods, construction materials, and industrial production. Energy-intensive industries raise prices. Households spend more on gasoline, utilities, and heating, leaving less for other goods. Firms then respond to changed demand patterns. Governments face pressure to intervene. The original energy shock becomes a broad inflationary impulse because energy sits near the center of the economic network.

Food prices operate similarly. Food is both essential and politically sensitive. A rise in food prices affects households unequally because lower-income households spend a larger share of income on necessities. Food inflation quickly becomes social stress. It cannot be postponed like the purchase of a luxury good. It cannot be substituted away from entirely. When food prices rise sharply, inflation becomes visible, emotional, and politically destabilizing. The official inflation rate may be moderate, but lived inflation may be severe for those whose budgets are concentrated in essentials.

Housing adds another layer. Rent is not simply another price. It is a long-term claim on household income. Rising rents enter inflation statistics, household stress, wage demands, labor mobility, family formation, and homelessness. Housing inflation is often slow-moving but deeply persistent because it reflects structural scarcity, land use rules, financing conditions, income inequality, investor demand, and local politics. When rents rise, workers may demand higher wages to remain in place. Employers may struggle to attract workers in high-cost regions. Public budgets face pressure for housing assistance. Families double up, move farther away, delay children, or accumulate debt. Housing inflation becomes a broader social process.

The second feedback mechanism is the wage-price loop. This is one of the most familiar inflationary concepts, but it is often discussed too mechanically. In its simplest form, rising prices lead workers to demand higher wages. Higher wages raise business costs. Firms raise prices. Higher prices lead workers to demand further wage increases. The loop continues. This can happen, but the actual process depends on institutions. Do workers have bargaining power? Are unions strong? Are contracts indexed? Are labor markets tight? Do firms have pricing power? Are profit margins flexible? Is productivity rising? Are public institutions credible? Does society have mechanisms for coordinating wage and price behavior?

A wage-price spiral is not automatic. In many modern economies, workers have limited bargaining power. Prices may rise without wages keeping pace. In that case, the burden of inflation falls on labor through declining real wages. The absence of a wage-price spiral does not mean inflation is painless. It may mean workers are too weak to defend themselves. A society can control inflation partly by suppressing wage growth, but such control carries moral and political costs. If workers absorb price increases while firms protect profits, inflation becomes a transfer of purchasing power away from labor.

This is why the phrase "wage-price spiral" can be misleading when used carelessly. It can imply that workers are the primary danger in inflation, even when wages are responding to prior price increases or when profits are rising. A complexity approach asks a more precise question: which actors are successfully passing on costs? If firms pass costs to consumers, landlords pass scarcity to tenants, creditors pass risk to borrowers, and workers cannot pass higher living costs to employers, then inflation is not a wage-price spiral. It is a price-wage squeeze. The distinction matters because it changes both policy and moral interpretation.

The third feedback mechanism is the expectation loop. Expectations are central because inflation is partly about the future. If households and firms believe prices will keep rising, they behave differently. Households may accelerate purchases. Firms may raise prices preemptively. Workers may demand higher wages. Lenders may demand higher interest rates. Investors may shift portfolios. Landlords may adjust rents upward in anticipation of market conditions. These behaviors can make inflation more persistent.

Expectations are not formed in isolation. They are social, institutional, and narrative. People learn from recent experience. They listen to media, employers, politicians, central banks, family members, and market signals. A household that sees grocery prices rise every week may distrust official claims that inflation is temporary. A firm that sees competitors raising prices may do the same. A worker who has lost purchasing power may assume future wages must rise just to stay even. A landlord who sees housing scarcity may raise rents because tenants have few alternatives. Expectations become embedded when they are repeatedly confirmed by experience.

Central banks worry intensely about expectations because they can become self-fulfilling. If people trust that inflation will return to target, temporary shocks may fade. If people lose confidence, the same shock can become persistent. But credibility is not only a matter of central bank communication. It is also a matter of social reality. If households are told that inflation is under control while essential costs continue to rise, credibility suffers. If unemployment is used to suppress wages while concentrated firms retain pricing power, legitimacy suffers. If inflation policy appears to protect financial markets more than workers, trust suffers. Expectations are anchored not only by words, but by perceived fairness.

The fourth feedback mechanism is the market power loop. In competitive theory, firms cannot raise prices much above cost because competitors would undercut them. But real markets often contain concentration, brand power, supply bottlenecks, patents, platform control, local monopolies, switching costs, or consumer dependency. In such markets, firms may have room to increase prices beyond cost pressures. They may use inflationary environments as cover, knowing that customers expect prices to rise and have difficulty distinguishing necessary cost pass-through from margin expansion.

This does not mean all price increases during inflation are opportunistic or abusive. Firms do face real cost increases. But market structure determines how those costs are distributed. A firm in a concentrated industry may preserve margins by raising prices quickly. A small business in a competitive market may be squeezed between rising input costs and customers unable to pay more. A dominant platform may raise fees because dependent sellers lack alternatives. A landlord in a tight housing market may raise rent because tenants cannot easily move. A hospital system with regional dominance may raise prices because patients have limited choice. Inflation reveals where pricing power resides.

Market power also changes inflation dynamics because it weakens balancing feedback. In competitive markets, high prices attract entry, substitution, and pressure. In concentrated or constrained markets, high prices may persist. If housing supply is politically restricted, rising rents do not automatically produce sufficient new housing. If a few firms dominate meat processing, shipping, pharmaceuticals, software, or digital platforms, price competition may be weak. If supply chains depend on scarce inputs, firms with control over those inputs gain leverage. Inflation then becomes tied to the structure of competition.

This has important policy implications. If inflation is partly driven by market power, interest-rate hikes alone may reduce demand without addressing pricing structures. They may slow the economy, weaken workers, and reduce investment, while leaving concentration intact. Competition policy, supply expansion, public options, transparency rules, anti-gouging enforcement in emergencies, and sector-specific regulation may be necessary complements. Monetary policy is powerful, but it is not omnipotent. It can suppress demand, but it cannot build houses, unclog ports, produce energy, reform zoning, reduce monopoly, or coordinate supply chains by itself.

The fifth feedback mechanism is the supply-chain loop. Modern production relies on networks of inputs, transportation, inventories, labor, financing, and timing. A disruption in one node can raise costs elsewhere. A shortage of semiconductors can reduce automobile production. Reduced automobile production raises car prices. Higher car prices affect consumer budgets, insurance values, rental fleets, and used-car markets. A port backlog delays retail goods. Delays create shortages. Shortages raise prices. Higher prices shift consumer behavior. Firms order more than needed to protect themselves, worsening bottlenecks. Defensive behavior by each firm can produce collective stress.

Supply-chain inflation is nonlinear because it involves coordination failure. A shortage in one input can idle entire production lines. A delay in one port can ripple through warehouses, trucks, stores, and factories. A labor shortage in logistics can affect goods far beyond that labor market. A weather event, war, pandemic, cyberattack, or shipping disruption can produce price effects that seem disproportionate to the initial cause because production systems are tightly coupled. Lean efficiency becomes inflationary when it lacks buffers.

The response to supply-chain inflation also creates feedback. Firms may increase inventories to avoid future shortages. This can temporarily increase demand for goods and storage. They may diversify suppliers, raising costs. Governments may subsidize domestic production, altering investment patterns. Consumers may switch brands or buy earlier. Retailers may overorder, then later face excess inventory and discounting. Inflation can therefore emerge from shortages and later give way to disinflation or sectoral price declines as supply catches up. The process is dynamic, uneven, and path-dependent.

The sixth feedback mechanism is the fiscal-monetary loop. Government spending, taxation, borrowing, and central bank policy interact with inflation. Fiscal support can stabilize households and firms during crises. It can prevent recessions, reduce poverty, and support demand. But if fiscal expansion occurs when supply is constrained, it can contribute to price pressure. Conversely, fiscal austerity can reduce demand, but it can also weaken productive capacity, public investment, and social resilience. The inflationary effect of fiscal policy depends on timing, composition, financing, distribution, and supply conditions.

Money matters, but not mechanically. An increase in the money supply does not automatically produce proportional inflation. If banks do not lend, households do not spend, firms do not invest, or the economy has idle capacity, monetary expansion may have limited consumer price effects. It may instead inflate asset prices. If supply is constrained and demand rises quickly, spending can push prices higher. If public transfers go to households with urgent needs, they may support consumption. If they go to wealthy households, they may increase savings or asset purchases. If spending builds productive capacity, it may reduce inflationary pressure over time. If spending merely bids up scarce goods, it may raise prices.

Central banks intervene through interest rates, balance-sheet policy, communication, and regulatory influence. Higher rates reduce borrowing, cool asset markets, slow investment, strengthen currency in some cases, and signal anti-inflation commitment. But rate hikes also affect debt service, bank balance sheets, housing construction, small business financing, public budgets, and unemployment. Their effects are delayed and uneven. Monetary policy is a blunt instrument in a complex economy. It can reduce inflation by slowing demand, but it may also reduce supply if it discourages investment in housing, energy, productive capacity, or innovation.

This creates a policy dilemma. If central banks act too slowly, inflation expectations may become unanchored. If they act too aggressively, they may cause recession, financial stress, unemployment, and political backlash. The optimal path depends on the source and persistence of inflation, the strength of labor markets, the structure of debt, the resilience of banks, the credibility of institutions, and the distribution of pain. There is no simple rule that works across all inflationary regimes.

Inflation is also connected to debt through a complex feedback loop. Inflation can reduce the real value of fixed-rate debt, benefiting some borrowers. It can harm creditors receiving payments in depreciated money. But central bank responses to inflation often raise interest rates, which can increase debt burdens for variable-rate borrowers, new borrowers, firms refinancing debt, governments rolling over obligations, and households seeking mortgages. Inflation may appear to help debtors in one channel while harming them through another.

For households, the interaction can be severe. Prices rise. Wages lag. Households use credit cards or loans to maintain consumption. Interest rates rise. Debt service increases. Households cut spending. Reduced spending affects businesses. Businesses cut costs or raise prices where possible. Workers face insecurity. The inflation-debt loop can become a trap for households without buffers. For governments, inflation may raise nominal tax revenues, but interest costs may rise, public wage demands may increase, and social spending pressures may grow. For firms, inflation may increase revenue in nominal terms, but input costs, financing costs, and uncertainty may reduce investment.

Inflation also interacts with asset markets. Low interest rates and monetary expansion may support asset prices. Rising asset prices can increase wealth for owners, supporting consumption among the affluent and widening inequality. When inflation rises and central banks tighten, asset prices may fall. This affects household wealth, pensions, business financing, and financial stability. If asset markets have become inflated during a period of low rates, anti-inflation policy can reveal hidden fragility. The fight against consumer price inflation may trigger asset deflation. The two forms of price movement are connected, even though public debate often treats them separately.

One of the most politically explosive aspects of inflation is its uneven distribution. Inflation does not affect everyone equally. A homeowner with a fixed-rate mortgage, rising wages, and appreciating assets experiences inflation differently from a renter with stagnant pay and rising grocery bills. A firm with pricing power experiences inflation differently from a small supplier squeezed by input costs. A government with long-term fixed-rate debt experiences inflation differently from a household with credit-card debt. A worker in a unionized sector experiences inflation differently from a gig worker. A wealthy investor can hedge; a poor household cannot.

This unevenness means that inflation is always distributive. The official rate may be one number, but lived inflation differs across class, age, region, tenure, occupation, and balance-sheet position. Older homeowners, young renters, debtors, creditors, wage earners, landlords, exporters, importers, urban households, rural households, and firms in different sectors all experience inflation differently. Aggregate inflation is an average of unequal pressures.

The politics of inflation emerges from this inequality of experience. When citizens feel that official statistics do not match their lives, trust declines. When policymakers speak in aggregates while households experience essentials rising faster than wages, public anger grows. When central banks focus on wage restraint while corporations appear to raise prices freely, legitimacy suffers. When governments provide relief that is perceived as insufficient, excessive, unfair, or poorly targeted, inflation becomes a moral dispute. Inflation is not merely a problem of purchasing power. It is a problem of recognition.

Inflation also affects time. It shortens horizons. Households under inflationary pressure focus on immediate costs. Firms become uncertain about future prices and demand. Workers worry that wage gains will vanish. Lenders demand protection. Governments face pressure for quick relief. Long-term investment may suffer because uncertainty increases. Inflation therefore changes the psychology of planning. A low and stable inflation environment allows contracts, savings, investment, and wages to be negotiated with some confidence. A high and volatile inflation environment makes the future harder to read.

This uncertainty can be self-reinforcing. If firms cannot predict input costs, they may raise prices more than necessary as insurance. If workers cannot predict living costs, they may demand higher wages. If lenders cannot predict inflation, they may demand higher interest rates. If households cannot predict prices, they may buy durable goods earlier or reduce discretionary spending sharply. The attempt to protect against uncertainty can make inflation more unstable. Volatility becomes a feedback loop.

Inflation also alters moral language. During stable times, price increases may be interpreted as ordinary market behavior. During inflation, they become suspect. Citizens ask whether firms are exploiting crisis, whether workers are demanding too much, whether government spent irresponsibly, whether central banks failed, whether foreigners, unions, corporations, or political parties are to blame. Inflation invites accusation because it is experienced as loss without clear individual consent. No one votes to reduce the value of their paycheck. No one signs a contract agreeing to higher grocery bills. Inflation feels like theft, even when no single thief exists.

This moral anger can be politically dangerous. Leaders may channel it toward simple explanations. They may blame immigrants, foreign governments, central bankers, corporations, unions, welfare recipients, or political opponents. Some targets may have real relevance; others may be scapegoats. The challenge is to distinguish partial causes from totalizing narratives. Complexity economics helps by showing that inflation is usually a system process. It can include excessive demand, supply shocks, market power, fiscal choices, monetary errors, geopolitical disruption, and expectations all at once. The presence of one cause does not negate the presence of others.

The danger of single-cause inflation narratives is that they produce single-lever policy. If inflation is only monetary, raise rates and ignore supply, power, and distribution. If inflation is only corporate greed, punish firms and ignore demand, energy, and monetary conditions. If inflation is only wages, discipline labor and ignore profits, rents, and supply chains. If inflation is only government spending, cut budgets and ignore private pricing power, global shocks, and household vulnerability. If inflation is only supply chains, wait for bottlenecks to clear and ignore expectations. Each explanation becomes harmful when it pretends to be complete.

A complexity approach does not avoid responsibility by multiplying causes. Rather, it assigns responsibility more precisely. Central banks are responsible for understanding monetary conditions and expectations.

Governments are responsible for fiscal design, public investment, social protection, and supply capacity. Firms are responsible for pricing behavior, market conduct, and margin choices. Regulators are responsible for competition, transparency, and systemic resilience. Labor institutions are responsible for wage coordination and worker voice. Energy policy is responsible for vulnerability to commodity shocks. Housing policy is responsible for rent pressures. Supply-chain policy is responsible for strategic fragility. Inflation is collective in origin, but responsibility is not dissolved. It is distributed across the system.

The policy response to inflation must therefore be multidimensional. Monetary policy may be necessary, especially when inflation becomes broad, persistent, or expectation-driven. But monetary policy should not be asked to solve every inflation problem alone. If housing scarcity is driving rent inflation, housing supply, tenant protection, land use reform, public housing, and anti-speculation measures matter. If energy volatility is central, energy diversification, efficiency, storage, grid investment, and strategic reserves matter. If supply chains are fragile, redundancy, domestic capacity, logistics infrastructure, and strategic inventories matter. If market concentration permits excessive pricing, antitrust and competition policy matter. If households are suffering, targeted fiscal relief matters. If wages are falling behind, labor policy matters.

The art is coordination. A central bank tightening while fiscal policy stimulates broadly may produce conflict. Fiscal austerity during supply-side investment needs may weaken long-term resilience. Housing policy that relies only on demand subsidies may raise rents. Energy policy that delays transition may leave the economy exposed to commodity shocks. Antitrust policy that moves too slowly may allow pricing power to persist. Inflation governance requires institutions capable of seeing across domains. It is not the responsibility of one agency alone.

A more sophisticated inflation policy begins by diagnosing the inflation regime. Is inflation concentrated in energy, food, housing, services, imports, or wages? Are price increases broadening or narrowing? Are wages leading prices or following them? Are profits rising, falling, or normalizing? Are supply bottlenecks easing or worsening? Are expectations anchored? Are households using debt to maintain consumption? Are firms investing in capacity or merely raising prices? Are interest-rate-sensitive sectors already slowing? Are vulnerable households protected? Are financial institutions exposed to rate shocks? These questions are not ideological. They are necessary for competent governance.

The diagnosis must also distinguish between level effects and ongoing inflation. A one-time price increase raises the price level but does not necessarily create continuing inflation. If oil prices jump and then stabilize, the price level is higher, but inflation may decline unless the shock propagates through wages, expectations, and other prices. Policymakers often struggle with this distinction because households continue to feel pain even after the inflation rate falls. Prices may stop rising rapidly, but they rarely return to prior levels. Disinflation is not the same as restoration of purchasing power. Citizens may hear that inflation has improved while still facing permanently higher costs.

This gap between statistical improvement and lived experience is politically important. If wages do not catch up, lower inflation does not repair the loss. If rents remain high, slower rent growth does not make housing affordable. If grocery prices stabilize at elevated levels, families still feel squeezed. If insurance premiums rise and stay high, households do not feel relief. Policymakers must communicate honestly. Saying inflation is falling is not the same as saying life is affordable. Price stability is necessary, but affordability depends on income, housing, healthcare, childcare, debt, and public goods.

Inflation also reveals the limits of gross domestic product as a measure of prosperity. An economy can grow while households feel worse because essentials rise faster than incomes. Corporate revenues can increase because prices rise, not because real wellbeing improves. Nominal wages can rise while real wages stagnate. Asset owners can benefit from inflation in certain contexts while renters and wage earners suffer. The aggregate economy may appear resilient while daily life becomes more precarious. Inflation forces us to ask what prosperity means when money values change.

The relationship between inflation and inequality is especially important. Inflation can widen inequality if asset owners are protected, firms with pricing power expand margins, and wages lag. It can also reduce certain forms of inequality if tight labor markets raise wages at the bottom and fixed-rate debt is eroded. The outcome depends on institutions. If workers have bargaining power, inflation may be partially offset by wage gains. If they do not, real wages fall. If housing is owned broadly with fixed-rate mortgages, some households benefit. If many rent, housing inflation intensifies inequality. If public benefits are indexed, vulnerable households are protected. If not, they fall behind. Inflation has no single distributive effect. It depends on system design.

This is why inflation cannot be morally evaluated without asking who is protected. A policy regime that achieves low inflation by maintaining worker insecurity, suppressing wages, weakening unions, and tolerating housing scarcity may be stable in a narrow price sense but unjust and fragile in a broader social sense. Conversely, a policy regime that allows inflation to accelerate without protecting purchasing power can destroy trust and harm the poor. The goal should not be inflation tolerance or inflation obsession. The goal should be stable purchasing power within an economy that distributes security fairly.

The historical memory of inflation matters because it shapes institutional response. Societies that have experienced high inflation often develop strong anti-inflation norms. Central banks gain independence. Wage indexation may be avoided. Fiscal rules may tighten. Citizens become sensitive to price instability. These norms can be stabilizing, but they can also produce overcorrection if every price shock is treated as the beginning of runaway inflation. Societies that have experienced long periods of low inflation may underestimate inflation risk and respond too slowly. Memory is part of the feedback system.

Inflation memory is also generational. Older citizens who lived through severe inflation may interpret price increases differently from younger citizens who grew up in low-inflation environments. Young adults facing rent, student debt, healthcare costs, and unstable work may experience inflation as one more betrayal in a broader affordability crisis. Homeowners with fixed mortgages may feel insulated from certain pressures. Retirees on fixed incomes may fear erosion of savings. Workers in strong labor markets may see inflation through wage negotiations. The public does not experience inflation as a single collective body. It experiences inflation through generational and class position.

The media environment further shapes inflation feedback. Constant reporting on rising prices can increase salience. Stories of shortages can encourage hoarding. Political messaging can intensify blame. Social media can spread anecdotes faster than official data. Corporate announcements can normalize price increases. Central bank statements can move markets before policy changes occur. Information is not neutral. It changes behavior. The inflation process is partly communicative.

This is not an argument for hiding information. Transparency is essential. But policymakers and institutions must understand that communication is itself an intervention. A central bank that speaks too casually may lose credibility. A government that dismisses public pain may appear indifferent. A firm that attributes all price increases to costs while profits rise may invite distrust. Media that presents every price movement as crisis may intensify anxiety. In a feedback system, words matter.

A democratic inflation policy must therefore include honest public explanation. Citizens should be told that inflation can have multiple causes, that policy involves tradeoffs, that different groups experience inflation differently, and that restoring price stability does not automatically restore affordability. They should also be told who is being asked to sacrifice and why. If unemployment is expected to rise as part of anti-inflation policy, leaders should say so plainly and justify how workers will be protected. If firms are benefiting from pricing power, competition policy should respond. If households need relief, relief should be targeted to avoid fueling broad demand while protecting essentials. Legitimacy requires truthfulness.

The moral failure of many inflation debates is that they treat pain as abstract. Raising interest rates is discussed as cooling demand. But demand is people's spending, employment, investment, and plans. Slowing wage growth means workers have less bargaining power. Reducing consumption means households delay or forgo needs. Lowering housing demand through higher mortgage rates may reduce price pressure but can also lock renters out and discourage construction. Cutting public spending may reduce deficits but harm services. Every anti-inflation policy has a human channel. A humane economics does not deny tradeoffs. It refuses to hide them.

This point leads to a broader claim: inflation governance must distinguish between reducing inflation and building an anti-inflationary society. Reducing inflation is the immediate task of slowing price increases. Building an anti-inflationary society means designing institutions that are less prone to inflationary feedback in the first place. That requires resilient supply chains, competitive markets, affordable housing, stable energy systems, strong public capacity, credible monetary institutions, fair wage-setting mechanisms, lower household precarity, and social trust. A society that ignores these foundations will repeatedly rely on painful emergency tools.

Affordable housing is anti-inflationary because rent is a major household cost and a driver of wage pressure. Energy resilience is anti-inflationary because volatile fuel costs propagate through the economy. Competitive markets are anti-inflationary because firms have less room to raise prices beyond costs. Public health capacity is anti-inflationary because pandemics and health shocks disrupt labor and production. Infrastructure investment is anti-inflationary because bottlenecks raise costs. Labor institutions can be anti-inflationary if they coordinate wage growth with productivity and fairness rather than forcing chaotic conflict. Social insurance is anti-inflationary when it prevents panic behavior and stabilizes demand during shocks.

This broader view challenges the narrow idea that inflation control belongs only to central banks. Central banks are essential, but they are often asked to compensate for failures elsewhere. If housing policy creates scarcity, central banks face rent inflation. If energy policy creates dependence, central banks face fuel shocks. If antitrust policy tolerates concentration, central banks face pricing power. If supply-chain policy ignores resilience, central banks face bottlenecks. If fiscal policy is poorly designed, central banks face demand surges or social distress. If labor institutions are weak, central banks face distributional conflict without coordination. Monetary policy becomes the emergency brake on a poorly designed vehicle.

A complexity economics approach asks us to redesign the vehicle. The goal is an economy in which shocks do not automatically become inflationary cascades. This does not mean eliminating inflation risk. No society can do that. It means reducing vulnerability. It means building buffers, diversifying supply, limiting pricing power, protecting households, coordinating policy, and maintaining trust. It means recognizing that inflation prevention is part of industrial policy, housing policy, labor policy, competition policy, energy policy, and social policy.

Inflation also raises questions about democracy. Democratic governments are vulnerable to inflation because inflation produces immediate public anger. Citizens may punish incumbents regardless of the causes. This can create incentives for denial, blame shifting, or short-term relief that worsens longer-term pressures. At the same time, authoritarian or technocratic approaches can impose anti-inflation pain without accountability. The challenge is democratic competence: the ability to explain, coordinate, and act in ways that are effective and perceived as fair.

Fairness is not decorative. It affects compliance and expectations. If citizens believe anti-inflation policy is unfair, they may resist it politically and behaviorally. Workers may demand more aggressive wage increases if they believe firms are profiting excessively. Firms may raise prices more readily if they believe competitors are doing so. Households may distrust official guidance if they believe elites are insulated. A fair inflation policy is not merely morally preferable. It is more likely to be credible.

The issue of profit margins during inflation illustrates this relationship. If firms face real cost increases and maintain margins, price increases may be understandable. If firms expand margins during widespread hardship, public anger is justified. The policy response should not be crude hostility toward business. Firms need profits to invest, employ, and innovate. But neither should policymakers pretend that all price increases are neutral market signals. Transparency, competition, and accountability are needed so that inflation does not become a cover for extraction.

Similarly, wage increases should not be treated automatically as inflationary danger. If wages rise because productivity rises, because low-wage workers gain bargaining power, or because wages are catching up after price increases, they may be part of restoring fairness. If wage growth persistently exceeds productivity in ways that force ongoing price increases, then inflation risk rises. The question is not whether wages rise, but how wage growth relates to productivity, profits, prices, and distribution. A society obsessed with restraining wages while ignoring rents, profits, and asset prices has confused price stability with class discipline.

Inflation also forces a reconsideration of the relationship between price stability and full employment. Traditional policy often treats them as a tradeoff. Lower unemployment may increase wage pressure and inflation. Higher unemployment may reduce inflation. This relationship can exist, but it is not fixed. Institutions matter. An economy with strong training, childcare, mobility, competition, healthcare, and labor coordination may sustain higher employment without destabilizing inflation. An economy with bottlenecks, housing scarcity, weak competition, and volatile energy may face inflation at lower levels of employment. The inflation-employment tradeoff is partly designed by the structure of the economy.

This means societies should not accept unemployment as the only tool of inflation control. Unemployment is socially costly. It damages income, health, families, skills, bargaining power, and dignity. It also falls unevenly. Workers with less education, less wealth, weaker networks, and marginalized identities often bear the brunt. If inflation can be reduced through supply repair, competition, targeted fiscal policy, energy resilience, housing reform, and coordinated wage-setting, those tools should be used. Monetary tightening may still be necessary, but it should not be the sole instrument because it often works through human distress.

A nonlinear view also reminds us that deflation is not the opposite of inflation in a simple moral sense. Falling prices may sound appealing to households suffering from inflation, but widespread deflation can create its own dangerous feedback loops. If consumers expect prices to fall, they delay purchases. Delayed purchases reduce business revenue. Firms cut wages or employment. Lower income reduces demand further. Debt burdens rise in real terms. Defaults increase. Investment declines. Deflation can become a trap. The goal is not falling prices across the economy. The goal is stable prices and rising real living standards.

Disinflation, the slowing of inflation, is often necessary after an inflationary episode. But the path matters. A soft landing occurs when inflation falls without severe recession. A hard landing occurs when inflation falls through major unemployment, financial stress, or demand collapse. Whether a soft landing is possible depends on the sources of inflation and the resilience of the system. If supply bottlenecks ease, energy prices stabilize, wage growth moderates, and expectations remain anchored, inflation can fall with less pain. If inflation is deeply embedded, policy may become harsher. Again, the outcome depends on feedback.

One of the most important lessons is that inflation policy should not wait until inflation becomes entrenched, but neither should it overreact to every temporary shock. This requires judgment. If policymakers dismiss early inflation as transitory when feedback loops are strengthening, they may act too late. If they treat every supply shock as demand overheating, they may act too harshly. Complexity does not provide a simple rule. It requires real-time diagnosis, humility, and adaptation. It requires institutions capable of learning from incoming data without being trapped by ideology.

Ideology is a major obstacle to understanding inflation. Some traditions see inflation everywhere as the result of government spending and monetary excess. Others see it primarily as corporate greed or class conflict. Others focus on wages, unions, or labor markets. Others emphasize external shocks. Each tradition has insights. Each becomes dangerous when it refuses the others. Inflation is often a meeting point of multiple mechanisms. The question is empirical and institutional: which mechanisms are active now, how strongly, and through what feedback?

A complexity framework encourages plural causation. It allows us to say that fiscal stimulus supported demand, supply chains restricted goods, energy shocks raised costs, market concentration enabled price increases, wages adjusted unevenly, expectations mattered, and monetary policy shaped financial conditions. These claims can all be true at the same time. The analytical challenge is weighting them and understanding their interactions. The political challenge is preventing partial truths from becoming weapons of blame.

Inflation can also be viewed as a stress test of the social contract. In stable times, societies may avoid confronting distributional questions. Inflation brings them forward. Who deserves protection? Should wages be allowed to catch up? Should profits be scrutinized? Should rents be regulated? Should public benefits be indexed? Should central banks prioritize price stability even at the cost of unemployment? Should governments subsidize energy or invest in transition? Should debtors be protected from rate shocks? Should essential goods be treated differently from discretionary goods? Inflation forces societies to reveal their priorities.

A humane and realistic approach would begin with essentials. Inflation in essential goods is more dangerous than inflation in luxuries because essentials determine dignity and survival. Food, shelter, energy, healthcare, childcare, transportation, and insurance are not easily avoided. When these costs rise, households lose freedom. Therefore, anti-inflation policy should pay special attention to essential-cost systems. Building affordable housing, reducing healthcare cost inflation, stabilizing energy, supporting childcare supply, and ensuring competitive food systems are not merely social policies. They are inflation-resilience policies.

This essential-cost perspective also clarifies why people may feel inflation even when certain consumer goods become cheaper. A lower price for electronics does not compensate for unaffordable rent. Cheap entertainment does not solve medical debt. Discounted imported goods do not offset childcare costs. An economy can deliver abundance in discretionary goods while failing in foundational goods. Inflation in the foundations of life has a greater moral and political effect than inflation in optional consumption. Any serious inflation analysis must distinguish between them.

The role of healthcare deserves special attention. In many economies, healthcare costs rise through complex interactions among providers, insurers, pharmaceuticals, technology, regulation, aging, market power, and public policy. Medical inflation affects wages, public budgets, household debt, employer costs, and labor mobility. If employers bear healthcare costs, rising premiums affect compensation and hiring. If households bear costs directly, insecurity rises. If governments bear costs, fiscal pressure increases. Healthcare inflation is not simply sectoral. It feeds into the entire economy.

Insurance more broadly is becoming an increasingly important inflation channel, especially under conditions of climate risk. As disasters become more frequent or severe, insurance premiums rise. Higher premiums affect homeowners, renters, businesses, agriculture, local governments, and lenders. In some regions, insurance withdrawal can damage housing markets and public finance. Climate-related inflation is therefore not limited to energy transition costs. It includes the rising price of risk itself. A nonlinear economy under ecological stress may experience inflation through insurance, food, infrastructure, migration, and disaster recovery.

This illustrates a broader point: inflation in the twenty-first century may increasingly be shaped by physical limits. Climate change, water scarcity, crop failures, heat stress, energy transition, critical minerals, geopolitical conflict, and infrastructure vulnerability can all produce price instability. Traditional inflation tools were not designed for a world in which ecological systems repeatedly shock economic systems. Raising interest rates cannot make rain fall, rebuild a burned grid, restore a failed crop, or stabilize an insurance market by itself. Monetary policy must be complemented by climate resilience and industrial transformation.

Geopolitics also changes inflation dynamics. Globalization helped produce low inflation for decades by expanding labor supply, lowering production costs, increasing trade, and disciplining domestic producers. But geopolitical fragmentation, war, sanctions, export controls, strategic competition, and reshoring can raise costs or increase volatility. A world organized around resilience and security may be less cheap than a world organized solely around efficiency. The challenge is to manage this transition without allowing necessary resilience to become a justification for avoidable price increases, corruption, or protectionist inefficiency.

This brings us back to the central theme: inflation is a process of adjustment in a complex system. It is not simply too much money chasing too few goods. Sometimes it is too much purchasing power relative to current supply. Sometimes it is too little resilience. Sometimes it is too much market power. Sometimes it is too much dependence on volatile inputs. Sometimes it is too much debt sensitivity. Sometimes it is too little trust. Sometimes it is too little productive investment. Sometimes it is an unavoidable signal that real resources are constrained and society must choose how to allocate them.

The question is how to govern the process fairly and effectively. A good inflation regime would include several principles. First, diagnose before prescribing. Second, distinguish temporary price-level shocks from persistent inflation. Third, protect essential purchasing power for vulnerable households. Fourth, avoid relying exclusively on unemployment as the adjustment mechanism. Fifth, address supply bottlenecks directly. Sixth, limit market power where it amplifies price increases. Seventh, coordinate fiscal and monetary policy. Eighth, invest in resilience so future shocks do not cascade. Ninth, communicate honestly. Tenth, preserve legitimacy by sharing burdens fairly.

These principles do not eliminate tradeoffs. Inflation governance will always involve difficult choices. But they improve the quality of those choices. They prevent policymakers from mistaking one tool for a complete strategy. They also prevent the public from being forced into false debates between inflation control and social justice. Price stability and justice are not enemies. Durable price stability may require a just and resilient economy. An unjust economy can suppress inflation for a time through weak labor and austerity, but it may build political and social instability. A just economy that ignores inflation will also fail because inflation harms the vulnerable and destroys trust. The task is integration.

Inflation should therefore be understood as both a warning and a mirror. It warns that some part of the system is under stress: demand, supply, energy, housing, labor, finance, expectations, or trust. It mirrors the power structure by showing who can defend themselves and who cannot. It reveals whether institutions can coordinate adjustment or merely impose pain. It reveals whether policymakers understand the system they govern. It reveals whether citizens believe sacrifice is shared.

In a nonlinear world, inflation is rarely just inflation. It is a cascade of signals moving through the economy. It tells us about supply chains, housing scarcity, energy dependence, market concentration, labor power, fiscal choices, monetary credibility, climate vulnerability, geopolitical exposure, and social trust. The mistake is to compress all of this into a single explanation and then declare the problem solved by a single lever.

The end of simple economic explanations requires a new inflation realism. This realism recognizes that inflation can be dangerous and must be controlled. It also recognizes that the method of control matters. It refuses to treat workers as the default shock absorber. It refuses to ignore corporate pricing power. It refuses to pretend that central banks can repair broken supply systems. It refuses to define success only as a lower inflation rate while affordability remains broken. It insists that price stability be embedded in a broader architecture of resilience, fairness, and democratic legitimacy.

Inflation as a feedback process teaches us that economic systems speak through prices, but prices do not speak clearly by themselves. They must be interpreted. A rising price may signal scarcity, speculation, market power, panic, cost pressure, public failure, or genuine demand. A good society does not silence price signals, but neither does it worship them. It asks what produced them and what consequences they produce in return. It listens to prices, but it also listens to households, workers, firms, communities, and institutions.

To understand inflation is to understand a society in motion. It is to see how an energy shock becomes a grocery bill, how a rent increase becomes a wage demand, how a supply bottleneck becomes a political crisis, how a central bank decision becomes a mortgage payment, how corporate pricing becomes public anger, how household anxiety becomes market behavior, and how trust becomes an economic variable. Inflation is not a simple line moving upward on a chart. It is a web of feedback.

The chapters that follow will deepen this systems perspective. Debt will show how obligations magnify shocks. Inequality will show how advantage compounds. Housing will show how scarcity becomes self-reinforcing. Labor markets will show how power and networks shape adjustment. Supply chains will show how efficiency becomes fragility. Financial markets will show how expectations become cascades. Technology will show how innovation becomes concentration or shared capability depending on governance. Public policy will show how institutions must learn to govern feedback rather than merely react to symptoms.

Inflation belongs near the beginning of this inquiry because it is the economic problem most citizens feel immediately and most politicians fear. It is also one of the clearest examples of nonlinear economic life. It begins somewhere, spreads unevenly, changes expectations, redistributes burdens, invites blame, alters policy, and can either fade or become embedded depending on the feedback loops it activates. It is never merely a number. It is a social process measured in prices.

The old explanations are not enough. Money matters, but money is not the whole story. Demand matters, but demand has structure. Supply matters, but supply has networks. Wages matter, but wages reflect power. Profits matter, but profits reflect competition and control. Expectations matter, but expectations reflect trust and experience. Policy matters, but policy operates through institutions and distribution. Inflation is the place where these forces meet.

A society that understands inflation as feedback will govern differently. It will build housing before rent becomes crisis. It will diversify energy before fuel shocks become household hardship. It will regulate finance before rate hikes expose fragility. It will protect competition before pricing power becomes entrenched. It will strengthen labor institutions before wage conflict becomes chaotic. It will maintain public trust before communication fails. It will protect vulnerable households before inflation becomes despair. It will treat price stability not as a narrow technical target, but as part of the moral architecture of a stable economy.

The end of simple inflation thinking is not the abandonment of discipline. It is the beginning of deeper discipline. It asks us to see inflation as a dynamic process, to identify the loops that sustain it, to design policy that acts on causes rather than symptoms, and to distribute the burden of adjustment fairly. In a nonlinear world, inflation is not merely too much money or too few goods. It is the economy arguing with itself over scarcity, power, time, and trust.

The question is whether democratic societies can learn to govern that argument wisely.

# Chapter 6

# Debt, Leverage, and Systemic Fragility

Debt is one of the most powerful instruments in economic life because it allows the future to be brought into the present. A household borrows to buy a home before it has accumulated the full price. A student borrows to finance education before earning the income that education may produce. A business borrows to build a factory, hire workers, develop technology, or expand production before revenues arrive. A government borrows to build infrastructure, fight a war, stabilize a recession, or invest in public goods before tax revenues are sufficient. Credit is the bridge between possibility and realization. Without debt, modern capitalism would be smaller, slower, and less dynamic.

Yet the same bridge can become a trap. Debt binds the future to fixed claims made in the present. It converts uncertainty into obligation. It assumes that tomorrow's income, revenue, growth, or tax base will be sufficient to honor yesterday's promises. When that assumption holds, debt supports prosperity. When it fails, debt magnifies distress. A household that loses income while carrying debt does not merely become poorer. It becomes vulnerable to default, penalties, damaged credit, and reduced future options. A firm with falling revenue and high debt does not merely earn less profit. It may be forced to cut investment, fire workers, sell assets, or declare bankruptcy. A government with rising interest costs does not merely face a budget problem. It may face a legitimacy crisis if debt service competes with public needs.

Debt is therefore nonlinear. A little debt can increase freedom. Too much debt can destroy it. A loan can create opportunity when income is stable, interest rates are low, and the borrowed funds finance productive capacity. The same loan can create fragility when income falls, rates rise, asset prices decline, or refinancing becomes difficult. Debt does not have one meaning. Its meaning depends on the system in which it is embedded. It depends on who borrows, who lends, at what rate, for what purpose, with what collateral, under what institutional rules, and under what macroeconomic conditions.

This chapter argues that debt becomes dangerous when it is joined to leverage, optimism, asset inflation, and interconnected balance sheets. Debt by itself is a promise. Leverage is the multiplication of exposure through borrowed money. A household uses leverage when it buys a home with a mortgage far larger than its savings. A firm uses leverage when it finances expansion through borrowing rather than equity. A financial institution uses leverage when it holds large assets against a small capital cushion. Leverage magnifies gains when conditions are favorable. It also magnifies losses when conditions reverse.

The nonlinear danger lies in the fact that leverage changes the behavior of the system. Rising asset prices make borrowers and lenders feel safer. The apparent safety encourages more borrowing. More borrowing supports further asset purchases. Higher asset prices strengthen collateral values. Stronger collateral values permit still more borrowing. The loop appears virtuous while prices rise. But when prices fall, the same loop reverses. Collateral weakens. Lenders tighten. Borrowers sell. Forced selling pushes prices lower. Lower prices weaken other balance sheets. The system does not adjust smoothly. It cascades.

Debt is often discussed as if it were merely an accounting category. How much does a household owe? How much does a corporation owe? What is the ratio of public debt to gross domestic product? What are the interest costs? These questions matter, but they are incomplete. Debt is not only a stock. It is a relationship across time. It is a claim held by one party against another. It links the wellbeing of borrowers and lenders. It connects present confidence to future income. It distributes risk. It creates hierarchies of obligation. It can discipline, empower, exploit, stabilize, or destabilize.

A complexity economics approach therefore asks not simply how much debt exists, but how debt is structured. Is it short term or long term? Fixed rate or variable rate? Domestic or foreign currency? Secured or unsecured? Productive or speculative? Widely distributed or concentrated? Held by stable institutions or fragile intermediaries? Supported by income or by asset appreciation? Used to build capacity or to compensate for stagnation? These distinctions determine whether debt supports resilience or creates fragility.

The productive use of debt is easy to understand. A city borrows to build a bridge that supports commerce for generations. A company borrows to purchase machinery that raises productivity. A family borrows to buy a modest home that provides shelter and stability. A government borrows during recession to prevent collapse in income and employment. In these cases, debt can align present financing with future benefit. It allows societies to invest before they possess all the necessary resources in cash. It spreads cost over time in ways that can be both efficient and fair.

But debt becomes destructive when it finances extraction rather than capacity, speculation rather than production, or survival rather than opportunity. A household that borrows to pay medical bills is not investing in future income. It is converting vulnerability into obligation. A student who borrows for a credential that does not produce adequate earnings is not purchasing mobility. The student is purchasing risk. A corporation that borrows to repurchase its own shares may enrich shareholders and executives without increasing productive capacity. A government that borrows because tax systems have been hollowed out by elite influence may be financing political avoidance rather than public investment. A financial system that extends credit mainly to inflate existing assets is not deepening prosperity. It is increasing claims on future income without creating corresponding real capacity.

This distinction between capacity-building debt and fragility-building debt is central. Debt is sustainable when it helps generate the income, productivity, stability, or public value needed to service it. Debt is fragile when it depends on continued asset appreciation, low interest rates, loose refinancing conditions, or the inability of borrowers to escape. The difference is not always obvious during the boom. Fragility-building debt often looks successful at first. Asset prices rise. Consumption increases. Corporate profits improve. Tax revenues grow. Defaults remain low. Confidence expands. The system appears strong because borrowing itself is producing the appearance of strength.

This is one of the central insights associated with financial instability theory: stability can breed instability. When the economy is calm, actors become more willing to borrow. When defaults are low, lenders reduce caution. When asset prices rise, risk models appear favorable. When volatility is subdued, leverage increases. When leverage increases, the system becomes more sensitive to shocks. The longer stability lasts, the more people assume it will continue. Their behavior then undermines the conditions that made stability possible. Calm becomes the seedbed of crisis.

This pattern can be seen across financial history. Credit booms rarely feel dangerous while they are underway. They feel like opportunity. Banks are lending. Households are buying. Firms are expanding. Investors are earning. Governments are collecting revenue. Rising asset prices validate optimism. Skeptics appear foolish because the data seem to contradict them. If defaults are low, why worry about debt? If collateral values are rising, why worry about lending standards? If markets are liquid, why worry about exit? If everyone is making money, why question the structure?

The answer is that debt changes the consequences of reversal. An unleveraged investor who owns an asset that falls in value may suffer a loss, but the investor can wait. A leveraged investor may be forced to sell. A household that owns a home outright can endure a decline in home value. A household with a large mortgage and job loss may face foreclosure. A firm with cash reserves can survive a revenue shock. A heavily indebted firm may be pushed into layoffs or bankruptcy. A bank with strong capital can absorb losses. A highly leveraged institution may fail if confidence disappears. Leverage turns patience into urgency.

This is why liquidity matters. Liquidity is the ability to meet obligations, sell assets, or obtain funding without severe loss. During good times, liquidity appears abundant. Buyers are available. Credit is accessible. Assets can be sold. Markets function. But liquidity is often a property of confidence, not a permanent feature of the world. When many actors try to sell the same assets at the same time, liquidity disappears. Prices fall sharply. Assets once considered safe become difficult to value. Lenders demand more collateral. Borrowers scramble for cash. The system discovers that liquidity was plentiful only when few needed it.

Debt, leverage, and liquidity interact in dangerous ways. Borrowers often assume that refinancing will be available when debts mature. Firms roll over bonds. Banks rely on short-term funding. Governments issue new debt to pay old debt. Households refinance mortgages. This can work for years. But when confidence shifts, refinancing risk becomes crisis. A borrower may be solvent in the long run but unable to meet immediate obligations. A bank may hold assets that will pay eventually, but if depositors withdraw now, it must sell into a falling market. A government may have future tax capacity, but if investors refuse to roll over debt at reasonable rates, pressure intensifies. The timing of obligations becomes as important as the size of obligations.

In a nonlinear economy, maturity structure is therefore crucial. Short-term debt creates vulnerability because it must be refinanced frequently. Long-term fixed-rate debt provides breathing room. Variable-rate debt shifts interest-rate risk to borrowers. Foreign-currency debt creates vulnerability because borrowers may owe in a currency they cannot create. Secured debt can reduce lender risk but increase borrower vulnerability if collateral values fall. Complex debt instruments can obscure where risk resides. Debt is never only how much. It is when, to whom, in what currency, at what rate, and under what conditions.

Household debt provides a direct window into the moral meaning of leverage. A household balance sheet is not an abstraction. It is a map of daily life. Mortgage payments, rent, credit cards, student loans, car loans, medical debt, payday loans, and personal loans shape what families can do. Debt can help households build assets or smooth consumption. But it can also discipline them through fear. A worker with heavy debt may be less likely to quit a bad job, challenge an employer, start a business, relocate, or take time for caregiving. Debt narrows the horizon of freedom.

Modern economies often use household debt to compensate for failures elsewhere. If wages stagnate but housing, education, healthcare, child-care, and transportation costs rise, households borrow to maintain the standard of life that income no longer supports. Credit fills the gap left by weak wage growth and inadequate public goods. This allows consumption to continue, but it transfers risk to households. The economy appears stable because families keep spending. Beneath the surface, insecurity accumulates.

This is a profound policy failure. When households borrow to invest in opportunity, debt may support mobility. When households borrow to survive ordinary life, debt becomes evidence of systemic dysfunction. Medical debt reflects a failure of healthcare financing. Student debt reflects both opportunity-seeking and the rising price of credentials. Credit-card debt may reflect consumption choices, but it also reflects income volatility, emergency costs, and inadequate savings. Auto debt often reflects the necessity of transportation in regions without adequate public transit. Household debt should not be moralized without examining the structure that made borrowing necessary.

The nonlinear danger of household debt appears during downturns. A household with no savings and high obligations cannot easily absorb job loss, illness, rent increase, or interest-rate shock. It cuts spending, misses payments, borrows at higher cost, or defaults. When many households face stress simultaneously, the effects spread. Consumption falls. Businesses lose revenue. Layoffs increase. Housing markets weaken. Public services face pressure. Credit losses rise. What begins as private distress becomes macroeconomic contraction.

Debt also affects mental and civic life. Chronic indebtedness produces stress, shame, anxiety, and reduced social participation. It can delay marriage, childbirth, entrepreneurship, relocation, education, and retirement. It can weaken trust in institutions if people believe the economic system requires them to mortgage their future for basic goods. A society organized around household debt may preserve consumption while corroding dignity.

Corporate debt operates differently, but it too can create systemic fragility. Debt can allow firms to expand, invest, innovate, and survive temporary shocks. But when corporate borrowing is used to finance share buybacks, mergers, speculative acquisitions, or private equity extraction, it may increase financial vulnerability without increasing productive capacity. A firm loaded with debt becomes less able to withstand downturns. It may cut workers, reduce research, sell assets, squeeze suppliers, raise prices, or lobby for public support when conditions deteriorate.

Highly leveraged firms can transmit shocks through labor markets and supply chains. A debt-burdened company facing lower revenue may lay off workers quickly because debt service cannot be postponed. It may delay payments to suppliers, creating stress elsewhere. It may reduce maintenance, training, or investment, weakening long-term productivity. It may raise prices if it has market power. It may seek concessions from workers or public subsidies from governments. Corporate leverage thus becomes a social issue, not merely a private financial decision.

Private equity illustrates the broader problem of financial structure. In some cases, private equity can improve management, provide capital, and restructure failing businesses. In other cases, it can use debt to acquire companies, extract fees, sell assets, reduce labor costs, and leave operating firms more fragile. The gains accrue to financial owners, while workers, suppliers, customers, communities, and creditors bear risk if the company struggles. The moral issue is not debt itself, but the use of debt to transfer value upward while increasing vulnerability below.

Financial-sector leverage is even more dangerous because financial institutions sit at the center of payment, credit, and confidence networks. Banks borrow short and lend long. They hold assets whose value may fluctuate. They rely on depositor trust, interbank markets, collateral, and regulatory guarantees. When banks are well capitalized and well regulated, they support economic life. When they are highly leveraged, opaque, or dependent on unstable funding, they become channels of contagion.

The banking system is inherently fragile because confidence is essential. A bank may be solvent on paper, but if depositors demand cash at the same time, the bank may be forced to sell assets quickly. If those assets have fallen in value, the bank realizes losses. If depositors see this, more may withdraw. The fear of failure creates failure. This is why banking systems require deposit insurance, lender-of-last-resort facilities, supervision, capital standards, liquidity requirements, and resolution mechanisms. Banking cannot be treated as an ordinary market because panic can destroy even institutions that might survive under calm conditions.

Shadow banking complicates this further. Credit creation and maturity transformation do not occur only in traditional banks. Money market funds, broker-dealers, securitization vehicles, hedge funds, private credit funds, and other nonbank institutions can create bank-like fragility without bank-like regulation. They may rely on short-term funding, collateral, and investor confidence. They may promise liquidity while holding less liquid assets. When stress occurs, withdrawals, margin calls, asset sales, and funding freezes can create cascades. Risk migrates to where rules are weakest.

This migration is a recurring problem in financial regulation. After one form of leverage is constrained, another may grow elsewhere. Regulate banks, and risk may move to shadow banks. Limit one instrument, and a new instrument appears. Tighten mortgage lending standards, and credit may move through less regulated channels. Financial systems adapt. Regulation must therefore be dynamic. It cannot assume that last crisis's instruments will be next crisis's instruments. It must monitor leverage, liquidity, maturity mismatch, interconnectedness, and incentives across the entire financial system.

Asset prices are the bridge between debt and fragility. Debt is often secured by collateral: homes, commercial real estate, securities, inventories, land, or future cash flows. When asset prices rise, collateral values rise. Borrowers appear safer. Lenders extend more credit. This can raise asset prices further. The feedback loop supports expansion. But when asset prices fall, collateral weakens. Loan-to-value ratios worsen. Lenders demand more collateral or reduce credit. Borrowers sell assets. Prices fall further. The system tightens exactly when support is needed.

This collateral loop is central to financial crises. It shows why falling asset prices can have consequences far beyond the owners of those assets. A decline in housing prices can reduce household wealth, trigger defaults, damage mortgage-backed securities, weaken banks, reduce lending, and lower consumption. A decline in commercial real estate values can affect landlords, banks, municipal revenues, construction, pension funds, and local employment. A decline in bond prices can affect bank balance sheets, insurance companies, pension funds, and government borrowing costs. Asset prices are not merely market signals. They are balance-sheet foundations.

This is why monetary policy interacts so powerfully with leverage. Low interest rates can support borrowing, asset prices, and debt service. They can be appropriate when demand is weak and inflation is low. But prolonged low rates can also encourage risk-taking, search for yield, rising asset valuations, and greater leverage. When inflation later forces rates upward, the system may discover vulnerabilities built during the low-rate period. Borrowers face higher refinancing costs. Asset prices fall as discount rates rise. Banks holding long-term assets may face losses. Housing affordability worsens. Governments pay more to borrow. Monetary tightening becomes not only an anti-inflation tool, but a stress test of the debt structure.

The interest rate is therefore not merely the price of money. It is a systemic variable that changes the distribution of pressure across balance sheets. Savers, borrowers, banks, governments, homeowners, renters, firms, investors, and foreign exchange markets all respond differently. A higher rate may reduce inflationary pressure by slowing demand, but it may also expose leverage, reduce housing construction, increase public debt service, and trigger financial instability. A lower rate may support employment and investment, but it may also inflate assets and encourage leverage. No interest-rate policy is neutral in a leveraged economy.

Public debt requires a careful and nonideological analysis. Governments are not households. A sovereign government with its own currency, credible institutions, productive capacity, and deep domestic capital markets has far more flexibility than a household or firm. It can tax, issue currency, regulate banks, and influence interest rates. Public borrowing can be essential during recession, war, disaster, or long-term investment. A government that refuses to borrow for productive infrastructure, climate resilience, public health, education, or social stabilization may be fiscally cautious in the narrow sense but economically reckless in the broader sense.

At the same time, public debt is not meaningless. Interest costs can crowd out other spending if they rise sharply. Heavy debt can create political conflict over taxation, spending, inflation, and intergenerational fairness. External debt in foreign currency can create serious vulnerability. Loss of institutional credibility can increase borrowing costs. Public debt becomes dangerous when it is used to avoid necessary taxation, finance recurring transfers to powerful groups without productive purpose, rescue private excess without reform, or compensate for structural stagnation. The issue is not whether debt is good or bad. The issue is whether debt builds the future or mortgages it.

The public debt debate is often trapped between two simplifications. One side treats government debt as if it were household debt and assumes that borrowing is inherently irresponsible. The other side treats sovereign borrowing capacity as if it removed meaningful constraints. Both views are incomplete. Governments can and should borrow when borrowing prevents collapse, supports investment, or distributes costs fairly across generations. But borrowing is not a substitute for political choice. A society must still ask what it is borrowing for, who benefits, who pays, whether the spending expands capacity, and whether the debt structure is resilient under changing rates.

The distinction between productive and unproductive public debt is essential. Borrowing to build resilient infrastructure, improve child health, expand education, accelerate energy transition, or prevent depression can increase future capacity. Borrowing to finance tax cuts that primarily increase asset wealth, or to rescue financial institutions without changing incentives, may increase fragility. Borrowing to maintain consumption in a crisis may be necessary, but if repeated because wages are inadequate and public goods are weak, it signals deeper failure. Public debt must be assessed in relation to public purpose.

Sovereign debt crises show how confidence can become nonlinear. Investors may lend to a government for years, then suddenly demand higher rates. Higher rates worsen debt dynamics. Worsened dynamics increase fear. Fear raises rates further. A solvency concern becomes a liquidity crisis, and a liquidity crisis can become a solvency crisis. Governments may impose austerity to restore confidence. Austerity may reduce growth, lower tax revenue, increase unemployment, and worsen the debt ratio. The attempt to reassure markets can deepen the problem if the underlying issue is growth, social capacity, or institutional legitimacy.

Currency matters enormously. Countries that borrow in a currency they cannot issue face harder constraints. If their currency depreciates, foreign-currency debts become more expensive in domestic terms. If global rates rise, refinancing becomes difficult. If export revenues fall, debt service becomes harder. External debt can subordinate domestic policy to creditor confidence. This is one reason international financial architecture is a moral issue. Debt crises in developing economies often involve not only fiscal choices, but commodity dependence, exchange-rate vulnerability, global interest rates, inherited debt, climate shocks, and creditor power.

International debt reveals the hierarchy of the global economy. Some countries borrow cheaply in their own currencies. Others borrow expensively in foreign currencies. Some can respond to crisis with fiscal expansion. Others are forced into austerity. Some can issue reserve assets. Others depend on capital flows. Debt is not only an economic relationship. It is a geopolitical relationship. It determines policy space, vulnerability, and sovereignty.

Systemic fragility emerges when many balance sheets are linked. A balance sheet is a statement of assets, liabilities, and equity. But in a complex economy, one actor's asset is another actor's liability. A household's mortgage is a bank's asset. A government bond is an investor's asset and the state's liability. A corporate bond is a pension fund's asset and a firm's obligation. A deposit is a household's asset and a bank's liability. These links create interdependence. Distress travels because obligations connect actors.

This balance-sheet perspective is crucial. Traditional economic discussion often focuses on flows: income, spending, output, employment, and inflation. Flows matter. But crises often begin in stocks: accumulated debt, asset values, collateral, capital cushions, reserves, and obligations. A household may have adequate income in normal times but insufficient net worth to absorb shock. A bank may have current earnings but fragile assets. A government may have current tax revenue but large refinancing needs. Balance sheets determine resilience.

A balance-sheet recession occurs when households or firms focus on paying down debt rather than spending or investing. Even low interest rates may not stimulate borrowing if actors are repairing balance sheets. This can make recovery slow. The private sector attempts to become safer by deleveraging. But if everyone deleverages at once, demand falls, income falls, and the burden of debt may become heavier. What is rationally individually becomes harmful collectively. This is another form of the paradox of composition.

Deleveraging is especially painful because it often follows a boom in which debt financed inflated asset prices. During the boom, households feel wealthier, firms expand, banks lend, and governments benefit from revenue. During the bust, balance sheets must adjust. If asset values fall but debts remain fixed, net worth collapses. Borrowers cut spending to rebuild. Lenders restrict credit. The economy enters a slow repair process. Without public intervention, debt overhang can suppress growth for years.

This is why debt restructuring can be economically necessary. Moralistic approaches to debt often insist that debts must always be paid in full because contracts matter. Contracts do matter. Credit systems depend on trust. But when debts become unpayable, pretending otherwise can destroy value. A bankrupt household cannot spend. A bankrupt firm cannot invest. A bankrupt country cannot grow. Debt restructuring recognizes that the future cannot be governed entirely by promises made under prior conditions. It is not always a reward for irresponsibility. It can be a mechanism of systemic recovery.

Bankruptcy law is therefore a central institution of capitalism. It allows failure to be reorganized rather than endlessly punished. It distinguishes between fraud, misfortune, and unsustainable obligation. It permits assets and people to return to productive life. A society without humane bankruptcy turns debt into permanent bondage. A society with overly permissive bankruptcy may weaken lending discipline. The challenge is balance. But the existence of bankruptcy itself recognizes a complexity truth: rigid enforcement of all promises can destroy the system in which promises have value.

Debt relief is politically contentious because it raises issues of fairness. Why should one borrower receive relief when another repaid? Why should taxpayers support debtors? Why should creditors absorb losses? These questions are legitimate. But fairness must be understood systemically. If debts were incurred under predatory terms, inflated costs, public policy failures, or macroeconomic shocks, moral responsibility is shared. If debt overhang harms the broader economy, relief may benefit even those not directly relieved. If the alternative is stagnation, foreclosure, despair, or crisis, restructuring may be the more just and efficient path.

Student debt illustrates the tension between individual obligation and systemic design. Borrowers signed contracts, but the broader system encouraged borrowing as the path to opportunity while tuition rose, public support declined, credentials became more necessary, and labor market returns became unequal. Some degrees produced high income. Others did not. Some institutions served students well. Others exploited them. A simple moral story of personal responsibility is inadequate. A simple story of universal victimhood is also incomplete. The complexity question is how education finance became a debt system and whether that system supports human development or traps young adults in delayed adulthood.

Medical debt is morally even clearer. Illness is not a consumer preference. A person does not choose cancer, injury, childbirth complications, or chronic disease in the way one chooses a luxury purchase. Medical debt converts vulnerability into financial punishment. It damages credit, savings, housing stability, and mental health. A society that allows illness to become debt has made a political choice about who bears the cost of human fragility. Complexity economics reveals the feedback: medical insecurity reduces labor mobility, increases stress, worsens health, reduces productivity, and deepens inequality. Healthcare finance is not separate from macroeconomic resilience.

Housing debt has a dual character. A mortgage can be a path to stability and wealth. It can also become a mechanism of exclusion, speculation, and crisis. When housing prices rise faster than incomes, households borrow more to enter the market. Larger mortgages make households sensitive to interest rates and income shocks. Rising prices enrich existing owners, who may resist new supply. Credit availability supports demand, which supports prices. The system becomes dependent on continued appreciation. Housing debt then links shelter, wealth, banking, local politics, and inequality.

The global financial crisis showed how dangerous this linkage can become. Mortgages were not merely household loans. They were inputs into securities, derivatives, bank assets, investor portfolios, and global funding markets. A mortgage payment in one community became part of a financial instrument held by institutions across the world. When households defaulted, the losses did not remain local. They traveled through securitized structures, ratings, leverage, and confidence networks. The crisis was not only about bad borrowers or bad lenders. It was about a system that transformed household debt into systemic exposure.

This transformation is one of the defining features of modern finance. Debt claims are packaged, traded, insured, leveraged, and used as collateral. This can distribute risk, but it can also obscure it. If no one knows where losses will fall, uncertainty spreads. If instruments are too complex to value under stress, markets freeze. If institutions rely on models that assume liquidity and correlation patterns that fail in crisis, risk is underestimated. Complexity becomes not knowledge, but opacity.

Financial opacity creates moral hazard. If institutions profit from risk-taking but expect rescue when risk becomes systemic, they have incentives to increase leverage. If creditors believe certain firms are too important to fail, they lend more cheaply. If executives are rewarded for short-term gains, they may ignore long-term fragility. If regulators are captured, under-resourced, or ideologically committed to market discipline, they may act too late. The system teaches actors what behavior is rewarded. If leverage is rewarded in booms and rescued in busts, leverage will return.

Macroprudential policy is the attempt to govern the system as a system. Traditional microprudential regulation asks whether individual institutions are safe. Macroprudential regulation asks whether the collective behavior of institutions is making the whole system fragile. Each bank may appear prudent if judged alone, but if all banks hold similar assets, rely on similar funding, or follow similar models, the system may be vulnerable. Each lender may believe a mortgage is safe because housing prices are rising, but widespread lending may be causing the price rise. Each investor may hedge risk, but if hedges depend on counterparties that fail together, the protection is fragile.

Macroprudential thinking is complexity thinking applied to finance. It focuses on leverage, liquidity, interconnectedness, procyclicality, concentration, and common exposure. It recognizes that risk is endogenous. Risk is not simply out there in the world, waiting to be measured. It is created by the behavior of the system. When actors believe risk is low, they take actions that can make risk higher. When they believe risk is high, they take actions that can make crisis worse. Regulation must therefore lean against the cycle, building buffers in good times so that systems can absorb bad times.

Countercyclical capital buffers are one example. Banks should hold more capital when credit is expanding rapidly, asset prices are rising, and risk appears low. Loan-to-value limits can restrain speculative borrowing. Debt-to-income limits can protect households. Liquidity requirements can reduce funding fragility. Stress tests can examine how institutions perform under severe scenarios. Resolution rules can allow failing institutions to be wound down without destroying the system. Transparency rules can reduce opacity. But these tools require political will. During booms, restraint is unpopular. Everyone appears to be winning. Regulation is accused of blocking prosperity. The regulator's task is hardest precisely when intervention is most needed.

This is a general feature of nonlinear systems. Preventive policy is least popular before the tipping point and most demanded after it. Before crisis, warnings seem abstract. After crisis, they seem obvious. A society that wants stability must learn to respect unpopular caution. It must value those who ask whether apparent prosperity is being purchased with hidden fragility.

Debt and leverage also shape inequality. The wealthy use debt differently from the poor. Wealthy households borrow against assets, often at lower rates, to invest, reduce taxes, or manage liquidity. Poor households borrow at higher rates to cover emergencies, consumption needs, or essential services. For the wealthy, debt can be a tool of wealth management. For the poor, debt can be a trap. The same financial instrument has different meanings depending on position in the economic hierarchy.

This inequality is visible in interest rates. Risk-based pricing means that those with fewer resources often pay more to borrow. Poor credit, unstable income, lack of collateral, and financial exclusion raise costs. Higher costs make repayment harder. Difficulty repaying worsens credit. The loop reinforces disadvantage. Meanwhile, those with assets borrow cheaply, invest, and accumulate more. Credit markets can therefore amplify inequality even when formally open to all.

Predatory lending intensifies this dynamic. Payday loans, abusive fees, high-cost credit cards, exploitative student programs, subprime auto loans, and deceptive mortgage products extract from vulnerability. They are profitable because some households lack alternatives. The market does not merely serve need. It monetizes desperation. Regulation of predatory credit is not paternalism. It is protection against feedback loops that convert insecurity into permanent extraction.

Debt also shapes race, gender, and geography through historical patterns of exclusion and discrimination. Communities denied fair access to credit, housing, education, and wealth-building opportunities often enter modern credit markets with fewer buffers and higher costs. Predatory lending has frequently targeted marginalized communities. Student debt burdens can fall disproportionately on those whose families lack wealth. Medical debt burdens those without secure insurance. These patterns are not accidental. They reflect the historical embedding of inequality in financial systems.

The moral status of debt cannot be separated from the conditions under which it is incurred. A contract signed under desperation, exclusion, misinformation, or structural necessity is not morally equivalent to a contract signed with abundant alternatives. Formal consent is not always substantive freedom. This does not mean borrowers bear no responsibility. It means responsibility must be understood relationally. Lenders, regulators, employers, educational institutions, healthcare systems, and governments also shape the choices borrowers face.

Leverage also influences corporate and political power. Firms with access to cheap credit can acquire competitors, buy back shares, invest in technology, and survive downturns. Firms without access may fail or be acquired. Financial conditions can therefore shape market concentration. Low rates may encourage mergers and private equity deals. High rates may favor cash-rich incumbents. Credit is not neutral. It allocates power.

Government responses to debt crises also distribute power. Bailouts can stabilize systems, but they can also entrench moral hazard and public anger if they protect financial elites while ordinary borrowers suffer. A rescue that saves banks without restructuring household debt may restore credit markets while deepening distrust. A rescue that protects depositors and the payment system while imposing losses on managers, shareholders, and unsecured creditors may preserve stability with more fairness. The design of rescue matters. Crisis response is moral architecture under pressure.

This is why the phrase "too big to fail" is so corrosive. It tells citizens that some institutions are so central that their mistakes cannot be allowed to bring them down. If true, such institutions are not ordinary private firms. They are public risks under private control. They require stricter obligations, size limits, capital standards, resolution plans, and accountability. No institution should be allowed to become so systemically dangerous that democracy must rescue it without conditions. Systemic importance should bring systemic responsibility.

Debt also influences political narratives. Debtors are often moralized as irresponsible, while creditors are moralized as prudent. This is too simple. Creditors can be reckless. Lenders can profit from bad loans. Investors can chase yield. Governments can borrow wisely. Households can borrow out of necessity. Firms can borrow productively or extractively. The moral meaning of debt depends on purpose, terms, alternatives, and consequences.

A society that moralizes debt only at the bottom and normalizes debt at the top has revealed its class structure. Poor borrowers are scolded. Large corporations are restructured. Banks are rescued. Governments debate austerity for social programs while tolerating tax avoidance and financial bailouts. The language of responsibility is applied unevenly. Complexity economics insists on symmetry: all debt relationships should be judged by their systemic effects and moral conditions.

Debt has a psychological power because it turns the future into a creditor. It colonizes imagination. The indebted person thinks not only about what is possible, but about what is owed. This can motivate discipline, but it can also produce fear. Societies with high household indebtedness may become less entrepreneurial in a deep sense, even while celebrating entrepreneurship rhetorically. People cannot take risks when failure means ruin. Broad security, not insecurity, is often the foundation of genuine risk-taking.

This reverses a common ideology. Some argue that insecurity creates discipline and productivity. But extreme insecurity can make people cautious, stressed, and short-term in their thinking. A worker without healthcare, savings, or debt relief cannot easily start a business, move for a better job, return to school, or challenge exploitation. A society that wants innovation should not burden ordinary life with catastrophic downside risk. It should provide enough security for people to experiment.

The same logic applies to firms. A productive economy needs failure, but failure should reallocate resources rather than destroy human lives and communities unnecessarily. Bankruptcy, unemployment insurance, retraining, regional investment, and portable benefits allow economic adaptation without social devastation. Debt systems should permit renewal. Permanent punishment for failure reduces dynamism.

Climate change introduces new debt and fragility dynamics. Governments will need to borrow for adaptation, infrastructure, energy transition, disaster recovery, and resilience. Households may face rising insurance costs, property devaluation, and relocation expenses. Municipalities may face declining tax bases in high-risk areas. Banks and insurers may hold assets exposed to climate risk. Developing countries may face debt burdens from disasters they did little to cause. Climate shocks can therefore become debt shocks.

The financial system may underestimate climate risk because losses are uncertain, delayed, and nonlinear. Property values may remain high in risky areas until insurance becomes unavailable, infrastructure fails, or migration begins. Municipal bonds may appear safe until tax bases erode. Agricultural loans may appear sound until drought patterns change. Disaster recovery borrowing may accumulate. Climate risk can reprice assets suddenly. Debt contracts written under old assumptions may become fragile in a new physical world.

This reinforces the central argument: debt is a claim on the future, but the future is changing. When ecological, technological, demographic, and geopolitical conditions shift, past debt assumptions may become invalid. A resilient society must consider how future shocks affect present obligations. It must not build financial systems on the fantasy of continuity.

Technology also affects debt dynamics. Digital lending can expand access, but it can also accelerate predatory credit, algorithmic discrimination, and behavioral manipulation. Buy-now-pay-later systems can fragment debt into small obligations that appear harmless but accumulate. Platform workers may borrow against uncertain income. Data-driven credit scoring may include or exclude in opaque ways. Financial technology does not eliminate the moral issues of debt. It transforms them.

At the macro level, technology-driven market concentration can increase corporate cash piles for dominant firms while smaller firms rely more heavily on credit. Platform economies can shift risk to workers and suppliers. Automation can increase income volatility for some workers, making debt burdens more dangerous. Artificial intelligence may reshape labor markets in ways that affect household creditworthiness, public revenues, and social insurance needs. Debt systems must be evaluated in relation to technological disruption.

Debt, leverage, and systemic fragility ultimately force us to rethink economic governance. The question is not how to eliminate debt. That would be neither possible nor desirable. The question is how to govern debt so that it finances real prosperity rather than fragility, dependency, and extraction. This requires a broad architecture.

First, credit should be directed toward productive and socially valuable uses. Housing finance should support shelter and stability, not speculative scarcity. Student finance should support education that produces real opportunity, not institutional price inflation. Corporate finance should support investment and innovation, not merely financial engineering. Public borrowing should build capacity, resilience, and shared prosperity.

Second, leverage must be restrained where it creates systemic risk. Financial institutions should hold adequate capital and liquidity. Shadow banking should be monitored. Leverage should not be allowed to migrate into darkness. Margin requirements, collateral rules, and stress tests should recognize correlated behavior and fire-sale risk. Regulation should be strongest during booms, when risk appears lowest.

Third, household balance sheets should be protected through fair wages, affordable essentials, social insurance, healthcare security, consumer protection, and humane bankruptcy. A society that relies on private debt to fund basic needs has confused credit access with freedom. Real freedom requires that households not be forced into costly debt to survive ordinary life.

Fourth, debt restructuring must be available when obligations become destructive. This applies to households, firms, municipalities, and sovereigns. The goal should be to preserve productive capacity, human dignity, and systemic stability while maintaining reasonable lending discipline. Punitive debt systems may satisfy moral anger, but they can destroy economic value.

Fifth, crisis rescues must be designed with accountability. If public support is necessary to prevent systemic collapse, it should come with conditions: losses for equity holders where appropriate, management accountability, restrictions on future risk-taking, protections for households and workers, and structural reform. Public rescue without reform teaches the system to repeat the behavior that made rescue necessary.

Sixth, public debt should be evaluated by purpose and capacity, not by slogans. Borrowing for investment, stabilization, and resilience can be responsible. Borrowing to avoid fair taxation, finance extraction, or postpone reform can be irresponsible. Fiscal sustainability is not only about debt ratios. It is about the relationship among growth, interest rates, public purpose, institutional credibility, and social legitimacy.

Seventh, the global debt system must recognize unequal vulnerability. Countries facing climate shocks, commodity dependence, foreign-currency debt, and volatile capital flows require fairer restructuring mechanisms. A global economy that imposes austerity on fragile societies while ignoring the systemic causes of their vulnerability will generate instability, migration, underdevelopment, and resentment. Debt justice is not charity. It is systemic realism.

The moral core of debt policy is the recognition that obligations must serve life, not dominate it. Contracts matter because trust matters. But contracts exist within society. When debt destroys families, hollows communities, destabilizes economies, or subordinates democracy to creditors, the system has lost proportion. Debt should finance human flourishing, not become a substitute for it.

This chapter has treated debt as a nonlinear process because debt changes the consequences of time, uncertainty, and shock. In a low-debt system, a downturn may be painful but manageable. In a highly leveraged system, the same downturn can become crisis. In a society where households have savings and public supports, job loss may be temporary hardship. In a society where households are indebted and unsupported, job loss can become foreclosure, bankruptcy, illness, and social decline. In a financial system with buffers, asset price declines can be absorbed. In a leveraged system, they can cascade. Structure determines outcome.

Debt, leverage, and systemic fragility are therefore central to a complexity economics inquiry. They show how a system can look strong while becoming weak. They show how private decisions can create public risk. They show how balance sheets connect households, firms, banks, governments, and markets. They show how confidence can stabilize or destroy. They show how inequality shapes the meaning of borrowing. They show how policy must act before crisis, not merely after it.

The next chapter turns to inequality and cumulative advantage. The connection is direct. Debt and inequality reinforce one another. Wealthy households use debt to accumulate assets. Poor households use debt to survive. Asset owners borrow cheaply. Vulnerable borrowers pay more. Financial crises destroy wealth at the bottom and often create opportunities for those with cash at the top. Public rescues can stabilize systems while leaving structural inequality intact. Debt is one of the mechanisms through which inequality compounds.

In a nonlinear world, debt is never just debt. It is a structure of promises, power, time, and vulnerability. It can build bridges to the future, or it can turn the future into a burden that crushes the present. It can support investment, or it can inflate bubbles. It can spread opportunity, or it can deepen dependency. It can stabilize a recession, or it can transmit crisis. It can enable freedom, or it can discipline the desperate.

The task of economic governance is not to fear debt, but to civilize it. Debt must be embedded in institutions that distinguish productive investment from extraction, opportunity from desperation, resilience from fragility, and public purpose from private gain. Leverage must be watched most carefully when confidence is highest. Balance sheets must be understood as social structures, not merely financial statements. Credit must be governed as a public utility of economic possibility.

A society that understands debt only as individual obligation will repeatedly miss its systemic danger. A society that understands debt as a complex network of claims will ask better questions. Who owes? Who owns the claim? What financed the debt? What happens if rates rise? What happens if asset prices fall? Who has buffers? Who is exposed? What obligations are productive, and which are extractive? What risks are private, and which will become public? What future is being built, and what future is being mortgaged?

These questions are the beginning of wisdom in a leveraged world. Without them, prosperity may become a balance-sheet illusion, stability may become a prelude to crisis, and the promise of credit may become the machinery of collapse. With them, debt can be restored to its proper role: not as master of economic life, but as a disciplined instrument of investment, resilience, and shared human possibility.

## Chapter 7

# Inequality and the Cumulative Advantage Machine

INEQUALITY IS OFTEN described as a gap. The image is familiar: a gap between rich and poor, between wages and profits, between owners and workers, between neighborhoods, between schools, between those who inherit and those who borrow, between those who are secure and those who live one disruption away from ruin. This language is useful because inequality is visible as distance. Some households have more income, more wealth, more security, more opportunity, and more influence than others. The gap can be measured, charted, debated, and compared across nations and eras.

But the language of gaps is not enough. A gap is static. It describes difference at a point in time. It does not explain how the difference was produced, why it persists, why it widens, or why it becomes difficult to reverse. Inequality in a nonlinear economy is not merely a gap. It is a machine. It is a cumulative advantage machine, a system of institutions, markets, norms, policies, networks, and feedback loops through which advantage produces further advantage and disadvantage produces further disadvantage.

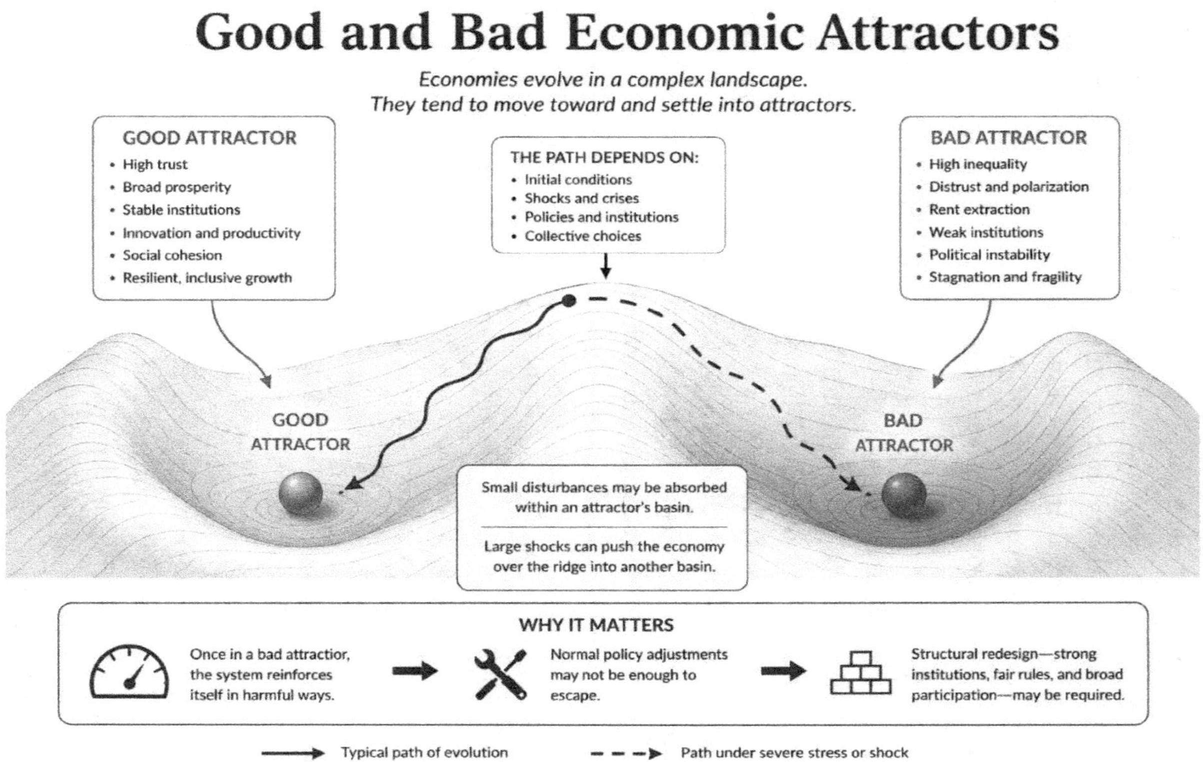


*Figure 4.0 – Good and Bad Economic Attractors*

This is the central argument of this chapter: inequality is not simply the unequal distribution of rewards after economic activity has occurred. It is an active force that shapes the future structure of economic activity itself. Wealth alters opportunity. Opportunity alters income. Income alters housing. Housing alters education. Education alters labor market access. Labor market access alters savings. Savings alter resilience. Resilience alters risk-taking. Risk-taking alters wealth. Wealth alters political influence. Political influence alters rules. Rules alter markets. Markets alter wealth. The system is recursive. Inequality does not merely result from the economy. It helps govern the economy.

Simple explanations of inequality are attractive because they reduce moral discomfort. They tell us that unequal outcomes mainly reflect unequal effort, talent, thrift, ambition, or risk-taking. These factors are not irrelevant. Human beings differ in skill, motivation, judgment, discipline, luck, and aspiration. No serious account of economic life should deny individual agency. But individual agency operates inside systems that distribute starting points, constraints, buffers, information, networks, and risks unequally. To treat inequality only as the result of personal choices is to begin the story too late.

The child born into a wealthy household does not merely receive more money. That child receives a different environment of possibility. The household may provide stable housing, safe neighborhoods, high-quality schools, tutoring, extracurricular activities, healthcare, books, technology, travel, social confidence, college preparation, unpaid internships, professional networks, and protection from catastrophic mistakes. Failure is cushioned. Experimentation is encouraged. Risk is survivable. Time is available. Stress is lower. The future is imagined as open.

The child born into poverty, or even into chronic insecurity, enters a different world. Housing may be unstable. Schools may be underfunded. Parents may be overworked, underpaid, indebted, or stressed. Healthcare may be delayed. Nutrition may be less reliable. Neighborhood violence may shape daily behavior. Transportation may be difficult. Quiet study space may be scarce. Social networks may provide love and resilience, but not access to elite institutions. Mistakes are costly. Risk is dangerous. Time is consumed by survival. The future is not absent, but it is constrained.

These differences accumulate before the labor market has a chance to reward anyone. They shape the development of health, confidence, cognition, aspirations, credentials, habits, expectations, and social belonging. By the time individuals appear in economic data as workers, borrowers, consumers, students, tenants, or taxpayers, inequality has already done much of its work. The market then interprets the resulting differences as if they were primarily individual properties. The system produces unequal capacities, then claims merely to measure them.

This is why complexity economics is essential to understanding inequality. A complexity approach asks how unequal outcomes emerge from interactions over time. It asks how small differences become large differences, how early advantages compound, how institutions amplify or dampen disparities, how networks transmit opportunity, how power reshapes rules, and how inequality becomes self-reinforcing. It refuses to treat the distribution of income and wealth as a mere aftereffect. Distribution is part of the system's structure.

The simplest form of cumulative advantage is financial compounding. Wealth earns returns. Returns increase wealth. Increased wealth earns greater returns. A household with savings can invest in stocks, bonds, real estate, retirement accounts, businesses, education, and tax-advantaged vehicles. It can diversify risk. It can wait through downturns. It can borrow at low rates against collateral. It can hire accountants, attorneys, and advisers. It can use time as an ally.

A household without wealth experiences time differently. It may rely on wages alone. It may pay rent without building equity. It may borrow at higher interest rates. It may pay late fees, overdraft fees, credit-card interest, or payday loan charges. It may sell assets during emergencies. It may be unable to invest because all income is absorbed by necessities. It may avoid beneficial risks because failure would be catastrophic. It may experience time as pressure rather than compounding. In the wealth economy, patience is rewarded. In the insecurity economy, delay is punished.

This difference is one of the great moral facts of capitalism. Capital can wait; labor often cannot. The owner of assets can choose when to sell, whether to borrow, where to invest, and how long to hold. The worker who needs a paycheck must sell labor on schedule. The renter must pay monthly. The debtor must meet due dates. The uninsured patient must face the bill. The household without savings lives under the discipline of time. This discipline is rarely visible in theories that treat market exchange as voluntary interaction among equal agents. Formal freedom can coexist with unequal urgency.

Debt intensifies this asymmetry. For the wealthy, debt can be a tool. For the poor, it can be a trap. A wealthy household may borrow against assets at low rates to invest, manage taxes, or bridge liquidity. A low-income household may borrow at high rates to cover rent, medical bills, transportation, or groceries. One form of debt expands opportunity; the other narrows it. One borrower uses leverage to acquire assets; the other uses credit to survive. The same financial system produces freedom at the top and discipline at the bottom.

Housing is perhaps the most powerful cumulative advantage machine in modern economic life. Housing is shelter, but it is also wealth, collateral, school access, neighborhood membership, tax advantage, political identity, and intergenerational transfer. Homeownership has long been one of the principal pathways through which middle-class families build wealth. A family buys a home. The home appreciates. Mortgage payments build equity. Equity can finance education, business formation, retirement, or assistance to children. Property ownership stabilizes residence and connects families to local institutions. In many cases, homeownership becomes a platform for further mobility.

But housing wealth is not evenly accessible. Families that already possess savings can make down payments. They can qualify for favorable mortgages. They can buy in neighborhoods where property values appreciate. They can help children purchase homes. Families without wealth rent longer, face rising rents, struggle to save, and miss appreciation. If prices rise faster than wages, the gap widens. Owners gain wealth because housing becomes expensive. Nonowners become excluded because housing becomes expensive. The same price movement enriches one group and burdens another.

This is a nonlinear process. Rising home values do not simply increase wealth. They alter politics. Existing homeowners often oppose new construction that might reduce scarcity, change neighborhood character, or affect property values. Local governments may depend on property tax bases and respond more to homeowners than renters. Zoning rules restrict supply. Restricted supply raises prices further. Higher prices increase homeowner wealth and strengthen resistance to change. Renters, young households, and newcomers are often less organized and less represented. The housing market becomes a feedback loop between scarcity and political power.

The result is not merely unequal housing consumption. It is unequal access to opportunity. Neighborhoods differ in schools, safety, transportation, jobs, environmental quality, healthcare, social networks, and public services. A child's address can shape educational attainment, health outcomes, peer networks, exposure to violence, commute times, and future earnings. Housing inequality becomes educational inequality, health inequality, labor market inequality, and wealth inequality. The place where one sleeps becomes part of the structure of one's future.

Education is often presented as the solution to inequality. In one sense, this is correct. Education expands human capability, increases income potential, deepens civic participation, and opens doors. But education is also shaped by inequality before it can reduce it. The quality of schooling is often linked to neighborhood wealth. Families with resources supplement education through tutoring, enrichment, test preparation, technology, summer programs, and college advising. They can navigate admissions systems, unpaid internships, and professional pipelines. They can absorb the cost of delayed earnings.

Education can therefore become both ladder and filter. It can enable mobility, but it can also reproduce class advantage. Credentials become more important as good jobs require formal qualifications. Families with resources are better able to secure those credentials. Elite institutions become gateways to elite networks. The labor market then rewards credentials as if they were pure evidence of merit, ignoring the unequal conditions under which credentials were acquired. Meritocracy becomes plausible because selection occurs through exams, grades, degrees, and resumes. But the inputs into those achievements are deeply unequal.

This is not an argument against merit. It is an argument against confusing merit with unassisted achievement. Talent exists everywhere. Opportunity does not. A society that wastes talent because of poverty, poor schools, housing instability, healthcare insecurity, or discrimination is not merely unjust. It is inefficient in the deepest sense. It fails to develop human capability. It narrows the field of invention, leadership, science, art, entrepreneurship, and citizenship. Inequality is not only a distributional problem. It is a loss of social intelligence.

Health is another feedback loop. Health affects learning, work, earnings, savings, and family stability. Inequality affects health through nutrition, stress, environmental exposure, medical access, neighborhood safety, work conditions, and time. Poor health reduces income. Lower income worsens health. Medical bills create debt. Debt creates stress. Stress worsens health. The loop is both biological and economic. A society that allows health to depend heavily on income builds inequality into the body.

Chronic stress is especially important. Insecure housing, unstable work, debt, unsafe neighborhoods, discrimination, and the constant need to manage scarcity impose physiological and psychological burdens. Scarcity consumes attention. It narrows planning. It increases the cost of mistakes. It can make short-term decisions rational even when they appear imprudent from a position of security. The poor are often judged for choices made under conditions that the secure never face. Complexity economics asks us to examine the decision environment before moralizing the decision.

Labor markets are central to cumulative advantage because wages remain the primary source of income for most households. Yet labor markets do not simply reward productivity in a neutral way. They are structured by bargaining power, institutions, technology, discrimination, credentialing, geography, firm concentration, unionization, scheduling practices, care responsibilities, immigration status, and social norms. Workers do not enter labor markets as isolated units of human capital. They enter as people embedded in families, places, debts, health conditions, and histories.

When labor power is weak, productivity gains can be captured by capital. Wages stagnate. Benefits erode. Work becomes precarious. Workers rely more heavily on debt. Families struggle to save. Children inherit insecurity. Weak labor power therefore feeds inequality across generations.

When labor power is strong, wage gains can support household stability, demand, savings, health, and mobility. Strong labor institutions can serve as balancing feedback against cumulative advantage at the top.

The decline of unions in many sectors has therefore had consequences beyond wages. Unions historically provided workers with voice, solidarity, political representation, training, workplace dignity, and a counterweight to employer power. Their weakening reduced the capacity of workers to claim a fair share of productivity and to influence policy. Corporate power grew. Executive compensation rose. Shareholder value became more dominant. Labor's voice in democracy weakened. Inequality rose not merely because the market changed, but because institutions that once dampened inequality were dismantled or weakened.

Market concentration reinforces this process. When a small number of firms dominate a labor market, workers have fewer outside options. Economists call this monopsony power, but the lived experience is simpler: if there are few good employers nearby, workers cannot easily leave. Firms can suppress wages, impose schedules, limit benefits, or restrict mobility. Noncompete agreements, no-poach arrangements, franchise structures, subcontracting, gig platforms, and algorithmic management can all weaken worker bargaining power. The labor market may appear voluntary while practical alternatives are scarce.

This is another example of how inequality hides behind formal freedom. A worker is legally free to quit, but quitting may mean losing healthcare, income, housing stability, childcare arrangements, or immigration security. A renter is legally free to move, but moving may require savings, transportation, credit, and access to another affordable unit. A debtor is legally free not to borrow again, but emergencies may force borrowing. The language of choice becomes misleading when options are unequal.

Social networks are another major mechanism of cumulative advantage. Jobs, internships, investment opportunities, mentors, information, recommendations, and institutional knowledge often move through networks. Those born into advantaged networks gain access to opportunities that are never publicly visible. They learn how to speak, dress, apply, negotiate, and belong in elite settings. They receive informal guidance about which schools matter, which fields pay, which neighborhoods appreciate, which risks are worth taking, and which mistakes can be repaired. Networks convert social belonging into economic opportunity.

Those outside such networks may possess talent and ambition but lack information and access. They may not know which credentials matter, how to finance education wisely, how to enter professional fields, how to negotiate salaries, how to evaluate debt, or how to avoid predatory institutions. They may be judged for not navigating systems they were never taught to see. Inequality is therefore partly an information ecology. Some people inherit maps; others inherit obstacles.

Inheritance itself is the most direct form of cumulative advantage. Wealth transfers across generations through gifts, inheritances, trusts, housing assistance, tuition payments, business capital, family loans, and informal support. Even modest family help can be decisive: a down payment, a debt-free college education, a place to live during transition, seed money for a business, help during unemployment, or childcare support. These transfers reduce risk and accelerate mobility. They also make unequal starting points appear later as individual success.

A society may celebrate self-made achievement while ignoring the hidden infrastructure of family support. Many people work hard, but not all hard work begins from the same foundation. A debt-free graduate can take an unpaid internship; an indebted graduate may need immediate income. A young adult with family housing support can move to an expensive city; another cannot. An aspiring entrepreneur with family backing can fail and try again; another must choose a stable paycheck. The cumulative advantage machine often works quietly through the reduction of downside risk.

Risk is distributed unequally in another sense. The wealthy can diversify. They hold multiple assets, income streams, insurance policies, and legal protections. The poor are concentrated. They depend on one job, one landlord, one car, one fragile health condition, one paycheck. A single shock can cascade. Car trouble leads to missed work. Missed work leads to lost wages. Lost wages lead to late rent. Late rent leads to fees or eviction risk. Eviction damages credit. Damaged credit raises future housing costs. The cascade begins with a small event but becomes life-altering because buffers are absent.

This is why poverty is expensive. The poor often pay more for credit, banking, transportation, housing, insurance, and time. They may live farther from work, rely on older cars, pay higher interest, face late fees, lack bulk purchasing power, and spend hours navigating bureaucracies. They may be unable to take advantage of discounts that require upfront payment. They may buy cheaper goods that wear out faster. The market often charges insecurity a premium. Poverty is not merely low income. It is a condition in which the cost of living is raised by lack of buffers.

Wealth, by contrast, often receives discounts. The wealthy qualify for lower interest rates, better financial products, tax planning, bulk purchasing, professional advice, safer neighborhoods, better schools, and appreciating assets. They can pay bills on time, avoid fees, buy durable goods, and negotiate from strength. The system calls this creditworthiness, prudence, or efficiency. But it is also feedback. Resources reduce costs, and lower costs preserve resources.

Tax policy can either interrupt or reinforce cumulative advantage. Progressive taxation, estate taxation, capital gains taxation, public investment, and social insurance can dampen inequality. Preferential treatment of capital income, weak estate taxation, loopholes, tax avoidance, regressive consumption taxes, and underfunded public goods can amplify inequality. Tax systems are not neutral mechanisms of revenue collection. They define which kinds of income society privileges and which public capacities it funds.

Modern tax systems often treat capital more favorably than labor. Capital gains may be taxed at lower rates than wages. Unrealized gains can accumulate without taxation. Wealth can be borrowed against, avoiding sale and tax liability. Estates can be structured to reduce taxation. Corporations can shift profits. High earners can hire experts to minimize obligations. Workers receive paychecks with taxes withheld. The result is a system in which those who live from labor often face more direct taxation than those who accumulate through capital. This reinforces the cumulative advantage machine.

Public goods are the other side of taxation. When public education, healthcare, transportation, childcare, housing, and infrastructure are strong, they reduce the dependence of opportunity on family wealth.

When they are weak, private wealth substitutes for public provision. Wealthy families buy what the public system does not provide. Poor families go without. The decline of public goods therefore privatizes opportunity. It turns citizenship into purchasing power.

This is one of the most important mechanisms through which inequality becomes self-reinforcing. If public schools are underfunded, wealthy families use private schools, tutoring, or residential sorting. If public transportation is poor, families need cars. If public healthcare is inadequate, employment becomes tied to insurance. If public childcare is unaffordable, parents, often mothers, reduce work or career advancement. If public universities become expensive, students borrow. Each private solution works better for those with resources. The more society relies on private solutions to public needs, the more inequality compounds.

Political power is the cumulative advantage machine's most dangerous component. Wealth does not remain confined to markets. It enters politics through campaign contributions, lobbying, litigation, media ownership, philanthropy, think tanks, industry associations, regulatory participation, and social access. Wealth shapes what issues are debated, which reforms are considered realistic, which candidates are viable, which policies are framed as responsible, and which forms of suffering remain invisible. The rich do not need to control everything to influence the boundaries of possibility.

This influence creates a feedback loop. Economic inequality increases political inequality. Political inequality shapes rules. Rules increase economic inequality. Tax policy, labor law, antitrust enforcement, financial regulation, housing policy, trade policy, intellectual property, bankruptcy law, education funding, and campaign finance all shape distribution. If those who benefit most from existing arrangements have disproportionate influence over these rules, inequality becomes institutionally protected.

Democracy is supposed to provide corrective feedback. If economic outcomes become too unequal, citizens can vote for reform. But this corrective mechanism weakens when money shapes politics, when districts are segregated by income, when media systems fragment, when voter suppression occurs, when lobbying dominates technical policy, and when citizens lose faith that political action can change material life. Inequality then becomes not only an economic problem, but a democratic problem. It corrodes the capacity of society to correct itself.

The relationship between inequality and trust is central. Extreme inequality tells citizens that they do not share a common fate. The wealthy live in different neighborhoods, attend different schools, use different healthcare systems, travel through different social networks, and experience public institutions differently. The poor and middle classes may come to believe that rules are written by and for others. Trust declines. Declining trust makes collective action harder. Public investment becomes harder. Taxation becomes more contested. Reform becomes more suspicious. Low trust then protects inequality because shared sacrifice becomes politically impossible.

Inequality also affects the meaning of law. Laws are formally equal, but their consequences depend on resources. A fine punishes the poor more than the rich. Bail requirements can detain the poor and release the wealthy. Legal complexity favors those who can hire counsel. Regulatory systems may burden small firms while large firms employ compliance departments. Bankruptcy can be navigated more effectively by those with advice. Tax audits are experienced differently by workers and corporations. Formal equality before the law can coexist with substantive inequality in legal capacity.

The moral effect is corrosive. When citizens see that wealth purchases better outcomes in education, healthcare, justice, housing, politics, and crisis response, they no longer experience society as a fair system of cooperation. They may comply outwardly while withdrawing inwardly. They may become cynical, resentful, or attracted to movements promising rupture. Inequality becomes a source of political instability because it undermines the belief that institutions deserve loyalty.

The cumulative advantage machine also shapes culture. In unequal societies, status competition intensifies. People compare themselves to those above them. Consumption becomes a signal of worth. Families spend more to secure positional goods: housing in good school districts, elite education, safe neighborhoods, credentials, technology, and enrichment. These expenditures may be rational for individuals, but collectively they intensify stress and inequality. The arms race for status consumes income and attention.

A positional good is valuable partly because others do not have it. Elite school admission, exclusive neighborhoods, prestigious credentials, luxury goods, and certain professional networks derive value from scarcity. When economic life becomes organized around positional competition, growth does not necessarily reduce anxiety. People may earn more but feel no more secure because the cost of maintaining status rises. Inequality therefore generates not only deprivation at the bottom, but insecurity in the middle and insulation at the top.

This status dynamic helps explain why inequality can produce political resentment even among those who are not poor. People evaluate their position relationally. If they feel they are falling behind, losing respect, or being displaced, they may experience economic change as humiliation. A community may resent not only material loss, but loss of status, recognition, and future. Economic decline becomes cultural grievance. Demagogues exploit this by offering simplified narratives of blame. Inequality and insecurity become political fuel.

Regional inequality deepens this process. Prosperous metropolitan areas attract capital, talent, universities, technology firms, cultural institutions, and public investment. Their success generates further success. High wages attract skilled workers. Skilled workers attract firms. Firms attract venture capital. Venture capital supports innovation. Innovation raises wages and property values. The region becomes a cumulative advantage machine. But success also creates housing scarcity, segregation, and exclusion if not governed wisely.

Declining regions face the opposite loop. Job loss reduces income. Reduced income weakens local businesses. Tax bases decline. Public services deteriorate. Young people leave. Employers hesitate to invest. Housing may lose value. Health problems rise. Civic institutions weaken. Political resentment grows. The region becomes trapped in cumulative disadvantage. National averages then obscure divergent trajectories. One country contains multiple economies.

This regional divergence matters for democracy. Citizens living in different economic realities may interpret the same national data differently. A booming stock market means little in a town where factories closed and young people left. Low unemployment means little if available jobs are low-wage and insecure. National growth means little if the gains are concentrated elsewhere. A politics built on aggregate prosperity will fail if large regions experience decline as abandonment.

Racial and gender inequalities further reveal how cumulative advantage is historically structured. Past exclusion from property, education, labor protections, voting rights, credit, and public benefits does not disappear when formal rules change. It leaves wealth gaps, neighborhood patterns, school inequalities, health disparities, occupational segregation, and political mistrust. Discrimination can be outlawed, yet the accumulated effects of discrimination remain embedded in assets, institutions, and geography.

Gender inequality operates through care, labor markets, wages, occupational sorting, violence, health, and social expectations. Care work, often performed by women and often underpaid or unpaid, subsidizes the rest of the economy. When childcare is expensive, paid leave is limited, and eldercare is unsupported, family responsibilities reduce labor market opportunities. Career interruptions reduce earnings, savings, promotions, and retirement wealth. The market then treats these outcomes as individual choices, ignoring the institutional absence of support for care. A society that does not value care builds gender inequality into its economic structure.

Race and gender also interact with debt, housing, education, and labor markets. Groups historically denied wealth accumulation rely more heavily on debt for education or emergencies. Discrimination in housing and lending affects neighborhood access and wealth formation. Occupational segregation affects wages and benefits. Health disparities affect earnings and costs. Political underrepresentation affects policy. Cumulative advantage and disadvantage are not abstract. They travel through specific histories.

The cumulative advantage machine is strengthened by narrative. Societies tell stories that justify their distributions. The most powerful story is meritocracy: people rise according to talent and effort. Meritocracy contains an important moral aspiration. A society should reward contribution more than inherited privilege. But when meritocratic language is used to legitimize outcomes produced by unequal starting points, it becomes ideology. It turns advantage into virtue and disadvantage into failure.

The ideology of meritocracy is emotionally powerful because it flatters the successful and disciplines the unsuccessful. The successful can believe their position reflects worth. The unsuccessful can be told to improve themselves rather than question the system. Public policy then focuses on individual mobility while neglecting structural reform. Education, training, financial literacy, and personal responsibility become substitutes for labor power, housing justice, tax reform, healthcare, public investment, and democratic accountability.

Individual development matters. Education matters. Skill matters. Responsibility matters. But they cannot carry the burden placed upon them by a structurally unequal society. A job training program cannot overcome a regional economy without good jobs. Financial literacy cannot compensate for poverty wages, medical debt, and predatory lending. Grit cannot overcome unaffordable housing. Entrepreneurship cannot flourish where families lack savings and healthcare security. Merit requires institutions that allow merit to develop.

Inequality also affects macroeconomic stability. When income and wealth concentrate at the top, aggregate demand can weaken because the wealthy save a larger share of income than lower-income households. Credit may fill the demand gap, leading to household indebtedness. Asset markets may absorb surplus wealth, producing bubbles. Political pressure for tax cuts may reduce public investment. The economy may become dependent on debt, asset appreciation, and speculative finance rather than broad wage growth. Inequality is therefore connected to debt and fragility.

This connection is one of the book's central systems arguments. Weak wage growth leads households to borrow. Borrowing sustains consumption. Consumption sustains profits. Profits accumulate at the top. Surplus wealth seeks returns in financial markets. Financial markets expand credit and asset speculation. Asset owners become wealthier. Housing and education become more expensive. Households borrow more. The loop links inequality, debt, finance, and asset inflation. It is not an accident that societies with high inequality often face household debt burdens and financial instability. The two can reinforce one another.

Inequality also affects inflation. If low-income households receive income gains, spending may rise on necessities, especially where supply is constrained. If wealthy households receive gains, asset prices may rise. If firms have market power, they may raise prices. If wages lag prices, inequality worsens. If central banks respond to inflation by weakening labor markets, inequality may deepen. Inflation is therefore not separate from distribution. It is one of the processes through which groups struggle over real income.

The relationship between inequality and technology is equally important. New technologies can create broad benefits, but they can also amplify cumulative advantage. Skilled workers may gain more than less-skilled workers. Owners of capital may gain more than labor. Platforms may capture network effects. Data advantages may entrench incumbents. Intellectual property may create monopoly rents. Automation may displace some workers while enriching firms and consumers. Artificial intelligence may increase productivity while concentrating control over infrastructure, data, and models. Technology does not automatically reduce inequality. It follows the institutional channels through which gains are distributed.

If workers have bargaining power, public investment supports broad access, competition policy limits concentration, education systems are inclusive, and social insurance cushions transition, technology can support shared prosperity. If labor is weak, markets are concentrated, education is unequal, and gains flow to capital, technology can deepen inequality. The effect of technology is not predetermined. It is governed by the cumulative advantage machine already in place.

The same applies to globalization. Trade can reduce prices, expand markets, and support development. It can also displace workers, weaken bargaining power, and enrich capital if adjustment mechanisms are weak. The gains from globalization are real, but they are not automatically shared. Communities exposed to import competition may suffer job loss, declining tax bases, social stress, and political resentment. Consumers benefit from cheaper goods, but workers in affected regions may experience durable harm. Averages conceal distribution. Policy determines whether trade becomes shared prosperity or concentrated gain.

The moral question is not whether economic change should occur. Change is inevitable. The moral question is whether the risks of change are distributed fairly and whether those harmed are included in the future being built. A society that celebrates innovation while abandoning displaced workers converts progress into betrayal. A society that opens markets while failing to support affected communities converts efficiency into resentment. A society that allows wealth to capture the gains of change while socializing the losses deepens illegitimacy.

Inequality becomes especially dangerous when it hardens into class separation. Class separation occurs when groups no longer share institutions, spaces, risks, or expectations. The wealthy exit public schools, private security replaces public safety, private healthcare replaces public health, gated communities replace common neighborhoods, private transport replaces public transit, philanthropy substitutes for taxation, and elite networks replace democratic deliberation. Exit reduces solidarity. Those who exit public systems have less incentive to fund them. Public systems decline. Decline encourages more exit. The loop continues.

This is one of the central dangers of inequality: it destroys the common world. Democracy depends on some sense of shared fate. Citizens need not be equal in all respects, but they must believe that institutions belong to all, that rules apply broadly, and that public goods matter. Extreme inequality fragments that belief. It creates separate realities. The affluent experience society as opportunity; the insecure experience it as extraction or abandonment. Politics becomes less a debate over policy and more a struggle over recognition and resentment.

The cumulative advantage machine is not inevitable. It is designed, even when no single designer exists. It is produced by laws, markets, norms, tax codes, zoning rules, school funding formulas, labor institutions, financial regulations, healthcare systems, family policies, corporate governance, and political structures. Because it is designed, it can be redesigned. Complexity economics does not say that inequality is natural and unavoidable. It says that inequality is produced by feedback loops that can be strengthened, weakened, redirected, or interrupted.

A serious inequality agenda must therefore operate at multiple points in the system. It must begin early in life, before disadvantage compounds. Early childhood health, nutrition, parental leave, childcare, safe housing, and high-quality education are not merely compassionate policies. They are anti-inequality infrastructure. They change developmental trajectories before gaps become entrenched. The returns are not only economic, but moral and democratic.

Education reform must address both quality and context. Schools matter, but schools cannot fully compensate for poverty, housing instability, hunger, untreated illness, violence, and family stress. A child cannot learn well if life outside school is chaotic. Equal opportunity requires equalizing the conditions under which learning occurs. This means investing in neighborhoods, health, housing, libraries, mentoring, after-school programs, and family support. It also means reducing the dependence of school quality on local wealth.

Housing policy must be treated as inequality policy. Affordable housing, zoning reform, social housing, tenant protections, anti-displacement measures, fair lending, public land use, and transit investment all shape opportunity. Housing should not be governed solely as an asset market for existing owners. It is social infrastructure. A society that allows shelter to become a speculative scarcity machine should not be surprised when inequality hardens.

Labor policy must rebuild bargaining power. Higher minimum wages, sectoral bargaining, union rights, wage boards, portable benefits, predictable scheduling, enforcement against wage theft, limits on misclassification, and antitrust action against labor market monopsony can all change the distribution of income. Work must become a source of dignity and security, not merely survival. A society cannot solve inequality if wages remain insufficient and worker voice remains weak.

Healthcare policy must reduce the link between illness and financial ruin. Universal or broadly secure access to healthcare, mental health services, preventive care, and prescription drugs reduces inequality by protecting human capability. It also supports labor mobility and entrepreneurship by reducing dependence on employer-provided insurance. Health security is economic freedom.

Tax and wealth policy must address accumulated advantage. Progressive taxation, capital gains reform, estate taxation, closing loopholes, wealth reporting, inheritance taxation, and enforcement against avoidance can reduce the compounding of wealth at the top. But taxation alone is not enough. Public revenue must finance universal goods, social insurance, infrastructure, education, climate resilience, and wealth-building opportunities for those historically excluded.

Financial policy must distinguish inclusion from extraction. Access to credit is important, but access to predatory credit is not empowerment. Fair banking, postal banking or public banking options, community development finance, consumer protection, debt relief, humane bankruptcy, and regulation of high-cost lending can reduce the cost of poverty. Asset-building policies, such as baby bonds, matched savings, down payment assistance, employee ownership, and retirement access, can help create buffers.

Competition policy must address concentration. Monopoly and oligopoly can raise prices, suppress wages, reduce innovation, and increase political influence. Antitrust is therefore inequality policy. It protects not only consumers, but workers, suppliers, entrepreneurs, and democracy. In digital markets, competition policy must address data, interoperability, platform governance, and acquisitions that eliminate future rivals.

Political reform is necessary because inequality cannot be durably reduced if wealth continues to dominate rule-making. Campaign finance reform, lobbying transparency, voting rights, district fairness, public financing, ethics rules, and regulatory capacity all matter. Democracy must regain the ability to act on behalf of the broad public. Without political equality, economic equality remains fragile.

Regional policy must address geographic divergence. Public investment, infrastructure, universities, broadband, clean energy, transportation, small business ecosystems, healthcare, and place-based development can help declining regions build new trajectories. But regional policy must avoid nostalgia. The goal is not to recreate the past exactly. It is to build dignified futures in places that have been left behind.

Care policy must be central. Paid leave, childcare, eldercare, disability support, and recognition of care work reduce gender inequality and support family stability. Care is not outside the economy. It is the human foundation of the economy. A society that ignores care relies on invisible labor and then misreads the resulting inequalities as personal choices.

These reforms are not isolated programs. They are interventions in feedback loops. Early childhood investment changes educational and health trajectories. Housing reform changes wealth and opportunity. Labor power changes income distribution and demand. Healthcare security changes risk-taking and mobility. Tax reform changes compounding at the top. Political reform changes rule-making. Competition policy changes market power. Care policy changes gendered opportunity. The goal is not simply to narrow the gap after the fact. It is to redesign the machine.

Critics often argue that inequality is necessary for incentives. Some inequality is indeed likely in any free and dynamic society. People make different choices, take different risks, develop different skills, and contribute in different ways. Perfect equality is neither possible nor desirable if it requires suppressing freedom, creativity, and pluralism. But this observation does not justify extreme inequality, inherited privilege, political capture, or insecurity. The question is not whether all differences should disappear. The question is whether inequality becomes so large and self-reinforcing that it undermines freedom, opportunity, dignity, democracy, and systemic stability.

A morally defensible economy can tolerate unequal rewards if several conditions hold. Starting points must not be radically unequal. Basic needs must be secure. Public goods must be strong. Labor must have bargaining power. Markets must be competitive. Political voice must be equal. Wealth must not purchase domination. Failure must not mean ruin. Opportunity must be real, not rhetorical. Under these conditions, inequality may reflect genuine pluralism and contribution. Without them, inequality becomes hierarchy disguised as merit.

The cumulative advantage machine violates these conditions because it turns yesterday's inequality into tomorrow's structure. It allows wealth to buy the conditions for more wealth. It allows poverty to generate the conditions for more poverty. It transforms markets, schools, neighborhoods, health, politics, and law into channels of reproduction. It tells individuals to compete while assigning unequal equipment, unequal fields, unequal referees, and unequal consequences for losing.

A complexity economics approach reveals that inequality is inefficient, unstable, and morally corrosive. It is inefficient because it wastes talent, reduces broad demand, encourages rent-seeking, and diverts resources into status competition. It is unstable because it increases debt dependence, political resentment, and institutional distrust. It is morally corrosive because it teaches that human worth can be measured by market position and that those without wealth deserve less voice, less security, and less dignity.

Yet complexity also gives hope. If disadvantage compounds, so can opportunity. If wealth builds on itself, so can public investment. If trust declines through feedback, it can also be rebuilt through competence and fairness. If neighborhoods decline through disinvestment, they can recover through sustained commitment. If labor power erodes through institutional weakening, it can be restored through law and organization. If political capture reinforces inequality, democratic reform can reopen the system. Feedback loops can be changed.

A society committed to reducing inequality must focus not only on redistribution, but on predistribution and system design. Redistribution corrects outcomes after markets operate. Predistribution shapes the rules before outcomes emerge. Both are necessary. Tax and transfer systems can reduce poverty and provide security. But unless labor markets, housing systems, education, healthcare, finance, and political power are redesigned, inequality will continue to regenerate. The machine must be altered, not merely its output adjusted.

The language of the machine should not imply that human beings are mechanical. The cumulative advantage machine is made of human choices, institutions, and histories. It persists because people defend advantages, normalize arrangements, ignore hidden suffering, and benefit from systems they may not have consciously designed. It can change because people organize, legislate, build institutions, tell new stories, and widen the circle of concern. Economic systems are not natural facts. They are moral constructions.

The next chapter turns to housing markets and the dynamics of scarcity, one of the most powerful engines of cumulative advantage. Housing is where inequality becomes visible in space. It determines who lives near opportunity, who builds wealth, who attends which schools, who has stability, who faces displacement, and who gains from scarcity. To understand housing is to understand how inequality becomes geography.

This chapter's conclusion is straightforward: inequality is not a passive distribution. It is an active system. It compounds through wealth, housing, education, health, labor power, social networks, debt, taxation, market concentration, political influence, and public goods. It shapes the economy's future by shaping the people who participate in it and the rules under which they participate. It is one of the great nonlinear problems of our time.

The end of simple economic explanations requires us to stop asking only why some individuals earn more than others. We must ask how the system produces unequal life chances before earnings begin. We must ask how advantage travels across generations. We must ask how markets amplify inherited differences. We must ask how wealth becomes power and power becomes law. We must ask how insecurity becomes debt, how debt becomes constraint, how constraint becomes low mobility, and how low mobility becomes moral judgment.

Inequality is not merely a gap to be measured. It is a process to be understood and a structure to be redesigned. If left alone, it compounds. If justified ideologically, it hardens. If translated into political power, it protects itself. If ignored morally, it degrades democracy. But if confronted systemically, it can be reduced. A society can build counter-loops of inclusion: public goods, fair wages, affordable housing, health security, democratic voice, broad ownership, and shared investment. These are not acts of charity. They are acts of economic intelligence.

A nonlinear economy teaches that small differences can become large destinies. A just society teaches that destiny should not be assigned at birth. Between those two truths lies the work of democratic political economy.

## Chapter 8

# Housing Markets and the Dynamics of Scarcity

Housing is where the abstract economy becomes concrete. It is where income meets rent, where credit meets shelter, where wealth meets geography, where local politics meets family life, and where inequality becomes visible in streets, schools, commutes, neighborhoods, and household stress. Housing is not merely one market among many. It is the place where the economy enters the body of daily life. It determines where people sleep, where children learn, how long workers commute, whether families can form, whether savings can accumulate, whether communities remain intact, and whether citizens experience the economy as a system of possibility or exclusion.

For this reason, housing cannot be understood adequately through simple supply-and-demand diagrams, although supply and demand certainly matter. Housing prices rise when demand grows faster than supply. Rents rise when available units are scarce relative to households seeking them. Interest rates affect affordability. Construction costs affect supply. Wages affect purchasing power. These relationships are real. But they are only the beginning of the story, not the end. Housing markets are nonlinear systems shaped by feedback loops among land, credit, zoning, wealth, speculation, political power, neighborhood status, public infrastructure, and expectations.

The central argument of this chapter is that modern housing markets often operate as scarcity machines. Scarcity is not merely a natural condition produced by limited land or rising population. It is also produced, protected, financialized, and politically defended. Housing scarcity raises prices. Rising prices enrich existing owners. Owner wealth increases political influence. Political influence is used to restrict or shape new supply. Restricted supply sustains scarcity. Scarcity raises prices again. The loop repeats. What begins as a market imbalance becomes an institutional regime.

Housing is uniquely prone to this kind of feedback because it is both a basic human need and a major financial asset. Bread, electricity, healthcare, education, and transportation all have special social importance, but housing combines daily necessity with wealth accumulation in an especially powerful way. A home is shelter, but it is also collateral, investment, retirement security, tax advantage, neighborhood access, school access, status marker, and intergenerational transfer. This dual character makes housing morally and economically unstable. When the price of shelter rises, homeowners may become wealthier, but renters and first-time buyers become less secure. The same price increase is prosperity for one group and exclusion for another.

This conflict lies at the heart of the housing crisis. Societies often say they want housing to be affordable, but they also design systems in which millions of households depend on rising home values for wealth. These goals are in tension. If housing prices rise faster than wages, owners build wealth while nonowners fall behind. If housing prices stabilize or fall, affordability improves for buyers, but existing owners may feel that their accumulated wealth is threatened. A society that treats housing as the principal asset of the middle class creates a political constituency for scarcity. It asks homes to serve two functions at once: affordable shelter and appreciating investment. Over time, the investment function often dominates.

This is one reason housing crises become so difficult to solve. The policy problem is not merely technical. It is distributive. More housing may be socially necessary, but it may be opposed by those who fear congestion, school crowding, neighborhood change, environmental loss, parking

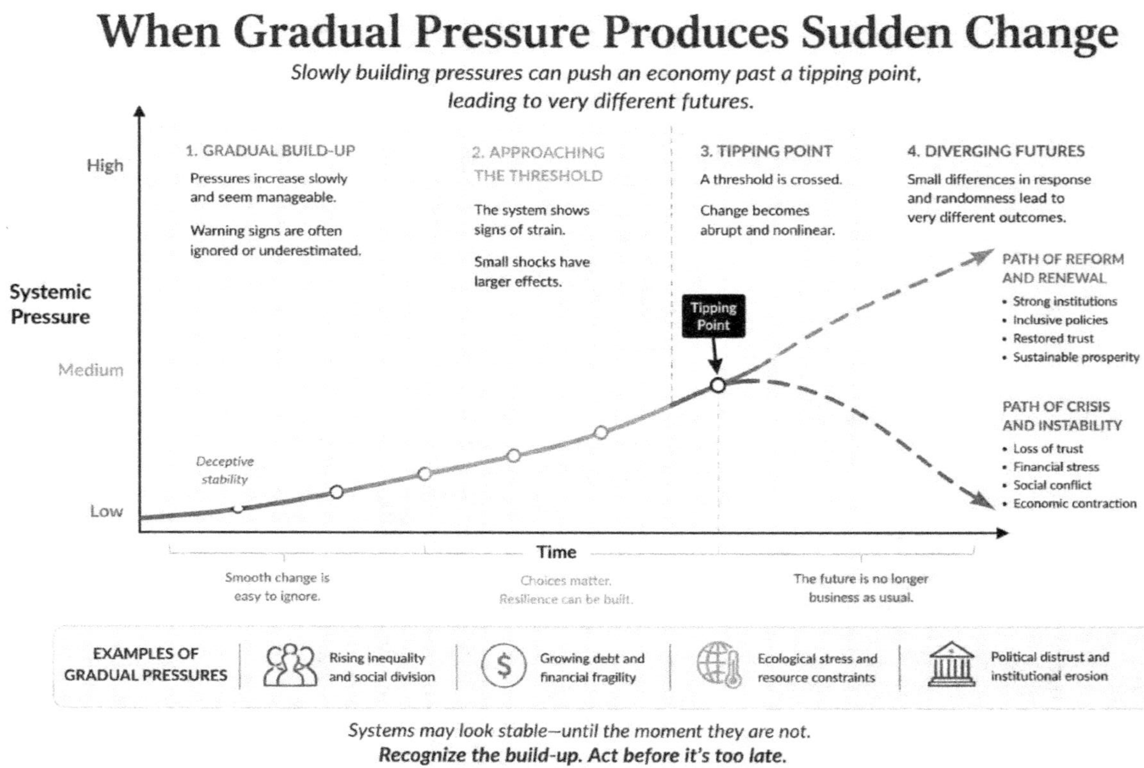


*Figure 5.0 – When Gradual Pressure Produces Sudden Change*

shortages, lower property values, or the arrival of poorer households. Some concerns are sincere and legitimate. Others mask exclusion. But in either case, local politics often gives greater voice to incumbent owners than to future residents, renters, young families, workers, or the unhoused. The people harmed by scarcity are frequently underrepresented in the institutions that govern scarcity.

This is a classic nonlinear problem. The system gives power to those who benefit from the current arrangement. Those who would benefit from reform often do not yet live in the jurisdiction, cannot afford to enter, or are too fragmented to influence local decisions. The existing residents vote, attend meetings, hire lawyers, organize neighborhood associations, and shape zoning boards. The absent future residents have no vote. Scarcity therefore protects itself through democratic forms that are local but not always broadly representative. The result is a political economy of incumbency.

Land is the first structural feature of housing nonlinearity. Unlike manufactured goods, land cannot be produced. Its location matters. A home near jobs, transit, schools, parks, safety, and cultural life is not equivalent to a home far from them. Housing is therefore deeply positional. Its value depends not only on the physical structure, but on its relationship to everything around it. Two identical houses can have radically different prices because they sit in different opportunity networks. Location is not a superficial attribute. It is the economic essence of housing.

This makes housing scarcity different from the scarcity of ordinary goods. If a factory produces too few chairs, additional production can increase supply. If one region produces too few homes near opportunity, the solution is harder because opportunity itself is geographically concentrated. Building far from jobs does not fully solve the problem if transportation is poor. Building without schools, healthcare, or infrastructure does not create a complete community. Building only luxury units in high-demand areas may increase total supply, but it may not address affordability for those most burdened unless broader supply, filtering, public investment, and affordability requirements are present. Housing supply must be understood as located supply.

The economic value of housing is therefore partly the value of access. A house gives access to a labor market, school district, peer network, transportation system, safety environment, tax base, and local public goods. When access is scarce, housing becomes expensive. When housing becomes expensive, access becomes class-based. The market then sorts households by income and wealth into different opportunity spaces. Inequality becomes geography. Geography becomes destiny.

Zoning is the institutional mechanism through which this sorting is often protected. Zoning determines what can be built where, at what density, for whom, and under what constraints. It may regulate height, lot size, setbacks, parking, use, occupancy, design, and approval processes. Zoning can protect health, safety, environmental quality, and neighborhood planning. But it can also restrict housing supply, exclude lower-income households, preserve racial and class segregation, and inflate property values. In many high-opportunity regions, zoning has become a scarcity device.

Large minimum lot sizes, bans on multifamily housing, parking mandates, discretionary approvals, environmental review abuse, historic preservation manipulation, and neighborhood veto points can all reduce new construction. When supply is restricted in high-demand areas, prices rise. Rising prices then become evidence of neighborhood desirability, which strengthens the desire to preserve existing form. The scarcity loop intensifies. A neighborhood becomes wealthy partly because not enough people are allowed to live there.

The moral issue is not that every neighborhood must be infinitely dense or that local concerns never matter. Communities need planning. Infrastructure has limits. Beauty matters. Trees matter. Schools and transit require capacity. The issue is that the costs of exclusion are often imposed on people outside the decision-making community. A suburb that restricts multifamily housing may preserve its quiet streets, but it also pushes workers farther away, raises regional rents, increases commute times, worsens environmental burdens, and limits access to high-quality schools. Local decisions create regional consequences.

Housing markets therefore reveal the limits of purely local governance. The people who benefit from restrictive decisions are concentrated and organized. The people harmed are dispersed across the region or excluded entirely. A city that fails to build enough housing does not merely harm its own residents. It affects regional labor markets, homelessness, transportation patterns, climate emissions, family formation, and economic productivity. Housing scarcity is a metropolitan and national problem, even when the decisions are local.

Credit is the second major feedback mechanism in housing. Housing prices are shaped not only by income and supply, but by the availability and cost of mortgage credit. When credit is cheap, buyers can bid more. When interest rates are low, a given monthly payment supports a larger loan. Larger loans support higher prices. Higher prices increase collateral values. Higher collateral values make lenders more comfortable. Credit expands. The loop can raise home prices faster than wages, especially in supply-constrained markets.

This relationship between credit and prices is central to housing nonlinearity. If supply is elastic, easier credit may lead to more construction and broader ownership. If supply is restricted, easier credit may primarily bid up the price of existing homes. In that case, policies intended to help buyers can enrich sellers. Down payment assistance, mortgage subsidies, tax advantages, and easy lending may help some households enter the market, but they may also raise prices if supply does not expand. Demand support without supply reform can become price support.

The mortgage system also ties households to interest-rate cycles. When rates are low, home prices often rise because buyers can finance larger purchases. When rates rise, affordability declines. But prices may not fall quickly if owners with low fixed-rate mortgages refuse to sell, creating a lock-in effect. Supply of existing homes declines. Buyers face both high prices and high rates. Construction may slow because financing becomes expensive. The market freezes rather than clears. Equilibrium thinking predicts adjustment, but housing often adjusts through volume, delay, overcrowding, and exclusion before it adjusts through affordable prices.

This lock-in effect shows why housing markets are sticky. Sellers resist lowering prices because homes are emotionally and financially important. Owners compare offers not only to current demand, but to remembered values, mortgage balances, retirement expectations, and neighborhood norms. Buyers hesitate when prices seem high. Builders hesitate when financing costs rise. Renters remain renters because entry costs are too high. The system may stall in a state of unaffordability. A market can fail to clear in a socially meaningful way while still recording transactions among those with sufficient resources.

Speculation is the third feedback mechanism. Housing becomes speculative when buyers purchase not only for use, but for expected appreciation. This can include individual investors, institutional landlords, short-term rental operators, foreign buyers, flippers, private equity funds, or ordinary households stretching to buy because they fear being permanently priced out. Speculation feeds on expectation. If people believe housing prices will continue to rise, they buy sooner, borrow more, or accept higher prices. Their behavior helps prices rise. Rising prices confirm the belief.

Speculation is not always irrational. If supply is restricted, demand is strong, and credit is available, betting on appreciation may be reasonable. The problem is that rational behavior under scarcity can deepen scarcity. Homes become assets to be accumulated rather than places to live. Investors may remove units from owner-occupancy or long-term rental markets. Short-term rentals may reduce local housing availability. Land banking may delay development. Luxury construction may chase returns rather than need. The market increasingly serves capital rather than shelter.

This transformation is especially harmful when institutional investors enter single-family or rental markets at scale. Large investors may bring management efficiency and capital for renovation, but they may also increase competition for homes, raise rents, impose fees, reduce tenant bargaining power, and treat neighborhoods as portfolios. At small scale, landlord ownership is a local relationship. At large scale, it can become an asset-management strategy. The function of housing changes when ownership is distant, financialized, and optimized for yield.

Financialization is the process through which housing is increasingly governed by financial logic. Homes become assets in portfolios. Rents become income streams. Mortgages become securities. Land becomes a store of value. Neighborhoods become investment opportunities.

This financial logic can mobilize capital for construction, but it can also detach housing from human need. The question becomes not, "What housing does this community require?" but, "What return does this asset produce?" A society that allows the second question to dominate the first should not be surprised when shelter becomes unaffordable.

The fourth feedback mechanism is wealth. Homeownership creates wealth through equity and appreciation. Wealth enables further homeownership, investment, education, and inheritance. Families that own homes in appreciating markets can assist children with down payments, college costs, or business formation. Children of homeowners may enter adulthood with support and eventually inherit property or proceeds. Renters pay monthly housing costs without building equity. They may face rent increases that make saving difficult. Their children receive less housing-based wealth. The divergence compounds.

Housing wealth also shapes retirement security. For many households, home equity is the largest asset. Rising home values can support borrowing, downsizing, reverse mortgages, or inheritance. But reliance on home equity makes society vulnerable to housing cycles and ties retirement security to property appreciation. It also creates a political constituency for high housing prices. If older households depend on home wealth, policies that improve affordability by reducing prices may feel threatening. Intergenerational conflict emerges.

Younger households face the other side of this arrangement. They are told that homeownership is the pathway to stability, but the pathway has become increasingly expensive. They face high rents while trying to save for down payments, student debt, insecure labor markets, childcare costs, and rising interest rates. If they delay homeownership, they miss years of appreciation. If they stretch to buy, they become vulnerable to debt stress. If they remain renters, they may face instability and limited wealth accumulation. The housing system turns age into an economic dividing line.

This generational dimension is not only financial. It affects family formation, fertility, geographic mobility, and political identity. Young adults may delay marriage or children because housing is unaffordable. Families may move farther from jobs, grandparents, and social networks. Workers may avoid high-opportunity regions because rents consume wage gains. Citizens may come to believe that the economic promises made to previous generations are no longer available. Housing scarcity becomes a narrative of broken intergenerational obligation.

The fifth feedback mechanism is labor mobility. Housing markets and labor markets are deeply connected. Workers need homes near jobs. Employers need workers who can afford to live near workplaces. When housing becomes scarce in productive regions, labor mobility declines. Workers cannot move to where wages are higher because housing costs absorb the gains. Employers struggle to hire teachers, nurses, service workers, public employees, and young professionals. Regional productivity suffers because people cannot access opportunity. The economy becomes less dynamic.

This is a major way housing scarcity harms growth. It prevents people from moving to places where they could be more productive. It traps some workers in low-opportunity regions and excludes others from high-opportunity regions. It forces long commutes that waste time, increase emissions, and damage health. It raises wage demands in expensive regions, increasing costs for employers and public services. It reduces entrepreneurship because people fear losing housing stability. Housing scarcity is not merely a social problem. It is a macroeconomic constraint.

Yet high-productivity regions often resist the housing needed to support their own prosperity. This is another paradox of housing politics. A region attracts firms, workers, universities, capital, and culture. Demand rises. Housing supply fails to keep pace. Prices rise. Incumbents become wealthier. Local resistance to development grows. Essential workers are pushed out. Commutes lengthen. Inequality deepens. The region becomes both prosperous and exclusionary. Its success creates the conditions for its dysfunction.

The sixth feedback mechanism is public finance. Local governments often rely heavily on property taxes. This can create incentives to favor high-value development, restrict low-income housing, or protect property values. Wealthy jurisdictions can fund better schools and services through high property tax bases. Better schools and services raise property values. Higher property values raise revenue. The loop reinforces local advantage. Poorer jurisdictions face the reverse: lower property values, weaker revenue, poorer services, and reduced attractiveness.

This connection between property wealth and public goods is one of the most powerful engines of inequality. If school quality depends on local wealth, then housing markets become educational markets. Families buy access to schools through home prices. Wealthy families can pay more for homes in desirable districts. Their children receive better-funded education. Better education supports future income. Future income supports homeownership in desirable districts. The loop reproduces class advantage. The market price of a house becomes a price of admission to public opportunity.

A society that funds opportunity through local property wealth should not claim to believe in equal opportunity. It has tied childhood development to real estate markets. It has converted public education into a partially privatized positional good. Reforming housing without reforming school finance is therefore incomplete. Reforming schools without addressing housing segregation is also incomplete. The systems are linked.

The seventh feedback mechanism is homelessness. Homelessness is often treated as an extreme social problem separate from ordinary housing markets. In reality, it is connected to the same scarcity system. When rents rise faster than incomes, households at the bottom lose stability. A medical bill, job loss, eviction, family conflict, or mental health crisis can become homelessness when affordable housing is unavailable. Homelessness then creates further barriers: health deterioration, trauma, job difficulty, legal problems, family separation, and social exclusion. Once someone loses housing, returning becomes harder.

Homelessness is a nonlinear threshold. A household may be strained for months or years, paying too much rent, falling behind on bills, relying on relatives, moving frequently, or living in overcrowded conditions. Then one shock pushes it past the threshold. The visible event may be eviction, but the underlying vulnerability was accumulated scarcity. Homelessness is not simply personal failure. It is often the final stage of a housing system that provides no margin for error.

The social costs are enormous. Emergency shelters, hospitals, police encounters, courts, sanitation, public health systems, schools, and charities all bear costs. More importantly, human beings bear suffering that cannot be reduced to fiscal measurement. Children lose stability. Adults lose dignity. Illness worsens. Communities experience visible evidence of institutional failure. Public spaces become arenas of conflict between compassion, fear, frustration, and neglect. Homelessness is the moral indictment of a housing system that has forgotten that shelter is a human necessity.

The eighth feedback mechanism is displacement. When neighborhoods become desirable, investment flows in. Buildings are renovated. Amenities improve. Rents rise. Property values rise. Higher-income households move in. Longtime residents may be priced out. Local businesses face higher rents. Cultural identity changes. The neighborhood improves by some measures while losing the people who endured its disinvestment. Displacement is not simply movement. It is the loss of social networks, memory, belonging, and informal support systems.

Gentrification is complex because investment in neglected neighborhoods is not inherently bad. Communities deserve safety, services, grocery stores, parks, schools, transit, and private investment. The problem arises when improvement is tied to exclusion. If the only way a neighborhood receives investment is by becoming unaffordable to existing residents, the market is rewarding displacement. A just housing policy must find ways to bring investment without removal. This requires tenant protections, community land trusts, affordable housing preservation, public investment, anti-speculation tools, and resident voice.

Displacement also has regional effects. Lower-income households pushed out of central or high-opportunity neighborhoods move farther from jobs and services. Their commutes lengthen. Transportation costs rise. Children change schools. Support networks weaken. Suburban poverty increases. Public agencies struggle to adapt. The apparent revitalization of one neighborhood may create hardship elsewhere. Housing policy must therefore look beyond neighborhood averages. Rising median income in a neighborhood may indicate improvement, displacement, or both.

The ninth feedback mechanism is race and historical exclusion. Housing markets have been shaped by racial covenants, redlining, discriminatory lending, exclusionary zoning, urban renewal, highway construction, segregation, appraisal bias, and unequal public investment. These histories are not past in any simple sense. They live on through wealth gaps, neighborhood boundaries, school quality, infrastructure, environmental exposure, and political representation. A family excluded from homeownership in one generation missed appreciation, equity, and inheritance in the next. A neighborhood denied credit suffered disinvestment. Disinvestment lowered property values. Lower values weakened tax bases. Weak tax bases affected schools and services. The loop continued.

Formal discrimination can be outlawed, but accumulated inequality remains. A housing market built on past exclusion cannot become fair merely by declaring equal access today. If one group has inherited home equity and another has inherited rent burden, equal mortgage terms do not equalize starting points. If neighborhoods remain segregated by wealth, school access remains unequal. If appraisal systems undervalue homes in minority neighborhoods, wealth accumulation is limited. If lending algorithms reproduce historical patterns, discrimination becomes technical. Housing justice must therefore address both current rules and accumulated consequences.

The tenth feedback mechanism is climate and insurance. Housing markets are increasingly shaped by environmental risk: floods, fires, heat, storms, drought, and sea-level rise. These risks affect insurance premiums, mortgage availability, public infrastructure costs, migration, and property values. Climate risk is nonlinear because property values may remain high until a threshold is crossed. Insurance may become unaffordable or unavailable. A major disaster may change perceptions. Lenders may tighten. Municipalities may face rising adaptation costs. Homeowners may be trapped in properties that lose value. Renters may face unsafe housing and displacement.

Climate risk also interacts with inequality. Wealthy households can insure, retrofit, relocate, or absorb losses. Poor households may live in more vulnerable areas, lack insurance, face poor construction quality, and have fewer resources for recovery. Disaster can become a wealth transfer if investors buy damaged properties cheaply while displaced residents cannot return. Public recovery funds may favor owners over renters. Climate change therefore threatens to create a new housing inequality regime, one in which the geography of risk increasingly shapes wealth and security.

This reinforces the need to treat housing as infrastructure. Homes must be safe, energy-efficient, climate-resilient, and connected to transit and public services. Sprawling housing patterns increase car dependency and emissions. Dense, well-planned housing near transit can reduce environmental harm. But density must be paired with affordability and livability. Climate policy and housing policy cannot be separated. A society cannot decarbonize fairly if low-income households are pushed to distant, car-dependent regions or exposed to unsafe housing.

The eleventh feedback mechanism is regulation and process. Many housing systems require multiple approvals, reviews, hearings, permits, lawsuits, and discretionary decisions. Some regulation protects safety, labor standards, environmental quality, and good planning. But excessive or unpredictable process can raise costs, delay construction, favor large developers who can navigate complexity, and empower opponents to block housing. Delay itself becomes a cost. Higher costs then lead developers to build only high-end units, because expensive projects require high rents or sale prices to be viable. The system produces luxury supply while failing to produce affordability.

This does not mean regulation should be abolished. Badly deregulated housing can produce unsafe buildings, environmental harm, displacement, corruption, and low-quality development. The question is what kind of regulation serves public purpose. Clear rules, by-right approvals for compliant projects, affordability requirements, design standards, tenant protections, infrastructure planning, and environmental safeguards can coexist with abundant housing. Uncertainty, veto points, and arbitrary delay are the problem. A housing system should regulate outcomes, not manufacture scarcity through procedural obstruction.

Construction costs matter as well. Materials, labor, land, financing, insurance, permitting, and infrastructure all affect what can be built. In some regions, even if zoning is loosened, high costs may prevent affordable construction without public subsidy. Affordable housing often requires public investment because the rents affordable to low-income households may not cover development and operating costs. This is not a market failure in the narrow sense. It is a structural reality: the poor need housing whose cost exceeds what their income can support in private markets. A civilized society responds by socializing part of the cost of shelter.

Public housing, social housing, nonprofit housing, housing vouchers, community land trusts, limited-equity cooperatives, inclusionary zoning, and public land development are all attempts to address this gap. Each has strengths and weaknesses. Public housing can provide deep affordability but requires sustained funding and good management. Vouchers can support household choice but may inflate rents if supply is scarce or landlords discriminate. Inclusionary zoning can produce affordable units but may be insufficient or raise costs if poorly designed. Community land trusts preserve affordability but require land acquisition and scale. No single tool solves housing scarcity. A systemic problem requires a portfolio of tools.

The concept of filtering is often invoked in housing debates. New market-rate housing, even if expensive, can reduce pressure over time as older units become more affordable. This can happen, especially in markets with abundant construction. But filtering is slow and can fail if supply remains restricted, high-income demand is strong, older units are renovated upward, or investors capture affordability. Filtering is not a substitute for direct affordability policy. It is part of a broader supply system. A city cannot rely only on luxury construction and hope affordability trickles down quickly enough to meet human need.

The debate between supply and affordability is often framed poorly. Some argue that only supply matters. Others argue that market-rate supply merely fuels gentrification and that only subsidized housing matters. Both positions are incomplete. Without sufficient supply, scarcity will raise prices and undermine affordability programs. Without affordability policy, supply may not reach those with the greatest need. A serious housing strategy must do both: build more housing overall and ensure that a meaningful share is affordable, stable, and protected from speculation.

Tenant protections are essential because markets adjust through people's lives. Renters need stability, fair leases, protection against unjust eviction, habitability standards, anti-discrimination enforcement, and reasonable limits on sudden rent shocks. But tenant protections must be designed alongside supply. If protections are too weak, renters are exposed to displacement and exploitation. If protections are rigid but supply is constrained, informal markets, deferred maintenance, or reduced mobility may emerge. The goal is not to choose between tenants and supply. The goal is a housing system that provides both stability and abundance.

Ownership policy must also be reconsidered. Homeownership can build wealth and stability, but it should not be the only path to dignity. Societies that treat renting as failure create unnecessary hierarchy. Many people rent because of age, mobility, income, preference, or circumstance. Renting should be secure, affordable, and respected. A renter should not be treated as a temporary citizen. Strong rental systems in many countries show that long-term renting can coexist with stability and dignity when law, supply, and tenant rights are well designed.

At the same time, broader asset ownership matters. If housing is the primary wealth-building tool, those excluded from ownership fall behind. Societies need alternative pathways to wealth: retirement accounts, employee ownership, public wealth funds, baby bonds, cooperative ownership, small business capital, and affordable financial products. Reducing the dependence of wealth accumulation on home price appreciation could make housing politics healthier. If families did not need homes to rise endlessly in value to feel secure, they might be less resistant to affordability.

This insight points to a larger institutional problem. Housing has been asked to compensate for weaknesses in retirement security, wage growth, public goods, and wealth distribution. When wages stagnate, home equity becomes a source of wealth. When pensions decline, homeownership becomes retirement insurance. When public schools vary by district, housing becomes education access. When healthcare and long-term care are expensive, home equity becomes a financial reserve. Housing becomes overloaded with social functions. The result is that affordability threatens security because security has been privatized through property.

A better society would reduce this burden. Strong pensions, universal healthcare, quality public schools, affordable education, secure wages, and broad wealth-building tools would allow housing to become more clearly what it should be: shelter, community, and reasonable stability. It would still be an asset, but not the central pillar of life security. Housing politics would become less zero-sum if families had other sources of protection.

The role of public land is particularly important. Land owned by government, transit agencies, schools, religious institutions, hospitals, or public authorities can be used for affordable and mixed-income housing. Public land allows society to reduce the cost component that often makes affordability difficult. Long-term ground leases can preserve public value while enabling development. Transit-oriented development can connect housing to opportunity while reducing car dependency. Land policy is often hidden, but it is central to housing justice.

Community land trusts offer another model. By separating land ownership from building ownership, they can preserve affordability over time. Residents may build equity, but resale prices are limited to keep homes affordable for future buyers. This interrupts speculative appreciation while supporting stability. The model is not sufficient alone at national scale, but it embodies an important principle: housing can be designed to serve both present residents and future affordability. Markets need not be organized solely around maximum appreciation.

Social housing also deserves renewed attention. Social housing is not simply emergency housing for the poorest. In its stronger forms, it can provide mixed-income, permanently affordable, publicly or nonprofit owned housing integrated into ordinary communities. It can create a housing sector outside speculative pressure. It can set benchmarks for quality and affordability. It requires public investment, competence, and long-term management. Done poorly, it can stigmatize residents or deteriorate. Done well, it can stabilize entire housing systems.

Housing vouchers help households afford private rentals, but their effectiveness depends on supply, landlord participation, anti-discrimination enforcement, and payment standards. In tight markets, vouchers may chase scarce units. Landlords may refuse them. Families may be unable to move to high-opportunity areas. Vouchers are necessary for many low-income households, but they cannot solve scarcity alone. Again, the nonlinear lesson is that demand support without supply and rights can be captured.

Rent regulation is similarly complex. It can protect tenants from sudden displacement and preserve community stability. It can also create distortions if poorly designed, especially if it discourages maintenance or new construction. The question is not whether rent regulation is inherently good or bad. The question is how it interacts with supply, subsidies, tenant rights, landlord obligations, and public investment. A nuanced approach may combine anti-gouging protections, predictable rent increases, vacancy rules, maintenance enforcement, and exemptions or incentives for new construction where appropriate. Simplicity fails because the system is complex.

Housing policy must also address vacancy and underuse. In some high-demand areas, homes are held vacant as investments, second homes, short-term rentals, or speculative assets. Vacancy taxes, restrictions on short-term rentals, transparency of ownership, and anti-money-laundering enforcement can help ensure that housing serves residents rather than idle capital. These tools are not substitutes for construction, but they address the misuse of scarce housing stock.

Short-term rentals illustrate the conflict between flexibility and housing need. Platforms can help homeowners earn income and travelers find lodging. But in tight markets, conversion of long-term housing to short-term rental use can reduce available homes and raise rents. Local economies may benefit from tourism while residents are displaced. The issue is not technology itself. It is governance. A platform-mediated market can turn spare rooms into income or entire neighborhoods into transient investment zones, depending on rules.

Transportation policy is housing policy. A home's affordability depends partly on transportation costs. Cheap housing far from jobs may not be affordable if commuting is expensive, unreliable, or time-consuming. Transit expands the effective supply of housing by connecting more places to opportunity. Walkable, transit-rich communities reduce household transportation burdens and environmental costs. Highway-centered development can produce sprawl, segregation, and car dependency. Housing affordability should be measured as housing plus transportation, not rent or mortgage alone.

Infrastructure policy is also housing policy. Water, sewer, schools, parks, transit, energy, broadband, and climate resilience determine where housing can be built and how livable it is. Some communities resist growth because infrastructure is inadequate. This suggests a coordination problem. Housing supply requires infrastructure investment. Infrastructure investment requires regional planning and public finance. If localities must absorb growth costs alone, they may resist. If regions share costs and benefits, housing becomes more feasible.

This points toward metropolitan governance. Housing markets operate regionally, but governance is often fragmented among municipalities. Each locality may restrict housing to protect itself, but collectively the region produces scarcity. Regional housing targets, fair-share requirements, state preemption of exclusionary zoning, infrastructure funding, and coordinated transit planning can reduce this fragmentation. Local voice matters, but local veto should not be absolute when regional need is severe.

Housing also requires better measurement. Policymakers often track median prices, rents, vacancy rates, permits, and starts. These are useful, but they do not fully capture lived housing stress. A serious housing analysis should ask: What share of households are rent-burdened? How many are severely burdened? How long are commutes? How many people are doubled up? How many households experience eviction filings? How many affordable units are lost each year? How many homes are vacant or used for short-term rental? How much income is needed to buy a starter home? How does housing cost affect fertility, mobility, health, and school stability? How does affordability vary by race, age, disability, and family structure?

The housing crisis often hides in adaptation. People cope before they appear in crisis statistics. Young adults live with parents longer. Families crowd into small apartments. Workers commute farther. Couples delay children. Tenants skip medical care to pay rent. Households take on debt. People stay in unsafe relationships because housing is unaffordable. Elderly homeowners remain in unsuitable homes because alternatives are too expensive. These adaptations reduce visible homelessness but increase invisible suffering. A housing system should not be judged only by the number of people on the street. It should be judged by how many lives are constrained by shelter insecurity.

The moral meaning of housing lies in this fact: without stable shelter, other freedoms become fragile. Education suffers. Health suffers. Work suffers. Family life suffers. Civic participation suffers. Safety suffers. The ability to plan suffers. Housing is not a reward for success. It is a foundation from which success becomes possible. A society that withholds stable housing until people succeed has reversed the order of human development.

This is why the slogan "housing is a human right" has force, even if policy design remains complex. To say housing is a human right does not mean every person receives any house in any place at any price. It means society has an obligation to ensure access to safe, stable, affordable shelter. It means housing cannot be governed solely by purchasing power. It means the market must be embedded in institutions that recognize shelter as a basic condition of dignity.

The opposing view says housing is a commodity, and commodities are allocated by markets. This view contains truth but not enough truth. Housing is bought, sold, rented, financed, maintained, and built through markets. Prices convey information. Developers need incentives. Owners bear costs. But housing is not like a luxury good. People cannot opt out of shelter. Children do not choose their housing market. Workers cannot participate in the economy without somewhere to live. Communities cannot survive without residents. Because housing is foundational, society must govern it differently from ordinary consumption.

A balanced housing philosophy would recognize four truths. First, markets are necessary for much housing production and allocation. Second, unregulated or badly regulated markets can produce exclusion, speculation, and instability. Third, public action is necessary to ensure affordability, fairness, and resilience. Fourth, public action must be competent, adaptive, and attentive to unintended consequences. The debate should not be market versus state. It should be how to design a housing system that produces enough homes, in the right places, at prices people can afford, while preserving dignity, community, and ecological responsibility.

The nonlinear nature of housing also means that small reforms can have large effects if they target the right loops. Reducing parking mandates can lower construction costs and increase feasible projects. Allowing accessory dwelling units can gently increase supply and support family flexibility. Legalizing multifamily housing near transit can expand opportunity. Streamlining approvals can reduce delay. Public land development can create affordable units in high-cost areas. Tenant right-to-counsel programs can reduce evictions. Emergency rental assistance can prevent homelessness. Land value taxation can discourage speculation. Each intervention changes a particular feedback loop.

But reform must be sequenced and coordinated. Upzoning without affordability protections may produce political backlash or displacement in vulnerable areas. Tenant protections without supply may preserve some households while worsening scarcity for others. Vouchers without landlord participation may fail. Public housing without maintenance funding may deteriorate. Climate resilience without affordability may produce green gentrification. Housing policy must be systemic because housing problems are systemic.

Public legitimacy is essential. Many residents fear development because they have seen growth produce displacement, luxury towers, traffic, speculation, or broken promises. Reformers must take these fears seriously without allowing fear to become veto. Communities need guarantees: affordable units, infrastructure investment, tenant protections, anti-displacement measures, school capacity, parks, transit, and meaningful but not obstructionist participation. Housing abundance must be linked to social trust. People are more likely to accept change if they believe the benefits will be shared.

The narrative of housing must also change. Too often, housing politics is framed as homeowners versus developers, renters versus landlords, growth versus preservation, density versus neighborhood character. These conflicts are real, but they obscure the larger question: What kind of society are we building if essential workers cannot live near work, young families cannot afford homes, children grow up in unstable housing, the unhoused sleep outside, and existing owners depend on scarcity for wealth? The housing crisis is not only a market problem. It is a statement about social priorities.

A more humane narrative would treat housing as part of the moral architecture of prosperity. Prosperity is not genuine if people cannot live where opportunity exists. A city is not successful if it becomes a playground for wealth and a workplace for commuters who cannot afford to reside there. A suburb is not virtuous if it preserves comfort by excluding those who serve it. A nation is not prosperous if younger generations inherit debt and rent burden while older generations depend on inflated property values. Housing reveals whether prosperity is shared or hoarded.

The connection between housing and democracy cannot be overstated. Stable housing supports civic participation. People vote, organize, volunteer, attend meetings, and form community ties when they are rooted. Housing instability weakens these capacities. Evictions disrupt political voice. Long commutes reduce time for citizenship. Segregation creates separate political realities. Homeowner dominance distorts local democracy. Homelessness exposes the failure of public responsibility. Housing is therefore democratic infrastructure.

Housing also shapes intergroup relations. Scarcity breeds conflict. Residents fear newcomers. Renters resent owners. Owners fear renters. Suburbs fear cities. Cities fear displacement. Generations blame one another. Immigrants may be scapegoated for housing shortages that policy created. Developers are treated as villains even when supply is needed. Government is blamed for both action and inaction. Scarcity turns social groups against one another because people are forced to compete for a basic need. Abundance, fairly governed, reduces conflict.

This is one of the deepest complexity lessons. When systems produce scarcity, politics becomes zero-sum. When systems produce security, cooperation becomes more plausible. Housing scarcity intensifies status competition, family stress, racial tension, generational resentment, and distrust. Housing security creates conditions for dignity, stability, and social peace. The question is not only how many units are built. It is what kind of social order housing policy creates.

A serious housing agenda for a nonlinear world would include at least ten elements. First, expand supply in high-demand and high-opportunity areas through zoning reform, by-right approvals, and infrastructure support. Second, build and preserve deeply affordable housing through public investment, nonprofit development, social housing, and public land. Third, protect renters through fair leases, eviction prevention, habitability standards, and anti-discrimination enforcement. Fourth, reduce speculation through vacancy taxes, short-term rental regulation, ownership transparency, and anti-flipping tools where appropriate. Fifth, reform property tax and school finance systems that tie opportunity to local wealth. Sixth, invest in transit-oriented development and infrastructure. Seventh, address homelessness through housing-first strategies, supportive services, and prevention. Eighth, expand pathways to ownership without inflating prices through shared equity, community land trusts, and targeted assistance tied to supply. Ninth, integrate climate resilience into housing policy. Tenth, build regional governance capable of overcoming fragmented local vetoes.

Such an agenda requires political courage because it challenges incumbent advantage. It asks homeowners to recognize that property rights exist within a broader society. It asks renters to be protected without freezing the system into scarcity. It asks developers to build within public purpose. It asks governments to invest competently. It asks regions to share responsibility. It asks citizens to see future residents as members of the community, even before they arrive.

The transition will not be easy. Housing systems are slow-moving. Buildings last decades. Land use rules are entrenched. Wealth is tied to property. Construction takes time. Local politics is intense. Financial interests are powerful. Public trust is low. But delay makes the problem worse. Every year of underbuilding increases scarcity. Every rent increase reduces savings. Every displaced family loses stability. Every young household priced out loses time. Every homeless person suffers injury to dignity. Every year of inflated home values deepens the political difficulty of reform.

The nonlinear nature of housing means that late action is more expensive than early action. Preventing displacement is easier than repairing it.

Preserving affordable units is cheaper than rebuilding them. Legalizing housing before prices explode is easier than doing so after homeowners become millionaires through scarcity. Maintaining public housing is cheaper than restoring it after deterioration. Investing in climate resilience before disaster is cheaper than rebuilding afterward. Housing policy rewards foresight and punishes denial.

This chapter has argued that housing markets are not simple markets. They are complex systems in which shelter, wealth, credit, land, politics, race, class, climate, infrastructure, and expectation interact. Housing scarcity is not merely the result of too many people seeking too few homes. It is often the product of feedback loops that make scarcity profitable, politically defended, and socially destructive. The housing market does not merely allocate shelter. It allocates opportunity, security, wealth, and belonging.

The next chapter turns to labor markets as adaptive networks. The connection is direct. Workers need homes near jobs. Employers need workers who can afford to live near workplaces. Housing costs shape wages, mobility, family decisions, and bargaining power. A labor market cannot function well when housing markets exclude the labor force. Likewise, housing affordability depends on wages, job stability, and worker power. Housing and labor are not separate systems. They are mutually constitutive.

The broader lesson is clear. A nonlinear economy cannot be governed by treating housing as a private asset alone. When housing becomes too scarce, too expensive, too speculative, and too tied to accumulated wealth, it destabilizes everything around it. It deepens inequality, burdens workers, weakens families, reduces mobility, fuels debt, strains public budgets, damages democracy, and converts opportunity into geography. The cost of housing scarcity is not only rent. It is the narrowing of human possibility.

A humane economy must begin from a different principle: shelter is foundational. Markets can help provide it, but markets must be governed so that the human purpose of housing is not subordinated to scarcity rents and asset inflation. Housing policy must build abundance, preserve affordability, protect stability, and reduce the political power of exclusion. It must treat homes not merely as investments, but as the places where human beings become capable of living full lives.

In a nonlinear world, housing is one of the clearest examples of when more becomes different. More scarcity becomes wealth for some and instability for others. More appreciation becomes political resistance. More resistance becomes less supply. Less supply becomes more inequality. More inequality becomes less democracy. But the reverse is also possible. More homes can become more mobility. More affordability can become more family stability. More stability can become better health, education, and work. More inclusion can become more trust. More trust can become better governance.

The housing system is a machine, but it is not an unchangeable one. It can be redesigned. The question is whether society has the moral imagination to see housing not as a privilege purchased in a scarcity market, but as the spatial foundation of freedom, dignity, and democratic life.

## Chapter 9

# Labor Markets as Adaptive Networks

Labor markets are often described in deceptively simple terms. Workers supply labor. Firms demand it. Wages adjust. If wages are too high, unemployment rises. If wages are too low, workers move elsewhere or employers raise pay to attract them. In this familiar picture, the labor market is a mechanism for matching workers to jobs and wages to productivity. People sell their labor, firms buy it, and the price of work reveals its value.

This model captures part of reality, but only part. Labor markets do involve supply, demand, wages, skills, productivity, and incentives. No serious theory of work can ignore these. But labor is not a commodity like wheat, steel, or software licenses. Labor is human time, energy, intelligence, care, attention, dignity, and life. Workers are not abstract units moving frictionlessly across a diagram. They are people embedded in families, neighborhoods, health conditions, debts, housing markets, transportation systems, educational histories, immigration statuses, social identities, and moral expectations. Jobs are not merely wage offers. They are bundles of power, schedule, status, risk, surveillance, meaning, benefits, mobility, and voice.

For this reason, labor markets are better understood as adaptive networks. They are networks because workers, firms, schools, unions, families, credentials, platforms, recruiters, professional associations, technologies, and public policies are connected in patterned ways. Information moves through these connections. Opportunities move through them. Exclusion moves through them. Bargaining power moves through them. They are adaptive because the actors within them learn, imitate, resist, evade, coordinate, and change. Firms alter hiring practices, wages, schedules, technologies, and organizational forms. Workers acquire skills, move, quit, organize, accept, bargain, or withdraw. Governments regulate, subsidize, tax, educate, and enforce. Technologies reshape tasks. Norms redefine what counts as good work. The labor market is not a static mechanism. It is an evolving social system.

The central argument of this chapter is that labor markets do not simply allocate workers to jobs. They produce social order. They determine who has security, who bears risk, who has voice, who can plan a life, who accumulates savings, who suffers exhaustion, who belongs to a community, and who receives dignity. Labor markets shape family formation, mental health, political participation, regional stability, inequality, inflation, debt, and democratic legitimacy. A society's labor market is therefore one of its most important moral institutions.

The simple supply-and-demand model becomes most misleading when it treats workers as mobile, informed, interchangeable, and free in the same way that capital is mobile and free. Capital can often move rapidly across sectors, regions, and borders. Workers cannot. They have spouses, children, parents, leases, mortgages, schools, medical needs, friendships, cultural ties, transportation limits, licenses, debts, and fears. A worker cannot instantly move from a declining town to a booming metropolitan area if housing costs are prohibitive. A parent cannot accept a higher-paying job if the schedule conflicts with childcare. A person with chronic illness cannot treat healthcare benefits as a minor detail. A worker without savings cannot quit an abusive workplace and search indefinitely for a better job. Labor market freedom is constrained by the conditions of life.

This is why housing and labor cannot be separated. Chapter 8 argued that housing markets allocate access to opportunity. Labor markets depend on that access. A job offer in a prosperous city means little if rent consumes the wage gain. A worker may be more productive in a high-opportunity region but unable to move because housing is unaffordable. Employers may complain of labor shortages while supporting or benefiting from local housing systems that exclude workers. Public servants, nurses, teachers, restaurant staff, caregivers, construction workers, retail employees, and young professionals may be essential to a regional economy yet unable to live near it. The labor market appears tight, but the true bottleneck is housing.

Transportation operates similarly. A worker's effective job market is not every job in the economy, but every reachable job. A position that is theoretically available may be practically unavailable if it requires a two-hour commute, unreliable transit, or car ownership the worker cannot afford. Transportation costs reduce real wages. Commute time reduces family time, health, education, and civic participation. Geographic mobility is therefore not simply a matter of willingness. It depends on infrastructure. A labor market is partly a transit network.

Care obligations also shape labor supply. Parents, especially mothers, make employment decisions within childcare constraints. Adult children care for aging parents. Spouses coordinate schedules. Workers with disabled family members need flexibility. The simple model treats labor supply as a choice between work and leisure. For many people, the choice is between paid work and unpaid care, between income and family responsibility, between career advancement and the needs of children or elders. A society that lacks affordable childcare, paid leave, eldercare support, and flexible work arrangements will misread care-constrained workers as less attached to the labor force. It will then interpret institutional failure as individual preference.

This misreading has profound consequences. If women reduce paid work because childcare is unaffordable, the economy loses talent and income. If caregivers leave jobs, household savings fall and future retirement security weakens. If parents face unpredictable schedules, children experience instability. If eldercare responsibilities force workers out of the labor market, families suffer financially and emotionally. Care is not outside the economy. It is the hidden infrastructure that allows the paid economy to function. Labor markets that ignore care are built on a false model of the worker as detached, unencumbered, and endlessly available.

Health is another constraint. A worker's ability to participate in the labor market depends on physical and mental health, access to treatment, disability accommodations, and the structure of health insurance. When healthcare is tied to employment, workers may remain in jobs they would otherwise leave. Economists call this job lock. The phrase is mild, but the reality is severe. A person may stay with an employer because a child needs medication, a spouse needs treatment, or a preexisting condition makes coverage essential. Labor market mobility is then limited not by wages alone, but by the fear of losing medical security.

Debt further disciplines labor. A worker with student loans, credit-card debt, medical debt, auto debt, or rent arrears may lack the freedom to search for better work, start a business, retrain, or join a strike. Debt makes the paycheck urgent. It shifts bargaining power toward employers because workers cannot easily withhold labor. Debt also shapes occupational choice. Graduates with large loans may choose higher-paying but less socially valuable or less fulfilling work. Households with mortgage obligations may resist relocation. Workers with car loans may accept jobs primarily to service debt. Debt turns the future into a claim on present labor.

Labor markets are also information networks. People rarely know all available jobs or all possible career paths. They learn about opportunities through family, friends, schools, online platforms, recruiters, former coworkers, unions, professional associations, community organizations, and social media. The quality of one's network affects the quality of opportunities one sees. Children of professionals often learn early how careers work, which credentials matter, how to interview, how to negotiate, and how to behave in elite workplaces. Others may possess talent but lack maps. The labor market then rewards navigation skills that are partly inherited.

This is why "equal opportunity" cannot be reduced to formal access. A job posting available online is not equally accessible if some applicants have mentors, referrals, unpaid internship experience, credential guidance, and financial support, while others do not. A labor market may appear open and meritocratic while still reproducing class advantage through networks. Hiring often relies on signals: degrees, internships, recommendations, prior employers, professional language, and cultural familiarity. These signals may correlate with ability, but they also correlate with privilege.

Credentials are especially important. In modern labor markets, credentials perform multiple functions. They certify skills, sort applicants, signal discipline, reduce employer uncertainty, and confer status. They can expand opportunity when they genuinely reflect capability and when access is broad. But they can also become barriers. Degree requirements may exclude capable workers whose skills were acquired through experience, military service, caregiving, informal work, community leadership, or nontraditional education. Licensing can protect safety and quality, but it can also restrict entry and raise costs. Credential inflation occurs when jobs require more formal education than the work itself demands, partly because employers use degrees as screening devices.

Credentialism links labor markets to inequality. Families with resources can help children accumulate credentials. They can pay tuition, support unpaid internships, subsidize test preparation, finance relocation, and cushion early career risk. Families without resources may rely on debt, work long hours while studying, attend lower-resourced institutions, or avoid training altogether. The labor market then treats credentials as individual achievements while ignoring unequal access to the credential pipeline. Merit becomes filtered through finance.

Skills matter, but the skills narrative is often overused. When workers are unemployed or underpaid, policymakers frequently say they need more education or training. Sometimes this is true. Technological change can create new skill needs. Workers should have access to lifelong learning. But skill deficits are not the cause of every labor market problem. A worker can be skilled and still underpaid if employers have power. A region can train workers and still lack jobs. A society can increase college attainment and still produce low wages if the labor market is polarized. Training cannot substitute for bargaining power, job creation, industrial policy, childcare, transportation, housing, antitrust, and labor standards.

The skills narrative is politically convenient because it individualizes structural problems. If wages are low, workers need skills. If communities decline, workers need retraining. If inequality rises, people need education. These claims contain enough truth to sound responsible, but they can obscure the deeper issue: the economy may not be generating enough dignified work with adequate pay, security, and voice. A humane labor policy must develop skills, but it must also improve the quality of jobs.

The quality of jobs is central. Employment alone is not enough. A job can provide income while destroying health, dignity, family life, or future prospects. Job quality includes wages, benefits, schedule stability, safety, autonomy, promotion pathways, training, respect, voice, and predictability. A labor market with low unemployment but widespread precarious work is not healthy in any deep sense. It may be formally tight while morally thin.

Precarity is a nonlinear condition. A small schedule change can destabilize childcare. A missed shift can cause rent arrears. A lack of paid sick leave can force a worker to choose between income and public health. A minor injury can produce lost wages and debt. A sudden cut in hours can trigger cascading hardship. The worker's vulnerability is not visible in the employment rate. It lies in the absence of buffers. A society that celebrates job numbers while ignoring precarity mistakes attachment to the labor market for security within it.

Wages are obviously central, but wages themselves must be understood as socially produced. The simple model suggests wages reflect productivity. In some contexts, this is approximately true. But the relationship between wages and productivity is mediated by institutions. Unions, minimum wages, labor law, monopsony power, discrimination, immigration status, public benefits, corporate governance, market concentration, outsourcing, subcontracting, and norms all affect how productivity gains are distributed. Workers may become more productive without receiving proportional wage gains if bargaining power is weak. Firms may capture the surplus. Executives and shareholders may capture even more.

This is why the labor share of income matters. When a larger share of national income flows to capital and a smaller share to labor, inequality tends to rise. Households depending on wages may rely more on debt. Demand may become dependent on credit or asset appreciation. Political resentment may grow. Labor's decline is therefore connected to the chapters on debt, inequality, inflation, and housing. Workers without bargaining power cannot easily defend purchasing power when prices rise. Workers without wage growth cannot save for homes. Workers without security cannot take risks. Labor markets sit at the center of the nonlinear economy.

Power is the missing variable in many labor market models. Employers and workers do not meet as equals. Employers often control hiring, scheduling, promotion, discipline, surveillance, benefits, and termination. They may have legal departments, human resources systems, data, and market knowledge. Workers may have limited savings, limited information, and urgent needs. The employment contract is formally voluntary, but its terms are shaped by unequal alternatives. A worker who must accept a job to avoid eviction does not bargain from the same position as a firm choosing among applicants.

Monopsony power is one way to describe this inequality. A labor market has monopsony characteristics when employers have wage-setting power because workers have limited alternatives. This can happen in small towns with few employers, specialized occupations, franchised industries, hospital systems, universities, warehouses, agriculture, or platform-mediated work. It can also happen through job search frictions, noncompete agreements, employer concentration, licensing barriers, discrimination, or lack of transportation. When workers cannot easily leave, employers can pay less than the value workers produce.

The existence of monopsony undermines the idea that wages naturally rise to reflect productivity. If employers have power, they may suppress wages, reduce benefits, or impose conditions that workers accept because alternatives are worse. Low wages do not necessarily prove low productivity. They may prove weak bargaining power. This distinction is morally crucial. A society that interprets low wages as evidence of low value will tolerate exploitation. A society that understands wage-setting power will ask how to rebalance the relationship.

Unions are one answer. Unions convert individual workers into collective actors. They reduce the isolation that gives employers power. They negotiate wages, benefits, schedules, safety, grievance procedures, and dignity. They also create political voice. A union is not merely an economic institution. It is a democratic institution inside the workplace. It teaches participation, leadership, solidarity, and collective problem-solving. It gives workers a way to contest arbitrary authority without losing their livelihood.

The decline of unions has weakened one of the labor market's most important balancing feedback loops. Without collective bargaining, workers negotiate individually. Individual negotiation favors those with rare skills, strong networks, high savings, or scarce credentials. Many workers lack such leverage. The result is wage dispersion, insecurity, and the normalization of employer discretion. Rebuilding worker voice is therefore not nostalgia. It is a systemic requirement for a labor market that produces dignity rather than dependency.

Critics argue that unions can protect insiders, reduce flexibility, raise costs, or resist necessary change. These concerns are not imaginary. Any institution can become rigid or exclusionary. But the answer is not a labor market without worker power. The answer is better worker institutions: democratic unions, sectoral bargaining, wage boards, works councils, portable benefits, training partnerships, and mechanisms that combine flexibility with security. The goal is not to freeze the economy. It is to ensure that adaptation does not mean unilateral employer power.

Sectoral bargaining deserves attention because many modern labor markets are fragmented. In a workplace-by-workplace bargaining system, unionization can be difficult in industries with small worksites, subcontracting, franchising, gig work, or high turnover. Sectoral bargaining sets standards across an industry or occupation, reducing the incentive for firms to compete by cutting labor standards. It can raise wages, reduce inequality, and create a more level playing field among employers. It also recognizes that labor markets are networks, not isolated firms.

The fissured workplace is one of the most important developments in modern labor markets. Firms increasingly outsource, subcontract, franchise, use temp agencies, rely on independent contractors, or structure work through platforms. The lead firm retains control over brand, strategy, technology, pricing, and standards, while legal responsibility for workers is shifted elsewhere. This allows firms to benefit from labor while distancing themselves from employment obligations. Workers may perform essential functions for a company without being its formal employees.

Fissuring weakens bargaining power and accountability. A janitor, driver, warehouse worker, delivery worker, security guard, or food service worker may be part of a large corporate ecosystem while employed by a contractor with thin margins. The lead firm can pressure costs downward. The contractor passes pressure to workers. If abuses occur, responsibility is fragmented. The labor market becomes a network of dependency hidden behind legal separation. Complexity economics is especially useful here because it looks at the network, not merely the formal contract.

Gig work and platform labor intensify these dynamics. Platforms match workers and customers through digital systems. They can provide flexibility, entry opportunities, and consumer convenience. But they can also shift risk to workers, use algorithmic management, control access to customers, set terms unilaterally, and classify workers as independent contractors. The worker may appear self-employed, but the platform may control pricing, visibility, ratings, deactivation, incentives, and data. Independence becomes ambiguous.

Algorithmic management changes the texture of work. Scheduling, productivity targets, route assignments, performance scores, customer ratings, surveillance, and discipline can be automated or semi-automated. Workers may not know how decisions are made. They may be managed by metrics they cannot contest. The boss becomes a system. This can increase efficiency, but it can also intensify stress, reduce autonomy, and hide power behind technical neutrality. A worker disciplined by an algorithm still experiences discipline. The fact that the decision is mediated by software does not make it apolitical.

Technology also reshapes task structure. Automation can replace some tasks, complement others, and create new work. Artificial intelligence may alter professional services, administration, coding, design, logistics, education, healthcare, law, finance, and creative industries. The effects will not be uniform. Some workers will become more productive and valuable. Others will face displacement, deskilling, surveillance, or wage pressure. Firms that own or control technology may capture gains.

Workers may receive gains only if institutions support bargaining, training, mobility, and redistribution.

Technological change is therefore not destiny. It is mediated by institutions. A technology can be used to augment workers or replace them. It can reduce drudgery or intensify monitoring. It can shorten work time or increase employer expectations. It can democratize knowledge or concentrate power. It can create broad productivity gains or narrow monopoly rents. The labor market outcome depends on ownership, governance, competition, education, labor power, and public policy.

This is one reason the phrase "future of work" can be misleading. The future of work is not something that simply arrives. It is built. Firms design jobs. Governments set rules. Workers organize. Consumers make demands. Technologies are deployed within power structures. A society that treats technological displacement as inevitable may fail to govern it. A society that insists on human-centered technological adoption can shape outcomes differently. The future of work is a political economy question.

Immigration also reveals the networked nature of labor markets. Migrants move through family networks, employer demand, legal status, recruitment systems, global inequalities, conflict, climate stress, and aspiration. They fill essential roles in agriculture, care, construction, hospitality, healthcare, domestic work, technology, and entrepreneurship. Immigration can expand labor supply, support growth, and enrich society. It can also be exploited by employers when workers lack legal protections or fear deportation. The effect of immigration on wages and labor conditions depends heavily on institutions.

A humane labor market must protect immigrant workers not only for their sake, but for the sake of all workers. If some workers can be underpaid, threatened, or excluded from labor rights, employers can use their vulnerability to weaken standards more broadly. Legal precarity becomes a tool of labor market segmentation. Strong enforcement, paths to legal status, anti-retaliation protections, and equal labor rights prevent a race to the bottom. The issue is not immigrants versus native workers. The issue is whether the labor market allows vulnerability to be exploited.

Discrimination remains a powerful force in labor networks. Race, gender, age, disability, class background, accent, criminal history, caregiving status, and appearance can shape hiring, pay, promotion, discipline, and credibility. Discrimination is not always explicit. It can operate through networks, referrals, stereotypes, algorithmic screening, occupational sorting, evaluation criteria, customer preferences, and informal culture. A labor market can appear meritocratic while reproducing exclusion through subtle mechanisms.

Occupational segregation is a major example. Groups are concentrated in different sectors and roles, often due to historical exclusion, care responsibilities, educational inequality, social norms, discrimination, and network pathways. Work associated with women, care, service, or marginalized communities is often undervalued. The wage attached to a job may reflect social power as much as economic contribution. Care work is essential, but often poorly paid. The market price of care does not reflect its social value because the people needing care often cannot pay the full cost and the workers providing care often lack bargaining power. Without public support, the care economy remains structurally undervalued.

This exposes a deeper problem in the idea that wages measure value. Some of the most socially necessary work is poorly paid: childcare, eldercare, home health, cleaning, food service, teaching assistants, agricultural labor, and many forms of public service. Some highly paid work may generate private returns without comparable social value, especially in speculative finance, rent extraction, or monopolistic markets. The wage is not a moral measure. It is an outcome of market demand, scarcity, bargaining power, institutional rules, and social valuation. A humane economy cannot confuse pay with worth.

Labor markets also shape identity. Work is not only income. It is a source of recognition, routine, community, self-respect, and contribution. The loss of work can therefore damage more than a household budget. It can damage meaning. The degradation of work can produce humiliation even when income remains. A person subjected to unpredictable scheduling, surveillance, disrespect, or arbitrary discipline may experience work as domination. A society that treats such suffering as merely a private employment matter misses the moral importance of work.

Dignity at work requires more than wages. It requires respect, safety, voice, predictability, and the ability to participate in decisions that shape one's life. A high wage can coexist with burnout. A low wage can coexist with pride if the work is respected and secure, although dignity should never be used to justify poor pay. The ideal labor market is not one in which every person becomes a high-earning professional. It is one in which every socially necessary worker receives enough pay, security, respect, and voice to live a full human life.

Unemployment must also be understood nonlinearly. A short spell of unemployment can be painful but manageable for a worker with savings, networks, and strong demand for skills. For a worker without buffers, unemployment can cascade into debt, eviction, health stress, family strain, and long-term earnings loss. Long-term unemployment can erode skills, confidence, employer perceptions, social networks, and mental health. It can become self-reinforcing. Employers may discriminate against applicants with employment gaps. Workers may withdraw from search. Communities with high unemployment may lose businesses and tax revenue. The harm exceeds lost income.

This is why recessions have long shadows. Workers entering the labor market during downturns may suffer lower earnings for years. Communities hit by plant closures may not recover quickly, especially if jobs are specialized and local institutions weaken. Children in households affected by unemployment may experience stress that affects education and health. A temporary macroeconomic shock can become a permanent life trajectory. Equilibrium thinking expects labor markets to recover. Complexity thinking asks what scars remain.

Hysteresis is the term often used for this persistence. It means that temporary shocks can have lasting effects. In labor markets, hysteresis occurs when unemployment reduces future employability, when firms reduce training, when workers leave the labor force, when communities decline, or when investment patterns shift. Policy that tolerates high unemployment in the belief that the economy will naturally return to full health may cause avoidable long-term damage. Full employment is not merely a short-run goal. It is a way of preserving human capability.

Full employment also changes power. When jobs are plentiful, workers have more options. They can quit bad jobs, demand better pay, negotiate schedules, and refuse abuse. Employers must compete for labor. Wages at the bottom may rise. Labor force participation may increase. Formerly marginalized workers may gain opportunity. Full employment is therefore not only an aggregate condition. It is a democratic condition within the labor market. It reduces domination by increasing exit options.

This is one reason inflation policy must be careful. If the primary tool for reducing inflation is weakening the labor market, then workers bear the burden through unemployment and reduced bargaining power. Sometimes demand reduction may be necessary to restore price stability. But a society should not use worker insecurity as its default stabilization device. Inflation may arise from supply chains, energy, housing, market power, and expectations. To respond primarily through unemployment is often both inefficient and unjust. Labor market pain should not be the universal solvent for economic disorder.

Public policy can strengthen labor markets in multiple ways. Minimum wages set a wage floor. Earned income supports can raise after-tax income. Unemployment insurance provides a buffer during job loss. Paid leave supports care. Childcare policy expands labor force participation. Healthcare security improves mobility. Training and apprenticeships develop skills. Antitrust reduces employer power. Labor law supports organizing. Public employment can provide work when private demand fails. Industrial policy can create jobs in strategic sectors. Immigration reform can reduce exploitation. Disability policy can support inclusion. Procurement standards can raise job quality in publicly funded sectors.

These policies are often debated separately, but they interact. A minimum wage works better with enforcement and predictable scheduling. Training works better when good jobs exist. Childcare works better when wages make employment worthwhile. Healthcare security works better when workers can move jobs without losing coverage. Antitrust works better when workers can organize. Industrial policy works better when it includes labor standards. Labor market policy must be systemic because labor markets are networks.

Employer responsibility is also central. Firms are not passive takers of labor market conditions. They design jobs. They choose whether to invest in training, reduce turnover, share gains, respect workers, provide predictable schedules, and build internal mobility. Some firms compete through low wages and high turnover. Others compete through skill, quality, productivity, and loyalty. Public policy can influence which model dominates. If low-road employers can undercut high-road employers by suppressing labor standards, the labor market rewards degradation. Standards can prevent a race to the bottom and create room for better business models.

The distinction between high-road and low-road employment is important. A high-road labor strategy treats workers as assets: training them, paying decently, involving them in problem-solving, and building long-term relationships. A low-road strategy treats workers as costs to be minimized and replaced. Low-road strategies can appear efficient in the short run, especially when labor is abundant and regulations are weak. But they often generate turnover, low morale, poor service, weak productivity, and social harm. The public bears part of the cost through income support, healthcare, housing assistance, family stress, and community instability. Low wages are often subsidized by society.

This is why public benefits should not be understood only as assistance to workers. They can also be indirect subsidies to low-wage employers if firms pay wages insufficient for basic life and public programs fill the gap. Such programs may be necessary to protect households, but they should not excuse business models built on poverty wages. A just system protects workers while raising labor standards. Otherwise, public compassion becomes private subsidy.

Labor markets also depend on enforcement. Rights without enforcement are fragile. Minimum wage laws, safety standards, anti-discrimination rules, overtime protections, misclassification rules, and organizing rights matter only if workers can assert them without retaliation and agencies can investigate violations. Low-wage workers often face the greatest abuses and the least ability to complain. Fear of job loss, immigration consequences, blacklisting, or schedule retaliation can silence workers. Enforcement must therefore be proactive, not solely complaint-based.

The informal economy complicates labor policy. Some workers operate outside formal contracts, tax systems, or legal protections. Informal work can provide survival income, flexibility, and community exchange. It can also involve exploitation, unsafe conditions, and lack of benefits. Informality often grows when formal labor markets fail to provide adequate jobs or when legal barriers exclude workers. A humane approach should not simply punish informal workers. It should ask why formality is inaccessible or unattractive and how to extend protections without destroying livelihoods.

The labor market is also shaped by macroeconomic demand. Firms hire when they expect customers. Workers find jobs when demand supports production. Public austerity can weaken labor markets by reducing demand and public employment. Investment in infrastructure, care, clean energy, education, and health can create jobs while building social capacity. Fiscal policy is labor policy. Monetary policy is labor policy. Trade policy is labor policy. Housing policy is labor policy. The separation of policy domains obscures how workers experience the economy as a whole.

Regional labor markets deserve special attention. National employment statistics can conceal local decline. A country may have low unemployment while certain towns, rural regions, or former industrial areas experience underemployment, low wages, addiction, poor health, and out-migration. Jobs are geographically embedded. When a major employer closes, the damage spreads through suppliers, restaurants, schools, tax bases, housing values, and civic institutions. The effect is not simply the number of jobs lost. It is the weakening of a local economic ecosystem.

Place-based policy is necessary because workers cannot always move and because communities matter. The advice to "move to opportunity" ignores housing costs, family ties, culture, care, and dignity. It also implies that places can be abandoned without consequence. A democratic society cannot write off regions as inefficient. It must invest in new forms of opportunity: broadband, community colleges, clean energy, advanced manufacturing, healthcare, care work, small business ecosystems, transportation, and public institutions. Regional renewal is labor market policy.

At the same time, place-based policy must avoid romanticizing every existing industry. Not all jobs can or should be preserved forever. Technological change, climate necessity, and global shifts will alter work. The moral obligation is not to freeze the economy, but to ensure that workers and communities are not sacrificed without support. Adaptation must be shared. Workers asked to bear transition costs should receive income support, retraining, relocation assistance where desired, pension protection, healthcare, and meaningful participation in planning.

The concept of just transition is therefore central to labor markets in a nonlinear world. Climate policy, automation, trade, and industrial restructuring all create winners and losers. A transition is unjust when the benefits are broad or concentrated at the top while the costs fall on specific workers and communities. A just transition recognizes contribution, protects dignity, and builds new opportunities before old ones disappear. It prevents necessary change from becoming social betrayal.

Labor markets also affect democratic politics through the experience of agency. Workplaces are often the institutions where adults experience authority most directly. If work is hierarchical, arbitrary, surveilled, and voiceless, citizens may carry those experiences into political life. A democracy that ends at the workplace door is incomplete. Worker voice can therefore strengthen democratic culture. It teaches negotiation, participation, solidarity, and accountability. Conversely, labor markets organized around fear and domination can habituate people to powerlessness or resentment.

This connection between workplace democracy and political democracy is underappreciated. Citizens who spend much of life without voice may struggle to believe in public voice. Citizens who experience institutions as rigged may generalize distrust. Citizens who feel humiliated at work may become receptive to political narratives of humiliation. Labor dignity is not only an economic matter. It is a civic matter.

The rise of remote work adds another layer. Remote work can increase flexibility, reduce commuting, expand access for some workers, and alter regional economies. It can also blur boundaries between work and home, intensify isolation, shift costs to workers, and create new inequalities between jobs that can be remote and jobs that cannot. Professionals with remote options may gain bargaining power and geographic flexibility. Service workers tied to place may not. Cities may change as office demand shifts. Housing markets in remote-friendly regions may heat up. The labor market adapts, and the adaptation produces new spatial and class dynamics.

Remote work also reveals that many job structures once treated as necessary were institutional habits. If work can be done flexibly, then rigid schedules may have been about control rather than productivity. Yet flexibility should not become privilege for the professional class alone. Care workers, retail workers, manufacturing workers, and service workers also need predictability, autonomy, and humane scheduling, even if their work cannot be remote. The future of work should not deepen the dignity gap between laptop workers and embodied workers.

The pandemic exposed the moral hierarchy of labor. Many workers labeled "essential" were also low-paid, exposed to health risks, and granted limited voice. Society depended on grocery workers, delivery drivers, nurses, aides, cleaners, teachers, warehouse workers, farmworkers, and public employees, yet often compensated them poorly. The crisis revealed a contradiction: work that is essential to society is not necessarily rewarded by the market. This should have forced a deeper revaluation of labor. In many cases, it produced temporary praise without durable structural change.

A complexity approach asks why essential work is undervalued. The answer lies in bargaining power, social status, gender, race, immigration, public funding, consumer price expectations, and institutional design. Care work is underpaid partly because those needing care often cannot pay high prices and because society has historically treated care as natural female labor rather than skilled social contribution. Food and delivery work are underpaid partly because consumers expect low prices and workers are replaceable in weak labor markets. Public service may be underpaid because budgets are constrained and tax politics are hostile. Wages reflect power as well as value.

Labor markets also distribute risk through benefits. Employer-provided benefits, such as health insurance, retirement plans, paid leave, and training, attach security to specific jobs. This can reward stable employment, but it can also create inequality between workers with good jobs and workers with bad jobs, between full-time employees and contractors, between large firms and small firms, between unionized and nonunionized sectors. Portable benefits could reduce this divide by attaching protections to workers rather than jobs. In an adaptive labor market, security must move with people.

The old model of a lifetime job with one employer has weakened in many sectors. Workers change jobs, careers, locations, and employment forms. Some choose flexibility. Others are forced into instability. Social insurance should reflect this reality. Retirement savings, healthcare, unemployment protection, training funds, paid leave, and workers' compensation should not disappear because a worker changes jobs or works through a platform. A dynamic economy requires portable security. Otherwise, flexibility becomes a euphemism for risk shifting.

The idea of flexicurity captures this balance: firms may need flexibility to adapt, but workers need security to live. The conflict between flexibility and security is often exaggerated. A society can make it easier for firms to change while protecting workers from ruin. Strong unemployment insurance, retraining, wage insurance, healthcare, childcare, active labor market policy, and worker voice can support adaptation. The worst system combines employer flexibility with worker insecurity. The best system combines economic adaptability with human stability.

Active labor market policy is especially important. It includes training, job search assistance, apprenticeships, wage subsidies, public employment services, relocation support, and partnerships with employers. But it must be designed carefully. Training should be linked to real jobs. Workers should not be blamed if jobs are absent. Programs should include income support so people can participate. Employers should have obligations, not merely receive subsidies. Outcomes should be monitored. Active labor policy is not a slogan. It is institutional capacity.

Apprenticeships and vocational pathways can reduce credential inequality when they are high quality, respected, and connected to good wages. Societies that treat non-college pathways as second-class waste talent and deepen resentment. Not every person needs a four-year degree to contribute meaningfully or earn dignity. A plural labor market should include academic, technical, vocational, entrepreneurial, care, artistic, and public service pathways. The hierarchy of credentials should not become a hierarchy of human worth.

Public employment can also play a role. When private markets fail to provide enough work or when communities need services, public jobs can build infrastructure, care systems, environmental resilience, and civic capacity. Public employment is sometimes dismissed as inefficient, but unemployment itself is wasteful. The question is whether public work is well designed, meaningful, and accountable. A society with unmet needs and unemployed workers has a coordination failure. Public institutions can help solve it.

The labor market also requires wage floors that reflect social dignity. A minimum wage is not merely an economic variable. It is a moral statement about the lowest acceptable price of human labor in a civilized society. If full-time work leaves a person unable to afford shelter, food, healthcare, transportation, and basic participation, the labor market has failed. Wage floors must be designed with attention to local costs, small business conditions, enforcement, and inflation. But the principle remains: work should not reproduce poverty.

Wage policy must also consider wage compression and internal fairness. Extreme gaps within firms can damage morale and legitimacy. Executive compensation many hundreds of times worker pay communicates a hierarchy of worth that cannot be justified by productivity alone. Firms are social organizations, not merely contracts. Their pay structures shape culture, loyalty, and public trust. Corporate governance that prioritizes shareholders and executives while treating workers as costs contributes to inequality and resentment.

Employee ownership and profit-sharing can help align workers with firm success. If workers contribute to productivity, they should share in gains. Employee stock ownership plans, cooperatives, gain-sharing, and broad-based profit-sharing are not magic solutions, but they can alter feedback loops. Workers with ownership stakes may build wealth, voice, and commitment. Firms may benefit from lower turnover and higher engagement. Ownership must be genuine, diversified, and protected from excessive risk. Workers should not have all wealth tied to one employer. But broader ownership is part of a more democratic labor market.

The relationship between labor and inflation is complex. Rising wages can contribute to inflation if they exceed productivity and are passed into prices. But wage growth can also restore purchasing power, reduce inequality, and support demand. The question is context. Are wages leading prices or catching up? Are profits rising? Is productivity increasing? Do firms have market power? Are wages rising at the bottom after years of stagnation? Is inflation driven by housing, energy, or supply chains rather than labor costs? A labor market analysis that treats wages as the main inflation threat while ignoring profits, rents, and bottlenecks is incomplete.

A more coordinated wage-setting system can reduce conflict. In some economies, unions, employers, and government institutions negotiate wage norms that balance inflation, productivity, and fairness. Such coordination is difficult in fragmented labor markets, but the principle matters. When each firm, worker, and sector acts defensively, inflation can become a conflict spiral. Institutions can mediate the conflict. Labor voice need not be inflationary if embedded in systems of coordination and productivity.

Labor markets also influence debt. Low wages and insecure work increase borrowing for basic needs. Stable wages reduce reliance on credit. Employment benefits affect medical debt. Predictable schedules affect ability to pay bills. Job loss affects mortgage defaults and rent arrears. Labor insecurity is therefore a driver of household fragility. A society cannot solve debt problems without improving work.

Labor markets influence housing as well. Wages determine affordability. Job locations determine demand. Work-from-home patterns reshape geography. Construction labor shortages affect housing supply. Care wages affect availability of childcare, which affects labor supply. Public-sector wages affect schools, healthcare, and local government services. Every chapter of this book connects through labor because labor is the human interface of the economy.

A systems view of labor markets must also consider exit from the labor force. People may leave paid work because of retirement, disability, caregiving, discouragement, illness, education, incarceration, addiction, or family needs. Some exits are chosen and healthy. Others represent social failure. A low unemployment rate can hide discouraged workers who stopped searching. Labor force participation, underemployment, involuntary part-time work, job quality, and wage growth all matter. A labor market cannot be judged by one number.

The same is true of productivity. Economies seek productivity growth because it allows higher living standards. But productivity gains do not automatically become shared prosperity. If gains flow mainly to capital, executives, or consumers through lower prices while workers receive little security, social conflict may grow. If productivity is achieved through speedup, surveillance, stress, and burnout, measured output may rise while human wellbeing falls. A humane productivity agenda should focus on technology, training, infrastructure, management quality, worker voice, and fair distribution.

Management quality is often neglected. Poor management wastes talent, creates stress, increases turnover, suppresses initiative, and reduces productivity. Good management can empower workers, improve processes, support learning, and increase dignity. The labor market is not only about wages and skills. It is about how work is organized. Hierarchical, fear-based workplaces may extract effort but destroy creativity and trust. Participatory workplaces may produce better information and adaptation. Worker voice is therefore also an efficiency tool.

Trust inside firms matters. Workers who trust management may share ideas, report problems, cooperate, and invest effort. Workers who distrust management may withhold information, disengage, or leave. Employers who distrust workers may rely on surveillance and control, which can further reduce trust. This is a feedback loop. High-trust workplaces can become more productive and humane. Low-trust workplaces can become coercive and inefficient. Labor policy usually operates at the legal level, but workplace culture is also economic infrastructure.

The adaptive network perspective also highlights the role of norms. What is considered a fair wage? How much notice should workers receive for schedules? Is it acceptable to contact employees after hours? Should service workers tolerate abuse from customers? Is unionization legitimate? Should layoffs be a first response to pressure or a last resort? Should firms train workers or expect workers to arrive fully formed? Norms shape behavior even without law. Law can reinforce norms, and norms can support law. A society that normalizes precarious work will produce more of it.

Customers are part of labor markets too. Consumer demand for low prices, fast delivery, extended hours, and convenience shapes working conditions. But consumers often do not see the labor embedded in goods and services. Same-day delivery means warehouse pressure and driver risk. Cheap food may mean low farm wages or restaurant instability. Low-cost care may mean underpaid caregivers. The market hides labor behind price. A moral economy makes labor visible.

This does not mean consumers alone are responsible. Many consumers seek low prices because their own wages are constrained. Firms compete by lowering labor costs because markets reward them. Public policy tolerates the structure. The point is that labor markets connect people in hidden ways. One person's convenience may be another person's precarity. A complexity economics approach reveals those connections and asks whether they are just.

Global labor networks extend the same issue across borders. Goods consumed in wealthy countries may be produced by workers in poorer countries under difficult conditions. Global supply chains can create jobs and development, but they can also exploit weak labor protections, suppress wages, and shift risk. Trade policy, corporate accountability, labor standards, and development policy must address these networks. A national labor market is embedded in a global labor system. Domestic workers and foreign workers should not be pitted against one another in a race to the bottom.

Labor rights should be understood as human rights within economic life. The right to organize, the right to safe work, the right to fair pay, the right to be free from discrimination, the right to rest, the right to care for family, and the right to dignity are not external constraints on the economy. They are conditions of a civilized economy. Markets without labor rights become systems of domination. States without labor rights become complicit in exploitation.

This is not anti-market. It is pro-human market design. Labor markets can be dynamic, innovative, and productive while respecting workers. In fact, dignity can improve performance. Workers who are healthy, secure, trained, respected, and heard are more capable of contribution. A society that treats labor as disposable wastes intelligence and undermines trust. The best economy is not the one that extracts the most from workers at the lowest cost. It is the one that develops human capability and channels it toward shared prosperity.

The policy architecture for labor markets as adaptive networks should rest on several principles. First, full employment should be a central goal because it strengthens worker bargaining power and preserves human capability. Second, job quality should be measured and improved, not assumed from employment counts. Third, worker voice should be strengthened through unions, sectoral bargaining, works councils, and democratic workplace institutions. Fourth, wage floors and labor standards should prevent competition through exploitation. Fifth, benefits should be portable and social insurance strong, allowing mobility without insecurity. Sixth, care infrastructure should be treated as labor market infrastructure. Seventh, training should be linked to real opportunity and supported by income. Eighth, antitrust should address labor market power. Ninth, technology should be governed to augment workers and distribute gains. Tenth, regional investment should bring opportunity to places as well as helping workers move where they choose.

These principles would not eliminate labor market conflict. Work will always involve negotiation among wages, profits, prices, productivity, autonomy, and organization. But they would shift the balance from domination toward cooperation. They would recognize that the labor market is not a natural force to which society must submit. It is an institutional system that can be designed.

The chapters before this one have shown how inflation, debt, inequality, and housing operate through feedback loops. Labor markets connect them. Inflation affects real wages. Debt affects worker freedom. Inequality affects opportunity and bargaining power. Housing affects mobility.

Technology affects tasks and power. Supply chains affect jobs. Financial markets affect corporate behavior. Public policy affects all of them. A worker standing in a workplace is not standing outside these systems. The worker is where they meet.

The next chapter turns to supply chains and the fragility of efficiency. The connection is direct. Supply chains are labor systems as well as logistics systems. Warehouses, ports, factories, farms, trucking routes, ships, railroads, retail stores, and delivery networks all depend on workers. When supply chains are optimized for cost and speed, labor is often squeezed for flexibility. When shocks arrive, essential workers absorb risk. The fragility of supply chains is partly the fragility of labor arrangements hidden inside them.

This chapter's central claim is that labor markets must be understood as adaptive networks of human beings, institutions, power, and place. Wages matter, but they do not exhaust the meaning of work. Skills matter, but they do not explain unequal opportunity alone. Mobility matters, but it depends on housing, care, transportation, health, and debt. Technology matters, but its effects are governed. Markets matter, but they are embedded in law and power. Labor is not merely an input. It is life organized through economic institutions.

A society that misunderstands labor will misunderstand prosperity. It may celebrate low unemployment while ignoring exhaustion. It may celebrate flexibility while shifting risk. It may celebrate productivity while suppressing wages. It may celebrate innovation while displacing workers without support. It may celebrate consumer convenience while hiding labor exploitation. It may celebrate meritocracy while ignoring unequal networks. It may celebrate freedom while workers lack real alternatives.

A complexity economics approach demands a richer standard. A good labor market is one in which people can find meaningful work, earn enough to live, develop skills, care for family, participate in decisions, move without ruin, recover from shocks, and share in the gains of productivity. It is one in which employers can adapt and compete without relying on exploitation. It is one in which technology broadens human capability. It is one in which work supports democracy rather than corroding it.

Labor markets are adaptive networks. If they reward low wages, insecurity, surveillance, and fragmentation, those patterns will spread. If they reward skill, dignity, voice, trust, and shared prosperity, those patterns can spread as well. The labor market teaches society what human effort is worth. The question is whether it teaches that work is a commodity to be minimized or a human contribution to be honored.

In a nonlinear world, the answer matters far beyond the workplace. It shapes inequality, inflation, debt, housing, family life, political trust, and democratic survival. A society that wants stability must build labor markets that produce security. A society that wants innovation must build labor markets that develop people. A society that wants democracy must build labor markets that give workers voice. A society that wants prosperity must remember that prosperity begins not with capital alone, nor technology alone, nor consumption alone, but with human beings whose labor turns possibility into the material life of the world.

## Chapter 10

# Supply Chains and the Fragility of Efficiency

Supply chains are the hidden circulatory system of modern economic life. They move food from farms to stores, medicine from laboratories to hospitals, semiconductors from fabrication plants to automobiles, lumber from forests to construction sites, oil and gas through pipelines and tankers, rare minerals into batteries, computer parts into data centers, and finished goods from factories to homes. Most of the time, they remain invisible. Their success is measured by the absence of attention. Shelves are stocked. Packages arrive. Factories receive inputs. Restaurants receive food. Hospitals receive equipment. Consumers click a button and expect the world to organize itself around delivery.

But supply chains become visible when they fail. A missing part stops an assembly line. A blocked shipping lane delays goods across continents. A port backlog raises prices. A pandemic closes factories and exposes dependency. A war disrupts energy, fertilizer, grain, and metals. A drought lowers river levels and restricts transport. A cyberattack disables logistics. A labor shortage slows trucking, warehousing, or healthcare. A natural disaster damages a critical facility. Suddenly, what looked like a smooth global system becomes a fragile web of dependencies. The modern economy discovers that efficiency is not the same as resilience.

The central argument of this chapter is that supply chains reveal one of the deepest contradictions of modern capitalism: systems optimized for efficiency under normal conditions may become dangerously fragile under stress. For decades, firms were rewarded for reducing inventories, consolidating suppliers, outsourcing production, minimizing costs, standardizing parts, and accelerating logistics. These strategies often worked. They lowered prices, raised profits, expanded consumer choice, and supported global integration. They also removed buffers. They reduced slack. They concentrated risk. They created dependencies that were invisible until disruption arrived.

This is not a simple argument against globalization, trade, or efficiency. Efficiency matters. Waste is costly. International specialization can raise living standards. Global trade can support development, innovation, and peace when embedded in fair institutions. The problem is not that firms sought efficiency. The problem is that efficiency was defined too narrowly. It was measured in terms of cost, speed, inventory turnover, and return on capital, while resilience, redundancy, labor stability, geographic diversity, public capacity, and strategic security were treated as secondary or wasteful. The system became efficient in the sense that it carried less slack, but fragile in the sense that it had less capacity to absorb shocks.

A supply chain is a network. It is composed of producers, suppliers, transporters, warehouses, ports, data systems, insurers, financiers, regulators, workers, energy systems, and customers. Each node depends on others. A factory depends on parts. Parts depend on raw materials. Raw materials depend on extraction, refining, energy, labor, transport, and political stability. A retailer depends on inventory, logistics software, truck drivers, warehouse workers, shipping containers, and consumer demand. A hospital depends on medicines, personal protective equipment, oxygen, syringes, diagnostic tools, cleaning supplies, and staffing. These dependencies form chains, but the word "chain" is actually too linear. Modern production is closer to a web.

Because supply chains are networks, they behave nonlinearly. A disruption at one node can produce disproportionate effects if that node is central, irreplaceable, or tightly coupled to many others. A small component can stop production of a large product. A shortage of microchips can reduce automobile output. A shortage of packaging can limit food distribution. A shortage of active pharmaceutical ingredients can affect healthcare. A labor disruption at a port can delay thousands of products. A storm damaging one industrial region can ripple across sectors. The importance of a node is not measured only by its size. It is measured by its position in the network.

This is why supply-chain fragility often surprises people. The missing input may be small, cheap, or obscure. Yet without it, the final product cannot be completed. A car is not produced when 99 percent of its parts are available. A medicine is not delivered if one critical ingredient is missing. A building is delayed if key materials are unavailable. A meal is not served if food, staff, packaging, and energy do not arrive together. Complex production requires coordination across many parts. Failure in one part can prevent the whole.

The old economic imagination often treated supply as an aggregate curve. If demand rises, supply responds. If prices rise, firms produce more. If shortages occur, higher prices attract investment. These mechanisms exist, but supply chains show why adjustment is neither instant nor smooth. Production takes time. Factories cannot be built overnight. Workers require training. Inputs have their own inputs. Transportation capacity is limited. Contracts, standards, certifications, and regulations shape substitution. A firm cannot always replace a supplier quickly, especially when parts are specialized. A country cannot instantly rebuild an industry after decades of offshoring. Price signals can reveal scarcity, but they cannot always cure it quickly.

This distinction is central to nonlinear economics. A price increase is information, not capacity. If shipping costs rise because ports are congested, the higher price signals scarcity in logistics. But the signal does not immediately create more docks, cranes, truck drivers, warehouses, or chassis. If semiconductor prices rise, the signal may encourage investment, but fabrication plants require enormous capital, specialized knowledge, equipment, water, energy, and time. If food prices rise because drought damages crops, the price signal cannot make rain fall. If energy prices rise because of war, new energy infrastructure may take years. The market signal moves faster than the physical system.

Supply chains therefore reveal the materiality of the economy. Financial markets move at the speed of information. Production moves at the speed of bodies, machines, ships, roads, mines, farms, factories, and institutions. Modern capitalism often forgets this difference because digital transactions make the economy feel instantaneous. A consumer order appears with a click. A payment clears electronically. A firm adjusts a spreadsheet. But the actual good still travels through physical space. It must be made, moved, stored, inspected, delivered, and used. The digital interface hides the material system.

The pursuit of lean production intensified this illusion. Lean systems reduce waste, minimize inventories, and coordinate production closely with demand. When well designed, they can improve quality, reduce cost, and increase responsiveness. The problem arises when lean becomes brittle. Just-in-time inventory systems depend on reliability. If inputs arrive exactly when needed, firms can reduce storage costs and working capital. But if disruption occurs, there is little buffer. The factory stops. The retailer runs out. The hospital lacks supplies. What once looked like wasteful inventory is revealed as a form of resilience.

Inventory is stored time. It is a buffer against uncertainty. It allows a system to continue operating when inputs are delayed. Reducing inventory improves financial efficiency, but it reduces shock absorption. This tradeoff was often ignored or minimized because normal conditions lasted long enough for firms to treat reliability as natural. The longer a system functions smoothly, the more managers are tempted to remove slack. The removal of slack then increases vulnerability to rare but severe disruption. Stability breeds fragility.

This pattern is familiar from financial markets. When volatility is low, leverage rises. When leverage rises, the system becomes fragile. Supply chains follow a parallel logic. When disruptions are rare, inventories fall. When inventories fall, disruption becomes more damaging. When suppliers are reliable, firms consolidate suppliers. When suppliers are consolidated, supplier failure becomes more dangerous. When transport is cheap, production spreads globally. When production spreads globally, logistics shocks travel widely. The system learns the wrong lesson from stability. It concludes that buffers are unnecessary because buffers have not recently been needed.

Efficiency also encouraged supplier concentration. Firms often reduced the number of suppliers to gain bargaining power, simplify coordination, ensure quality, and lower costs. This can be rational. Managing hundreds of suppliers is expensive. Concentration can deepen relationships and improve performance. But concentration creates single points of failure. If a critical supplier fails, there may be no immediate substitute. If multiple firms rely on the same supplier, a disruption affects an entire industry. If the supplier is located in a region exposed to disaster, conflict, or political risk, the vulnerability is geographic as well as commercial.

Single-source and sole-source dependencies are especially dangerous. A single-source arrangement means a firm chooses one supplier, even though others may exist. A sole-source situation means only one supplier can provide the input. Both can reduce cost under normal conditions and raise danger under stress. In complex products, firms may not even fully understand their lower-tier dependencies. A company may know its direct suppliers but not the suppliers of those suppliers. Hidden concentration can exist deep in the network. A shock then reveals that many firms depended on the same obscure input, region, or facility.

The bullwhip effect illustrates another nonlinear feature of supply chains. Small changes in consumer demand can produce larger changes upstream as each participant adjusts orders based on expectations. A retailer sees demand rise and orders more from a wholesaler. The wholesaler, fearing continued demand, orders even more from manufacturers. Manufacturers increase production or orders for inputs. If the initial demand increase was temporary, the system later finds itself with excess inventory. The result is oscillation: shortage, overordering, glut, discounting, and production cuts. The bullwhip effect shows that supply chains are not passive pipes. They are expectation systems.

During disruption, defensive behavior intensifies the bullwhip. Firms that fear shortages may order more than they need. This hoarding behavior is rational individually but destabilizing collectively. If every firm doubles orders to protect itself, suppliers see artificial demand. They allocate scarce goods, raise prices, or expand capacity that may later prove excessive. When the panic ends, inventories pile up. Firms cancel orders.

Producers are left exposed. The supply chain swings from scarcity to surplus. This is the paradox of composition applied to logistics.

Consumers can participate in the same dynamic. If households fear toilet paper, baby formula, gasoline, medicine, or food shortages, they buy more than usual. Increased buying creates the shortage they feared. Retailers impose limits. Media amplify fear. Supply systems strain. Eventually, households have extra inventory and demand falls. A temporary disruption becomes a social episode because expectations spread through networks. The supply chain is not only physical. It is psychological.

Labor is central to supply-chain resilience. Goods do not move themselves. Workers load ships, drive trucks, operate warehouses, harvest crops, process meat, manufacture parts, inspect quality, maintain equipment, design software, repair vehicles, stock shelves, and deliver packages. Supply-chain efficiency has often depended on labor flexibility, low wages, subcontracting, long hours, unpredictable schedules, and intense productivity monitoring. Workers absorb the volatility that firms seek to remove from balance sheets.

The pandemic made this visible. Workers in logistics, healthcare, food production, retail, agriculture, delivery, manufacturing, and transportation were called essential. Yet many had limited protections, modest pay, health risks, and little voice. The supply chain continued because human beings exposed themselves to danger. When workers became ill, quit, demanded better conditions, or could not access childcare, supply chains slowed. Labor was not a separate issue from logistics. It was the living infrastructure of logistics.

This reveals a moral contradiction. A supply chain cannot be resilient if the workers who sustain it are treated as disposable. Low wages, poor safety, weak benefits, and burnout may reduce costs in the short run, but they create turnover, absenteeism, labor shortages, and social resentment. A warehouse optimized for speed but built on exhaustion is fragile. A trucking system dependent on underpaid or overworked drivers is fragile. A food system dependent on vulnerable migrant labor is fragile. A healthcare supply chain dependent on burned-out nurses and aides is fragile. Labor dignity is supply-chain resilience.

The same point applies to suppliers. Large firms may pressure suppliers to reduce costs, shorten delivery times, and hold inventory risk. Suppliers with thin margins have less capacity to invest in resilience. They may underpay workers, reduce maintenance, rely on debt, or avoid redundancy. The lead firm appears efficient because costs and risks have been pushed down the chain. But when disruption occurs, the weakness of suppliers returns to the lead firm as shortage. Efficiency achieved through risk transfer is often fragility disguised as discipline.

Financialization has reinforced this pattern. Firms rewarded by investors for high returns on capital may reduce inventories, outsource assets, sell facilities, subcontract labor, and prioritize shareholder payouts. These choices can improve financial metrics. But they may also weaken the physical and organizational capacity of production. If every firm seeks to minimize working capital, the system as a whole carries less inventory. If every firm seeks to outsource risk, risk accumulates in weaker parts of the network. If every firm prioritizes short-term returns, long-term resilience is underprovided.

This is a key example of the difference between private optimization and system optimization. What is efficient for one firm may be inefficient for society if it increases systemic vulnerability. A firm that relies on one low-cost overseas supplier may reduce consumer prices and increase profits. If many firms do the same for critical goods, the nation may become dependent on a fragile foreign supply base. A firm that keeps minimal inventory may improve financial performance. If many firms do so, the economy becomes vulnerable to disruption. A firm that cuts labor costs may compete effectively. If many firms do so, household income, worker stability, and supply reliability may decline. The collective outcome differs from the individual incentive.

This is why supply chains require public policy. Markets coordinate much production, but they do not automatically produce the socially optimal level of resilience. Firms bear some costs of disruption, but not all. When shortages affect hospitals, national security, food supply, energy, inflation, or employment, the public bears costs. When supply disruption raises prices, households suffer. When critical industries disappear, communities suffer. When dependence on unstable regions creates geopolitical vulnerability, the nation suffers. Resilience has public-good characteristics. Because no single firm can capture all the benefits of systemic resilience, firms underinvest in it.

The underinvestment is especially severe for low-probability, high-impact events. Firms may discount rare shocks because preparing for them reduces current profits. Executives may not be in office when the shock arrives. Investors may punish firms that carry higher inventory or redundant capacity. Consumers may choose cheaper goods without seeing the resilience tradeoff. Governments may assume private markets have handled the risk. Then the crisis arrives, and the public discovers that no one owned responsibility for the system as a whole.

Supply chains also reveal the fragility of global interdependence. Globalization allowed firms to locate production where costs were lower, skills were available, regulations were favorable, or clusters had formed. This produced real gains. Consumers benefited from lower prices. Developing countries gained manufacturing jobs and export income. Firms gained scale. Innovation moved through global networks. But globalization also created dependencies on distant suppliers, long shipping routes, political stability, currency conditions, and international rules. The world economy became more connected, and therefore more exposed to cascading disruption.

The moral evaluation of globalization must therefore be nuanced. It is not enough to say globalization was good because it lowered prices and reduced poverty in some countries. It is not enough to say it was bad because it displaced workers and weakened domestic capacity. Both are true in part. Globalization created abundance and vulnerability, opportunity and dislocation, efficiency and dependency. Its effects depended on institutions, labor standards, industrial policy, adjustment support, trade rules, currency regimes, and corporate strategies. A complexity approach refuses totalizing stories.

The central failure was not global trade itself. It was the ideology that treated global efficiency as self-justifying and assumed that displaced workers, hollowed-out regions, strategic dependencies, and fragile supply systems would adjust smoothly. The adjustment was not smooth. Some communities lost manufacturing ecosystems that could not be easily rebuilt. Workers were told to retrain, but new jobs were often lower paid or located elsewhere. Domestic production capacity disappeared in sectors that later proved important. Firms saved money, consumers saved money, and shareholders gained, but the social costs were uneven and often ignored.

The loss of manufacturing capacity is not only about jobs. Manufacturing ecosystems contain skills, suppliers, engineers, tacit knowledge, maintenance capabilities, training systems, machine-tool expertise, and innovation pathways. Once these ecosystems decline, rebuilding them is difficult. Knowledge is embodied in workers, firms, routines, and supplier relationships. A country cannot always buy back productive capacity quickly because capacity is not merely equipment. It is a network of capabilities.

This is why the phrase "industrial commons" matters. An industrial commons is the shared base of knowledge, suppliers, workers, institutions, and infrastructure that supports production. Firms may draw from this commons without individually owning it. When production is offshored or domestic ecosystems erode, the commons weakens. Innovation may eventually follow production elsewhere because engineers and manufacturers learn from proximity. The loss is not visible immediately in consumer prices. It appears later as reduced resilience, weaker innovation, and strategic dependence.

The pandemic exposed such dependencies in medical supplies, pharmaceuticals, personal protective equipment, semiconductors, and logistics. Societies discovered that critical goods were often produced through distant, concentrated, and fragile networks. Hospitals lacked masks and gowns. Pharmaceutical ingredients depended on foreign production. Semiconductor shortages affected autos, appliances, and electronics. The crisis did not prove that everything must be produced domestically. It did prove that critical supply chains require mapping, redundancy, transparency, and public strategy.

The semiconductor example is especially instructive. Semiconductors are essential inputs into automobiles, phones, computers, defense systems, medical devices, energy infrastructure, artificial intelligence, and industrial machinery. Their production requires highly specialized facilities, equipment, chemicals, talent, intellectual property, and supply networks. Capacity is geographically concentrated. Building new fabrication plants takes years and enormous investment. A shortage in this sector can affect large parts of the economy. The market price of chips cannot instantly create the fabrication capacity needed. This is supply-chain nonlinearity at the heart of modern technology.

Food supply chains have their own fragilities. Food appears abundant in wealthy societies, but the system depends on energy, fertilizer, water, weather, transportation, labor, packaging, processing plants, refrigeration, and trade. Concentration in meatpacking or food processing can create bottlenecks. Climate events can reduce yields. War can disrupt grain and fertilizer. Fuel prices affect transport and farm costs. Labor conditions affect harvests and processing. Food price spikes harm low-income households most because food is essential. Food security is therefore not only an agricultural issue. It is a supply-chain, climate, labor, trade, and justice issue.

Energy supply chains are even more central. Energy is the input into almost every input. Oil, gas, electricity, coal, uranium, batteries, transmission equipment, transformers, solar panels, wind turbines, critical minerals, and refining capacity form the energy foundation of economic life. Energy shocks propagate through transportation, production, heating, food, and inflation. Dependence on a few producers, chokepoints, or fuel types creates vulnerability. The transition to clean energy reduces some fossil-fuel risks but creates new supply-chain needs for minerals, grid equipment, storage, and manufacturing. Energy resilience requires diversification, storage, efficiency, domestic and allied capacity, and public planning.

Critical minerals illustrate the new geography of supply-chain dependence. Batteries, electronics, renewable energy systems, defense technologies, and digital infrastructure depend on minerals such as lithium, cobalt, nickel, rare earth elements, graphite, and copper. Extraction and processing can be geographically concentrated, environmentally damaging, and politically complex. The energy transition cannot be separated from mining, labor rights, indigenous rights, environmental justice, recycling, and geopolitical strategy. A clean technology supply chain can reproduce old extractive patterns if not governed ethically.

Supply chains are also shaped by chokepoints. Chokepoints are narrow passages, facilities, or systems through which large flows must pass. Shipping canals, straits, major ports, rail hubs, pipelines, data cables, cloud providers, payment systems, and critical suppliers can all be chokepoints. Chokepoints create efficiency because concentrating flow can reduce cost. They create vulnerability because disruption can have outsized effects. A ship stuck in a canal, a cyberattack on a port, a conflict near a strait, or failure of a major cloud provider can affect global activity. The map of supply chains is also a map of power.

Geopolitics enters through these chokepoints. Nations can use export controls, sanctions, tariffs, port access, shipping routes, energy supply, technology standards, and investment rules as instruments of power. Firms that once optimized mainly for cost must now consider political risk. Governments that once assumed global markets would provide must consider strategic autonomy. The era of pure efficiency is giving way to an era in which resilience, security, and political alignment matter more. The question is how to manage this transition without abandoning the benefits of openness.

Reshoring and friend-shoring are responses to fragility. Reshoring brings production back domestically. Friend-shoring moves production to allied or trusted countries. Near-shoring moves production closer to end markets. These strategies can reduce some risks, but they are not simple solutions. Domestic production may be more expensive. Allied countries may have their own vulnerabilities. Concentrating production domestically can create local single points of failure. Protectionism can invite retaliation or inefficiency. Supply-chain resilience does not require autarky. It requires diversified, transparent, flexible, and ethically governed networks.

The goal should be strategic diversification. Critical goods should not depend on a single firm, region, route, or political relationship. Redundancy should be built intentionally. Some domestic capacity may be essential for national security, healthcare, energy, and infrastructure. Some international trade remains valuable and necessary. The question is not whether a product is foreign or domestic, but whether the system can survive disruption. A resilient supply chain may include domestic production, allied production, strategic reserves, substitute inputs, recycling, demand management, and emergency coordination.

Strategic reserves are another form of buffer. Governments may store oil, medical supplies, food, rare materials, or essential equipment. Firms may maintain safety stock. Public agencies may support emergency manufacturing capacity. Such reserves are often criticized as costly or inefficient. They require storage, rotation, maintenance, and governance. But their value appears during crisis. A society that refuses to pay for preparedness may pay far more for emergency scarcity. The difficulty is ensuring that reserves are well managed and not treated as symbolic substitutes for broader resilience.

Information is central to supply-chain governance. Many governments and even firms lack full visibility into supply networks. Direct suppliers may be known, but lower-tier suppliers may be obscure. Critical dependencies may be hidden in subcontracting layers. Data may be proprietary. Firms may resist disclosure. Without mapping, policymakers cannot identify vulnerabilities. Supply-chain transparency is therefore a public good. It allows risk assessment, emergency planning, labor enforcement, environmental accountability, and strategic investment.

But transparency must be used wisely. Data alone does not create resilience. A government may know a dependency exists but lack tools to address it. A firm may map suppliers but choose not to diversify because cost pressures dominate. Public policy must align incentives with resilience. This can include reporting requirements, stress testing, procurement standards, tax incentives, public investment, stockpiling, competition policy, and emergency powers. The supply chain must be governed as a system, not merely observed.

Stress testing is a useful concept borrowed from finance. Banks are tested against severe scenarios to see whether they can survive. Supply chains could be similarly tested. What happens if a major port closes? If a key supplier fails? If a pandemic disrupts labor? If a cyberattack disables logistics software? If energy prices spike? If a major exporting country restricts supply? If climate events damage a region? Stress testing does not predict the future exactly. It reveals fragility. It forces firms and governments to ask what conditions would break the system.

Procurement policy can also build resilience. Governments purchase enormous quantities of goods and services. They can use this purchasing power to require domestic or allied capacity for critical goods, labor standards, environmental standards, supplier diversity, cybersecurity, and resilience planning. Public procurement can create markets for resilient production. It can also be misused if captured by political favoritism or inefficient incumbents. Competence and accountability are essential. But procurement is one of the most powerful tools for shaping supply chains before crisis.

Competition policy matters because concentrated supply chains are fragile. When a few firms dominate production, processing, shipping, or distribution, disruption at one firm can affect many. Concentration can also increase pricing power during shortages. Antitrust is therefore not only about consumer prices in normal times. It is about resilience under stress. Competitive diversity can be a buffer. Multiple firms, suppliers, and regions reduce the probability that one failure becomes systemic. A market with redundant capacity may look less efficient, but it may be healthier.

However, redundancy has costs. A society must decide which goods require redundancy and how much. Not every product needs domestic backup or strategic reserves. Some goods are nonessential, easily substituted, or low risk. Others are critical: food, water, energy, medicine, medical equipment, semiconductors, defense inputs, communications, payment systems, and infrastructure components. Resilience policy must be targeted. If everything is treated as critical, resources are wasted. If nothing is treated as critical, society is exposed. The art is classification, not panic.

Climate change requires a new supply-chain imagination. Extreme weather can damage crops, factories, roads, ports, railways, power grids, water systems, and communities. Heat can reduce labor productivity. Drought can limit river transport and hydroelectric power. Floods can damage warehouses and homes. Fires can disrupt utilities and insurance. Sea-level rise threatens ports. Climate risk is not a distant environmental concern. It is a supply-chain risk. As climate shocks increase, past assumptions about reliability may fail.

Climate adaptation should therefore be integrated into supply-chain planning. Ports need resilience. Warehouses need flood protection. Energy systems need redundancy. Food systems need crop diversity and water management. Transportation networks need alternative routes. Firms need climate-risk mapping. Governments need regional planning. Insurance markets need reform. The private sector alone may underinvest because benefits are long term and widely shared. Public investment is necessary.

Cybersecurity is another emerging source of fragility. Supply chains depend on software, communications, cloud services, logistics platforms, digital payments, inventory systems, and industrial control systems. A cyberattack can stop production, delay shipping, compromise data, disrupt energy, or damage trust. Digital efficiency creates digital dependency. Firms may outsource critical functions to a few cloud providers or software vendors. This can improve capability but create systemic risk. Cyber resilience is now supply-chain resilience.

Data systems can also produce fragility through opacity and automation. Automated ordering, pricing, routing, and inventory systems may respond quickly to signals, but they can also amplify errors. If algorithms misread demand, overorder, underorder, or respond similarly across firms, volatility can increase. If platforms control market access, suppliers and sellers become dependent on opaque rules. If logistics software fails, physical goods may be stranded. The digital layer of supply chains must be governed for reliability, transparency, and accountability.

The moral dimension of supply chains extends beyond resilience to labor and environmental justice. Low prices often depend on hidden costs: unsafe factories, low wages, child labor, forced labor, environmental damage, pollution, carbon emissions, and weak regulation. Consumers in wealthy countries may enjoy cheap goods while workers and communities elsewhere bear harm. Supply chains allow distance to obscure responsibility. A shirt, phone, battery, or piece of furniture arrives as a product, not as a history of labor and extraction. A moral political economy must make that history visible.

This does not mean every consumer must trace every product personally. That is impossible. It means institutions must enforce standards. Firms should be responsible for due diligence in their supply networks. Governments should regulate imports tied to forced labor or severe environmental harm. Trade agreements should include labor and environmental protections. Investors should consider supply-chain risk and ethics. Consumers should not be asked to solve systemic problems through individual shopping choices alone. Moral supply chains require public rules.

Environmental costs are often externalized through supply chains. Production may move to countries with weaker environmental protections. Emissions may be counted territorially rather than by consumption. Waste may be exported. Mining may damage local communities. The consumer price does not reflect the full ecological cost. Efficiency measured by price can therefore be false efficiency. It is cheap because someone else, somewhere else, or some future generation pays. A nonlinear economy eventually receives those costs back through climate change, health damage, migration, conflict, and biodiversity loss.

Supply chains also raise questions of sovereignty and democracy. When essential production is controlled by private firms operating across borders, democratic governments may struggle to secure public needs. A government can regulate domestic firms, but supply chains cross jurisdictions. A corporation can shift production, sourcing, profits, and legal responsibility. Workers and communities affected by decisions may have little voice. Democratic accountability weakens when the economy's material foundations are governed by transnational private networks. This does not require rejecting global trade. It requires democratic coordination across borders and stronger public capacity.

Public capacity is crucial. Governments cannot manage supply-chain risk if they lack expertise, data, industrial knowledge, procurement competence, and planning institutions. Decades of market-oriented ideology often weakened public capacity by assuming that private firms would handle production while government merely set broad rules. But crises reveal the need for competent public institutions that understand industries, coordinate emergency response, invest in infrastructure, support innovation, and negotiate with firms from a position of knowledge. A hollow state cannot govern complex supply chains.

Industrial policy is the public effort to shape the structure of production. It can include subsidies, loans, public research, tax credits, procurement, training, infrastructure, standards, trade policy, and coordination. For many years, industrial policy was dismissed in some circles as inefficient government picking winners. Yet every economy has industrial policy in some form, even if implicit. Tax codes, defense spending, infrastructure, trade agreements, intellectual property, education funding, and regulation all shape industries. The real question is whether industrial policy is conscious, competent, democratic, and aligned with public purpose.

Supply-chain fragility has revived industrial policy because societies now see that production structure matters. A country that cannot produce or access critical goods is vulnerable. A country that loses manufacturing ecosystems may lose innovation capacity. A country that depends on adversarial suppliers for essential inputs faces strategic risk. But industrial policy must avoid becoming corporate welfare. Public support should come with public obligations: labor standards, domestic investment, technology sharing where appropriate, environmental standards, profit-sharing, anti-buyback restrictions, accountability, and performance measures. If public money builds supply-chain resilience, public value should be returned.

The distribution of costs and benefits matters. Resilience investments may raise prices in the short run. Domestic production may cost more than lowest-cost imports. Strategic reserves require funding. Workers may need training. Consumers may pay slightly more for goods that are more reliable, ethical, and secure. But the alternative is often hidden cost: shortages, inflation spikes, unemployment, emergency spending, geopolitical vulnerability, and human suffering. Cheapness is not the same as affordability if it creates future crisis. A resilient economy may cost more visibly and less catastrophically.

This distinction is central to the book's argument. Linear thinking looks at the immediate price. Complexity thinking looks at the system cost. A supply chain that produces a low price today by relying on forced labor, environmental destruction, single-source suppliers, fragile logistics, and geopolitical dependency is not truly cheap. It is deferring cost into risk. A supply chain that costs slightly more but supports decent labor, environmental sustainability, supplier diversity, and shock absorption may be more efficient over time. Efficiency must be redefined to include resilience.

This redefinition requires new metrics. Firms and policymakers should not measure supply chains only by cost, speed, and inventory turnover. They should measure supplier diversity, geographic concentration, inventory buffers, substitution capacity, labor stability, emissions, climate exposure, cyber risk, financial health of suppliers, dependence on chokepoints, and recovery time after disruption. The key question is not only, "How cheaply can this system operate when everything goes right?" It is also, "How well does this system perform when something goes wrong?"

Recovery time is a crucial metric. A resilient system is not one that never fails. No system can guarantee that. A resilient system fails gracefully and recovers quickly. It has alternatives, buffers, information, trust, and coordination. It prevents local failure from becoming systemic collapse. It protects vulnerable people during disruption. It learns after shocks. Resilience is not rigidity. It is adaptive capacity.

Adaptive capacity depends on diversity. Biological ecosystems are more resilient when they contain diversity because different species respond differently to shocks. Economic systems are similar. A supply chain with multiple suppliers, regions, transport routes, technologies, and firms can adapt better than one optimized around a single pathway. Diversity may reduce short-term efficiency, but it increases optionality. In uncertain environments, optionality has value. It allows systems to respond to unknown shocks.

Modularity is another resilience principle. A modular system contains parts that can fail without bringing down the whole. If components are standardized and interchangeable, substitution becomes easier. If systems are tightly integrated and customized, failure can be harder to manage. Modularity can conflict with efficiency or performance, but it can improve resilience. In supply chains, this may mean designing products with substitute parts, maintaining multiple qualified suppliers, using open standards, or reducing excessive complexity where possible.

Local capacity also matters. Global networks are valuable, but local and regional production can provide speed, flexibility, and emergency response. Local food systems, distributed energy, regional manufacturing, repair capacity, and community-based logistics can complement global trade. The goal is not to replace global systems entirely. It is to avoid total dependence on distant systems for everything. A resilient economy combines scales: local, regional, national, allied, and global.

Repair and maintenance deserve more attention. Modern economies often focus on production and consumption while undervaluing repair. A society with strong repair capacity can extend the life of goods, reduce waste, respond to shortages, and preserve functionality during disruption. Skilled trades, spare parts, maintenance workers, machine shops, and local technical knowledge are resilience assets. Yet they are often undervalued compared with new production or digital services. Supply-chain resilience requires honoring practical capabilities.

The circular economy is relevant here. Recycling, reuse, remanufacturing, repair, and material recovery can reduce dependence on virgin inputs and fragile supply chains. Critical minerals, plastics, metals, electronics, and construction materials can be managed more sustainably. A circular economy is not only environmental policy. It is supply-chain policy. It creates domestic material streams, reduces waste, and lowers exposure to extraction bottlenecks. But circular systems require design, infrastructure, regulation, and markets. They do not emerge automatically from good intentions.

Demand management is another overlooked tool. During shortages, societies often focus only on increasing supply. But demand can also be managed through conservation, substitution, rationing in emergencies, efficiency standards, public communication, and price design. Energy efficiency reduces exposure to fuel shocks. Public transit reduces dependence on gasoline. Reducing food waste reduces pressure on agricultural supply chains. Standardization can reduce parts complexity. Demand-side resilience is not austerity. It is intelligent use of resources.

Emergency rationing is politically sensitive, but in severe crises it may be fairer than price allocation alone. If essential goods are scarce, allowing prices to rise without limit may allocate goods to those with money rather than those with need. Temporary rationing, priority allocation, anti-hoarding rules, and public procurement may be necessary for medical supplies, vaccines, fuel, food, or disaster materials. Markets are useful, but emergencies require moral allocation. A society should decide in advance how essential scarcity will be governed.

Inflation connects directly to supply-chain fragility. When supply systems fail, prices rise. If the goods are essential or central inputs, the price increases spread. Energy, food, transportation, semiconductors, housing materials, and medical supplies can all transmit inflation. Supply-chain inflation is especially difficult because monetary policy can reduce demand but cannot immediately repair supply. Raising interest rates may cool spending, but it does not unclog a port, build a chip plant, end a war, produce fertilizer, or train truck drivers. It may even reduce investment needed to expand capacity.

This does not mean monetary policy is irrelevant. If supply shocks trigger broad inflation expectations, monetary action may be necessary. But supply-chain inflation requires supply-chain policy. Infrastructure investment, competition policy, strategic reserves, logistics modernization, energy resilience, and industrial capacity all matter. Price stability depends partly on physical resilience. Central banks cannot be the only inflation managers in a supply-constrained world.

Supply chains also connect to inequality. Shortages and price spikes harm low-income households more because they spend a larger share of income on essentials. Wealthy households can absorb delays, pay higher prices, buy substitutes, stock up, or use premium services. Poor households cannot. A supply-chain crisis becomes a class crisis when essentials are scarce. The distribution of buffers determines the distribution of pain.

Small businesses are also vulnerable. Large firms may have purchasing power, inventory systems, logistics contracts, and access to capital. Small firms may face higher input prices, delayed deliveries, and inability to pass costs to customers. They may be squeezed between suppliers and consumers. A supply-chain shock can therefore increase market concentration if large firms survive and small firms fail. Crisis becomes an opportunity for consolidation. Resilience policy should protect competitive diversity, not only national capacity.

This is another reason public support during crises must be designed carefully. If emergency credit, subsidies, or supply allocations favor large incumbents, the system may become more concentrated after the crisis. If small firms lack access, communities lose local businesses. If workers are not protected, labor shortages and hardship deepen. Crisis response shapes the post-crisis economy. Cascades do not end when the immediate disruption passes. They leave institutional and market traces.

Supply-chain fragility also affects public trust. When citizens cannot obtain basic goods, when prices rise suddenly, when leaders appear unprepared, or when firms seem to profit from scarcity, trust declines. People begin to doubt competence. They may hoard, blame, or turn to conspiracy narratives. Supply-chain failure becomes political failure. The state is judged not only by laws and speeches, but by whether society can provide food, medicine, energy, and functioning infrastructure. Material reliability is a foundation of legitimacy.

This is an old truth rediscovered in modern form. States have always been judged by their ability to secure basic goods, maintain roads, manage disasters, and protect life. Market societies sometimes forget this because private firms provide most goods most of the time. But when the private system fails, citizens turn to public authority. If public authority lacks tools, legitimacy suffers. The distinction between public and private becomes less important than the practical question: can the system deliver what life requires?

A democratic society must therefore build supply-chain resilience openly and fairly. It should not use resilience as a cover for nationalism, corruption, corporate favoritism, or permanent emergency powers. It should explain tradeoffs. It should identify critical goods. It should involve workers, firms, communities, scientists, engineers, and local governments. It should protect labor and environmental standards. It should coordinate with allies. It should maintain transparency. Resilience should strengthen democracy, not bypass it.

International cooperation remains essential. No country can or should produce everything. Many supply-chain risks are global: pandemics, climate change, shipping security, cyberattacks, financial instability, forced labor, and environmental degradation. Cooperation can include shared reserves, mutual aid agreements, diversified production among allies, common labor standards, climate adaptation finance, technology partnerships, and crisis communication. Resilience should not become a retreat into isolation. It should become a more intelligent form of interdependence.

Interdependence is not the enemy. Blind interdependence is. Interdependence with transparency, redundancy, standards, mutual obligation, and democratic oversight can be a source of peace and prosperity. Interdependence without buffers, ethics, or strategic awareness becomes vulnerability. The goal is not to cut the world apart, but to connect it more wisely.

This chapter's argument can be summarized through a simple distinction: efficiency asks how to minimize cost under expected conditions; resilience asks how to preserve function under unexpected conditions. A healthy economy needs both. Too much inefficiency wastes resources and burdens households. Too little resilience invites catastrophic failure. The problem of recent decades is that efficiency was often elevated into an ideology. Anything that did not contribute to immediate cost reduction was suspect. Inventories were waste. Redundant suppliers were waste. Domestic capacity was waste. Public stockpiles were waste. Worker slack was waste. The crisis revealed that some of this so-called waste was actually insurance.

Insurance always looks unnecessary before the loss. This is why resilience requires a different political imagination. It requires valuing what does not happen: the shortage avoided, the factory that keeps running, the hospital that has supplies, the household that does not face a price spike, the community that does not lose jobs, the country that does not become dependent on a hostile power. Prevention is harder to celebrate than rescue, but it is more humane.

The moral question is whether society is willing to pay for durability. A cheap system that breaks under stress is not just a technical failure. It is a failure of responsibility. It shifts costs onto those least able to bear them:

workers, low-income households, patients, small firms, future generations, and communities without alternatives. The affluent can often buy their way around scarcity. The vulnerable cannot. Resilience is therefore a justice issue.

The next chapter turns to financial markets, herding, and cascades. The connection is direct. Supply chains and financial markets share a common pattern: systems optimized for return under normal conditions can become fragile under stress. In finance, leverage replaces inventory as the hidden vulnerability. In supply chains, just-in-time logistics replaces capital buffers. In both cases, private actors may reduce their own costs while increasing systemic risk. In both cases, calm can breed overconfidence. In both cases, crisis reveals interdependence.

Supply chains also connect back to every prior chapter. They shape inflation through shortages and costs. They interact with debt because firms and households face stress when goods and prices move unexpectedly. They reinforce inequality because shortages harm those without buffers. They connect to housing through construction materials, labor, land, and infrastructure. They depend on labor markets and worker dignity. They reveal nonlinearity through chokepoints, bullwhip effects, and cascades. They show why equilibrium thinking fails when supply cannot adjust smoothly.

A complexity economics approach asks us to see supply chains as living systems of production, not invisible plumbing. They require maintenance, trust, redundancy, labor, knowledge, and public stewardship. They can create abundance, but they can also transmit fragility. They can connect the world, but they can also hide exploitation. They can lower prices, but they can also defer costs into future crises. They are not morally neutral. They embody choices about labor, place, environment, security, and time.

The old economics of supply chains celebrated optimization. The new economics must ask what is being optimized and at whose risk. If the answer is short-term cost at the expense of workers, communities, ecosystems, and systemic resilience, then the optimization is false. If the answer is reliable provision of essential goods, decent work, environmental responsibility, innovation, and adaptability, then efficiency can be reconciled with resilience.

Supply chains teach one of the most important lessons of a nonlinear world: the absence of failure is not proof of strength. A system may function for years because conditions remain favorable. That does not mean it is prepared. A bridge may stand until the flood arrives. A bank may profit until liquidity disappears. A housing market may rise until a generation is excluded. A supply chain may deliver until a critical node fails. The task of governance is to see fragility before collapse, to value buffers before crisis, and to build systems that do not depend on permanent good luck.

The economy of the future will face more shocks, not fewer. Climate instability, geopolitical conflict, cyber risk, pandemics, technological dependency, resource constraints, and political fragmentation will test supply systems repeatedly. A society that clings to the old model of lowest-cost optimization will experience recurring surprise. A society that builds resilience will still face shocks, but it will face them with capacity, fairness, and legitimacy.

The choice is not between efficiency and resilience. The choice is between shallow efficiency and deep efficiency. Shallow efficiency minimizes visible cost today. Deep efficiency includes the cost of failure, the value of preparedness, the dignity of labor, the importance of public trust, and the survival of critical functions. Deep efficiency understands that a system that collapses is not efficient. It was merely underpriced.

Supply chains are the material proof that the economy is not a machine operating in frictionless space. It is a world of ships, ports, roads, warehouses, workers, software, energy, land, weather, politics, and time. It is a world in which a missing part can stop an industry, a port delay can raise prices, a labor shortage can expose dependence, a war can reorder production, and a climate shock can travel through grocery bills. To understand supply chains is to understand that economic life is embodied, connected, and vulnerable.

A humane political economy must therefore govern supply chains not as private cost-minimization devices alone, but as systems that sustain social life. Food, medicine, energy, housing materials, communications, and critical technologies are not ordinary commodities in moments of crisis. They are conditions of collective survival. The institutions that produce and distribute them must be judged by more than price.

The fragility of efficiency is not an argument for waste. It is an argument for wisdom. It asks us to distinguish waste from redundancy, cheapness from value, speed from reliability, and profit from resilience. It asks us to design supply systems that can bend without breaking. It asks us to honor the workers who make continuity possible. It asks us to remember that the economy's hidden networks become visible only when they fail, and that a just society should not wait for failure before learning how much it depends on them.

In a nonlinear world, supply chains are not background. They are destiny in motion. They determine whether abundance is real or fragile, whether efficiency serves life or endangers it, whether interdependence becomes solidarity or vulnerability. The lesson is clear: a society that removes every buffer in the name of efficiency should not be shocked when the system cannot absorb shock. A society that builds resilience may appear less efficient in calm times, but it will prove wiser in crisis.

The future belongs not to the cheapest supply chain, but to the most intelligently resilient one. That is the lesson modern economies must learn before the next cascade arrives.

## Chapter 11

# Financial Markets, Herding, and Cascades

FINANCIAL MARKETS ARE often described as the nervous system of capitalism. They gather information, price risk, allocate capital, reward innovation, discipline failure, and translate expectations about the future into present values. A stock price expresses a judgment about future earnings. A bond yield expresses a judgment about creditworthiness, inflation, and time. A currency value expresses a judgment about national credibility, interest rates, trade, and confidence. A commodity price expresses a judgment about scarcity, demand, storage, weather, geopolitics, and production. Financial markets are, in this sense, systems of collective interpretation. They do not merely record the economy. They think about it.

This is the source of their power and their danger. Financial markets are valuable because they can aggregate dispersed information faster than any central planner. Millions of investors, lenders, traders, analysts, firms, households, and institutions bring their judgments into prices. Capital moves toward promising uses and away from failing ones. Risk is transferred. Savings become investment. Entrepreneurs obtain funding. Governments finance infrastructure. Households receive mortgages. Firms issue bonds and equity. Pension funds invest for retirement. In their best form, financial markets convert uncertainty into organized economic possibility.

But financial markets are not neutral mirrors of value. They are social systems filled with feedback loops, incentives, narratives, imitation, leverage, fear, ambition, and institutional pressure. They do not simply discover the future. They help create it. A rising stock price can lower a firm's cost of capital, attract talent, validate strategy, support acquisitions, and strengthen the firm's actual prospects. A falling stock price can raise financing costs, damage confidence, trigger downgrades, encourage employee departures, and weaken the firm it appears merely to evaluate. A sovereign bond selloff can raise borrowing costs, worsen fiscal conditions, and make default more likely. A bank run can destroy an institution because people fear it may be destroyed. Expectations become causes.

This reflexive quality makes financial markets profoundly nonlinear. Prices shape beliefs, beliefs shape behavior, behavior shapes prices, and prices shape fundamentals. Herding emerges when investors watch one another. Cascades occur when selling, withdrawal, margin calls, downgrades, and fear spread through interconnected balance sheets. Financial instability rarely comes from one bad judgment alone. It comes from the interaction of judgments, incentives, leverage, and liquidity. A market can be wrong collectively not because every participant is foolish, but because each participant is responding rationally to the behavior of others.

The central argument of this chapter is that financial markets are not merely information-processing mechanisms. They are amplification systems. They can amplify knowledge, investment, and innovation. They can also amplify error, speculation, panic, inequality, and crisis. When governed well, they serve productive enterprise and social resilience. When governed poorly, they become engines of self-reinforcing boom and bust. The problem is not finance itself. The problem is finance detached from its proper purpose: to support the real economy, allocate capital responsibly, and distribute risk without endangering society.

The elegant theory of efficient markets begins with an important insight. Financial prices often incorporate information quickly. If a company reports strong earnings, investors respond. If inflation rises, bond yields may move. If a war threatens oil supply, energy prices adjust. If a central bank changes interest rates, currencies and stocks react. No single person needs to command this response. Markets coordinate interpretation through prices. This is remarkable. It is one of the most powerful forms of decentralized intelligence in economic life.

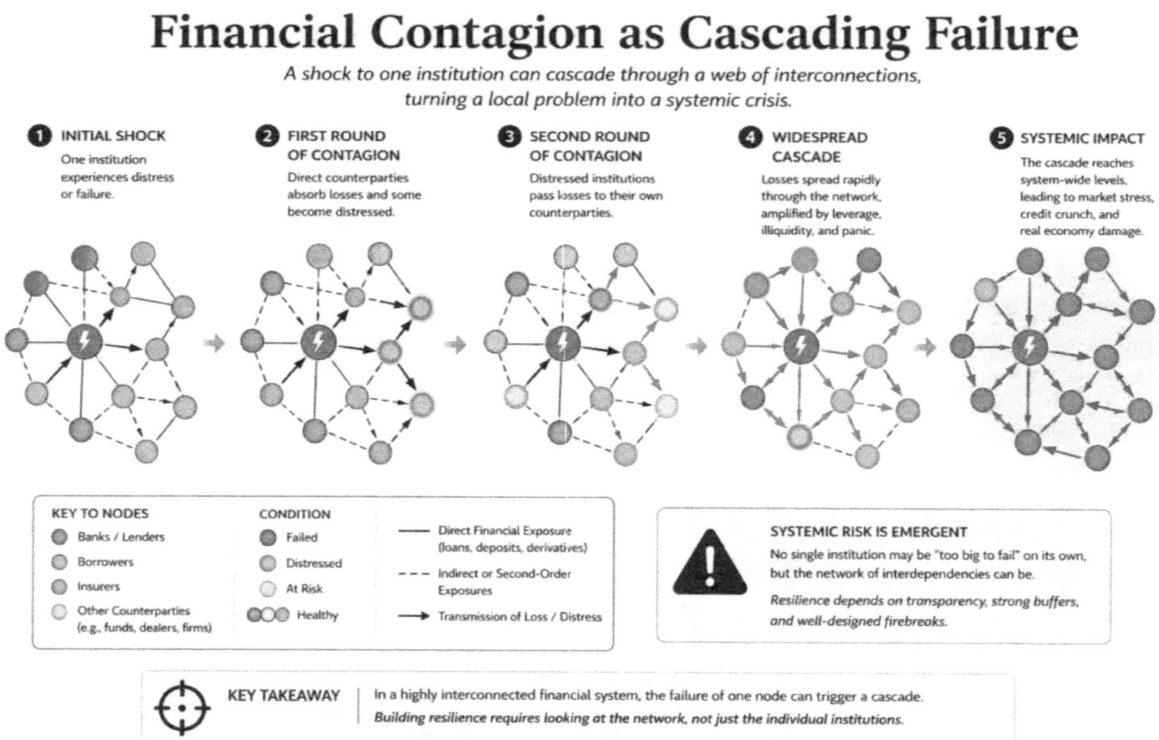


*Figure 6.0 – Financial Contagion as Cascading Failure*

Yet the efficient-market ideal becomes misleading when it assumes that prices reliably reflect fundamental value. Markets do not process information in a vacuum. They process information through institutions, incentives, models, narratives, time horizons, and crowd psychology. Investors are not isolated calculators. They are professionals competing against benchmarks, funds seeking flows, traders managing risk limits, algorithms reacting to signals, households watching headlines, firms issuing guidance, analysts interpreting stories, and central banks shaping expectations. Their behavior is interconnected.

The price of an asset is not only a judgment about fundamentals. It is also a judgment about what others will judge. An investor may believe a stock is overvalued and still buy it if the investor expects others to keep buying. A fund manager may privately doubt a bubble but fear underperforming competitors. A bank may loosen standards because rivals are gaining market share. A trader may sell not because the asset is worthless, but because others are selling and liquidity may vanish. The market is a hall of mirrors in which beliefs about beliefs matter.

This is the foundation of herding. Herding occurs when actors imitate or follow the behavior of others rather than relying solely on their independent assessment. Herding is often portrayed as irrational, but it can be rational under uncertainty. If others appear to possess information, following them may seem sensible. If one's career depends on relative performance, being wrong with the crowd may be safer than being right alone. If liquidity is uncertain, leaving early may be prudent. If prices rise persistently, the market itself appears to be providing evidence. Herding becomes rational at the individual level and dangerous at the collective level.

Professional finance often intensifies herding. Fund managers are judged against peers and benchmarks. If a manager avoids a booming sector and the sector continues rising, clients may withdraw funds. If the manager joins the crowd and the sector later falls, the manager can say that everyone was exposed. Career risk encourages conformity. The fear is not merely losing money. It is losing money differently from others. This creates a powerful incentive to participate in trends even when doubts remain.

This dynamic helps explain bubbles. A bubble is not simply an episode of stupidity. It is a social process through which rising prices become their own justification. A new technology, financial innovation, housing market, commodity, cryptocurrency, or business model captures imagination. Early gains attract attention. Attention brings new buyers. New buyers raise prices. Rising prices validate the narrative. Media coverage expands. Skeptics are mocked. Credit becomes more available. Valuation metrics are revised. Old rules are declared obsolete. The boom becomes a story about a new era.

Narratives are essential to bubbles. Financial markets do not trade only numbers. They trade stories about the future. A company is not merely a set of cash flows. It is a story about growth, dominance, disruption, management, technology, or transformation. A housing market is not merely shelter. It is a story about safety, scarcity, status, and inevitable appreciation. A currency is not merely a medium of exchange. It is a story about national strength and institutional credibility. A commodity is not merely a material input. It is a story about scarcity and demand. When a narrative becomes widely believed, capital flows toward it and helps make it temporarily true.

This is why bubbles can persist longer than skeptics expect. The rising price is not an external fact separate from the story. It is part of the story's evidence. Investors who doubt the fundamentals may still profit if they enter before others. This creates the logic of the greater fool, although many participants would not describe it that way. They may believe the asset is expensive but still expect to sell to someone more optimistic. The bubble becomes a coordination game. The danger is not merely being wrong. It is being late.

Leverage magnifies the bubble. Borrowed money allows investors to buy more assets than their own capital would permit. Rising prices increase collateral values. Higher collateral values support more borrowing. More borrowing supports more buying. The feedback loop accelerates. During the boom, leverage appears to increase returns without increasing visible risk. Volatility may be low. Defaults may be low. Liquidity may be abundant. The system seems safe precisely because the boom has not yet reversed.

But leverage changes the nature of decline. An unleveraged investor can wait. A leveraged investor may be forced to sell. If prices fall, collateral values decline. Lenders demand additional margin. Borrowers sell assets to meet margin calls. Selling pushes prices lower. Lower prices trigger more margin calls. This is a cascade. It is not a sequence of independent decisions. It is a system-wide mechanism of forced adjustment. Prices fall not only because beliefs changed, but because balance sheets require action.

Liquidity is the second great amplifier. Liquidity means the ability to sell an asset quickly at a price close to its perceived value. In calm markets, liquidity appears plentiful. Traders buy and sell. Spreads are narrow. Assets are easily financed. Models assume exit is possible. But liquidity can disappear when everyone wants to sell at once. A market that was deep yesterday becomes thin today. Prices gap downward. Assets cannot be sold without large losses. Institutions discover that liquidity was not a permanent property of the asset. It was a social condition dependent on confidence.

This is one of the most dangerous illusions in finance. Many assets appear liquid because markets are liquid in normal times. But their liquidity under stress may be much lower. If funds promise investors daily withdrawals while holding assets that cannot be sold quickly, they create a mismatch. If banks rely on short-term funding while holding long-term assets, they create a mismatch. If traders finance positions overnight, they create a mismatch. If pension funds or insurers use leverage tied to collateral values, they create a mismatch. When stress arrives, liquidity needs become synchronized. Everyone wants cash at once.

Cash becomes the ultimate asset in crisis because it settles obligations. A firm may own valuable assets and still fail if it cannot meet immediate claims. A bank may have long-term assets and still collapse if depositors withdraw. A fund may hold securities that will eventually recover but still be forced to sell to meet redemptions. Finance is therefore governed by time. Long-term value can be destroyed by short-term pressure. A market can be fundamentally solvent but immediately illiquid. If illiquidity persists, solvency can fail. This is the nonlinear movement from fear to fact.

Financial cascades often begin in one of several ways: an asset price falls, a borrower defaults, a funding source disappears, a rating changes, a rumor spreads, a policy shifts, or a shock alters expectations. The initial event may be modest. The cascade depends on the system's structure. Are institutions leveraged? Are they holding similar assets? Are their funding sources short term? Are they connected through derivatives or collateral? Are investors crowded into the same trade? Are risk models similar? Are there credible backstops? Are regulators trusted? The shock is only the spark. Fragility is the fuel.

The global financial crisis demonstrated this with devastating clarity. The trigger was housing and mortgage credit, but the crisis spread because mortgage debt had been transformed into securities, derivatives, bank assets, shadow-bank funding structures, and global portfolios. The system was tightly connected through leverage and confidence. Rising home prices had supported lending. Lending had supported home prices. Mortgage products had been packaged and rated. Investors had relied on ratings. Institutions had financed long-term assets with short-term funding. When housing prices fell and defaults rose, the losses were not contained. They moved through the network.

The crisis was a failure of market discipline because the actors who were supposed to discipline risk were part of the risk-generating system. Mortgage originators did not always hold the loans they made. Rating agencies were paid by issuers. Investors relied on models that underestimated correlated losses. Regulators trusted financial innovation too much. Banks moved exposures off balance sheet or into complex structures. Compensation systems rewarded short-term gains. Shareholders enjoyed profits during the boom. Taxpayers absorbed catastrophic risk during the bust. The system rewarded fragility until fragility became public.

This is the central moral problem of financial markets: private gain often precedes public risk. In normal times, profits flow to shareholders, executives, traders, and investors. In crisis, the state may be forced to intervene to protect the payment system, depositors, credit flows, employment, and the broader economy. If public rescue is necessary, then finance is not merely private enterprise. It is a public utility wrapped in private incentives. That does not mean finance should be nationalized wholesale. It means financial institutions must be governed with public obligations equal to their systemic importance.

Too-big-to-fail institutions present a special danger. If an institution is so large, interconnected, or central that its collapse would endanger the economy, then markets may assume it will be rescued. This lowers its funding costs and encourages risk-taking. Managers may claim private autonomy while benefiting from implicit public support. Such institutions occupy an ambiguous zone: private in profit, public in danger. Democracy should not tolerate this ambiguity without strict regulation, credible resolution mechanisms, capital requirements, size constraints where necessary, and accountability for management.

The problem extends beyond traditional banks. Shadow banking, private credit, hedge funds, money market funds, derivatives markets, stablecoins, and other nonbank financial structures can create systemic risk. They may promise liquidity, use leverage, rely on collateral, or become central to credit provision without the same regulatory safeguards as banks. Risk often migrates to the least regulated space because finance is adaptive. Once rules are written for one sector, innovation may move risk elsewhere. Regulation must follow function, not merely legal form. If an institution behaves like a bank in systemic terms, it should be supervised for bank-like risks.

Herding is strengthened by common models. Modern financial institutions often use similar risk models, data sources, benchmarks, and regulatory metrics. This can create the illusion of scientific precision while increasing systemic similarity. If many institutions measure risk the same way, they may buy the same assets during calm periods and sell the same assets during stress. If models rely on recent historical volatility, they may declare assets safe precisely when long calm has encouraged leverage. If correlations are assumed to be stable, crises may reveal that correlations rise when diversification is most needed. The model does not simply describe behavior. It can shape behavior.

This creates model risk at the systemic level. A model can be wrong not only because its assumptions fail, but because widespread use of the model changes the market. If many traders follow similar signals, their trades move prices. If many funds rebalance based on volatility targets, rising volatility triggers selling. If many institutions use value-at-risk constraints, price declines force risk reduction. If many investors track the same index, index inclusion attracts flows and exclusion triggers outflows. Financial models become part of the feedback system. They are not outside observers.

Algorithmic trading accelerates this process. Algorithms can process information and execute trades faster than humans. They can improve liquidity, reduce transaction costs, and detect patterns. But they can also amplify speed, correlation, and opacity. If algorithms respond to similar signals, selling can intensify quickly. If market-making algorithms withdraw during stress, liquidity can vanish. If automated systems interact in unexpected ways, flash crashes can occur. Speed becomes a source of fragility when governance and human judgment cannot respond as quickly as the system moves.

The rise of passive investing creates another complex dynamic. Index funds and exchange-traded funds provide low-cost diversification for investors, which is a major benefit. They have democratized access to broad market returns. But at large scale, passive flows can alter market structure. Money flows into securities because they are in an index, not necessarily because of independent evaluation. Large asset managers gain governance power over corporations. Market movements may become more correlated as investors buy and sell baskets of assets. Passive investing is not bad, but like any dominant structure, it changes the system.

Financial markets also produce inequality through asset ownership. When asset prices rise, those who own assets gain wealth. Those who depend mainly on wages do not benefit directly. Monetary policy that supports asset prices may stabilize the economy, but it can also widen wealth inequality if gains accrue disproportionately to asset owners. Low interest rates may raise stock and housing prices. Quantitative easing may support financial markets. These policies may be necessary in crisis, but their distributional effects should not be ignored. Stabilization can become unequal if not paired with labor, housing, tax, and social policy.

This is one reason many citizens distrust financial rescue. They see markets fall and receive support. They see banks protected. They see asset prices recover. But they may also see wages stagnate, debts remain, homes lost, rents rise, and public services strained. The technical justification for rescue may be valid: allowing financial collapse would harm everyone. But legitimacy depends on design. Rescue without justice breeds anger. A system that rescues finance while abandoning households teaches citizens that risk is socialized upward and discipline is imposed downward.

The politics of finance is therefore inseparable from democracy. Financial markets can discipline governments through bond yields, currency pressure, capital flight, and investor sentiment. Sometimes this discipline prevents irresponsible policy. Sometimes it constrains democratic choices. Governments that depend on market confidence may hesitate to invest, redistribute, regulate, or respond to social needs. The phrase "the markets will not like it" becomes a political argument. Financial power shapes the boundaries of policy.

This does not mean governments can ignore financial markets. Public borrowing requires trust. Inflation, currency stability, debt sustainability, and institutional credibility matter. But democratic societies must not allow financial markets to become unelected sovereigns. The challenge is to build fiscal, monetary, and financial institutions that maintain credibility while preserving democratic capacity. A state captured by markets cannot govern justice. A state that ignores markets may face crisis. The answer is neither submission nor denial. It is disciplined public sovereignty.

Sovereign debt markets reveal this tension. Investors buy government bonds based on expectations about inflation, growth, fiscal policy, central bank action, political stability, and currency risk. If confidence declines, yields rise. Higher yields raise debt service costs. Higher costs worsen fiscal projections. Worsened projections raise investor concern. A feedback loop can emerge. In extreme cases, market fear helps create the crisis it fears. A country may be pushed toward austerity, default, or external support. The line between market discipline and self-fulfilling panic can be thin.

Currency markets operate similarly. A falling currency can improve exports, but it can also raise import prices and inflation, especially for energy, food, and foreign-currency debt. If investors expect depreciation, they may sell the currency, causing depreciation. Central banks may raise rates to defend the currency, slowing the economy. Governments may face political pressure. A currency crisis can become a national legitimacy crisis because money is not merely a financial instrument. It is a symbol of state credibility.

Financial markets are also vulnerable to contagion across borders. A crisis in one country can lead investors to reassess risks in others. They may sell assets in countries that appear similar, even if fundamentals differ. Funds facing losses in one market may sell assets in another to raise cash. Currency depreciation in one region may trigger fear elsewhere. Global finance connects economies through portfolios, funding markets, banks, investor narratives, and risk appetite. Contagion is not always rational in a fundamental sense, but it is rational as liquidity behavior. If investors fear others will flee, they flee first.

Emerging markets often bear the burden of global financial cycles. When interest rates are low in advanced economies, capital may flow into higher-yielding assets abroad. This can support investment, but it can also inflate credit and currency values. When global rates rise or risk appetite falls, capital flows reverse. Borrowing costs rise. Currencies weaken. Debt burdens increase. Domestic policy space narrows. A country may suffer crisis not only because of its own policies, but because of the global financial cycle. Finance transmits power internationally.

This is why the global financial architecture is a moral issue. Countries do not participate in global markets on equal terms. Some issue reserve currencies. Others borrow in foreign currency. Some can stabilize crisis through central bank balance sheets. Others face capital flight. Some receive rapid liquidity support. Others face austerity conditions. Global finance can support development, but it can also subordinate weaker economies to volatile capital and creditor power. A just international order would include fairer debt restructuring, liquidity facilities, capital-flow management tools, climate finance, and development-oriented investment.

Financialization is the broader process through which financial motives, markets, and metrics expand into the rest of the economy. Firms become increasingly focused on shareholder value, stock prices, buybacks, leverage, mergers, and financial returns. Households become dependent on credit, mortgages, retirement accounts, and asset appreciation. Governments become sensitive to bond markets and ratings. Universities, hospitals, housing, infrastructure, and even care systems are evaluated through financial logic. Finance moves from serving the economy to shaping it.

Financialization changes corporate behavior. If executives are compensated heavily in stock, they have incentives to raise share prices. This may encourage innovation and efficiency, but it may also encourage buybacks, cost cutting, wage suppression, mergers, tax avoidance, underinvestment, and short-termism. A firm may choose to return cash to shareholders rather than invest in workers, capacity, or resilience. Financial markets then reward the behavior, reinforcing it. The stock price becomes not only a measure of performance, but a governor of strategy.

Share buybacks illustrate the ambiguity. Buybacks can be reasonable if a firm has excess cash and no productive investment opportunities. They can return capital to shareholders who may invest elsewhere. But buybacks become problematic when they are used to manipulate earnings per share, enrich executives, substitute for investment, or distribute cash after public support. If firms use profits to buy shares while underinvesting in workers, supply capacity, safety, or research, financial performance may improve while social productivity weakens. The market rewards extraction from the firm rather than investment through the firm.

Private equity, hedge funds, and activist investors can sometimes improve inefficient firms, challenge complacent management, and reallocate capital. They can also intensify financial pressure. A firm acquired with debt may be forced to cut costs, sell assets, raise prices, reduce staffing, or focus on short-term cash flow. Workers, suppliers, customers, and communities may bear the consequences. The question is not whether private capital is inherently good or bad. It is whether financial control improves productive capacity or extracts value while increasing fragility.

Financial markets also transform housing, as Chapter 8 argued. Mortgages become securities. Rental housing becomes an asset class. Institutional investors buy homes. Short-term return expectations shape shelter. When finance enters housing, it can expand capital for construction and ownership. It can also intensify speculation, raise rents, and detach housing from local need. The value of a home becomes a financial yield. The tenant becomes a revenue stream. The neighborhood becomes a portfolio. Financialization of housing turns a basic need into a vehicle of accumulation.

A similar pattern appears in healthcare, education, and infrastructure. When essential services are governed by financial return, social purpose may be subordinated. Hospitals may be loaded with debt. Nursing homes may be acquired and cost-cut. Colleges may raise tuition because credit is available. Infrastructure may be privatized through contracts that guarantee returns while shifting risks to the public. Finance can bring capital, but capital has claims. If the claims exceed the social purpose, the institution is distorted.

Speculation is not limited to financial assets. It can enter commodities, housing, land, carbon credits, cryptocurrencies, art, collectibles, and even essential goods. Speculation can improve liquidity and price discovery, but it can also amplify volatility. When financial investors enter commodity markets at scale, price movements may reflect portfolio flows as well as physical supply and demand. When farmland becomes an investment vehicle, food systems change. When water rights are financialized, ethical concerns intensify. The boundary between productive investment and speculative claim becomes politically important.

Cryptocurrency and digital assets illustrate several themes of this chapter: narrative, herding, reflexivity, speculation, technological promise, and regulatory lag. Some digital assets emerged from a critique of centralized money and finance. Some innovations may have future value in payments, contracts, or decentralized systems. But much of the digital asset boom displayed classic speculative dynamics: rising prices, charismatic narratives, fear of missing out, leverage, opaque institutions, celebrity promotion, regulatory gaps, and retail exposure. The lesson is not that all digital financial innovation is worthless. It is that new technology does not repeal old financial psychology.

Retail investors are increasingly drawn into financial markets through apps, social media, commission-free trading, options, cryptocurrencies, meme stocks, and online communities. This democratizes access in one sense. Ordinary people can invest, coordinate, learn, and challenge institutions. But it also exposes households to volatility, manipulation, leverage, and speculative narratives. If wages are stagnant and wealth inequality high, speculation may appear as one of the few available paths to financial mobility. The casino becomes attractive when the escalator is broken.

This is a moral warning. A society in which ordinary people turn to speculative finance because work, housing, and public goods no longer provide security is not financially democratized in the deepest sense. It is desperate. Investment opportunity should be broad, but broad investment is healthiest when households have stable income, savings, education, consumer protection, and long horizons. Speculation should not be the substitute for shared prosperity.

Financial education is useful, but it cannot solve structural financial vulnerability by itself. Teaching households about compound interest, diversification, debt, and risk is valuable. But a household cannot budget its way out of poverty wages, medical debt, unaffordable rent, predatory lending, or volatile work. Financial literacy becomes ideological when used to shift responsibility from institutions to individuals. A just financial system requires both informed citizens and fair structures.

Regulation is essential because financial markets are adaptive and crisis-prone. The goal is not to eliminate risk. Risk-taking is necessary for investment and innovation. The goal is to prevent private risk-taking from creating systemic catastrophe or predatory harm. This requires capital requirements, liquidity rules, consumer protection, transparency, derivatives oversight, resolution regimes, limits on leverage, stress testing, market conduct rules, antitrust, fiduciary duties, and macroprudential supervision. Regulation should focus on function, incentives, and system effects.

Capital requirements force financial institutions to fund themselves with more equity relative to debt. This reduces the probability that losses wipe out the institution. Liquidity requirements ensure that institutions can meet short-term demands. Stress tests examine severe scenarios. Resolution planning allows failure without chaos. Derivatives clearing and margin rules reduce counterparty opacity. Consumer protection prevents abusive lending and deceptive products. These tools are not anti-market. They are the guardrails that allow markets to function without endangering society.

The challenge is political economy. Financial sectors are powerful. They have resources, expertise, lobbying capacity, and revolving-door relationships. They can argue that regulation reduces lending, innovation, competitiveness, or growth. Sometimes these concerns are valid. Overregulation can stifle useful finance. But underregulation can produce catastrophe. Because the benefits of deregulation are often immediate and the costs delayed, political systems are vulnerable to financial influence during calm periods. After crisis, reform becomes possible. As memories fade, pressure for deregulation returns. This is a regulatory cycle driven by collective amnesia.

Complexity economics suggests that regulation should be countercyclical. It should tighten when risk appears low and credit grows rapidly. It should build buffers during booms. It should resist the pressure to relax standards because "this time is different." It should recognize that stability can breed instability. Regulators must be willing to disappoint markets before markets disappoint society. This requires independence, expertise, democratic legitimacy, and moral courage.

Central banks occupy a unique position. They are guardians of money, lenders of last resort, managers of interest rates, and often supervisors of financial institutions. In crisis, central banks provide liquidity to prevent panic. This role is necessary because financial markets can collapse through self-fulfilling fear. But lender-of-last-resort support creates moral hazard if institutions expect rescue. Central banks must therefore distinguish liquidity support from solvency support, protect the system without protecting reckless managers, and coordinate with fiscal authorities where public losses are involved.

The lender-of-last-resort function reflects a deep truth: financial markets sometimes need public authority to stop cascades. Pure market discipline can be destructive when everyone seeks safety at once. A central bank can create liquidity when private liquidity disappears. A deposit insurance system can prevent bank runs. A fiscal authority can recapitalize institutions or support households. The state is the ultimate backstop of financial capitalism. This is why the state has the right and duty to set rules before crisis.

Public backstops should be designed to protect people and systems, not privileges. Deposit insurance protects ordinary depositors and payment stability. Emergency lending protects liquidity. But shareholders, executives, and unsecured creditors should not automatically be shielded from loss. If public power prevents collapse, public conditions should follow. These may include limits on dividends, buybacks, executive compensation, risk-taking, and future structure. Rescue should be paired with reform. Otherwise crisis becomes a subsidy for repetition.

Financial markets also shape time horizons. Short-term trading, quarterly earnings, mark-to-market pressure, and performance benchmarks can shorten corporate and investor horizons. Long-term investment in research, workers, resilience, and infrastructure may be undervalued if markets demand immediate returns. Pension funds and sovereign wealth funds can provide longer-term capital, but they too may face performance pressures. A society that wants long-term prosperity must align financial incentives with long-term value. Otherwise finance will reward immediate extraction over durable capacity.

Long-term value includes environmental and social risk. Climate change is a financial risk because it affects property, insurance, agriculture, infrastructure, energy, migration, and public budgets. Transition risk affects fossil fuel assets and carbon-intensive industries. Physical risk affects homes, ports, factories, and municipal bonds. Liability risk may emerge as courts and regulators respond. Financial markets are beginning to price these risks, but pricing may be delayed and nonlinear. Assets can remain overvalued until perception shifts suddenly. Climate risk may produce financial cascades if insurance withdraws, property values fall, or energy transitions disorderly.

Sustainable finance attempts to incorporate environmental, social, and governance factors into investment. In principle, this can improve risk assessment and direct capital toward better uses. In practice, it can become vague, politicized, or used for marketing without real change. The deeper issue is that financial markets alone cannot solve climate change. They can support transition, but public policy must set standards, prices, infrastructure, and investment direction. Markets can allocate within a framework. They cannot substitute for collective choice.

This is a recurring theme: finance is powerful, but it must be embedded. It must be embedded in law, public purpose, democratic accountability, productive investment, and moral limits. Disembedded finance becomes self-referential. It generates claims on future income without necessarily increasing real capacity. It turns homes, education, healthcare, commodities, and infrastructure into yield-bearing assets. It confuses liquidity with wealth, price with value, and speculation with progress. Embedded finance serves life. Disembedded finance begins to govern it.

The distinction between price and value is central. Financial markets produce prices continuously. But value is broader. A forest has ecological value beyond its timber price. A hospital has social value beyond its cash flow. A home has human value beyond its asset price. A worker has dignity beyond wage cost. A stable community has value beyond real estate appreciation. A resilient supply chain has value beyond short-term profit. Financial markets tend to price what can be claimed, traded, discounted, and owned. They struggle with what is shared, long term, relational, or morally significant. Public institutions must therefore protect values that markets underprice.

This does not mean prices are meaningless. Prices are indispensable signals. But they are not complete moral judgments. A high stock price does not prove social contribution. A low wage does not prove low human worth. A profitable firm is not necessarily a beneficial firm. A cheap product is not necessarily a socially efficient product. A rising housing market is not necessarily a healthy housing system. Financial prices must be interpreted within a broader political economy.

The governance of finance should be guided by several principles. First, finance should serve productive and socially useful investment rather than extraction. Second, leverage should be constrained where it creates systemic risk. Third, liquidity promises should match asset liquidity. Fourth, public backstops should carry public obligations. Fifth, consumer and investor protection should prevent predation and manipulation. Sixth, market concentration and too-big-to-fail power should be limited. Seventh, financial innovation should be evaluated by social function, not novelty alone. Eighth, long-term resilience should be rewarded. Ninth, global finance should include fair mechanisms for crisis liquidity and debt restructuring. Tenth, democratic institutions must retain authority over the rules of finance.

These principles do not require hostility toward markets. They require respect for their power. Fire is useful because it is governed. Electricity is useful because it is regulated. Medicine is useful because it is tested. Finance is useful when disciplined by institutions that prevent its destructive tendencies from overwhelming its productive ones. The alternative is periodic crisis, public rescue, inequality, and distrust.

Financial markets are especially dangerous when they colonize public imagination. If society begins to treat stock indexes as the primary measure of economic health, it will misunderstand itself. A rising stock market may coexist with stagnant wages, unaffordable housing, medical debt, precarious work, and regional decline. Asset prices can rise because profits rise, but also because interest rates fall, buybacks expand, market power grows, or investors expect future monopoly rents. The stock market is not the economy. It is one part of the economy, heavily weighted toward asset owners and large firms.

Similarly, gross financial wealth is not the same as shared prosperity. A society can become wealthier on paper while more fragile in reality. Housing values can rise while young families are excluded. Equity values can rise while firms underinvest. Bond markets can rally while public goods decay. Private wealth can accumulate while public capacity weakens. The balance sheet of the wealthy can improve while the life chances of the majority stagnate. A financialized society may confuse capitalization with civilization.

The psychology of markets encourages this confusion because numbers move constantly and visibly. A stock price updates every second. The condition of a child in an underfunded school does not. A bond yield moves instantly. The erosion of trust takes years. A cryptocurrency can double in a week. The rebuilding of a community takes a generation. Finance privileges what can be measured, priced, and traded now. Democratic political economy must also value what matures slowly: education, health, trust, infrastructure, ecological stability, worker skill, and civic life.

Herding also affects public policy. Policymakers can herd around ideas just as investors herd around assets. A dominant policy narrative can take hold: deregulation is always efficient, markets always discipline risk, austerity always restores confidence, low inflation always means stability, financial innovation always spreads risk, shareholder value always improves performance. These narratives can persist until crisis breaks them. The collapse of one narrative then produces another. Intellectual herding is as dangerous as financial herding because it shapes the rules under which markets operate.

This book argues for a different intellectual posture. It does not deny the usefulness of markets, prices, finance, or risk-taking. It denies that these systems are self-justifying or self-stabilizing. Financial markets require moral and institutional architecture. They require humility because uncertainty is real. They require restraint because leverage seduces. They require transparency because opacity hides fragility. They require public authority because panic is contagious. They require justice because rescue without fairness destroys legitimacy.

The next chapter turns to technological change and disruptive feedback. The connection is direct. Financial markets often fund technological innovation, but they also inflate technology bubbles, reward platform dominance, and shape the direction of innovation. Venture capital can support experimentation, but it can also encourage winner-take-all strategies, labor disruption, and growth without profits. Public markets can provide capital, but they can also pressure firms toward short-term valuation. Technology and finance together can produce extraordinary progress or extraordinary concentration.

The broader lesson of this chapter is that finance must be understood as a nonlinear system of belief, leverage, liquidity, and power. Financial markets do not merely allocate capital. They shape the future by deciding which futures receive funding. They do not merely price risk. They create risk through leverage and herding. They do not merely reflect confidence. They generate or destroy confidence through feedback. They do not merely serve the real economy. They can dominate it if not governed.

Cascades are the signature danger. A decline in confidence becomes selling. Selling becomes price decline. Price decline becomes margin call. Margin call becomes forced sale. Forced sale becomes further decline. A rumor becomes withdrawal. Withdrawal becomes illiquidity. Illiquidity becomes insolvency. A downgrade becomes funding pressure. Funding pressure becomes default risk. Default risk becomes higher yields. Higher yields become fiscal stress. Financial cascades transform fear into fact.

A society that understands this will not wait for panic before regulating leverage. It will not confuse liquidity in calm markets with resilience in crisis. It will not allow institutions to become too important to fail and too powerful to discipline. It will not celebrate rising asset prices while ignoring who owns the assets. It will not permit financial innovation to outrun public understanding. It will not rescue markets without rescuing legitimacy. It will remember that finance is a servant of human prosperity, not its master.

The end of simple economic explanations requires us to abandon the fantasy that financial markets naturally move toward correct valuation and stable equilibrium. They may do so at times. They may also overshoot, imitate, panic, speculate, concentrate, and cascade. Their intelligence is real, but incomplete. Their discipline is useful, but uneven. Their power is enormous, but not inherently wise.

Financial markets are among humanity's most sophisticated systems of collective expectation. They can mobilize capital across continents, fund discovery, support enterprise, and help societies invest in the future. But because they are systems of expectation, they are also vulnerable to dreams, delusions, fear, and stampede. The question is not whether to trust or distrust them absolutely. The question is how to govern them so that their energy serves a democratic and humane economy.

In a nonlinear world, the price of an asset is never just a price. It is a signal, a story, an incentive, a claim, a feedback mechanism, and sometimes a trigger. To understand finance is to understand how belief becomes balance sheet, how balance sheet becomes action, how action becomes market movement, and how market movement becomes social consequence. A wise society will treat that power with respect, skepticism, and discipline.

Financial markets can help build the future. They can also turn the future into a bubble. The difference depends on whether finance remains anchored to productive purpose, moral responsibility, and public governance. Without those anchors, herding becomes mania, leverage becomes fragility, liquidity becomes illusion, and markets become cascades waiting for a shock. With them, finance can become what it should be: a disciplined system for funding real prosperity in a world that will always be uncertain.

# Chapter 12

# Technological Change and Disruptive Feedback

Technological change is often described as progress. A new tool appears. Productivity rises. Costs fall. Communication accelerates. Knowledge expands. New industries emerge. Old limitations disappear. Society becomes richer, faster, more connected, and more capable. This story contains truth. Technology has lifted living standards, extended life expectancy, transformed agriculture, expanded education, enabled global communication, created entire industries, and opened forms of human possibility that earlier generations could not imagine. To deny the creative power of technology would be foolish.

Yet the language of progress can also conceal. Technology does not simply arrive as a neutral force and distribute benefits automatically. It enters societies already organized by power, inequality, law, markets, culture, and institutions. It changes incentives. It creates winners and losers. It restructures work. It shifts bargaining power. It alters the scale at which firms operate. It creates new dependencies. It destroys some skills while increasing the value of others. It changes how people communicate, shop, learn, organize, borrow, invest, date, vote, and understand themselves. Technology is not merely a set of tools. It is a system of feedback.

The central argument of this chapter is that technological change is nonlinear because it is disruptive, cumulative, and institutionally mediated. A small technical advantage can become market dominance. A new platform can become infrastructure. A productivity tool can become a labor surveillance system. A communication network can become a channel of misinformation. A data system can become a mechanism of prediction and control. A medical innovation can extend life, but also increase costs if embedded in a profit-driven system. Artificial intelligence can augment human creativity, but also displace workers, concentrate power, and destabilize trust if poorly governed. Technology does not have one destiny. Its effects depend on feedback loops among innovation, markets, finance, labor, law, culture, and politics.

The old economic imagination often treats technology as an external force that improves productivity. In many models, technological progress appears as a shift in the production function, allowing more output from the same inputs. This is useful as a first approximation. Better machines, software, logistics, medicine, energy systems, and knowledge can indeed allow societies to produce more with less. But technology is not merely an input into production. It reorganizes the entire system of production and distribution. It changes who owns the tools, who controls the data, who captures the gains, who bears the risks, and what forms of life become possible or impossible.

Technological change is therefore never only technical. It is political economy in motion.

The first feedback loop of technological change is adoption. A technology becomes more valuable as more people use it. This is especially true for communication systems, social networks, payment platforms, marketplaces, operating systems, and digital standards. A telephone is useful only if others have telephones. A social platform becomes valuable because other users, creators, advertisers, and communities are present. A marketplace attracts buyers because sellers are there, and sellers because buyers are there. A payment system becomes more useful as more merchants accept it. The value of the technology grows with the network.

This is the logic of network effects. Network effects create increasing returns. Success breeds more success. Early adoption attracts later adoption. More users generate more data, more complementary services, more investment, more developer activity, and more cultural familiarity. The technology becomes easier to use because everyone else is using it.

Eventually, switching becomes costly. Users do not necessarily remain because the technology is best in an abstract sense, but because the network is there. Dominance becomes self-reinforcing.

This is a central reason digital markets often do not behave like the competitive markets of classical imagination. In ordinary markets, high profits attract competitors. Competition reduces profits. Prices fall. Innovation spreads. But in network markets, an early leader may become stronger as it grows. More users create more value, and more value attracts more users. Data improves services, and better services attract more data. Developers build tools for the dominant platform, making the platform more useful. Advertisers follow attention. Sellers follow customers. Customers follow sellers. The loop becomes difficult to break.

The result can be winner-take-most markets. This does not mean the dominant firm is always undeserving. It may have innovated brilliantly. It may have solved real problems. It may have built reliable infrastructure. But the system can shift from competition on the merits to competition shaped by lock-in. Once a platform becomes central, rivals face barriers unrelated to product quality alone. They must overcome user habits, network size, data advantages, switching costs, brand trust, complementary services, and capital access. The market's past shapes its future.

This is path dependence. In technological systems, early events can have long consequences. A standard adopted early may persist. A platform that gains scale may become embedded. A firm that controls a key interface may shape the ecosystem around it. A protocol, operating system, app store, cloud service, or search engine may become part of the economic environment. Once technology becomes infrastructure, private design choices acquire public consequences.

This shift from tool to infrastructure is one of the most important nonlinear transformations in modern capitalism. A search engine begins as a tool for finding information. At scale, it shapes what information is visible. A social network begins as a tool for connection. At scale, it shapes public discourse, identity, politics, and social comparison. A delivery platform begins as a convenience. At scale, it reshapes restaurants, urban logistics, labor conditions, and consumer expectations. A cloud provider begins as a technical service. At scale, it becomes part of the operating infrastructure of firms, governments, schools, hospitals, and financial systems. A digital payment system begins as convenience. At scale, it becomes part of commercial life.

At that point, the question changes. We should no longer ask only whether the technology is useful. We must ask who governs it. Who sets the rules? Who has access? Who owns the data? Who can be excluded? Who audits the system? Who benefits from dependency? Who bears the risks of failure? When private platforms become public infrastructure, public obligations should follow. The greater the systemic role, the greater the democratic responsibility.

The second feedback loop is data accumulation. Digital technologies generate data through use. Search queries, purchases, location traces, clicks, messages, medical records, educational activity, workplace productivity metrics, financial transactions, viewing habits, and social interactions can all become data. Data can improve services, personalize results, reduce fraud, support research, predict demand, optimize logistics, and guide innovation. But data can also enable surveillance, manipulation, discrimination, price targeting, behavioral prediction, and power concentration.

Data creates increasing returns because firms with more users often collect more data. More data improves algorithms. Better algorithms improve service quality, advertising effectiveness, product recommendations, fraud detection, or user engagement. Improved services attract more users. More users generate more data. The loop reinforces the dominant firm. Data becomes not merely a byproduct of business, but a strategic asset.

This changes the nature of competition. A new entrant may have a better idea but lack data. It may not be able to train models, target customers, detect fraud, or personalize services as effectively. Users may be reluctant to switch because their histories, contacts, preferences, files, purchases, and reputations are locked into existing systems. The incumbent's advantage grows through use. The market becomes less contestable.

Data also changes power between firms and consumers. In theory, consumers choose among services. In practice, firms may know far more about consumers than consumers know about firms. Firms can predict vulnerability, target desire, test behavioral responses, and personalize persuasion. Prices, advertisements, feeds, recommendations, and offers can be adjusted based on data. The consumer becomes transparent to the firm, while the firm's algorithms remain opaque to the consumer. This asymmetry undermines the ideal of informed choice.

Behavioral extraction occurs when firms profit by capturing attention, shaping habits, and nudging behavior in ways that serve revenue more than wellbeing. A platform may maximize engagement because engagement sells advertising. Content that provokes anger, envy, fear, or compulsion may keep users online. The system learns what captures attention and feeds it back. Human psychology becomes an input into profit optimization. The user is not merely served. The user is studied, predicted, and influenced.

This is a technological feedback loop with moral consequences. The platform measures behavior. The measurement informs algorithmic ranking. Ranking changes what users see. What users see changes behavior. Changed behavior produces more data. The system optimizes. But the optimization target matters. If the target is human flourishing, the loop may support learning, connection, and creativity. If the target is engagement or monetization alone, the loop may amplify addiction, polarization, misinformation, anxiety, and social comparison. Technology inherits the moral logic of its objective function.

The third feedback loop is labor substitution and augmentation. Technology can replace human tasks, complement human skills, or create new kinds of work. The same technology may do all three at once. Machines replaced some forms of manual labor while creating industrial jobs. Computers automated clerical tasks while increasing demand for analytical and technical work. The internet disrupted retail, media, travel, and advertising while creating digital services, logistics, software, and platform work. Artificial intelligence may automate routine cognitive tasks, augment professional work, create new creative tools, and destabilize occupations once considered secure.

The crucial question is not whether technology destroys jobs or creates jobs in the aggregate. Historically, economies have often created new work after technological disruption. But aggregate job counts do not settle the moral issue. Which jobs disappear? Which jobs are created? Where are they located? What do they pay? Who has access to them? How long does transition take? Who bears the income loss? What happens to communities built around declining industries? What happens to older workers, less-credentialed workers, caregivers, immigrants, disabled workers, and those without savings? A society can experience technological progress and human abandonment at the same time.

The simple story of creative destruction often glorifies the creative side while minimizing the destruction. Destruction is not merely the disappearance of inefficient firms. It is the disruption of lives, identities, towns, skills, and institutions. A factory closure is not only a reallocation of capital. It is lost wages, lost tax revenue, weakened schools, damaged health, family stress, outmigration, and political resentment. A profession disrupted by automation is not only an efficiency gain. It is a challenge to dignity, meaning, training pathways, and social status. A humane society can welcome innovation while refusing to treat displaced people as acceptable collateral damage.

Technology changes bargaining power. If a firm can automate tasks, it may gain leverage over workers. Even the credible threat of automation can discipline wage demands. If workers believe they are replaceable by software, robots, or cheaper global labor mediated through platforms, they may accept worse conditions. On the other hand, if technology increases the productivity of workers with scarce skills, those workers may gain bargaining power. Technological change can therefore widen inequality within labor markets. It can raise wages for some while suppressing wages for others.

The distribution of gains depends on institutions. If workers have unions, profit-sharing, strong labor markets, portable benefits, training access, and public support, productivity gains can be broadly shared. If labor is weak and capital owns the tools, gains flow upward. Automation does not automatically create inequality. It creates inequality when ownership, bargaining power, and policy allow the gains to concentrate. The machine does not decide distribution. Society does.

The fourth feedback loop is skill-biased opportunity. New technologies often increase demand for certain skills: engineering, data analysis, management, design, technical maintenance, scientific knowledge, digital literacy, and complex problem-solving. Workers with those skills gain. Schools and families with resources prepare children for such opportunities. High-income regions attract technology firms. Technology firms attract skilled workers. Skilled workers attract more firms. Wages rise. Housing prices rise. Public revenues rise. The region becomes a cumulative advantage machine.

Other regions fall behind. Workers whose skills are less in demand may face wage pressure. Local firms may struggle to adapt. Young people may leave. Tax bases weaken. Schools and training systems may suffer. Employers may not invest because the local skill base is thin. The region becomes trapped in cumulative disadvantage. Technology thus interacts with geography. It does not spread evenly across space. It clusters, and clustering creates feedback.

Agglomeration is powerful. Innovation often thrives where people, firms, universities, investors, suppliers, and skilled workers are near one another. Ideas move through networks. Startups spin out of established firms. Venture capital follows talent. Talent follows opportunity. Restaurants, culture, transportation, and amenities attract more talent. The region becomes more productive and more expensive. If housing supply fails, technological success produces exclusion. The innovation economy then becomes geographically narrow and socially stratified.

This is why technology policy cannot be separated from housing policy. A region may generate extraordinary technological wealth while pricing out teachers, nurses, artists, service workers, young families, and even many engineers. If only the highly paid can live near innovation, the social fabric frays. Long commutes increase. Inequality becomes visible in space. Resentment grows. A technology hub may be economically dynamic and morally unstable. Prosperity concentrated in a few regions is not national renewal.

The fifth feedback loop is financial acceleration. Technological change is shaped by finance. Venture capital, public markets, private equity, corporate acquisitions, and speculative narratives determine which technologies receive funding and which business models expand. Finance can support risk-taking and experimentation. It can fund companies before profits exist. It can allow ambitious projects to scale quickly. But it can also reward growth over sustainability, market capture over profitability, monopoly strategy over social value, and hype over substance.

The venture capital model often seeks outsized returns. This can encourage firms to pursue winner-take-all strategies. Grow fast. Capture users. Subsidize prices. Undercut incumbents. Build network effects. Collect data. Raise more capital. Expand into adjacent markets. Accept losses today in exchange for dominance tomorrow. If successful, the firm becomes valuable because it may eventually control a market. If unsuccessful, losses are absorbed by investors, workers, suppliers, or communities. This model can produce innovation, but it can also produce predatory growth.

Financial markets can also inflate technology bubbles. A new technological possibility captures imagination. Investors extrapolate enormous future profits. Capital floods the sector. Firms grow rapidly. Valuations rise. Talent moves in. Media amplify the story. Skeptics are dismissed as lacking vision. Some technologies eventually justify the optimism; many do not. When the bubble bursts, capital retreats, workers lose jobs, and trust declines. The technology may still matter, but the financial cycle distorts its development.

This distinction is important. A technology can be real and a bubble can still exist around it. Railroads were transformative, yet railroad speculation produced financial manias. The internet was transformative, yet internet stocks became wildly overvalued in particular moments. Artificial intelligence may be transformative, and still be surrounded by hype, overinvestment, inflated promises, and market concentration. The existence of genuine innovation does not validate every valuation, business model, or social claim attached to it. Financial excitement is not technological wisdom.

The sixth feedback loop is monopoly and acquisition. Dominant technology firms can buy potential competitors before they become threats. They can integrate vertically, control app stores or marketplaces, preference their own services, restrict interoperability, use data from dependent firms, and shape standards. The larger they become, the more resources they have to defend position. Their dominance attracts talent, capital, partners, and political influence. The market becomes less a field of open competition and more an ecosystem governed by a few private actors.

This raises a difficult question for antitrust policy. Traditional antitrust often focused on consumer prices. Many digital services appear free or low-cost to users. But the real price may be paid in data, attention, reduced competition, lower innovation, worker control, seller fees, dependency, or political influence. A platform can harm competition while charging consumers little. It can extract value from advertisers, sellers, developers, workers, or society as a whole. The old price-centered lens is too narrow for digital markets.

Competition policy in technology must examine data control, interoperability, switching costs, self-preferencing, acquisitions, platform governance, ecosystem dependency, and network effects. It must ask whether markets remain contestable. It must protect innovation not only from old monopolies, but from new ones. It must recognize that the absence of immediate price harm does not mean the absence of power. Technology markets can create private sovereignties, and private sovereignty requires democratic scrutiny.

The seventh feedback loop is institutional lag. Technologies change faster than laws, norms, and public understanding. A new platform, data practice, financial instrument, artificial intelligence system, or labor model can spread before society has decided how it should be governed. By the time regulation arrives, the technology may be entrenched. Users depend on it. Firms have built around it. Workers rely on it. Investors defend it. Policymakers fear disrupting it. The delay becomes a source of power. Innovation outruns democracy.

This pattern appears repeatedly. Social media expanded before societies understood its effects on mental health, privacy, politics, and misinformation. Gig platforms grew before labor law adapted to algorithmic management and worker classification. Digital advertising expanded before privacy rules caught up. Financial technology spread before consumer protections fully adjusted. Artificial intelligence systems are developing faster than many institutions can evaluate bias, accountability, intellectual property, employment effects, and safety. The speed of innovation creates governance gaps.

Institutional lag does not mean innovation should be stopped until every question is answered. That would be impossible and undesirable. But it does mean societies need adaptive governance. Rules must be flexible enough to learn, strong enough to prevent harm, and legitimate enough to command trust. Regulatory sandboxes, audits, transparency requirements, safety standards, liability rules, public-interest research, worker consultation, and democratic oversight can help. The goal is not to freeze technology. It is to govern the feedback loops before they harden into unaccountable systems.

The eighth feedback loop is surveillance and control. Digital tools allow employers, governments, platforms, insurers, lenders, schools, and advertisers to monitor behavior at unprecedented scale. Surveillance can improve safety, efficiency, fraud detection, logistics, and accountability. But it can also create domination. Workers can be tracked minute by minute. Consumers can be profiled. Students can be monitored. Citizens can be scored. Borrowers can be evaluated by opaque systems. Insurance can be personalized in ways that punish risk. People may change behavior because they know they are watched.

Surveillance changes power because information is asymmetrical. The watched often do not know how data is collected, interpreted, sold, or used. The watcher gains predictive capacity. Predictive capacity becomes control. In labor markets, surveillance can intensify work, reduce autonomy, and discourage organizing. In consumer markets, surveillance can enable manipulation. In finance, surveillance can enable inclusion or discrimination. In politics, surveillance can chill dissent. Technology that begins as measurement can become governance.

Algorithmic decision-making raises similar concerns. Algorithms may screen job applicants, set prices, approve loans, recommend prison sentences, detect fraud, rank content, assign workers, schedule shifts, evaluate performance, or diagnose disease. These systems can improve consistency and detect patterns humans miss. But they can also reproduce bias, hide accountability, and make decisions difficult to contest. If an algorithm denies a loan, lowers a worker's rating, increases an insurance premium, or filters a job application, who is responsible? The programmer? The firm? The data? The model? The regulator? Accountability can disappear into complexity.

Opacity is not merely a technical problem. It is a democratic problem. People subject to consequential decisions should have rights to explanation, appeal, correction, and human review. Systems affecting employment, credit, housing, healthcare, education, criminal justice, and public benefits require public standards. Efficiency cannot justify unchallengeable authority. A society governed by black boxes is not fully free.

The ninth feedback loop is misinformation and social trust. Communication technologies expand access to information, but they also change how information spreads. Content can move rapidly through networks. Emotional, sensational, or divisive material may travel faster than careful explanation. Recommendation algorithms can amplify engagement. Communities can form around shared belief, including false belief. Public trust can fragment. Democratic discourse can become more volatile.

This is not simply a problem of ignorant users. It is a system design problem. Platforms are structured by incentives. If advertising revenue depends on attention, and attention is captured by outrage or fear, the system may amplify harmful content. If content moderation is opaque or inconsistent, trust declines. If political actors learn to exploit platform dynamics, misinformation becomes strategic. If citizens lose faith in institutions, they become more vulnerable to alternative narratives. Technology interacts with distrust already present in society.

Information disorder has economic consequences. Public health guidance may be rejected. Inflation narratives may become conspiratorial. Financial scams may spread. Market rumors may move prices. Workers may distrust retraining programs. Citizens may reject climate policy. Elections may be delegitimized. Trust is economic infrastructure, and communication technologies can either support or corrode it. The governance of digital information is therefore part of economic governance.

The tenth feedback loop is productivity paradox and institutional adaptation. New technologies often take time to show up in productivity statistics because firms must reorganize work, train employees, build complementary infrastructure, and develop new business models. Electricity did not transform factories instantly. Computers required organizational change. Artificial intelligence may similarly require new workflows, skills, standards, and institutions. The mere existence of a technology does not guarantee immediate productivity gains. Adoption is social and organizational.

This matters because financial markets and political leaders often expect instant transformation. Firms may invest in technology without changing management. Workers may resist tools that threaten them. Organizations may automate bad processes rather than redesign them. Public institutions may lack expertise. Small businesses may lack capital. Schools may lag behind skill needs. The productivity effect depends on complementary systems. Technology is not magic. It is capability embedded in institutions.

The benefits of technology may also be mismeasured. Digital services can produce value that is not fully captured by prices. Free communication, search, maps, online learning, open-source software, and creative tools improve life in ways not always reflected in gross domestic product. At the same time, digital technologies can impose costs that are also undermeasured: distraction, anxiety, misinformation, surveillance, privacy loss, labor precarity, energy use, e-waste, and market concentration. Measurement struggles because technology changes the quality of life, not only output.

Artificial intelligence deserves special attention because it brings together many nonlinear dynamics at once: data, scale, labor substitution, augmentation, market concentration, misinformation, surveillance, intellectual property, finance, and institutional lag. AI systems can support medical research, education, logistics, language translation, coding, design, scientific discovery, administrative efficiency, accessibility, and creativity. They can help people perform tasks that once required specialized expertise. They can reduce drudgery and expand capability.

But AI can also concentrate power in firms with data, computing resources, talent, and capital. It can automate white-collar tasks, weaken labor bargaining power, produce biased decisions, generate convincing false content, intensify surveillance, and make intellectual work more precarious. It can flood information systems with synthetic material, making trust harder. It can be used for fraud, manipulation, cyberattacks, and political propaganda. It can change education by making old methods of assessment less reliable. It can alter the value of credentials and expertise. The effect of AI will depend on governance, ownership, access, labor institutions, public investment, and democratic oversight.

The key question is whether AI becomes a tool of broad human augmentation or a mechanism of concentrated control. If teachers, nurses, small businesses, public servants, researchers, artists, disabled people, and workers gain access to AI tools that improve capability, the technology can support shared prosperity. If AI is used primarily to reduce labor costs, monitor workers, replace creative work without fair compensation, manipulate consumers, and concentrate profits, it will deepen inequality. The technology contains both possibilities. Institutions will decide which feedback loop dominates.

Ownership is central. If productivity gains from AI accrue primarily to the owners of models, data centers, cloud infrastructure, intellectual property, and platforms, inequality will rise. If gains are shared through wages, reduced work time, public services, cooperative ownership, open tools, taxation, and broad access, AI can support social flourishing. The question of who owns the means of digital production is not antiquated. It has returned in new form. Data, models, compute, platforms, and networks are the new productive assets.

Public investment has a vital role. Many foundational technologies were built through public research, defense spending, universities, grants, procurement, and infrastructure. The internet, GPS, semiconductors, biotechnology, and clean energy technologies all drew heavily on public support. Yet private firms often capture much of the commercial gain. This does not mean private enterprise is unimportant. It is essential for scaling, refining, and deploying technologies. But public contribution should be recognized. When public investment creates technological possibility, public value should be returned through access, fair taxation, open standards, public-interest licensing, or shared benefits.

This point challenges the myth of the lone inventor or purely private innovator. Innovation is collective. It depends on public education, scientific research, infrastructure, legal systems, capital markets, skilled workers, prior discoveries, and cultural knowledge. The successful entrepreneur may be brilliant and courageous, but the platform of innovation is social. A society that forgets this allows private wealth to claim what collective effort made possible.

Intellectual property law shapes technological feedback. Patents and copyrights can encourage innovation by granting temporary rights. But excessive protection can block follow-on innovation, raise prices, create patent thickets, and strengthen incumbents. Weak protection can reduce incentives to invest. The balance is delicate. In medicine, intellectual property can support drug development but also create unaffordable prices. In software and AI, data and copyright questions affect creators, users, firms, and public knowledge. Innovation policy must balance reward with access.

Open systems can support innovation through shared knowledge, interoperability, and collaboration. Open-source software has become critical infrastructure. Open standards allow competition and compatibility. Public science enables discovery. But openness requires support. Maintaining open infrastructure often depends on underfunded communities or public institutions. A society that relies on open systems should invest in them. Otherwise, essential digital infrastructure may be fragile despite appearing free.

Technology also changes energy demand and ecological pressure. Data centers, artificial intelligence, blockchain systems, semiconductor fabrication, electric vehicles, battery production, and digital infrastructure require energy, water, minerals, land, and cooling. The digital economy is not immaterial. It has physical foundations. A society that treats digital technology as weightless will ignore its environmental footprint. Clean energy and efficient computing are therefore part of technology governance.

At the same time, technology is essential to ecological transition. Renewable energy, storage, smart grids, precision agriculture, building efficiency, electric transportation, climate modeling, carbon monitoring, materials science, and industrial decarbonization all require innovation. The question is whether technological optimism becomes an excuse for delay or a tool for transformation. Technology can help solve climate problems, but only if embedded in policy, investment, behavioral change, and justice. There is no purely technological escape from political economy.

The concept of rebound effects is important. Efficiency improvements can reduce the cost of using a resource, which may increase use. More efficient lighting can lower the cost of lighting and expand lighting use. More efficient vehicles can reduce driving costs and potentially increase miles driven. Digital efficiency can increase demand for computing. Efficiency gains are valuable, but their environmental benefits depend on policy and behavior. Technology alone may not reduce total resource use if savings are reinvested in more consumption. Nonlinearity again appears: less per unit can become more in total.

Military and geopolitical feedback should not be ignored. Technologies developed for civilian purposes can have military uses, and military technologies can spill into civilian life. Artificial intelligence, drones, cyber tools, satellites, biotechnology, quantum computing, and advanced manufacturing have strategic significance. Nations compete for technological leadership because technology shapes economic power and security. This can spur innovation, but also arms races, surveillance states, export controls, and geopolitical fragmentation. Technology is not only market competition. It is state competition.

Technological nationalism can protect strategic capacity, but it can also reduce cooperation, raise costs, and intensify conflict. Global challenges such as climate change, pandemics, cyber risk, and AI safety require international coordination. Yet technological competition encourages secrecy and rivalry. The world faces a dilemma: innovation is global, but governance is fragmented. A nonlinear technological order requires institutions capable of cooperation across borders, even among competitors.

Technological change also affects culture and human meaning. Work, art, friendship, memory, attention, identity, and community are shaped by tools. A society that communicates through platforms experiences time, selfhood, and politics differently. A person who works under algorithmic management experiences authority differently. A child educated through digital systems learns differently. An artist competing with generative systems faces a new question of authorship and value. A worker whose expertise is automated faces a question of identity. Technology changes what people do, but also how they understand what they do.

This is why technological governance cannot be left only to engineers, investors, or economists. It requires moral philosophy, democratic deliberation, labor voice, education, psychology, law, sociology, environmental science, and public participation. Technical feasibility is not the same as social desirability. A technology may be profitable and still harmful. It may be efficient and still degrading. It may be innovative and still unjust. The question should never be only, "Can we build it?" It should also be, "Should we build it, under what rules, for whose benefit, and with what safeguards?"

The precautionary principle is relevant, but it must be applied wisely. Excessive fear can block beneficial innovation. Reckless enthusiasm can cause harm. The challenge is adaptive precaution: identify high-risk uses, require testing and accountability, monitor effects, update rules, protect vulnerable groups, and allow beneficial experimentation. Not all technologies require the same level of oversight. A medical diagnostic system, autonomous weapon, financial trading algorithm, social media recommendation engine, educational assessment tool, and creative writing assistant pose different risks. Governance should be proportionate to harm, scale, and reversibility.

Scale matters again. A small experimental tool used by a few people may pose limited risk. The same tool deployed to millions, embedded in public services, or used in hiring, credit, policing, healthcare, or education becomes systemically important. Regulation should intensify with scale and consequence. The greater the reach, the greater the obligation to transparency, auditability, fairness, safety, and public accountability.

Labor must have a voice in technological adoption. Workers often know where technology helps and where it harms. They understand workflows, risks, customers, and practical realities. When technology is imposed from above, it may fail, intensify stress, or destroy trust. When workers participate in design and implementation, technology can improve productivity and dignity. Works councils, unions, worker committees, professional associations, and participatory design can help align technology with human needs. The people whose lives are reorganized by technology should not be treated as obstacles to progress.

Education systems must also adapt, but not by chasing every new tool. The deeper task is to cultivate judgment, creativity, ethical reasoning, collaboration, technical literacy, civic understanding, and lifelong learning. In a world where specific tasks change, people need foundations that allow adaptation. But education cannot be reduced to labor market preparation. Citizens also need to understand technology's social consequences. Digital literacy should include privacy, misinformation, algorithmic bias, data rights, and the political economy of platforms.

Lifelong learning must be real, not rhetorical. Workers cannot be told to retrain without time, income support, affordable programs, childcare, and clear pathways to jobs. Training systems should be linked to employers, unions, community colleges, public agencies, and regional development. A worker displaced by technology should not be handed a website and a slogan. The transition must be institutionally supported. Adaptation is a public responsibility.

Reduced work time is another possibility. If technology increases productivity, societies could choose shorter workweeks, more leisure, more caregiving time, earlier retirement options, or sabbaticals. But this requires distribution. Productivity gains must be shared as time, income, or public goods. Without bargaining power and policy, productivity gains may simply increase profits and output expectations. Technology could liberate time, but only if institutions make that liberation a social goal.

Universal basic income and related proposals arise from concerns about automation and insecurity. A guaranteed income could provide a floor, reduce poverty, support risk-taking, and protect people in volatile labor markets. Critics worry about cost, work incentives, inflation, political durability, and whether cash alone can replace public services. A complexity approach does not treat guaranteed income as a magic solution or dismiss it reflexively. It asks how income support interacts with housing, healthcare, labor markets, bargaining power, inflation, taxation, and public goods. Cash helps, but if landlords capture it through rent or healthcare remains unaffordable, the system adapts. Income policy must be part of a larger architecture.

Public options and universal basic services are alternative or complementary approaches. Healthcare, childcare, housing, transportation, education, broadband, and energy support can reduce dependence on wages and private markets for basic security. In a technologically disruptive economy, such services provide resilience. They allow people to change jobs, retrain, care for family, and participate in innovation without catastrophic risk. The best response to technological uncertainty may be a combination of income security, public services, worker power, and broad ownership.

Broad ownership is crucial. If technology increases returns to capital, then more people must own capital or share in its returns. Employee ownership, public wealth funds, social wealth funds, cooperative platforms, retirement access, baby bonds, and profit-sharing can democratize claims on technological productivity. Tax policy can also distribute gains. Without broader ownership, technological progress may intensify class division between those who own productive systems and those whose labor is increasingly replaceable or monitored by them.

Platform cooperatives offer one vision. Workers, users, or communities could own digital platforms and govern them democratically. Such models face challenges of capital, scale, technical expertise, and competition against dominant firms. But they demonstrate that technological form and ownership form are separable. A platform need not be owned by distant shareholders. It can be governed as a cooperative, public utility, nonprofit, or regulated infrastructure. Institutional imagination matters.

Data rights are another frontier. Individuals and communities may need rights to access, correct, delete, transfer, and control data. Data portability can reduce lock-in. Interoperability can support competition. Privacy rules can limit extraction. Collective data governance may be needed where data derives from communities or public systems. Data is relational. One person's data often reveals information about others. Therefore, purely individual consent may be insufficient. Data governance must recognize collective stakes.

The idea of digital public infrastructure is gaining importance. Societies need secure identity systems, payment systems, data exchanges, public clouds, open standards, and civic platforms that serve public purposes rather than extraction. If the digital foundations of society are entirely private and profit-maximizing, public capacity weakens. Digital public infrastructure can support inclusion, competition, and resilience if governed democratically. It can also become dangerous if used for surveillance or exclusion. Public does not automatically mean good. Design and accountability matter.

Technology also interacts with crisis. During emergencies, digital systems can support remote work, telemedicine, online education, logistics, public communication, and financial transfers. They can also expose digital divides. Households without broadband, devices, quiet space, or digital skills fall behind. Schools, health systems, and governments may struggle if technology is uneven. Digital access is therefore no longer luxury. It is participation infrastructure. A society that tolerates digital exclusion creates a new form of inequality.

The digital divide is not only access to devices. It includes quality of connection, affordability, technical support, skills, accessibility for disabled users, language access, privacy protection, and meaningful use. A child with a smartphone but no quiet place to study is not digitally equal. A worker with internet but no training is not fully included. A small business with broadband but no cybersecurity capacity remains vulnerable. Digital inclusion requires social support, not merely hardware.

The ethical use of technology requires institutional humility. Designers often do not foresee how tools will be used. Users adapt technologies creatively. Bad actors exploit systems. Business models evolve. Scale changes effects. A harmless feature at small scale may become harmful at large scale. A beneficial tool in one context may be destructive in another. Governance must therefore include monitoring and revision. Technology policy cannot be a one-time decision. It must be an ongoing process of democratic learning.

This chapter's argument can be summarized in a simple claim: technology is feedback, not fate. It does not determine society from outside. It enters society and amplifies existing structures. If a society is unequal, technology may amplify inequality. If labor is weak, technology may weaken workers further. If markets are concentrated, technology may deepen concentration. If public institutions are hollow, technology may outrun governance.

If trust is low, technology may spread distrust. But if institutions are democratic, inclusive, adaptive, and justice-oriented, technology can amplify capability, resilience, creativity, and shared prosperity.

The difference lies in design. Design includes technical design, but also institutional design. Who owns? Who governs? Who has access? Who pays? Who benefits? Who is protected? Who can appeal? Who audits? Who shares in gains? Who bears losses? These questions determine the social meaning of technology.

A complexity economics approach to technology would rest on several principles. First, treat technology as embedded in institutions, not as an external force. Second, govern network effects before they become unaccountable dominance. Third, protect data rights, privacy, and transparency. Fourth, strengthen labor voice in technological adoption. Fifth, distribute productivity gains through wages, ownership, public services, and taxation. Sixth, invest in education, lifelong learning, and public research. Seventh, support competition through interoperability, open standards, and antitrust. Eighth, regulate high-risk algorithmic systems with audit, appeal, and accountability. Ninth, build digital public infrastructure that serves democratic purposes. Tenth, align technological innovation with ecological sustainability and human flourishing.

These principles do not oppose innovation. They make innovation worthy of a democratic society. The goal is not to slow progress for its own sake. The goal is to prevent progress from becoming domination. The goal is not to punish successful firms. The goal is to ensure that success does not become private sovereignty. The goal is not to protect every old job forever. The goal is to protect people, communities, and dignity during transition. The goal is not to eliminate risk. The goal is to prevent technological risk from being imposed on those least able to bear it.

The next chapter turns to public policy under conditions of complexity. Technology makes that chapter necessary because it shows how quickly systems evolve beyond old categories. Is a platform a marketplace, employer, publisher, utility, infrastructure provider, data broker, or all of these at once? Is an AI model a tool, author, service, infrastructure, or decision-maker? Is a gig worker independent, dependent, entrepreneurial, or managed? Is data personal property, collective resource, corporate asset, or public concern? Old regulatory boxes strain under new realities. Public policy must learn to govern adaptive systems.

Technological change also ties together the earlier chapters. It affects inflation through productivity, energy demand, supply chains, and market power. It affects debt through financial technology, speculative bubbles, and productivity expectations. It affects inequality through skill premiums, ownership, platforms, data, and geography. It affects housing through remote work, urban clustering, and construction technology. It affects labor through automation, surveillance, and new job forms. It affects supply chains through logistics software, robotics, semiconductors, cyber risk, and critical minerals. It affects financial markets through algorithmic trading, valuations, and speculative narratives. Technology is not a separate chapter in economic life. It is a force moving through all chapters.

The moral challenge is to avoid both technological determinism and technological nostalgia. Determinism says technology will decide, and society must adapt. Nostalgia says technology is the source of decline, and society should return to an imagined past. Both are inadequate. Technology is neither savior nor demon. It is power. Power must be governed. The question is not whether society will change. It will. The question is whether change will be shaped by democratic purpose or by the narrow incentives of profit, control, and competition.

A humane economy should welcome invention that reduces suffering, expands knowledge, protects the planet, improves work, strengthens democracy, and broadens human possibility. It should resist technologies and business models that exploit attention, deepen inequality, destroy privacy, weaken labor, manipulate behavior, or concentrate unaccountable power. This requires discernment. Not every new thing is progress. Not every disruption is liberation. Not every efficiency is humane. Not every platform is a community. Not every algorithm is objective. Not every innovation deserves the society it asks us to become.

Technology tests our moral imagination because it expands what is possible before we decide what is desirable. It gives us capacities faster than it gives us wisdom. It allows prediction before accountability, automation before justice, connection before trust, scale before governance, and convenience before reflection. The task of political economy is to slow thought enough to guide action, without strangling creativity. It is to ask what kind of human beings our technologies encourage us to become.

In a nonlinear world, the consequences of technological choices can compound for decades. A platform standard becomes infrastructure. A data practice becomes a surveillance norm. A labor model becomes an industry template. A pricing algorithm becomes market behavior. An AI system becomes embedded in institutions. A generation grows up under a communication architecture that shapes attention and identity. Early choices matter because path dependence is real. The time to govern is before harmful feedback loops become irreversible.

The story of technology should therefore be rewritten. It is not simply the story of invention. It is the story of social choice under conditions of expanding power. It is the story of whether human beings use tools to deepen freedom or to intensify control. It is the story of whether productivity becomes shared time and dignity or concentrated wealth and insecurity. It is the story of whether intelligence becomes collective wisdom or automated manipulation. It is the story of whether innovation serves markets alone or the broader project of civilization.

Technological change is disruptive feedback. It disrupts because it changes tasks, firms, markets, regions, skills, and expectations. It feeds back because those changes alter the incentives and institutions that shape future technology. A platform becomes dominant and then influences regulation, culture, and innovation. A data system improves prediction and then changes behavior. A labor-saving technology changes wages and then changes demand for further automation. A financial bubble funds experimentation and then shapes which technologies survive. A communication network changes politics and then shapes the rules governing communication. Technology is both cause and consequence.

The end of simple economic explanations requires us to stop saying that technology by itself will solve inequality, climate change, labor insecurity, healthcare, education, or democratic distrust. It may help solve them. It may also worsen them. The result depends on governance. Markets will not automatically choose the humane path. States will not automatically choose the wise path. Citizens must deliberate, workers must have voice, institutions must learn, and power must be constrained.

Technology gives society new capacities. Complexity economics asks what feedback loops those capacities create. Moral political economy asks whether those loops support human flourishing. Democratic governance asks who gets to decide. These three questions must be asked together.

If we ask them well, technological change can become a source of shared renewal. It can reduce dangerous work, improve medicine, expand education, strengthen public services, accelerate climate transition, support disabled people, connect communities, and deepen creativity. It can help build a more resilient and humane economy. If we fail to ask them, technological change may deepen the very problems this book has traced: inequality, debt, labor insecurity, market concentration, supply fragility, financial speculation, and institutional distrust.

Technology is not the future. It is one of the forces from which the future is made. The future itself remains a political and moral question.

## Chapter 13

# Climate, Energy, and Ecological Constraint

Economics was built around the problem of scarcity, but modern economics often misunderstood the deepest scarcity of all. It studied the allocation of goods, labor, capital, and money, yet too often treated nature as background. Land appeared as an input. Energy appeared as a cost. Pollution appeared as an externality. Climate appeared, if it appeared at all, as an environmental issue separate from the main engine of growth. The economy was imagined as a circular flow among households, firms, governments, and markets, with nature entering only as raw material and leaving only as waste. The living world was treated as a source and a sink, not as the condition of possibility for economic life.

That assumption can no longer survive. Climate change, energy volatility, biodiversity loss, water stress, soil depletion, extreme weather, food insecurity, insurance instability, migration, and ecological degradation are forcing economics to confront a truth it should never have forgotten: the economy is embedded in the biosphere. It is not outside nature. It is not above nature. It is not a machine operating in empty space. It is a subsystem of the Earth's living and physical systems. Every factory, data center, home, farm, hospital, school, vehicle, supply chain, and financial market depends on energy, materials, climate stability, water, land, atmosphere, and ecological function. The economy breathes through the planet.

This chapter argues that climate, energy, and ecological constraint represent the most profound nonlinear challenge facing modern political economy. Climate change is not merely a gradual rise in average temperature. It is a destabilizing force operating through thresholds, feedback loops, tipping points, cascades, and unequal exposure. Energy is not merely another commodity. It is the master input into economic activity, the enabling force behind production, transport, heating, cooling, computation, agriculture, and modern life. Ecological constraint is not merely a moral concern for nature. It is a structural limit on the fantasy of unlimited growth within finite systems.

A complexity economics perspective is essential because ecological systems are nonlinear systems. They do not always respond gradually to pressure. A forest can absorb stress until drought, heat, pests, and fire push it into collapse. A fishery can sustain harvest until reproduction falls below recovery. A climate system can absorb greenhouse gases until feedbacks accelerate warming. A river system can support agriculture until drought, overuse, and heat make water scarcity structural. A coastal housing market can function until insurance withdraws and property values shift abruptly. A food system can appear stable until crop failures occur across multiple regions. More pressure does not always produce more of the same. Sometimes more becomes different.

The old economic language of externalities is useful, but inadequate. A carbon emission is an externality because the private actor emitting greenhouse gases does not bear the full social cost. A factory, vehicle, power plant, airline, or consumer imposes climate costs on others, including future generations. Pricing carbon can help correct this. But climate change is not merely a market failure in the narrow sense. It is a systems failure. It involves energy infrastructure, industrial policy, land use, transportation, agriculture, finance, housing, geopolitics, technology, labor markets, public trust, and democratic capacity. It is an externality so large that it challenges the institutional architecture of capitalism itself.

Climate change is also an intergenerational problem. The benefits of fossil-fuel use have been enjoyed largely in the present and past, while many of the costs fall on the future. Economic systems discount future harms, especially when they are uncertain, distant, or politically voiceless. But the atmosphere does not negotiate with discount rates. Carbon accumulates. Methane warms. Ice melts. Oceans absorb heat. Forests burn. Physical systems respond to cumulative reality, not to political convenience. A society may delay action, but delay is not neutral. Delay is an active choice to increase future constraint.

The first major feedback loop is the carbon-growth loop. Industrial capitalism grew through fossil energy. Coal powered factories, railways, steel, electricity, and urbanization. Oil transformed transportation, agriculture, military power, plastics, chemicals, and global trade. Natural gas reshaped heating, electricity, fertilizer, and industry. Fossil energy enabled extraordinary increases in productivity and living standards. It also filled the atmosphere with greenhouse gases. Growth generated emissions. Emissions generated warming. Warming now threatens the systems that support growth.

This loop exposes a contradiction at the center of modern prosperity. The same energy regime that created abundance now destabilizes the conditions of abundance. Fossil fuels made the modern economy possible, but continued dependence on them makes the modern economy fragile. The problem is not that energy use is immoral. Energy is essential to human development. The problem is that the dominant energy system has imposed costs that were not paid at the time of use. The bill arrives later, with interest, in the form of heat, storms, fires, droughts, floods, crop losses, disease risks, infrastructure damage, and human displacement.

Energy is the second central concept. It is impossible to understand the economy without understanding energy. Money circulates, but energy does the work. Labor requires food, transport, heating, cooling, and tools. Capital goods require materials and power. Digital systems require electricity, chips, cooling, and data centers. Agriculture requires sunlight, soil, water, fertilizer, machinery, and transport. Cities require energy for buildings, transit, sanitation, communication, and safety. Economic complexity rests on energy availability.

This is why energy shocks are so economically powerful. A rise in energy prices spreads through transportation, manufacturing, agriculture, utilities, housing, and consumer budgets. Energy inflation becomes food inflation, rent pressure, production cost pressure, and political anger. Energy dependence creates geopolitical vulnerability. Nations dependent on imported fuels are exposed to wars, sanctions, cartel behavior, shipping routes, currency movements, and infrastructure failures. Energy is not merely a sector. It is a systemic variable.

The transition to clean energy is therefore not simply an environmental project. It is an economic restructuring. It changes investment flows, labor demand, industrial strategy, supply chains, electricity grids, land use, mining, transportation, housing, geopolitics, and household costs. It creates new industries and disrupts old ones. It reduces some risks while creating others. It requires public coordination because energy systems are large, capital-intensive, networked, and slow to transform. The market can innovate powerfully within the transition, but the transition itself requires direction.

A simple story says that once clean energy becomes cheaper than fossil energy, the transition will happen automatically. Cost declines matter enormously, and they are a source of hope. But energy systems do not change through price alone. They are embedded in infrastructure, regulation, utilities, land use, transmission lines, permitting, finance, consumer behavior, political power, and incumbent interests. A cheaper technology can still diffuse slowly if grids are inadequate, permitting is blocked, financing is unavailable, supply chains are constrained, or incumbents resist. Price signals move faster than physical systems.

This is another example of nonlinearity. A solar panel or wind turbine is not just a device. It belongs to a system. Clean electricity requires generation, transmission, storage, balancing, demand management, permitting, interconnection, skilled labor, and regulatory design. Electric vehicles require batteries, charging networks, minerals, grid capacity, manufacturing, recycling, and consumer trust. Heat pumps require installation labor, building retrofits, financing, and public awareness. Green hydrogen, if used where appropriate, requires clean electricity, electrolyzers, storage, transport, and end-use applications. Technologies do not transform economies alone. Systems transform economies.

The third feedback loop is the fossil incumbent loop. Existing energy systems create powerful interests. Fossil-fuel companies, utilities, pipeline owners, petrochemical firms, industrial users, regions dependent on extraction, financial institutions, workers, and governments all have stakes in the current system. Infrastructure lasts decades. Political influence accumulates. Communities depend on jobs and tax revenue. Consumers depend on affordability. Governments depend on fuel taxes, royalties, or export revenues. The existing system defends itself because many lives and institutions are tied to it.

This does not make every defender of fossil energy corrupt or irrational. Some workers fear losing livelihoods. Some communities fear abandonment. Some countries depend on energy exports to fund public budgets. Some households fear higher energy bills. Some firms fear unreliable power. Some policymakers fear political backlash. The transition is not a morality play between enlightened reformers and villains alone. It is a complex restructuring of real dependencies. But acknowledging those dependencies does not justify delay. It means transition policy must be just, credible, and concrete.

A just transition is essential because climate policy will fail politically if it is experienced as elite moralism imposed on vulnerable communities. Workers in fossil-fuel sectors did not singlehandedly create the climate crisis. Many built the energy systems that powered modern life. Regions dependent on coal, oil, gas, refining, petrochemicals, or combustion-engine manufacturing deserve investment, retraining, pension protection, healthcare, infrastructure, and new industries. A policy that decarbonizes while abandoning workers will create resentment and resistance. A policy that protects workers while transforming the energy base can build legitimacy.

The same applies to households. Climate policy must not punish those already struggling with energy costs, rent, transportation, and debt. Carbon pricing, fuel regulations, building standards, and energy transitions can impose costs if poorly designed. Low-income households spend a larger share of income on energy and transportation. They may live in inefficient homes, lack access to transit, or be unable to afford electric vehicles or retrofits. A fair transition must include rebates, public investment, affordable transit, weatherization, clean-energy access, and protection against energy poverty. The burden of transition must not fall hardest on those least responsible for emissions.

The fourth feedback loop is the climate-damage loop. Climate change creates physical damage. Physical damage raises public and private costs. Resources diverted to repair are unavailable for investment in prevention. Repeated disasters weaken households, insurers, local governments, and infrastructure. Weakened systems become more vulnerable to future disasters. The loop can become self-reinforcing. A flood damages homes and roads. Property values decline or insurance costs rise. Local tax revenue weakens. The municipality has less capacity for adaptation. Future floods cause more damage. Residents with resources leave. Those without resources remain. Inequality deepens.

This dynamic is already reshaping the meaning of property. A house in a climate-exposed area may appear valuable until insurance premiums rise, lenders become cautious, infrastructure costs mount, or buyers reassess risk. The repricing may be gradual, or it may be sudden after a disaster or regulatory change. Climate risk can turn a household's main asset into a liability. It can destabilize municipal finance. It can produce migration. It can create political conflict over who pays for protection, retreat, rebuilding, or compensation.

Insurance is the price of risk, and climate change is raising the price of risk. When insurers can price risk accurately, premiums rise in vulnerable areas. When premiums rise too much, households cannot afford coverage. When insurers withdraw, mortgage markets may be affected because lenders require insurance. When governments subsidize insurance heavily, they may encourage rebuilding in risky places and socialize losses. When they do not, households may face ruin. Insurance markets are becoming a frontline institution of climate political economy.

This creates a moral dilemma. Should society subsidize people living in high-risk areas? Should it require retreat? Should it protect existing communities through public infrastructure? Should it allow insurance prices to signal risk fully, even if that destroys household wealth? There is no easy answer because homes are not merely assets. They are places of memory, identity, and community. But avoiding the question is itself a decision. Climate risk will force societies to confront the geography of safety.

The fifth feedback loop is food and water stress. Climate affects agriculture through heat, rainfall, drought, floods, pests, disease, soil moisture, and extreme events. Food systems are global and interconnected. A crop failure in one region can raise prices elsewhere. Multiple simultaneous failures can create severe price shocks. Water scarcity affects agriculture, energy production, industry, cities, and health. Groundwater depletion can sustain production for a time, but only by borrowing from the future. Once aquifers decline, rivers shrink, or snowpack changes, the system may enter a new regime.

Food and water stress are not only environmental issues. They are inflation issues, migration issues, security issues, and justice issues. Food price spikes harm poor households most. Farmers face income volatility. Governments face pressure to subsidize, import, ration, or restrict exports. Export restrictions by one country can worsen global scarcity. Water conflicts can emerge among agriculture, cities, industry, ecosystems, and regions. Climate stress can become political stress.

The sixth feedback loop is migration and instability. Climate change can contribute to displacement through drought, crop failure, sea-level rise, extreme heat, storms, fire, and water insecurity. Migration is often multi-causal; people move because of economics, violence, family, politics, and hope, not climate alone. But climate stress can intensify existing pressures. It can weaken livelihoods, increase food prices, deepen conflict, and make some regions less habitable. Migration then affects labor markets, housing, public services, politics, and international relations.

A humane climate economics must treat migration as adaptation, not merely crisis. People have always moved in response to environmental change. The question is whether movement is orderly, supported, rights-based, and integrated, or chaotic, coercive, and exploited. Wealthy societies that contributed heavily to historical emissions have moral obligations to support adaptation and protect displaced people. But domestic politics often turns migration into fear. Climate stress may therefore feed authoritarian and nationalist movements if societies fail to build institutions of humane transition.

The seventh feedback loop is biodiversity and ecological function. Climate is not the only ecological constraint. Pollinators, forests, wetlands, fisheries, soils, oceans, coral reefs, and microbial systems all support economic life in ways markets often underprice. Biodiversity contributes to food systems, medicine, water filtration, flood control, carbon storage, disease regulation, and cultural meaning. Ecological systems can degrade gradually, then collapse. A fishery may seem productive until population dynamics break. A forest may sequester carbon until drought and fire turn it into a source of emissions. Wetlands may appear economically idle until storms reveal their protective value.

The destruction of ecological function is often treated as development because the market values the converted asset more than the living system. A wetland becomes real estate. A forest becomes timber or pasture. A river becomes industrial input. A species disappears without a price. Gross domestic product may rise while natural capital falls. This is false accounting. It counts extraction as income and ignores depletion. A household that sells its roof to pay bills is not wealthier, even if cash flow rises. A society that destroys ecological foundations to increase measured output is doing the same at planetary scale.

Natural capital accounting attempts to correct this by valuing ecosystem services. This can be useful. It can make hidden benefits visible in policy analysis. But it also has limits. Not everything of value can be adequately priced. The existence of species, the integrity of landscapes, the sacredness of places, the rights of indigenous communities, and the beauty of the living world exceed monetary calculation. Economics must learn humility here. Valuation can inform decisions, but it should not be the only language of ecological responsibility.

The eighth feedback loop is inequality and exposure. Climate risk is unequal. Wealthy households can move, insure, retrofit, install cooling, buy generators, diversify assets, and recover from loss. Poor households often live in more exposed areas, in lower-quality housing, with less insurance, less savings, and less political voice. Outdoor workers face heat. Renters depend on landlords for repairs and energy efficiency. Elderly people, disabled people, children, and the medically vulnerable face greater risks.

Communities historically burdened by pollution often face climate stress as well. Climate change is not an equal-opportunity disaster.

This means climate policy must be justice policy. Adaptation resources should not flow only to wealthy coastal property, politically powerful districts, or areas with high property values. Heat protection, flood control, air quality, public cooling, resilient housing, clean transit, health services, and disaster recovery must prioritize vulnerability. Otherwise public policy will reproduce inequality by protecting the already protected. A society's climate response will reveal whose lives it values.

Energy transition also has unequal effects. If electric vehicles, solar panels, efficient appliances, and home retrofits are accessible mainly to affluent households, the benefits of lower operating costs will accumulate upward. Poor households may remain dependent on expensive fossil fuels, inefficient housing, and unreliable transit. If climate subsidies are structured through tax credits that require upfront spending, they may miss those with low tax liability or limited savings. Equity must be built into program design. The transition should reduce inequality, not green it.

The ninth feedback loop is finance. Climate risk affects financial markets through property values, insurance, municipal bonds, corporate assets, agricultural loans, energy investments, litigation, and transition risk. Financial institutions may hold assets that become stranded if fossil-fuel reserves cannot be burned, if infrastructure becomes obsolete, or if regulations change. They may also underestimate physical risk to real estate, supply chains, and public finance. If climate risks are repriced suddenly, financial cascades can follow.

Stranded assets are central to the transition. A fossil-fuel reserve has value on a company's books because it is expected to be extracted and sold. If climate policy, technology, or market shifts reduce future demand, some reserves may lose value. Infrastructure such as pipelines, refineries, coal plants, and combustion-engine manufacturing facilities may also become stranded. Investors, workers, regions, and governments tied to these assets face transition risk. The risk is not only environmental. It is financial and social.

This creates political resistance. Owners of carbon-intensive assets have incentives to delay transition, weaken regulation, promote doubt, or demand compensation. Workers and communities tied to those assets fear loss. Governments dependent on fossil revenues fear fiscal instability. The transition therefore requires both firmness and fairness. Society cannot allow incumbent interests to veto planetary stability. But it must support those whose livelihoods are disrupted by necessary change.

Green finance can help direct capital toward clean energy and resilience, but it cannot substitute for public policy. Investors need clear rules, credible standards, reliable permitting, infrastructure, and demand. Without policy, green finance may become branding. With policy, finance can scale transformation. Public investment can reduce risk, crowd in private capital, and support technologies that markets underfund. The state must help create the markets needed for decarbonization.

The tenth feedback loop is public trust. Climate policy requires sustained collective action over decades. It requires citizens to believe that burdens are fair, institutions are competent, benefits are real, and sacrifice is not being imposed by hypocritical elites. If trust is low, climate policy becomes vulnerable to conspiracy, backlash, and delay. If people believe the transition will enrich corporations, punish workers, raise living costs, or ignore rural communities, resistance grows. If they see tangible benefits, lower bills, cleaner air, good jobs, safer homes, better transit, and community investment, support strengthens.

This is why climate communication must move beyond abstract catastrophe alone. Fear can alert, but fear without agency produces denial or despair. A democratic climate politics must show practical pathways: jobs, health, energy independence, lower household costs, cleaner neighborhoods, resilient infrastructure, and intergenerational responsibility. It must be honest about costs and tradeoffs, but also concrete about benefits. It must connect planetary stability to daily life.

The eleventh feedback loop is governance capacity. Climate action requires permitting, planning, infrastructure, research, regulation, coordination, taxation, investment, emergency response, and international cooperation. A hollowed-out state cannot manage this transformation. Public agencies need expertise, data, engineers, planners, scientists, procurement capacity, legal authority, and democratic accountability. Markets can deploy capital and innovate, but public institutions must set direction, manage collective risks, and protect justice.

Permitting illustrates the complexity. Clean energy projects, transmission lines, housing, transit, mining, and infrastructure all require approvals. Environmental review protects communities and ecosystems, but it can also delay necessary climate projects if poorly designed or weaponized by incumbents. The solution is not to abandon review. It is to make it faster, fairer, more strategic, and more capable of distinguishing harmful projects from necessary transition infrastructure. A society cannot decarbonize if it cannot build. It also cannot decarbonize justly if building ignores communities and ecology. Governance must learn to do both.

Transmission is a key example. Clean electricity often must be generated where wind, sun, hydro, or other resources are abundant, then moved to where people live and work. Without transmission, clean energy projects cannot connect. Building transmission requires land, permits, regional coordination, cost allocation, and public acceptance. Local opposition can block projects with national climate importance. The system needs planning institutions capable of balancing local harms, regional benefits, ecological protection, and urgency. Fragmented governance can become climate obstruction.

Mining for transition minerals raises similar tensions. Clean technologies require materials. Mining can create environmental damage, labor abuse, water stress, and harm to indigenous communities. Ignoring these harms would reproduce extractive injustice. But refusing all mining while demanding rapid decarbonization is inconsistent. The answer is stronger standards, recycling, material efficiency, community consent, fair labor, environmental safeguards, and diversified supply. The clean economy must not be built on dirty extraction hidden elsewhere.

The twelfth feedback loop is growth itself. Modern economies are built around growth: rising output, incomes, consumption, productivity, tax revenue, profits, and investment. Growth can reduce poverty, support public goods, improve health, and create opportunity. But if growth depends on ever-increasing material throughput, emissions, land use, and ecological depletion, it becomes self-undermining. The question is not whether human wellbeing should improve. It should. The question is whether wellbeing must always require more extraction and waste.

This is where ecological economics challenges conventional economics. A finite planet cannot support infinite material expansion. Technological innovation can reduce resource intensity, but absolute decoupling at sufficient speed and scale is difficult. Some sectors can dematerialize; others cannot. A digital service still depends on energy and materials. A clean energy system still requires land, minerals, and infrastructure. Agriculture still requires soil, water, and ecological balance. The economy can become more efficient, but it cannot become immaterial.

A mature political economy must distinguish growth in human flourishing from growth in material throughput. More health, education, leisure, dignity, care, safety, creativity, and democratic participation need not require endless consumption of physical resources. Some forms of economic growth are necessary and good, especially for poorer societies and underprovided communities. Other forms are wasteful, status-driven, or ecologically destructive. The question is not growth or no growth in the abstract. The question is what grows, for whom, with what resource use, and toward what human end.

This is why gross domestic product is insufficient. GDP counts spending on disaster recovery as positive. It counts pollution cleanup but not the lost ecosystem. It counts medical treatment but not the suffering prevented by public health. It counts luxury consumption and essential care in the same monetary language. It does not distinguish resilience from repair, extraction from renewal, or useful production from defensive expenditure. Climate change will likely increase some forms of spending while reducing wellbeing. GDP may rise after a hurricane because rebuilding occurs, but society is not richer in any meaningful sense.

A complexity economics approach requires broader measures: emissions, energy intensity, material use, biodiversity, health, household security, inequality, resilience, leisure, public trust, housing affordability, and ecological stability. Prosperity must be judged by whether it can be sustained without destroying its foundations. An economy that grows by destabilizing climate is like a company that reports profits while ignoring the collapse of its main factory. The accounting is incomplete.

The thirteenth feedback loop is cultural expectation. Consumer societies teach people to associate wellbeing with acquisition. Advertising, status competition, planned obsolescence, and social comparison increase demand for goods, travel, space, and energy. Consumption becomes identity. People are told to solve insecurity through purchase, boredom through purchase, status anxiety through purchase, and belonging through purchase. The ecological cost of this culture is enormous. So is the psychological cost.

This does not mean ordinary people should be blamed for consumption patterns created by systems of work, advertising, inequality, and infrastructure. Many people consume because life is organized around consumption. Suburban design requires cars. Poor housing requires energy. Insecure status encourages visible spending. Long work hours encourage convenience consumption. Low wages make cheap goods necessary. The consumer is not sovereign in the simplistic sense. The consumer is shaped by the system.

A humane ecological economy would expand forms of wellbeing less dependent on material throughput: public parks, libraries, arts, community spaces, care, shorter work time, walkable neighborhoods, education, health, repair, sharing, durable goods, and public services. It would not impose austerity on the poor. It would reduce wasteful luxury emissions, planned obsolescence, and status arms races. It would ask affluent societies and households to distinguish sufficiency from excess. Ecological constraint is not a call for universal deprivation. It is a call for moral proportion.

The fourteenth feedback loop is public investment. Climate stability requires massive investment in energy, transit, buildings, grids, storage, research, adaptation, agriculture, water systems, and resilience. Public investment can create jobs, reduce long-term costs, crowd in private capital, and build legitimacy. Investment also has feedback effects. A better grid enables more clean energy. More clean energy reduces operating costs and emissions. Lower costs increase adoption. Adoption creates industries and political constituencies. Constituencies support further policy. The clean transition can become self-reinforcing if early public investment creates positive feedback.

This is the hopeful side of nonlinearity. Just as harmful systems can lock in, beneficial systems can tip toward transformation. Solar and wind cost declines, battery improvements, electric vehicle adoption, heat pump diffusion, building retrofits, and clean industrial technologies can create virtuous loops. More deployment leads to learning. Learning lowers costs. Lower costs increase deployment. Scale attracts investment. Investment improves technology. Technology improves performance. Policy can accelerate the loop.

But positive tipping points require intentional design. They do not emerge automatically everywhere. Some technologies face infrastructure bottlenecks, incumbent resistance, financing barriers, consumer uncertainty, or supply-chain constraints. Policy can push systems over thresholds: standards, subsidies, procurement, research, public finance, carbon pricing, infrastructure, and regulation can work together. Once a clean technology becomes cheaper, easier, trusted, and embedded, adoption accelerates. The goal is to create beneficial cascades before destructive climate cascades intensify.

Industrial policy is central here. Clean energy manufacturing, grid equipment, batteries, public transit, building retrofits, green steel, low-carbon cement, heat pumps, and climate-resilient infrastructure require coordinated investment. Markets can produce remarkable innovation, but they may underinvest in early-stage technologies, public infrastructure, and benefits that spill over to society. Public policy must shape the direction of innovation. The question is not whether government picks winners. The current system has already picked winners through fossil subsidies, infrastructure, tax policy, and regulatory choices. The question is whether public choices align with a livable future.

Carbon pricing remains important because prices matter. If emitting greenhouse gases is free or underpriced, markets will overuse the atmosphere. A carbon price can encourage efficiency, clean substitution, and innovation. But carbon pricing alone is not enough. It may be politically fragile if it raises household costs. It may not overcome infrastructure barriers. It may be insufficient for sectors with limited alternatives. It may be regressive without rebates. It may not drive public investment in grids, transit, and research. Carbon pricing should be part of a policy mix, not a substitute for governance.

Regulation is also necessary. Performance standards, clean electricity requirements, building codes, vehicle standards, methane rules, appliance efficiency, industrial emissions limits, and land-use protections can drive change where price signals are insufficient. Critics may call this command and control, but all markets operate within rules. The question is whether rules guide investment toward public purpose. Clear standards can create certainty for firms, accelerate innovation, and prevent laggards from undermining progress.

Adaptation policy must proceed alongside mitigation. Mitigation reduces future climate change by cutting emissions. Adaptation prepares for impacts already unavoidable. Societies need both. It is morally irresponsible to focus only on future emissions while ignoring people already exposed to heat, floods, fires, storms, drought, and disease. It is equally irresponsible to focus only on adaptation while allowing emissions to continue rising. Adaptation without mitigation becomes an endless and eventually impossible repair project. Mitigation without adaptation leaves vulnerable people unprotected. The two must be integrated.

Adaptation includes flood defenses, heat planning, resilient housing, water management, fire prevention, crop diversification, public health preparedness, urban trees, cooling centers, early-warning systems, insurance reform, managed retreat, and disaster recovery. Adaptation must be local, but supported nationally and globally. It must include community knowledge. It must prioritize the vulnerable. It must avoid maladaptation, such as protecting wealthy coastal property while encouraging continued development in high-risk areas or building infrastructure that shifts risk downstream. Adaptation is not merely engineering. It is justice under changing conditions.

Managed retreat is one of the hardest adaptation questions. Some places may become too risky or costly to protect indefinitely. Moving people away from danger can save lives and public resources, but it involves loss of home, culture, memory, and community. If done coercively or unfairly, it becomes injustice. If avoided until disaster, it becomes chaos. A humane policy would plan early, compensate fairly, preserve community ties where possible, and include residents in decision-making. Retreat should not mean abandonment. It should mean supported transition.

International justice is unavoidable. Wealthy industrialized nations produced a large share of historical emissions. Poorer nations often face severe climate impacts with fewer resources. They need finance for adaptation, clean development, disaster recovery, and energy access. A just climate order must support development without forcing countries to repeat the fossil-intensive path of the past. It must provide technology, finance, debt relief, and fair trade. Climate justice is not charity. It is responsibility for a shared atmospheric system shaped unequally by history.

Energy poverty must also be addressed globally. Hundreds of millions of people still lack reliable access to electricity or clean cooking. Development requires energy. The moral task is to provide abundant clean energy, not to freeze poor countries in low-energy poverty. Rich countries that grew through fossil energy cannot demand that poor countries remain poor in the name of climate. They must help finance clean development. Ecological constraint does not abolish the right to development. It requires a new model of development.

This new model must be based on sufficiency, resilience, and justice. Poor countries and poor communities need more energy, infrastructure, housing, healthcare, education, and material security. Wealthy societies need cleaner energy, less waste, more efficient systems, and a shift from status consumption to human flourishing. The same ecological policy cannot mean the same thing everywhere. Justice requires differentiation.

Debt and climate are deeply linked. Many vulnerable countries face high debt burdens while also needing climate investment. Disasters force governments to borrow for recovery. Debt service then reduces fiscal space for adaptation. Lack of adaptation increases future disaster damage. The loop is vicious. Climate-related debt traps are a major risk. A fair global system would include disaster clauses, debt restructuring, concessional finance, grants, and loss-and-damage mechanisms. Otherwise climate impacts will be compounded by financial extraction.

The relationship between climate and democracy is equally serious. Climate policy requires long-term planning, but democracies operate through election cycles. Climate impacts create emergencies that can strain institutions. Disinformation can weaken public support. Fossil interests can influence politics. Citizens may resist policies perceived as unfair. Authoritarian movements may exploit energy costs or migration fears. If democratic governments cannot deliver a fair transition, climate stress may feed anti-democratic politics. Conversely, authoritarian climate policy may impose costs without consent, producing repression. The challenge is democratic ecological governance.

Democratic ecological governance requires participation, fairness, competence, and honesty. Citizens must see the transition not as sacrifice demanded by distant experts, but as a collective project that improves life. Workers must have a voice. Communities must be consulted. Benefits must be tangible. Costs must be shared. Corruption must be prevented. Public institutions must deliver. Climate policy cannot be only a technocratic carbon plan. It must be a social contract.

The moral language of climate must also change. Too much climate discourse frames the problem as individual guilt: drive less, fly less, consume less, recycle more. Individual behavior matters, but the major systems are structural: energy grids, housing, transportation, agriculture, industry, finance, land use, and public policy. A person living in a car-dependent suburb with no transit, inefficient housing, and limited income does not have the same choices as an affluent household with solar panels, transit access, and flexibility. Moral responsibility must be proportionate to power and alternatives.

At the same time, affluent individuals and societies do have special responsibility. Luxury emissions, wasteful consumption, frequent flying, oversized homes, speculative resource use, and political resistance to change cannot be excused by structural arguments. The wealthy have more capacity to reduce harm and more responsibility for shaping institutions. Climate ethics must avoid blaming the powerless while refusing to excuse the powerful.

This chapter has emphasized constraint, but constraint is not the same as despair. Constraints can clarify purpose. A finite planet forces economics to ask what is enough, what is valuable, what should grow, what should shrink, and how prosperity can be sustained without destruction.

This is not an anti-human question. It is a deeply human one. A society that mistakes endless consumption for freedom may become less free as ecological systems destabilize. A society that builds sufficiency, care, resilience, and beauty may become richer in the ways that matter most.

Ecological constraint also invites innovation. Clean energy, circular production, regenerative agriculture, resilient cities, public transit, building retrofits, ecosystem restoration, water efficiency, and low-carbon industry can create meaningful work and public value. The transition can be a project of renewal if designed well. It can repair infrastructure, reduce pollution, improve health, reduce energy poverty, create jobs, and rebuild public trust. Climate policy should not be presented only as the avoidance of catastrophe. It should also be presented as the construction of a better economy.

But hope must be disciplined. Technological optimism without institutional change is inadequate. Markets alone will not protect the vulnerable. Innovation alone will not ensure justice. Adaptation alone will not prevent escalating damage. Carbon pricing alone will not transform infrastructure. Consumer choice alone will not redesign cities. International pledges alone will not cut emissions. A nonlinear problem requires a systems response.

A serious climate and energy agenda would include rapid decarbonization of electricity, electrification of transport and buildings where feasible, industrial decarbonization, methane reduction, grid expansion, storage, public transit, housing reform, building efficiency, clean-energy manufacturing, climate-resilient agriculture, ecosystem protection, adaptation investment, disaster preparedness, just transition support, carbon pricing with rebates where appropriate, strict regulation of emissions, climate finance for developing countries, and democratic accountability. These are not separate policies. They are components of a new economic architecture.

Energy abundance should remain a goal, but it must be clean abundance. Human development requires reliable energy. Hospitals, schools, homes, industry, agriculture, communication, and public services all need power. The ecological task is not to romanticize scarcity. It is to build energy systems that provide enough for dignified life without destabilizing the planet. Clean abundance, fairly distributed, can support prosperity within limits. The issue is not energy itself. The issue is the source, structure, ownership, and use of energy.

Ownership matters in the energy transition. If clean energy infrastructure is owned narrowly, the benefits may concentrate. If communities, public utilities, cooperatives, households, tribes, municipalities, and workers share ownership, the transition can build wealth more broadly. Energy democracy is not only a slogan. It is a way to ensure that the benefits of transition do not flow only to large firms and investors. Community solar, public power, cooperative utilities, and local ownership can create support and distribute gains.

The transition must also address reliability. Critics of clean energy often point to intermittency, grid stress, or storage needs. These are real challenges, not reasons for inaction. A reliable clean grid requires diversified resources, transmission, storage, demand response, firm clean power, smart planning, and regional coordination. Fossil systems also fail through price volatility, fuel supply disruptions, pollution, and climate damage. Reliability should be evaluated across the whole system, not through selective criticism. The question is how to design a clean system that is more reliable than the fossil system it replaces.

Energy efficiency remains one of the most powerful tools. The cleanest energy is often the energy not wasted. Insulation, efficient appliances, industrial efficiency, smart controls, public transit, compact land use, and building retrofits reduce demand and lower bills. Efficiency also improves resilience because it reduces exposure to price spikes and grid stress. But efficiency programs must reach low-income households and renters, not only homeowners with capital. Otherwise the benefits accumulate upward.

Land use is central to climate and energy. Sprawling development increases driving, infrastructure costs, land consumption, and emissions. Compact, walkable, transit-rich communities reduce energy demand and improve quality of life. But density must be humane, green, and affordable. Climate policy that ignores housing will fail, and housing policy that ignores climate will create new risks. Land is where ecological constraint, housing, transportation, and inequality meet.

Agriculture must also transform. Industrial agriculture has increased yields enormously, but it can depend heavily on fossil fuels, synthetic fertilizer, pesticides, monoculture, water depletion, and soil degradation. Regenerative practices, precision agriculture, crop diversity, soil health, reduced waste, methane reduction, sustainable livestock systems, and fair farm labor can reduce ecological harm. Food systems must be resilient to climate shocks while reducing their own emissions. The goal is not nostalgia for a preindustrial past. It is a scientifically informed agriculture that respects ecological function.

Urban policy is climate policy. Cities concentrate people, infrastructure, emissions, risk, and opportunity. They can be efficient and low-carbon if designed well, with transit, density, parks, shade, affordable housing, clean buildings, and resilient infrastructure. They can also become heat islands, inequality machines, flood zones, and centers of exclusion. Urban trees, reflective surfaces, stormwater systems, cooling centers, resilient public housing, and equitable transit all matter. Climate adaptation must be built into the ordinary fabric of city planning.

The private sector has an indispensable role. Firms innovate, invest, build, produce, and deploy. But voluntary corporate commitments are not enough. Some firms will lead; others will delay. Some will greenwash. Some will lobby against regulation while advertising sustainability. Clear rules are needed so that responsible firms are not undercut by irresponsible ones. Markets need standards. Corporate climate responsibility must include emissions reductions, supply-chain accountability, capital expenditure alignment, lobbying transparency, and worker transition plans.

Greenwashing is a serious problem because it erodes trust. If citizens believe climate policy is symbolic or captured by corporate marketing, legitimacy declines. Standards for disclosure, offsets, emissions accounting, and sustainability claims are necessary. Offsets require special caution. Some offsets may be legitimate, but many are uncertain, temporary, or difficult to verify. Reducing emissions at the source is more reliable than claiming neutrality through questionable accounting. A society cannot offset its way out of structural dependence on fossil fuels.

The concept of net zero can be useful, but also misleading. Net zero means remaining emissions are balanced by removals. Some removals will be necessary for hard-to-abate sectors. But if net zero becomes a justification for delaying reductions, it becomes dangerous. Carbon removal technologies may help, but they are not a substitute for rapid emissions cuts. Forests and soils can store carbon, but they are vulnerable to fire, drought, and land-use change. The atmosphere responds to actual concentrations, not accounting optimism. Climate policy must be grounded in physical reality.

Physical reality is the ultimate constraint. Economic systems can create money, credit, and contracts, but they cannot legislate away thermodynamics, atmospheric chemistry, ecological interdependence, or material limits. This does not make economics irrelevant. It makes economics more serious. The discipline must learn to operate within biophysical boundaries. It must ask how to allocate scarce ecological capacity, how to invest in resilience, how to distribute transition costs, and how to preserve human flourishing under constraint.

This is a return to the original meaning of economics as household management. The household is now planetary. The question is how to manage the shared home without exhausting its foundations. A household that spends down its savings, damages its roof, poisons its water, neglects its children, and declares itself prosperous because consumption is high is not well governed. Modern economies have too often done the planetary equivalent. Climate change is the audit.

The next chapter turns to public policy under conditions of complexity. Climate, energy, and ecological constraint make that chapter unavoidable. No single policy lever can solve a problem that spans energy systems, finance, housing, labor, technology, agriculture, trade, and democracy. The state must become more adaptive, more capable, more honest, and more just. Markets must be guided without being smothered. Citizens must be included without allowing every necessary project to be vetoed. Public institutions must learn to govern feedback loops, not merely respond to symptoms.

The lessons of this chapter connect to every prior chapter. Climate intensifies inflation through food, energy, insurance, and disasters. It affects debt through public recovery costs, stranded assets, and household losses. It deepens inequality through unequal exposure and unequal capacity to adapt. It affects housing through floods, fires, heat, insurance, and migration. It reshapes labor through heat stress, green jobs, displaced industries, and care burdens. It exposes supply-chain fragility through extreme weather and resource constraints. It affects financial markets through repricing, risk, and stranded assets. It interacts with technology through clean innovation, data centers, artificial intelligence, and critical minerals. Climate is not a separate issue. It is the systemic context of all future economics.

A nonlinear world teaches that ecological damage can accumulate quietly, then erupt suddenly. A heat wave, fire, flood, crop failure, insurance crisis, grid collapse, or migration surge may appear as a discrete event, but it is often the visible expression of long feedback loops. Emissions accumulated. Land was misused. Infrastructure was underbuilt. Inequality left people exposed. Political systems delayed. Then the shock arrived. The disaster was sudden; the vulnerability was not.

This recognition creates responsibility. We cannot claim surprise forever. We know enough to act. We know that emissions warm the planet. We know that warming increases risk. We know that the poor are more exposed. We know that fossil systems are politically entrenched. We know that clean technologies exist but require systems to scale. We know that delay raises cost. We know that public trust matters. We know that ecological stability is the foundation of economic stability. The question is not whether we have perfect certainty. The question is whether we have enough knowledge to govern responsibly. We do.

The end of simple economic explanations requires us to stop treating nature as an externality and start treating it as the ground of economic possibility. It requires us to stop treating energy as just another input and start treating it as the metabolic basis of civilization. It requires us to stop treating climate policy as a special environmental concern and start treating it as macroeconomic policy, industrial policy, housing policy, labor policy, financial policy, and democratic policy. It requires us to redefine prosperity so that it can endure.

A society that fails to respect ecological constraint will experience growth as instability. It will spend more repairing disasters, insuring losses, cooling cities, moving people, treating illness, rebuilding infrastructure, and fighting over scarcity. A society that respects constraint can redirect investment toward resilience, health, clean energy, and shared security. The choice is not between economy and ecology. There is no economy without ecology. The choice is between an economy that denies its foundations and one that learns to live within them.

Climate, energy, and ecological constraint are therefore not the final obstacle to prosperity. They are the conditions under which any future prosperity must be designed. The task is immense, but it is also clarifying. It asks economics to become more honest, more physical, more moral, and more democratic. It asks societies to build systems that can flourish without devouring their own ground.

In a nonlinear world, the planet is not passive background. It is an active system responding to what human economies do. The atmosphere remembers emissions. Oceans remember heat. Soils remember extraction. Communities remember disasters. Future generations will remember whether we acted in time.

The economy has long treated nature as if it were silent. Climate change is nature speaking back.

## Chapter 14

# Public Policy Under Conditions of Complexity

Public policy in a nonlinear world begins with humility. This does not mean timidity, resignation, or the abandonment of ambition. It means recognizing that economic systems are not machines that respond predictably to single levers. They are complex adaptive systems composed of households, firms, workers, banks, investors, governments, technologies, ecosystems, institutions, narratives, and expectations. They react to policy. They reinterpret policy. They adapt around policy. They amplify some interventions and absorb others. They produce unintended consequences, not because policymakers are always foolish, but because society is dynamic.

The great temptation of modern policy is simplification. A problem appears, and a lever is selected. Inflation rises, so interest rates must rise. Poverty persists, so people need jobs. Housing is expensive, so buyers need subsidies. Banks fail, so liquidity must be provided. Supply chains break, so production must be reshored. Workers fall behind, so they need training. Climate change worsens, so carbon must be priced. Each of these responses may contain truth. Each may be necessary in some circumstances. But none is sufficient if treated as a complete theory of the problem. Complexity does not deny the usefulness of policy levers. It denies the fantasy that one lever can govern a system.

The central argument of this chapter is that public policy under conditions of complexity must shift from mechanical control to adaptive governance. The task is not to find the one correct intervention that restores equilibrium. The task is to understand the feedback loops that generate the problem, identify leverage points, build institutional capacity, monitor consequences, adjust over time, distribute burdens fairly, and preserve legitimacy. Policy must become less like repairing a clock and more like tending an ecosystem. It must recognize interdependence, uncertainty, thresholds, adaptation, and the moral consequences of design.

This requires a different kind of policy imagination. Traditional policy often asks, "What is the market failure, and what corrective instrument should government apply?" This is a useful question. Externalities, information asymmetries, public goods, monopoly power, coordination failures, and inequality all justify intervention. But complexity pushes the inquiry further. It asks how the failure reproduces itself. It asks who benefits from the current feedback loop. It asks whether the proposed intervention will be captured, resisted, gamed, delayed, or amplified. It asks what will happen not only immediately, but after households, firms, investors, local governments, and political actors respond. It asks whether the policy creates resilience or new fragility.

Consider housing. A mechanical approach sees high prices and offers demand subsidies to buyers or renters. This may help some households. But if supply is constrained by zoning, land costs, local vetoes, financing barriers, and speculation, subsidies can raise prices further. The relief becomes partially capitalized into higher rents or home values. The policy helps at the margin while strengthening the scarcity machine. A complexity approach asks how to alter the loop: expand supply, preserve affordability, reduce speculation, reform zoning, protect tenants, use public land, coordinate regionally, and change the political incentives that reward exclusion. The problem is not only that housing costs too much. The problem is that the system is organized to keep scarcity valuable.

Consider inflation. A mechanical approach sees rising prices and tightens monetary policy. This may be necessary, especially if demand is excessive or expectations are becoming unanchored. But if inflation is driven by energy shocks, supply-chain bottlenecks, housing scarcity, climate stress,

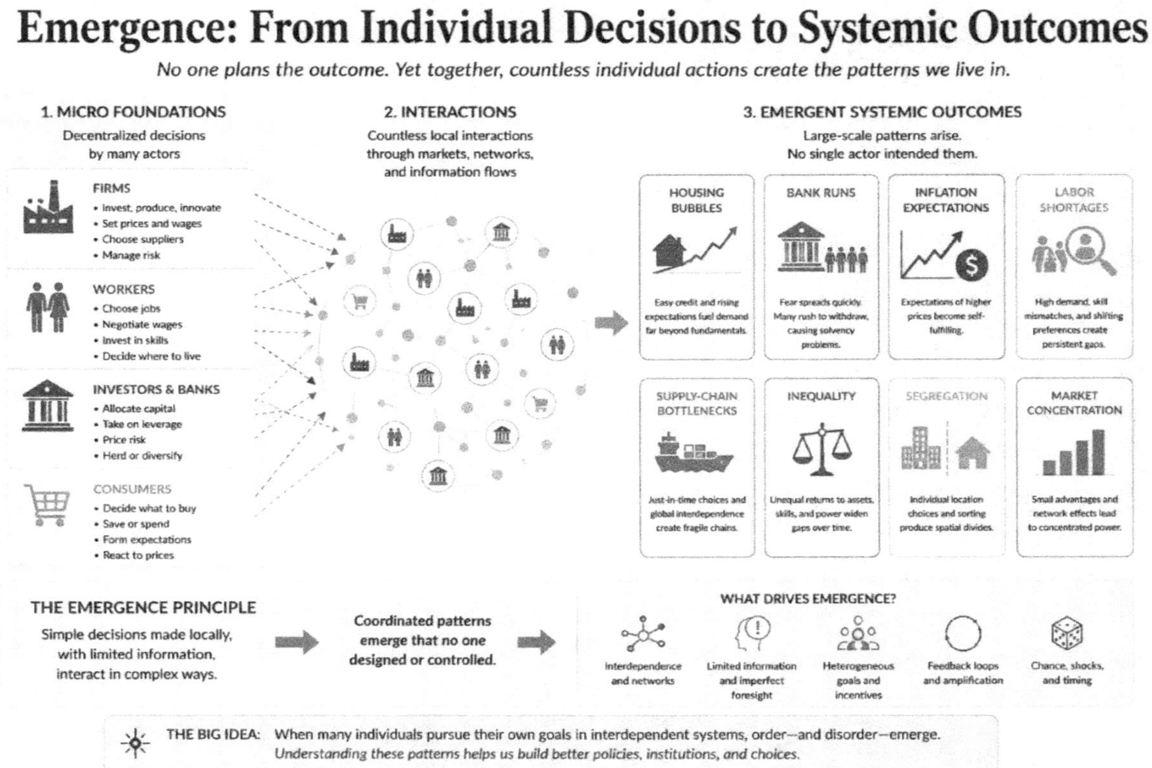


*Figure 7.0 – Emergence: From Individual Decisions to Systemic Outcomes*

market concentration, or geopolitical disruption, monetary tightening alone can impose pain without repairing sources. A complexity approach still respects price stability, but it asks which inflationary loops are active. It combines monetary policy with supply repair, competition policy, energy resilience, targeted fiscal relief, housing reform, and public communication. It treats inflation as a process, not merely a number.

Consider inequality. A mechanical approach may focus on taxes and transfers after market outcomes occur. Redistribution is necessary. It reduces poverty, supports demand, and expresses solidarity. But if the labor market produces low wages, housing markets compound wealth gaps, schools depend on local property wealth, healthcare insecurity burdens workers, political finance amplifies elite influence, and capital income receives preferential treatment, inequality will regenerate. A complexity approach combines redistribution with predistribution. It changes the rules before outcomes emerge: labor power, education, healthcare, housing, antitrust, tax design, inheritance, public goods, and democratic reform. It does not merely mop the floor while the pipe remains broken.

Consider climate. A mechanical approach may say, "Put a price on carbon." Carbon pricing is valuable because emissions impose social costs. But climate change is not only a pricing problem. It is an energy infrastructure problem, a land use problem, a transportation problem, a finance problem, a technology problem, a labor problem, a housing problem, a geopolitical problem, and a democratic problem. Carbon pricing without clean infrastructure, public investment, permitting reform, just transition, adaptation, and equity can produce backlash or insufficient change. A complexity approach uses prices, standards, investment, public planning, and social protection together.

The lesson is not that policy should become endlessly complicated or paralyzed by nuance. Complexity without decision becomes evasion. The lesson is that policy must be systemic enough to be effective. A simple policy can be powerful if it targets a leverage point. Automatic stabilizers, deposit insurance, vaccination, child allowances, unemployment insurance, interest-rate policy, bank capital requirements, and clean energy standards can all be relatively simple in form. Their power comes from the feedback loops they alter. Simplicity is valuable when it is grounded in systemic understanding. It is dangerous when it is a substitute for understanding.

Public policy under complexity begins by mapping the system. This does not require omniscience. No map is complete. But policymakers must identify the main actors, incentives, constraints, flows, stocks, feedback loops, delays, thresholds, and power relations. In a debt crisis, the map should include borrowers, lenders, maturity structures, interest rates, collateral values, refinancing needs, currency risk, legal rules, and confidence. In a labor market crisis, the map should include wages, bargaining power, childcare, housing, transportation, credentials, health, monopsony, technology, and regional conditions. In a supply-chain crisis, the map should include suppliers, bottlenecks, inventories, labor, logistics, chokepoints, substitutes, financing, and demand behavior.

Mapping changes the policy conversation. It prevents policymakers from treating symptoms as isolated. It reveals hidden dependencies. It shows where a small intervention might have large effects and where a large intervention might be absorbed. It identifies who has power to block reform. It clarifies which policies must be coordinated. It helps distinguish temporary shocks from structural regimes. It also reveals moral stakes, because every system map is also a map of exposure. It shows who has buffers and who does not, who can pass costs on and who must absorb them, who benefits from delay and who suffers from it.

The next task is identifying feedback loops. A policy that does not alter feedback may provide temporary relief but leave the system unchanged. For example, emergency rental assistance can prevent eviction, which is vital. But if rents keep rising because supply is restricted and wages are insufficient, the need returns. Debt relief can free households from crushing obligations, which may be just and economically beneficial. But if healthcare, education, and housing continue to force borrowing, debt will reaccumulate. Food aid can reduce hunger, but if wages, housing, and food systems remain unstable, hunger persists. Relief and structural reform are not substitutes. Relief prevents harm now; structural reform changes the loop.

Feedback analysis also helps distinguish stabilizing from destabilizing policy. A stabilizing policy dampens harmful swings. Unemployment insurance stabilizes household income and demand during downturns. Deposit insurance prevents bank runs. Automatic fiscal stabilizers support the economy when private spending falls. Progressive taxation dampens inequality and demand volatility. Bank capital buffers reduce financial amplification. Public health systems reduce epidemic cascades. Affordable housing reduces rent shocks and labor market strain. These policies may appear passive in normal times, but they are active stabilizers.

A destabilizing policy amplifies harmful swings, often unintentionally. Procyclical austerity during recession can reduce demand, lower revenue, and worsen debt burdens. Deregulation during a boom can encourage leverage precisely when caution is needed. Housing subsidies without supply reform can raise prices. Tax cuts during overheating can intensify inflation. Underfunding public health during calm periods can worsen crisis. Labor market policies that weaken worker power during already unequal conditions can deepen insecurity and debt. The effect of policy depends on timing and context. The same instrument can stabilize in one regime and destabilize in another.

Timing is crucial because complex systems contain delays. A policy may show benefits immediately and costs later, or costs immediately and benefits later. Infrastructure investment takes time. Education reforms take years. Climate mitigation takes decades to fully protect. Interest-rate changes affect the economy with lags. Housing supply reforms may take years to reduce pressure. Deregulation may produce growth before fragility appears. Austerity may reduce deficits now but weaken future capacity. Policy evaluation must therefore resist short-termism.

Democratic politics often struggles with delay. Voters feel immediate pain. Elected officials face election cycles. Media reward visible action. Financial markets demand quick signals. Bureaucracies measure annual budgets. Preventive policies are underappreciated because the disasters they avoid do not occur. This creates a bias toward reaction rather than prevention. Complexity economics demands the opposite. The highest form of policy intelligence is preventing cascades before they become visible. A society that only responds after breakdown will always be governed by emergency.

Prevention requires institutional memory. Financial crises, pandemics, supply shortages, energy shocks, housing bubbles, and climate disasters often produce reform immediately afterward. Over time, memory fades. Interest groups press for relaxation. Citizens grow tired of preparedness costs. Politicians declare old safeguards unnecessary. The system returns to fragility. Public institutions must preserve memory against the political erosion of caution. Stress tests, independent agencies, public reporting, scenario planning, and civic education can help. But memory is ultimately a moral discipline: the willingness to remember suffering after fear has passed.

Scenario planning is essential under uncertainty. Forecasting seeks the most likely future. Scenario planning considers multiple plausible futures, especially severe ones. What if inflation persists? What if energy prices spike? What if a major supplier fails? What if sea levels rise faster than expected? What if a cyberattack disables payment systems? What if a housing market freezes? What if a pandemic returns? What if unemployment rises quickly? Scenario planning does not predict precisely. It prepares broadly. It builds institutions that can respond to surprise.

This is the logic of robustness. A robust policy works reasonably well across different possible futures. It does not depend on perfect prediction. Social insurance is robust because someone will face unemployment, illness, disability, or caregiving needs, even if we do not know who. Bank capital is robust because financial losses will occur, even if we do not know where. Climate adaptation is robust because extreme weather will intensify, even if exact events are uncertain. Public health capacity is robust because infectious disease risk persists. A robust society invests in capacity before knowing the precise form of need.

Resilience is related but broader. Resilience is the ability of a system to absorb shock, maintain essential function, recover, learn, and adapt. It is not merely the ability to bounce back to the old state. Sometimes the old state was unjust or fragile. Resilience can mean transformation. A community rebuilding after disaster should not simply recreate the vulnerabilities that made disaster so harmful. A financial system after crisis should not return to the same incentives. A labor market after disruption should not reproduce precarity. Resilience is not nostalgia. It is adaptive continuity.

Public policy should therefore evaluate systems by stress performance, not only normal performance. A healthcare system should be judged not only by average efficiency, but by surge capacity. A supply chain should be judged not only by low cost, but by ability to maintain critical goods during disruption. A financial system should be judged not only by profitability, but by capital, liquidity, and failure containment. A housing system should be judged not only by property values, but by affordability under stress. A labor market should be judged not only by employment rates, but by income stability, job quality, and recovery after downturns. An economy that performs well only in calm conditions is not well governed.

This requires rethinking efficiency. In conventional policy discourse, efficiency often means minimizing waste, lowering cost, and allocating resources to their highest-valued uses. These are important goals. Waste matters. Public resources are limited. But efficiency measured without resilience is incomplete. Spare hospital beds may look inefficient until a pandemic. Inventory may look wasteful until a supply shock. Bank capital may look costly until a crisis. Public housing capacity may look expensive until homelessness rises. Energy redundancy may look unnecessary until a fuel shock. What appears inefficient in ordinary accounting may be deeply efficient in systemic accounting.

The challenge is to distinguish genuine waste from necessary buffer. Not every redundancy is wise. Not every public program is effective. Not every regulation protects. Not every stockpile is well managed. Complexity is not an excuse for sloppy government. It demands better government. Buffers should be targeted, maintained, evaluated, and updated. Resilience spending should be accountable. Institutions should learn from evidence. The point is not to glorify excess capacity everywhere, but to recognize that systems without adequate buffers shift costs into crisis.

Adaptive governance also requires feedback from implementation. Policies do not become real when passed into law. They become real through agencies, budgets, rules, forms, workers, courts, firms, citizens, technology systems, and local conditions. A beautiful policy design can fail if implementation is weak. A benefit that requires complex applications may not reach those who need it. A regulation without enforcement may become symbolic. A subsidy may be captured by intermediaries. A training program may not connect to jobs. A housing program may be delayed by permitting. Implementation is not administrative detail. It is policy substance.

Public capacity is therefore central. A state cannot govern complexity if it lacks skilled personnel, data systems, institutional memory, procurement ability, scientific expertise, local relationships, legal authority, and trust. Decades of anti-government ideology in many societies have weakened the very institutions needed to manage complex problems. Citizens are told government cannot work, resources are withdrawn, agencies degrade, performance worsens, and distrust is confirmed. This is a vicious loop. Public failure becomes evidence for further public weakening.

Rebuilding public capacity is not a matter of bureaucracy for its own sake. It is a condition of freedom. Citizens are not free when public institutions cannot provide clean water, safe food, functioning infrastructure, public health, fair courts, disaster response, stable money, affordable housing, labor standards, education, or ecological protection. Markets depend on public capacity. Contracts require courts. Finance requires regulation. Innovation requires research. Labor markets require education and law. Property requires public order. A capable state is not the enemy of markets. It is one of their conditions.

At the same time, the state must be democratic and accountable. Complexity should not become a justification for technocratic arrogance. Experts are necessary, but they are not sufficient. Data are necessary, but they do not settle values. Models are useful, but they are simplifications. Citizens have local knowledge, moral claims, and democratic rights. Policy under complexity must combine expertise with participation. It must listen to those affected, especially those with the least power. It must explain tradeoffs honestly. It must correct mistakes. It must earn trust.

Technocracy fails when it treats legitimacy as secondary. A policy can be technically sound and politically unstable if citizens experience it as unfair, opaque, or imposed. Climate policy that raises fuel costs without protecting low-income households invites backlash. Public health policy that asks for sacrifice without transparency loses compliance. Monetary policy that reduces inflation through unemployment while ignoring corporate pricing power may appear class-biased. Housing reform that accelerates development without tenant protections may be perceived as displacement. Legitimacy is not decorative. It is part of policy effectiveness.

Fairness is a stabilizing force. People are more willing to accept burdens when they believe burdens are shared, benefits are real, and institutions are honest. Fairness shapes compliance, trust, and expectation. An anti-inflation policy that demands wage restraint while allowing excessive profits will face resistance. A climate policy that asks ordinary households to pay while wealthy households continue high-emission lifestyles will lose moral authority. A financial rescue that protects banks but not households will produce anger. Policy must be evaluated not only by aggregate outcomes, but by perceived and actual justice.

This is why distributional analysis must be built into every major policy. Who benefits? Who pays? Who is exposed to risk? Who gains power? Who loses options? Who receives relief quickly? Who must navigate bureaucracy? Who is likely to be excluded? Which regions are affected? Which generations? Which racial, gender, disability, age, and income groups? Distribution is not an afterthought. It shapes feedback. A policy that deepens inequality may undermine legitimacy and create future instability even if it improves short-term efficiency.

Power analysis is equally important. Policies enter fields of power. Firms lobby. Wealthy households plan around taxes. Local incumbents resist housing. Financial institutions innovate around rules. Platforms shape regulation. Fossil interests delay transition. Professional associations protect licensing. Agencies may be captured. Courts reinterpret statutes. Policy design that ignores power will often fail. Complexity is not only interaction; it is unequal interaction. The system adapts, but not all actors adapt with equal resources.

Regulatory capture is one of the recurring dangers. Agencies created to regulate industries may come to identify with those industries, depend on their information, hire from them, or anticipate employment within them. Technical complexity can increase dependence on regulated firms.

The public may lack the expertise to monitor the relationship. Capture need not involve bribery. It can arise through worldview, access, information asymmetry, and social proximity. Preventing capture requires transparency, strong ethics rules, independent expertise, public-interest representation, adequate funding, and democratic oversight.

Policy must also anticipate gaming. Actors respond to rules. If benefits are means-tested, households may face cliffs or administrative burdens. If firms receive subsidies tied to job creation, they may relabel jobs or automate later. If banks face capital requirements on certain assets, risk may shift elsewhere. If schools are judged by test scores, teaching may narrow or manipulation may occur. If hospitals are reimbursed by procedure, procedures may increase. If police departments are judged by arrests, arrests may rise without safety improving. Metrics shape behavior.

This is Goodhart's law in practical governance: when a measure becomes a target, it can cease to be a good measure. Complexity-aware policy uses metrics but does not worship them. It combines quantitative indicators with qualitative feedback, audits, citizen experience, and institutional judgment. It updates measures when behavior changes. It avoids reducing complex goals to single numbers. A school is not only test scores. A hospital is not only throughput. A labor market is not only unemployment. An economy is not only GDP. A democracy is not only turnout. Metrics are tools, not truth itself.

The limits of prediction also matter. Policymakers often rely on models, and they should. Models discipline thought, clarify assumptions, estimate effects, and reveal tradeoffs. But models are not reality. They omit variables, simplify behavior, assume relationships, and rely on data from the past. In nonlinear systems, relationships can change. A model built on calm periods may fail in crisis. A model that assumes representative agents may miss distributional fragility. A model that treats expectations as stable may miss panic. A model that ignores networks may miss cascades. The responsible use of models requires pluralism and humility.

Model pluralism means using different models for different purposes. A macroeconomic model may estimate aggregate demand. A network model may identify contagion. A distributional model may show household effects. A systems dynamics model may trace feedback loops. A scenario model may explore uncertainty. A qualitative institutional analysis may reveal power and implementation. No single model can contain society. The policy process should compare perspectives rather than elevate one framework into dogma.

Experimentalism can help. Policies can be piloted, evaluated, revised, and scaled. Randomized trials can be useful for some interventions, especially where treatment can be clearly defined and outcomes measured. Natural experiments, administrative data, case studies, historical analysis, and community feedback are also valuable. But complex systems require caution in generalizing from one context to another. A program that works in one city may fail elsewhere because institutions, culture, labor markets, housing, transportation, and trust differ. Evidence matters, but context shapes evidence.

Adaptive policy should therefore include learning loops. Set goals. Implement. Measure. Listen. Revise. Scale what works. Stop what fails. Protect people during experimentation. Avoid locking in bad designs because of political pride. Create sunset clauses where appropriate. Use automatic triggers where conditions can be specified. Build review institutions. Treat policy as an evolving practice, not a one-time decree.

Automatic stabilizers are among the most elegant examples of complexity-aware policy. They respond without requiring new political action during crisis. When unemployment rises, unemployment insurance payments increase. When income falls, tax payments fall. When poverty rises, safety net spending expands. These automatic responses stabilize demand and households quickly. They avoid delays caused by legislative conflict. They are feedback devices built into government. Strong automatic stabilizers make societies more resilient.

Automatic triggers can be extended. Fiscal support could increase when unemployment rises above a threshold. Rental assistance could activate when eviction filings spike. Food support could expand when food prices rise sharply. Infrastructure funding could accelerate during downturns. Bank capital buffers could rise during credit booms and fall during stress. Climate disaster funds could be released based on measurable events. Policy can be designed to respond to conditions, not only political will.

However, automatic policy must be designed with care. Bad triggers can misfire. Indicators can be revised or manipulated. Automatic spending can create fiscal concerns if poorly bounded. Some decisions require judgment. The goal is not to automate democracy. It is to reduce harmful delay where conditions are clear and speed matters. Automatic stabilizers should complement democratic deliberation, not replace it.

Coordination is another central challenge. Complex problems cross agency boundaries. Housing involves local zoning, transportation, finance, labor, climate, schools, and health. Climate involves energy, industry, agriculture, housing, transportation, finance, trade, and labor. Public health involves healthcare, labor conditions, housing, education, transportation, and trust. Inflation involves monetary policy, fiscal policy, supply chains, competition, energy, housing, and wages. A fragmented state cannot manage interconnected problems if each agency optimizes its own narrow mission.

Whole-of-government coordination is often promised but difficult. Agencies have mandates, budgets, cultures, data systems, legal constraints, and political overseers. Coordination requires leadership, shared goals, institutional mechanisms, data interoperability, and accountability. It also requires avoiding the illusion that a central office can command complexity from above. Effective coordination often combines central strategy with local implementation, cross-agency teams, public dashboards, and continuous feedback.

Local knowledge matters. National policy sets resources and rights, but implementation occurs in places. Communities understand specific needs, histories, barriers, and trust relationships. A housing program in a rural area differs from one in a dense city. Workforce policy differs across regions. Climate adaptation differs by geography. Public health messages differ by culture and experience. Centralized policy that ignores local knowledge can fail. Local control that ignores regional and national consequences can also fail. The challenge is nested governance: decisions made at the level appropriate to the problem, coordinated across levels.

Federalism, where present, can be a strength or weakness under complexity. It allows experimentation, local adaptation, and policy learning. It can also create fragmentation, inequality, race-to-the-bottom competition, and paralysis. A state or province may innovate in healthcare, energy, labor standards, or housing. Another may undercut standards to attract business. Local governments may block housing needed regionally. National standards may be necessary for rights, climate, finance, and labor. The design of multi-level governance is itself a complexity problem.

Policy sequencing is another overlooked issue. The order of reforms affects outcomes. Deregulating housing supply before strengthening tenant protections may increase displacement fears. Expanding clean energy before building transmission may create bottlenecks. Raising carbon prices before providing rebates may create backlash. Offering training before jobs exist may waste effort. Tightening monetary policy before addressing financial fragility may expose crisis. Sequence matters because systems adapt to each step. Policy packages must be timed.

Complementarity matters as well. Some policies work only in combination. Childcare support increases labor force participation more effectively when jobs pay adequately. Training works better with employer demand. Housing vouchers work better with supply and landlord enforcement. Clean energy subsidies work better with permitting and grid investment. Minimum wages work better with enforcement and support for small firms where needed. Antitrust works better with data portability and interoperability in digital markets. Policy failure sometimes occurs not because an idea is wrong, but because its complements are missing.

This has implications for political communication. Policymakers often sell isolated programs because they are easier to explain. But citizens experience systems. A parent needs childcare, transportation, wages, healthcare, and housing together. A worker displaced by technology needs income support, training, jobs, benefits, and regional opportunity. A community facing climate risk needs adaptation, insurance reform, infrastructure, relocation options, and economic development. Policy should be communicated as an architecture, not a list of disconnected initiatives.

The word "architecture" is important. Public policy is not only intervention. It is design. Laws, taxes, subsidies, regulations, public investments, rights, and institutions create the structure within which private decisions occur. Markets then operate inside that structure. If housing scarcity is rewarded, scarcity grows. If financial leverage is rewarded, leverage grows. If pollution is free, pollution grows. If labor voice is weakened, insecurity grows. If public goods are underfunded, private inequality grows. Policy sets the rules of feedback.

A moral political economy therefore asks what behavior policy rewards. Does it reward extraction or investment? Speculation or production? Short-term profit or long-term resilience? Monopoly or competition? Wage suppression or shared productivity? Pollution or clean energy? Exclusionary zoning or inclusive housing? Predatory credit or fair finance? Preventive health or emergency treatment? The economy learns from incentives. Public policy teaches.

This teaching function is often invisible because laws become background. The mortgage interest deduction, zoning codes, bankruptcy rules, tax treatment of capital gains, union law, central bank mandates, bank capital rules, intellectual property terms, school funding formulas, procurement standards, and campaign finance rules all shape behavior. They are not natural. They are choices. Once established, they create interests that defend them. Complexity-aware policy must be historically aware because today's "market outcome" may be yesterday's political decision compounded over time.

Path dependence makes reform difficult. Existing systems create beneficiaries who resist change and harmed groups who may lack power. Infrastructure locks in behavior. Fossil-fuel systems, car-dependent suburbs, employer-based healthcare, fragmented school finance, private pension arrangements, and financialized housing all shape expectations. Reform must often work with legacy systems while building alternatives. Sudden rupture may be impossible or harmful. Gradual reform may be too slow. Policy must navigate between urgency and institutional reality.

This is especially true in climate and energy policy. Fossil infrastructure cannot disappear overnight without harming people. But delay worsens climate risk. A just transition requires phasing, investment, worker support, clean alternatives, and credible timelines. Similarly, housing scarcity cannot be solved overnight, but every delay raises costs. Financial reform must prevent crisis without choking productive credit. Labor reform must strengthen workers while allowing adaptation. Complexity policy is often the art of transition management.

Transitions require social contracts. People accept change when they believe they will not be abandoned. Workers accept technological change when they have retraining, income support, and voice. Communities accept clean energy infrastructure when they share benefits and are respected. Homeowners accept housing reform when infrastructure and affordability are addressed. Citizens accept climate policy when costs are fair. Firms accept regulation when rules are clear and competitors are held to the same standards. Trust lowers the cost of transition.

Trust, however, cannot be commanded. It must be earned through competence, honesty, fairness, and accountability. Governments lose trust when they overpromise, hide tradeoffs, favor insiders, ignore local concerns, or fail to deliver. They gain trust when policies work, mistakes are acknowledged, burdens are shared, and citizens are treated as adults. In complex systems, uncertainty is unavoidable. Pretending to certainty undermines trust when events change. Honest uncertainty is more credible than false precision.

Public communication must therefore change. Leaders should explain systems without drowning citizens in jargon. They should say why a problem has multiple causes, why no policy is costless, why timing matters, and how success will be judged. They should distinguish short-term relief from long-term reform. They should identify who will be helped and who may bear costs. They should not scapegoat convenient groups to avoid complexity. Democratic maturity requires truthful complexity made accessible.

This is difficult in a media environment that rewards outrage, simplicity, and conflict. Complex explanations are vulnerable to slogans. A housing crisis becomes "greedy developers" or "lazy renters" or "government regulation." Inflation becomes "money printing" or "corporate greed" or "wages." Climate policy becomes "war on energy" or "green salvation." Financial crisis becomes "irresponsible borrowers" or "evil banks." Each slogan contains fragments of reality or moral intuition, but each distorts when made total. Policy under complexity requires narrative discipline.

A good public narrative does not say, "Everything is complicated, so no one is responsible." That is fatalism disguised as sophistication. A good narrative says, "This problem is produced by interacting systems, and responsibility must be assigned at the level of those systems." Banks are responsible for risk. Regulators are responsible for oversight. Firms are responsible for pricing and labor practices. Governments are responsible for public investment and rules. Citizens are responsible for democratic participation. Wealthy actors with greater power have greater responsibility. Complexity clarifies responsibility by locating it in relationships and institutions.

Moral responsibility under complexity differs from blame in simple stories. Blame seeks a villain. Responsibility seeks leverage. Blame can mobilize anger, but it can also misdirect. Responsibility asks who has the capacity to change the loop. A landlord may raise rent because the market allows it. A developer may build luxury units because financing requires high returns. A homeowner may oppose density because wealth is tied to scarcity. A bank may lend aggressively because competitors do. Each actor makes choices, but the policy question is how to alter incentives, rules, and institutions so that better choices become rational and harmful choices are constrained.

This is the difference between moralism and moral political economy. Moralism condemns individuals without changing systems. Moral political economy redesigns systems while preserving moral judgment. It recognizes greed, fear, inertia, ambition, solidarity, and self-interest as recurring human forces. It builds institutions that channel them toward public good. It does not assume people will become angels. It also does not assume they must remain trapped in destructive incentives.

Complexity policy must be precautionary where harms are systemic, irreversible, or catastrophic. Climate change, financial collapse, pandemics, nuclear risk, ecological destruction, and certain technological dangers require action before full certainty. Waiting for proof beyond doubt can mean waiting until thresholds are crossed. Precaution does not mean banning everything risky. It means matching the burden of proof to the scale and reversibility of harm. A small reversible mistake may be tolerable. A global irreversible cascade demands caution.

The precautionary principle is often criticized for blocking innovation. This criticism has force when precaution becomes indiscriminate. But the opposite error is more dangerous in systemic domains: allowing private experimentation with public catastrophe. Financial instruments, chemical releases, data systems, artificial intelligence, environmental destruction, and public health risks can impose costs far beyond the experimenting actor. A democratic society must ask who benefits from risk and who bears it. Innovation should proceed with safeguards proportional to potential harm.

Policy must also recognize irreversibility. Some harms cannot be easily undone: species extinction, childhood developmental damage, lost schooling, community collapse, climate tipping points, long-term unemployment scars, destroyed trust, accumulated debt, or public health failures. When harms are irreversible or path-dependent, cost-benefit analysis must be careful. A policy that appears efficient in expected value terms may be reckless if downside risks are catastrophic. Irreversibility increases the moral value of prevention.

Cost-benefit analysis remains useful, but incomplete. It helps compare alternatives and prevent waste. But it struggles with distribution, dignity, uncertainty, irreversible loss, rights, and nonmarket values. The value of a stable climate, a childhood free from hunger, a community not displaced, a species preserved, or a democracy trusted cannot be fully captured in discounted dollars. Policy should use cost-benefit analysis as one input, not as a moral sovereign. Some values set constraints on optimization.

Rights-based frameworks are necessary where human dignity is at stake. Housing, healthcare, education, clean air, safe work, voting, and bodily security cannot be treated only as goods to be allocated by willingness to pay. Rights do not eliminate tradeoffs, but they establish obligations. They say that certain conditions are foundational to membership in society. Complexity economics can inform how to realize rights effectively, but it should not reduce rights to efficiency calculations.

The same applies to democracy itself. Democratic procedures are not merely instruments for producing policy outcomes. They are expressions of equal citizenship. Complexity can tempt elites to say that problems are too complicated for ordinary citizens. This is dangerous. Citizens need not master every technical detail to have legitimate authority over social goals. Experts can advise on means; democracy decides ends. The best policy systems combine expert competence with democratic accountability.

Participation can also improve policy. People affected by policy often understand barriers that experts miss. Low-income households know why benefits are hard to access. Workers know how technology changes the workplace. Tenants know how landlords evade rules. Patients know where healthcare systems fail. Farmers know land and water conditions. Local communities know flood patterns, transportation gaps, and trust relationships. Participation is not only morally valuable. It is epistemically valuable. It improves knowledge.

But participation must be designed. Public meetings dominated by the most organized incumbents can reproduce inequality. Comment processes can privilege those with time, education, and legal support. Local veto can block regional needs. Participatory processes must include underrepresented groups, compensate time where appropriate, provide accessible information, and distinguish consultation from obstruction. Democracy should broaden voice, not merely empower those already loud.

Complexity policy also requires administrative simplicity for citizens. Systems can be complex internally while simple at the point of use. A well-designed benefit should be easy to access. A tax credit should not require expert navigation by those without resources. A housing application should not be impossible. A healthcare system should not force patients through labyrinths. Administrative burden is a form of policy failure. It often excludes the most vulnerable. Government should absorb complexity so citizens do not have to.

Digital technology can help or harm. It can simplify applications, target services, detect fraud, and improve coordination. It can also create surveillance, exclusion, algorithmic error, and opaque decision-making. Public digital systems should be designed with privacy, accessibility, appeal rights, human support, and transparency. Efficiency should not come at the cost of dignity. A person denied benefits by an algorithm still needs food, shelter, or care. Administrative modernization must remain humane.

Fiscal policy under complexity must distinguish investment from mere expenditure. Public spending that builds capacity, health, education, infrastructure, resilience, and productivity should not be treated the same as spending that merely patches avoidable harm. Preventive spending may reduce future costs. Underinvestment can create hidden liabilities: bridges decay, children suffer, diseases spread, climate damage grows, workers lose skills, housing shortages deepen. Fiscal prudence should include the cost of neglect.

Debt-financed public investment can be responsible when it builds future capacity. But fiscal capacity is not unlimited. Interest rates, inflation, institutional credibility, currency structure, and political legitimacy matter. Complexity avoids both crude austerity and careless borrowing. It asks what borrowing finances, who benefits, whether capacity expands, what risks are created, and how debt interacts with the broader economy. Fiscal policy should be countercyclical, investment-oriented, and distributionally aware.

Tax policy under complexity should shape incentives and fund public goods. It should reduce inequality where inequality destabilizes democracy and opportunity. It should discourage harmful behavior such as pollution, speculation, and excessive leverage where appropriate. It should support work, investment, and broad prosperity. It should be enforceable, legitimate, and resistant to avoidance. A tax system that wealthy actors can easily escape destroys trust. Tax compliance depends not only on law, but on perceived fairness.

Regulation should be designed as market architecture, not merely market restriction. Rules define property, contracts, liability, competition, disclosure, safety, labor rights, environmental obligations, and financial stability. Markets do not exist before rules. They exist through rules. The question is not regulation versus freedom. The question is which rules create freedom for whom. A rule that prevents predatory lending increases freedom for borrowers. A rule that protects monopoly reduces freedom for competitors and consumers. A rule that supports worker voice increases freedom from domination. A rule that protects pollution reduces freedom for those who breathe the air. Regulatory philosophy must be substantive, not rhetorical.

Antitrust policy is a key example. Competition is not automatic. It must be protected against monopoly, collusion, platform dominance, and political influence. Antitrust under complexity must look beyond short-term consumer prices to market structure, innovation, labor power, supplier dependency, data control, and democratic influence. Concentrated private power can distort markets and politics. Competition policy is therefore part of democratic policy.

Industrial policy is another example. Public investment and strategic coordination can build capacity in clean energy, semiconductors, medical supplies, infrastructure, and other critical sectors. But industrial policy must be disciplined by public purpose. It should avoid becoming subsidy capture. Public support should carry conditions: labor standards, environmental performance, domestic or allied capacity where needed, accountability, profit-sharing or public return where appropriate, and performance evaluation. Industrial policy is not about replacing markets. It is about shaping the direction of markets where national resilience and public purpose require it.

Social policy is macroeconomic policy. Healthcare, childcare, housing, education, unemployment insurance, food security, and retirement systems are not merely welfare programs. They shape labor supply, productivity, mobility, entrepreneurship, household debt, health, and trust. A society with strong social infrastructure is more adaptable because people can take risks without ruin. Security is not the enemy of dynamism. It is often its precondition.

This point reverses a common assumption. Some argue that generous social protections reduce work and innovation. Poorly designed systems can create disincentives, and policy should be attentive to them. But insecurity can also reduce innovation by making people fearful. A worker without healthcare cannot easily start a business. A parent without childcare cannot take a better job. A family without housing stability cannot plan. A student buried in debt may avoid socially valuable work. Social policy can expand freedom by reducing catastrophic downside risk. The goal is capability, not dependency.

The concept of capability should guide public policy. The question is not only how much income people have, but what they are able to do and become. Can they live in safe housing? Receive healthcare? Learn? Work with dignity? Care for family? Move if they choose? Participate in democracy? Recover from shock? Breathe clean air? Build wealth? Capability connects economics to human flourishing. Complexity economics provides the systems analysis; capability provides the moral standard.

Policy under complexity must also be historically honest. Many current inequalities and institutional arrangements are the accumulated result of past policies: redlining, segregation, exclusionary zoning, labor law, tax preferences, infrastructure placement, school finance, financial deregulation, trade rules, and environmental sacrifice zones. The state has not been absent. It has shaped markets. Corrective policy is therefore not artificial interference in a natural order. It is the redesign of institutions that were always publicly structured.

Historical honesty also matters for trust. Communities harmed by past policy may distrust new initiatives. A climate project, housing redevelopment, public health campaign, or infrastructure plan may be evaluated through memories of displacement, neglect, discrimination, or broken promises. Policymakers must understand this. Trust cannot be demanded from people whose experience justifies skepticism. It must be rebuilt through consistency, respect, and material benefit.

Complexity also requires international policy. Inflation, finance, climate, migration, supply chains, technology, tax avoidance, pandemics, and energy markets cross borders. National policy remains essential, but no nation can fully govern these problems alone. International coordination is needed for climate finance, debt restructuring, tax cooperation, labor standards, trade rules, financial regulation, pandemic preparedness, cyber security, and technology governance. Yet global institutions often lack democratic legitimacy and enforcement capacity. The challenge is to build cooperation without erasing sovereignty or justice.

Global policy must recognize asymmetry. Wealthy nations, reserve-currency issuers, multinational corporations, and financial centers have more power than poor nations, workers, migrants, and climate-vulnerable communities. Rules that appear neutral may operate unequally. A complexity-aware international order would consider vulnerability, historical responsibility, development needs, and policy space. It would treat global stability as a shared good, not a privilege of the powerful.

All of this may sound demanding, and it is. Complexity raises the standard for governance. But the alternative is not simple governance that works. The alternative is simple governance that fails repeatedly. The crises of recent decades, financial collapse, housing unaffordability, supply-chain breakdown, inflation shocks, climate disasters, labor insecurity, technological disruption, and democratic distrust, reveal the cost of inadequate policy imagination. The world has become too interconnected for narrow tools and too unstable for complacency.

The answer is not to abandon markets. Markets remain indispensable systems of coordination, experimentation, and information. The answer is not to centralize everything. Central planning cannot master the full complexity of economic life. The answer is to build institutions that combine market dynamism with public purpose, decentralized adaptation with democratic rules, expert knowledge with citizen voice, efficiency with resilience, and innovation with justice. This is not ideological moderation for its own sake. It is systems realism.

A complexity-informed policy state would have several defining features. It would be anticipatory, looking for vulnerabilities before crisis. It would be adaptive, revising policies as systems respond. It would be preventive, valuing avoided harm. It would be distributive, examining who gains and who bears risk. It would be participatory, incorporating local knowledge and democratic legitimacy. It would be capable, staffed and funded to implement. It would be coordinated across domains. It would be precautionary where harms are irreversible. It would be transparent about uncertainty. It would be morally grounded in human dignity and shared flourishing.

Such a state would not be perfect. No institution is. It would make mistakes. It would face political conflict. It would require correction. Complexity does not promise policy omnipotence. It promises a better way to think about fallibility. A policy state that expects error can learn. A policy state that pretends certainty becomes brittle. The difference between failure and catastrophe often lies in the capacity to detect, admit, and adjust.

The culture of policymaking must therefore change. Admitting uncertainty should not be treated as weakness. Revising policy should not be treated as betrayal. Piloting programs should not be treated as indecision. Building buffers should not be treated as waste. Regulating booms should not be treated as hostility to prosperity. Listening to affected communities should not be treated as delay. Protecting future generations should not be treated as abstraction. These are habits of mature governance.

The moral center of public policy under complexity is responsibility across time and connection. A policy decision today affects people not yet visible, harms not yet measured, and feedback loops not yet fully activated. A zoning decision affects future residents. A carbon emission affects future generations. A bank capital rule affects crisis probability. A childcare policy affects future labor markets and children's development. A tax rule affects wealth concentration. A technology regulation affects power and privacy. Policy is the architecture of tomorrow's constraints and possibilities.

The next and final chapter, Economic Governance After Equilibrium, will draw together the book's central thesis. If the economy is not a self-correcting machine moving naturally toward balance, then governance cannot be limited to occasional correction at the margins. It must become the conscious design of resilient, fair, adaptive systems. The old question was how to restore equilibrium. The new question is how to govern nonlinear motion without sacrificing freedom, dignity, or democracy.

This chapter has argued that complexity does not make policy impossible. It makes simple policy illusions impossible. It teaches that problems are sustained by feedback loops, that interventions change behavior, that timing matters, that power adapts, that legitimacy affects outcomes, and that resilience must be designed before crisis. It asks policymakers to abandon both arrogance and fatalism. Arrogance says the system can be controlled from above with precise levers. Fatalism says the system is too complex to govern. Complexity rejects both. Systems cannot be perfectly controlled, but they can be shaped.

The task is not mastery. The task is stewardship. Stewardship means acting with knowledge of interdependence, respect for uncertainty, attention to the vulnerable, and responsibility for the future. It means building institutions that can learn. It means designing markets that serve human purposes. It means distributing risk fairly. It means preventing private incentives from producing public catastrophe. It means preserving democratic legitimacy in the face of necessary change.

A nonlinear world does not absolve policymakers of responsibility. It deepens responsibility. When systems amplify, small choices can have large consequences. When thresholds exist, delay can be dangerous. When cascades occur, prevention is humane. When feedback loops compound inequality, neutrality is complicity. When ecological systems respond to cumulative harm, short-termism becomes moral failure. When financial markets herd, regulation is public protection. When technology scales, governance must scale with it. When housing scarcity hardens, reform must address power. When labor insecurity spreads, dignity must be designed into institutions.

Public policy under conditions of complexity is therefore not merely technical. It is ethical. It asks what kind of society our systems are producing and whether those systems deserve loyalty. It asks whether prosperity is resilient or brittle, shared or hoarded, humane or extractive, democratic or captured. It asks whether institutions can learn before catastrophe. It asks whether citizens can be told the truth and invited into the work of repair.

The end of simple economic explanations is the beginning of serious public policy. It does not give us easy answers. It gives us better questions. What feedback loop is driving the problem? Where is the threshold? Who has buffers? Who bears risk? Who benefits from the current system? What will actors do in response to intervention? What must be coordinated? What harms are irreversible? What would resilience require? What would fairness require? What would legitimacy require? What does the future need from us now?

These are the questions of governance after simplicity. A society that asks them honestly may still struggle, but it will struggle intelligently. A society that refuses them will continue to be surprised by crises it helped create.

Complexity is not an excuse for inaction. It is a demand for wiser action. Public policy must rise to that demand.

## Chapter 15

# CONCLUSION: ECONOMIC GOVERNANCE AFTER EQUILIBRIUM

MODERN ECONOMICS WAS long animated by a promise of order. Markets, if left to operate within the right conditions, would coordinate human activity through prices. Supply and demand would adjust. Wages would reflect productivity. Interest rates would balance saving and investment. Competition would discipline excess profit. Capital would flow toward its most productive use. Shocks might disturb the system, but the system would tend toward correction. The economy, in this imagination, was not always fair, nor always calm, but it possessed an internal logic of balance. Equilibrium stood as the organizing metaphor of economic reason.

This book has argued that the equilibrium imagination is no longer adequate to the world we inhabit. It is not useless. It remains valuable in particular settings. Prices matter. Incentives matter. Scarcity matters. Tradeoffs matter. Markets can coordinate dispersed information with remarkable power. Competition can spur innovation. Monetary policy can influence demand. Fiscal policy can stabilize downturns. Supply and demand remain necessary concepts. But they are not sufficient. They become dangerous when transformed from tools into a worldview.

The central economic problems of our time do not behave like simple movements toward balance. Inflation does not arise from one cause alone, nor does it necessarily fade once a single lever is pulled. Debt does not remain harmless simply because it is manageable in calm periods. Inequality does not merely reflect differences in productivity or effort. Housing markets do not automatically produce affordable shelter when prices rise. Labor markets do not clear smoothly because workers are not frictionless commodities. Supply chains do not become resilient merely because firms optimize costs. Financial markets do not always process information wisely. Technology does not distribute its gains automatically. Climate change does not wait politely for markets to adjust. These systems are nonlinear, adaptive, interconnected, and morally charged.

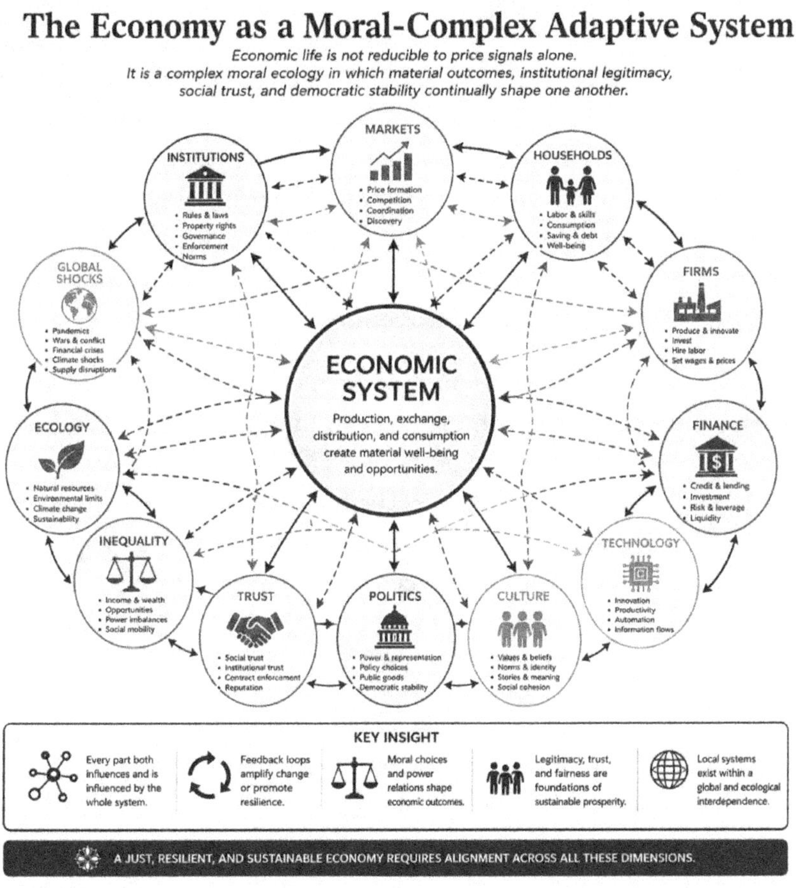


*Figure 8.0 – The Economy as a Moral-Complex Adaptive System*

The economy is not a machine returning naturally to balance. It is a complex adaptive order. It consists of households, firms, workers, investors, banks, governments, technologies, ecosystems, laws, norms, expectations, narratives, and power relations interacting across time. Its behavior emerges from feedback loops, thresholds, networks, incentives, institutions, and accumulated histories. It can generate stability, but it can also generate fragility. It can create prosperity, but also exclusion. It can innovate, but also concentrate. It can coordinate, but also cascade. It can appear calm while accumulating danger.

The end of equilibrium thinking does not mean the end of economic analysis. It means the beginning of a more realistic economics. It means replacing the question "What restores balance?" with deeper questions: What feedback loops are operating? Which loops stabilize and which amplify? Where are the thresholds? Who has buffers? Who bears risk? Who benefits from the current system? What happens if expectations change? What happens if one node fails? What is being optimized, and what is being ignored? What private incentives are producing public consequences? What does resilience require? What does justice require? What does democratic legitimacy require?

This is the meaning of economic governance after equilibrium. It is not rule by technocrats, nor command from above, nor the abandonment of markets. It is the conscious design and stewardship of economic systems under conditions of uncertainty, interdependence, and moral responsibility. It recognizes that markets must be embedded in institutions that shape their feedback. It recognizes that governments must be capable but humble, active but accountable, adaptive but principled. It recognizes that prosperity is not merely output, but the capacity of a society to sustain human flourishing through shock, change, and conflict.

The first lesson of this book is that linear thinking fails when causes return as consequences. A linear view assumes that a cause produces an effect in a proportional and traceable way. Raise a price, demand falls. Raise wages, labor supply changes. Raise interest rates, inflation declines. Reduce regulation, efficiency improves. Increase education, inequality falls. Sometimes such relationships hold. But often the effect feeds back into the cause. A rising price can lead buyers to purchase sooner, increasing demand. Rising asset values can encourage borrowing, which raises asset values further. Rising inequality can increase political influence, which produces rules that deepen inequality. Falling trust can produce behavior that confirms distrust. A shortage can produce hoarding, which worsens the shortage. A financial loss can produce selling, which creates more losses.

Feedback is the grammar of economic life. It is what makes the economy dynamic rather than mechanical. Feedback explains why the same policy can produce different effects in different contexts. It explains why small shocks can become large crises. It explains why systems can remain stable for long periods and then change suddenly. It explains why reform often disappoints when it treats symptoms rather than loops. It also explains why well-designed interventions can have powerful effects when they alter the right mechanism.

The second lesson is that thresholds matter. Societies often tolerate gradual deterioration because the visible system still functions. Debt rises, but defaults remain low. Housing prices rise, but transactions continue. Inequality rises, but growth persists. Trust erodes, but institutions operate. Supply chains thin, but goods arrive. Climate risks accumulate, but daily life continues. Financial leverage increases, but markets remain calm. The danger is that systems can cross thresholds before leaders recognize them. Once crossed, change accelerates.

A household can manage debt until one shock pushes it into default. A bank can appear solvent until depositors withdraw. A city can absorb rent increases until essential workers leave, families collapse into overcrowding, and homelessness rises. A democracy can tolerate inequality until citizens conclude that institutions no longer respond. A supply chain can function until a critical node fails. A climate system can absorb emissions until feedbacks intensify warming. A labor market can appear healthy until job quality, care burdens, debt, and housing costs produce widespread insecurity beneath low unemployment. Thresholds are often invisible until they have been crossed.

This is why governance must become anticipatory. It must detect vulnerability before collapse. It must measure not only averages but distributions. It must ask not only whether the system is working today, but whether it is becoming more fragile. It must not confuse calm with safety. The most dangerous moments in complex systems often occur when risk appears low because recent experience has encouraged overconfidence. Stability can breed instability. This is true in finance, supply chains, housing, climate, and politics.

The third lesson is that efficiency can become a source of fragility. Efficiency is valuable when it reduces waste, improves productivity, and expands access. But efficiency, defined too narrowly, can strip systems of the very buffers that allow them to withstand stress. A bank with minimal capital may be profitable until losses arrive. A supply chain with minimal inventory may be cheap until disruption occurs. A hospital with no surge capacity may be efficient until a pandemic. A household with no savings may manage until illness or job loss. A city with no affordable housing reserve may function until workers can no longer stay. An energy system dependent on one fuel or supplier may be cheap until a geopolitical shock.

A society that treats all redundancy as waste will eventually discover that some redundancy was insurance. Buffers are not always inefficient. They are stored resilience. Savings, capital requirements, inventories, public health capacity, affordable housing, unemployment insurance, diversified suppliers, energy reserves, public trust, and ecological protection all appear costly in normal times. Their value appears fully only when conditions change. To govern after equilibrium is to budget for resilience before catastrophe.

The fourth lesson is that distribution shapes system behavior. Inequality is not only a moral problem, nor only a statistical gap. It changes how the economy works. A dollar to a low-income household has different effects from a dollar to a billionaire. A household with savings responds differently to a shock than a household without them. A homeowner experiences inflation differently from a renter. A firm with pricing power responds differently to cost increases than a small supplier. A worker with bargaining power responds differently to labor demand than a worker trapped by debt, care obligations, or weak alternatives. A community with political influence shapes policy differently from one excluded from power.

Distribution affects demand, debt, trust, mobility, education, health, political stability, and crisis response. It determines who can wait and who must sell, who can move and who is trapped, who can pass costs forward and who absorbs them, who can recover and who cascades into hardship. A theory that treats aggregates as if distribution were secondary will repeatedly misunderstand instability. Averages can conceal the stress that produces crisis. The mean is not the system.

The fifth lesson is that power is endogenous to markets. Markets do not merely allocate resources among equal actors. They produce and reproduce power. Wealth buys influence. Market share creates bargaining strength. Data creates prediction. Platforms create dependency. Ownership creates control. Employer concentration weakens workers. Housing ownership shapes local politics. Financial institutions have become too important to fail. Fossil incumbents delay transition. Corporate lobbying shapes rules. Power then feeds back into markets by shaping law, regulation, taxation, competition, and public investment.

Equilibrium thinking often abstracts from power by imagining voluntary exchange among agents facing prices. Complexity economics brings power back into the center. It asks who sets the terms of exchange, who has alternatives, who controls infrastructure, who owns information, who can wait, who can lobby, who can exit, who can impose risk on others, and who can force the public to rescue private failure. Without power analysis, economics becomes a language for naturalizing politically constructed outcomes.

The sixth lesson is that institutions are not external to the economy. They are part of the economy. Property rights, contract law, bankruptcy rules, zoning codes, tax systems, labor law, monetary institutions, financial regulation, intellectual property, public education, healthcare systems, infrastructure, environmental rules, and political finance all shape market behavior. There is no pre-institutional market waiting to be freed. Markets are made through rules. The question is not whether government intervenes, but what structure of intervention already exists and whose interests it serves.

This insight changes the meaning of reform. Reform is not interference with a natural order. It is redesign of an existing order. Housing markets already reflect zoning, credit policy, tax preferences, school finance, land use, and infrastructure. Labor markets already reflect law, bargaining rules, immigration status, care policy, transportation, and employer power. Financial markets already reflect central banks, deposit insurance, regulation, tax law, disclosure rules, and public rescue expectations. Technology markets already reflect intellectual property, data rules, antitrust, public research, and procurement. Climate outcomes already reflect energy infrastructure, subsidies, regulations, land use, and global trade. The economy is always governed. The issue is whether it is governed consciously, democratically, and justly.

The seventh lesson is that legitimacy is economic infrastructure. Trust is not a soft variable outside the economy. It shapes compliance, investment, cooperation, expectations, and policy effectiveness. People pay taxes when they believe the system is broadly legitimate. Workers accept transition when they believe they will not be abandoned. Citizens accept anti-inflation measures when the burden is shared. Communities accept infrastructure when they are respected. Investors lend when institutions are credible. Households follow public health guidance when they trust authorities. Firms invest when rules are stable and fair.

Legitimacy can erode slowly and collapse quickly. Financial rescues that protect banks while households lose homes damage legitimacy. Inflation that raises essential costs while profits appear protected damages legitimacy. Housing systems that enrich owners while excluding the young damage legitimacy. Labor markets that praise essential workers while underpaying them damage legitimacy. Climate policies that burden the poor while the affluent continue excess emissions damage legitimacy. Technology systems that surveil, manipulate, and concentrate power damage legitimacy. Legitimacy is built by fairness, competence, honesty, and shared sacrifice. Without it, even technically sound policy can fail.

The eighth lesson is that narratives are causal. People act not only on prices and incentives, but on interpretations. If they believe inflation will persist, they behave differently. If they believe housing prices always rise, they bid differently. If they believe a bank is unsafe, they withdraw. If they believe the government is captured, they disengage. If they believe technology will replace them, they bargain differently. If they believe climate policy threatens their livelihoods, they resist. If they believe the future is closed, they may turn to anger or withdrawal.

Economic life is full of stories: the market is always right, hard work guarantees success, housing never falls, debt is harmless, government cannot work, technology will save us, climate action kills prosperity, inflation is always caused by one villain, financial innovation spreads risk, inequality reflects merit, austerity restores confidence. Some stories contain fragments of truth. Many become dangerous when made total. Public policy after equilibrium must tell better stories, stories that are truthful enough to handle complexity and clear enough to guide action.

The ninth lesson is that prevention is the highest form of economic intelligence. Modern politics often rewards crisis response more than crisis avoidance. Leaders are praised for rescuing banks, rebuilding after disasters, responding to shortages, or fighting inflation after it accelerates. Less visible is the value of bank capital that prevents failure, public health capacity that prevents spread, housing policy that prevents homelessness, climate adaptation that prevents loss, labor standards that prevent exploitation, antitrust that prevents domination, and social insurance that prevents household collapse. The avoided catastrophe rarely receives a monument.

Yet in a nonlinear world, prevention is everything. Once cascades begin, they are harder and more expensive to stop. Once inequality captures politics, reform becomes harder. Once housing scarcity hardens, incumbents become stronger. Once inflation expectations shift, adjustment becomes more painful. Once financial panic begins, an extraordinary rescue may be necessary. Once climate tipping points are crossed, restoration may be impossible. Prevention is not cautious in the timid sense. It is bold in the deepest sense because it refuses to wait for suffering to become undeniable.

The tenth lesson is that economics must become moral without becoming sentimental. Complexity does not eliminate tradeoffs. Resources are limited. Incentives matter. Poorly designed programs fail. Regulation can be captured. Public spending can be wasteful. Markets can solve problems that bureaucracies cannot. Prices communicate information.

Innovation requires risk. A serious moral economics must respect these realities. It must not confuse compassion with competence.

But competence without moral purpose is not enough. An economy can be efficient and cruel, productive and unjust, innovative and degrading, wealthy and unstable. The question is not only whether output grows, but whether the system supports dignity, security, capability, freedom, resilience, and democratic legitimacy. Economic governance after equilibrium must be morally explicit because every system distributes life chances. Neutrality is often a disguise for inherited power.

This book began with the end of simple economic explanations because the present crises reveal the inadequacy of single-cause thinking. Inflation is not only money, not only wages, not only corporate pricing, not only supply shocks, not only expectations. It is a feedback process. Debt is not only borrowing, nor only irresponsibility, nor only investment. It is a system of promises, leverage, and vulnerability. Inequality is not only a gap. It is a cumulative advantage machine. Housing is not only shelter, but also an investment. It is a system of scarcity that allocates opportunity. Labor is not only supply and demand. It is an adaptive network of human lives. Supply chains are not only logistics. They are fragile systems of interdependence. Financial markets are not only information processors. They are amplification systems. Technology is not only progress. It is disruptive feedback. Climate is not only an externality. It is the ecological context of all economic life.

What follows from this? First, economic policy must become more integrated. Inflation policy cannot belong only to central banks. It also involves energy, housing, supply chains, competition, wages, expectations, and fiscal choices. Housing policy cannot belong only to local zoning boards. It involves labor markets, schools, transportation, inequality, climate, finance, and democracy. Labor policy cannot be separated from care, health, housing, debt, technology, and regional development. Climate policy cannot be separated from industry, energy, housing, labor, finance, and global justice. Financial regulation cannot be separated from housing, debt, inequality, and public legitimacy.

Fragmented policy is one of the reasons complex problems persist. Each institution sees only part of the system. The central bank sees inflation. The housing agency sees subsidies. The labor department sees jobs. The energy regulator sees electricity. The financial supervisor sees balance sheets. The environmental agency sees emissions. The education department sees credentials. Each perspective matters, but the problem often lives between them. Governance after equilibrium requires coordination across domains. It requires institutions that can see systems rather than silos.

Second, policy must be adaptive. Because systems change, policy must learn. No design will be perfect at the start. Actors will respond. Conditions will shift. Technologies will evolve. Interest groups will adapt. Unintended consequences will appear. An adaptive state monitors outcomes, listens to affected communities, revises rules, and corrects errors. It does not treat revision as failure. In complex systems, refusal to revise is failure.

Adaptive policy should include automatic stabilizers, stress tests, early-warning indicators, public data, pilot programs, evaluation, sunset provisions, and institutional learning. It should build feedback into governance itself. If unemployment rises, support should expand. If credit grows dangerously, buffers should increase. If rents spike, assistance and supply responses should activate. If climate risk rises, adaptation should accelerate. If a policy is captured, it should be redesigned. The state must be capable of responding before the crisis becomes a collapse.

Third, policy must be distributionally aware from the beginning. It is not enough to maximize aggregate benefits and compensate later. Compensation often arrives late, poorly, or not at all. Communities damaged by trade, automation, climate policy, infrastructure, or financial crisis cannot be treated as afterthoughts. Distribution affects legitimacy and system performance. Policies should be designed around who is exposed, who has buffers, and who receives gains. This is not only justice. It is stability.

Fourth, governance must rebuild public capacity. Complex systems cannot be governed by slogans or by hollow institutions. Public agencies need expertise, data, staff, trust, and authority. They need the ability to procure, regulate, plan, coordinate, and implement. They need insulation from capture and accountability to democracy. The state must be neither omnipotent nor absent. It must be competent. A society that weakens public capacity and then complains that government fails is trapped in a self-fulfilling loop.

Fifth, markets must be designed to reward the right forms of behavior. If the tax code rewards speculation, speculation grows. If corporate governance rewards short-term share price, short-termism grows. If housing policy rewards scarcity, scarcity grows. If energy systems allow pollution without cost, emissions grow. If labor law weakens voice, insecurity grows. If financial regulation allows leverage, fragility grows. If technology markets reward data extraction and attention capture, manipulation grows. Incentives are moral instructions written into institutions. The economy learns what we reward.

Sixth, resilience must become a central measure of prosperity. A prosperous society is not one that maximizes output under ideal conditions while collapsing under stress. It is one that can absorb shocks without sacrificing the vulnerable, destroying trust, or abandoning the future. Resilience includes household savings, social insurance, affordable housing, public health, energy security, climate adaptation, bank capital, diversified supply chains, labor dignity, democratic legitimacy, and ecological stability. These are not luxuries. They are the foundations of durable prosperity.

Seventh, economic governance must become ecological. The economy cannot be governed as if nature were limitless. Climate stability, biodiversity, water, soil, air, and energy systems are not background conditions. They are the physical foundations of economic possibility. Ecological constraint does not mean the end of prosperity. It means the end of prosperity defined as unlimited extraction. The future requires clean energy, circular production, resilient agriculture, sustainable cities, climate adaptation, and a definition of flourishing that does not depend on endless material throughput.

Eighth, democracy must be strengthened, not bypassed. Complexity can tempt elites toward technocratic control, but this would be both morally wrong and practically fragile. Citizens must have a voice in the systems that shape their lives. Workers must have a voice in technological change. Tenants and communities must have a voice in housing policy. Vulnerable regions must have a voice in the climate transition. Consumers and users must have rights in digital systems. Democracy is not an obstacle to complex governance. It is a necessary source of legitimacy and knowledge.

At the same time, democracy must be capable of acting. Participation should not mean endless veto by incumbent interests. Local voice should not mean exclusionary zoning that harms regional affordability. Environmental review should not mean permanent obstruction of clean infrastructure. Public consultation should not mean capture by the most organized. Democratic governance must balance voice, expertise, urgency, rights, and the needs of those not yet represented, including future generations and excluded residents. The task is not simple, but it is essential.

What would economic governance after equilibrium look like in practice? It would not be a single program or ideology. It would be a governing orientation.

In inflation policy, it would combine monetary discipline with supply-side resilience, competition policy, housing reform, energy stability, targeted relief, and honest communication. It would ask not only whether demand is excessive, but which prices are rising, why they are rising, who can pass costs on, and who is falling behind.

In debt policy, it would distinguish productive borrowing from fragility-building leverage. It would regulate financial risk, protect households from predatory credit, provide humane bankruptcy, restructure unpayable obligations, and evaluate public debt by purpose, capacity, and resilience.

In inequality policy, it would redesign the cumulative advantage machine. It would invest early in children, strengthen public goods, build affordable housing, support labor power, tax accumulated advantage fairly, regulate monopoly, broaden ownership, and reform political finance.

In housing policy, it would treat shelter as social infrastructure. It would build enough homes, preserve affordability, protect tenants, reduce speculation, reform exclusionary zoning, use public land, integrate transit, address homelessness, and weaken the political power of scarcity.

In labor policy, it would treat workers as human beings embedded in networks of care, health, housing, debt, and dignity. It would pursue full employment, job quality, worker voice, wage floors, portable benefits, training, childcare, fair scheduling, and protection against monopsony and algorithmic domination.

In supply-chain policy, it would redefine efficiency to include resilience. It would map critical dependencies, diversify suppliers, maintain strategic reserves, support domestic and allied capacity where necessary, protect supply-chain workers, and build climate and cyber resilience.

In financial policy, it would discipline leverage, regulate shadow banking, prevent too-big-to-fail power, protect consumers, align finance with productive investment, respond to climate risk, and ensure that public rescue carries public obligations.

In technology policy, it would govern network effects, data power, artificial intelligence, platform dominance, surveillance, and labor disruption. It would invest in public research, digital public infrastructure, open standards, lifelong learning, worker voice, and broad sharing of productivity gains.

In climate and energy policy, it would accelerate clean energy, protect vulnerable households, support workers and regions in transition, invest in adaptation, reform land use, build resilient infrastructure, price and regulate emissions, and recognize ecological stability as the foundation of economic life.

In democratic policy, it would strengthen citizens' capacity to shape the economy through voting rights, campaign finance reform, transparency, public-interest regulation, civic institutions, labor voice, and accountable expertise. Economic governance after equilibrium must be democratic governance, or it will not endure.

The aim of these policies is not to eliminate uncertainty. That is impossible. Nor is it to eliminate markets, inequality, risk, failure, or change. Some inequality will exist. Some firms will fail. Some technologies will disrupt. Some risks must be taken. Some policies will disappoint. The goal is to create systems in which failure does not become catastrophe, success does not become domination, innovation does not become exclusion, efficiency does not become fragility, and growth does not destroy its foundations.

This is a more demanding standard than equilibrium. Equilibrium asks whether forces balance. Complexity asks whether systems are healthy. A system can be in balance and still be unjust. It can be stable and still be stagnant. It can be efficient and still be brittle. It can be profitable and still be extractive. It can grow and still erode the conditions of future life. Economic governance after equilibrium requires criteria beyond balance: resilience, fairness, adaptability, sustainability, dignity, and legitimacy.

The concept of the "good economy" must therefore be recovered. For too long, economic success has been measured through aggregates that conceal lived reality: gross domestic product, stock indexes, unemployment rates, inflation rates, productivity, debt ratios, and consumption. These indicators matter, but they are incomplete. A good economy is one in which people can live secure and meaningful lives. It provides decent work, affordable shelter, healthcare, education, care, mobility, clean air, stable communities, democratic voice, and protection from ruin. It develops human capability. It respects ecological limits. It shares risk fairly. It allows innovation without abandonment. It builds trust.

This is not utopian. It is practical. Societies that fail to provide these foundations face instability. Workers without dignity become resentful. Renters without hope become disillusioned. Young people without opportunity lose faith. Regions without investment decline. Households without buffers cascade into crisis. Citizens without trust reject institutions. Ecosystems without protection strike back through disaster. Democracies without economic legitimacy weaken. Moral failure becomes system failure.

The great error of simple economics was not that it valued markets. Markets deserve value. The error was imagining that markets could be abstracted from the moral and institutional conditions that make them useful. A market without fair rules becomes extraction. A market without competition becomes domination. A market without social insurance becomes fearful. A market without public goods becomes an inherited privilege. A market without ecological limits becomes destructive. A market without democratic accountability becomes private government. Markets are tools of civilization only when civilization governs them.

Economic governance after equilibrium is therefore not anti-market. It is anti-fatalism. It refuses to say that outcomes are natural when they are designed. It refuses to say that suffering is inevitable when it is produced by remediable feedback loops. It refuses to say that public purpose is impossible because systems are complex. Complexity does not absolve us of action. It requires wiser action.

The central ethical principle is systemic responsibility. Actors with greater power, greater knowledge, greater resources, and greater capacity to affect the system bear greater responsibility. A household trying to survive inflation does not bear the same responsibility as a corporation with pricing power. A worker with debt does not bear the same responsibility as a financial institution designing credit products. A renter excluded from local politics does not bear the same responsibility as homeowners protecting scarcity. A small country facing climate damage does not bear the same responsibility as wealthy industrialized nations that emitted for generations. Responsibility should follow power.

Systemic responsibility also applies to policymakers. Leaders are responsible not only for immediate decisions but for foreseeable feedback. If deregulation encourages leverage, a future crisis is not an accident. If zoning produces scarcity, unaffordability is not a mystery. If public goods are underfunded, inequality is not surprising. If climate action is delayed, disaster is not unforeseeable. If labor institutions are weakened, wage stagnation is not natural. If technology is allowed to scale without accountability, domination is to be expected. Complexity deepens responsibility because it reveals the pathways through which harm is produced.

This does not mean all consequences can be predicted. They cannot. It means that enough is often knowable to act more responsibly than we do. We know that debt and leverage can cascade. We know that inequality compounds. We know that housing scarcity enriches incumbents and excludes newcomers. We know that labor power shapes wages and dignity. We know that supply-chain efficiency without buffers creates fragility. We know that financial herding produces crises. We know that technology can concentrate power. We know that climate change creates nonlinear risks. We know that trust is easier to lose than to regain. The claim that society could not have known has become less credible.

A mature economics would teach citizens and leaders to see these patterns before they become disasters. It would make feedback loops visible. It would train attention to thresholds, buffers, distributions, and power. It would integrate history, psychology, institutions, ecology, and ethics. It would remain quantitative, but not merely quantitative. It would use models, but not worship them. It would respect markets, but not mythologize them. It would be understood that the economy is a human system embedded in the living world.

This book has used the language of complexity not to obscure economics, but to make it more honest. Complexity does not mean everything is too complicated to understand. It means the world must be understood through relationships. Inflation is related to supply chains, wages, energy, expectations, and power. Debt is related to asset prices, interest rates, confidence, and inequality. Inequality is related to housing, education, health, labor, wealth, and politics. Housing is related to zoning, credit, schools, local power, and family life. Labor is related to care, geography, technology, and bargaining power. Supply chains are related to efficiency, labor, climate, and geopolitics. Finance is related to belief, leverage, liquidity, and public rescue. Technology is related to ownership, data, labor, and democracy. Climate is related to energy, food, housing, finance, and survival. Complexity is not confusion. It is a connection.

A society that learns to think in connections will govern differently. It will not ask schools alone to solve poverty. It will not ask central banks alone to solve inflation. It will not ask training alone to solve labor insecurity. It will not ask markets alone to solve climate. It will not ask housing vouchers alone to solve scarcity. It will not ask individuals alone to solve debt. It will not ask technology alone to solve social failure. It will design systems in which policies reinforce rather than undermine one another.

This is the positive vision at the heart of the book. Feedback loops can be destructive, but they can also be constructive. Advantage can compound for the many, not only the few. Public investment can improve health, education, productivity, and trust. Affordable housing can increase mobility, family stability, access to labor, and wealth-building. Strong labor institutions can raise wages, demand, dignity, and democracy. Clean energy investment can reduce pollution, create jobs, stabilize energy costs, and protect the climate. Financial regulation can reduce crises, preserve trust, and direct capital to productive use. Technology can augment human capability if governed for inclusion. Social insurance can reduce fear and support adaptation. Democracy can create legitimacy when it delivers fairly.

The question is not whether systems will have feedback. They always will. The question is which feedback loops society chooses to cultivate. A vicious loop of inequality, insecurity, distrust, and extraction is not destiny. A virtuous loop of security, capability, investment, trust, and resilience is possible. It requires institutional design. It requires political will. It requires moral clarity. It requires the courage to challenge interests that benefit from harmful feedback.

The transition from equilibrium thinking to complexity governance will not be easy. Old ideas are deeply embedded. Many institutions are organized around narrow mandates. Powerful actors benefit from the current system. Citizens are often exhausted and distrustful. Media systems reward simplicity. Political polarization punishes nuance. Crises create urgency but also fear. Yet the difficulty of change does not make the old paradigm viable. The world is already nonlinear. The only question is whether our institutions will become intelligent enough to govern it.

Economic governance after equilibrium must also become intergenerational. Future generations cannot vote, lobby, purchase influence, or attend hearings. Yet they will inherit the debt, climate, infrastructure, institutions, technologies, and inequalities we leave behind. An equilibrium model focused on present exchange struggles to represent them. Complexity thinking makes them visible because it sees time as causal. Today's emissions, underinvestment, debt structures, housing shortages, educational inequalities, and institutional choices become tomorrow's constraints. Intergenerational justice is not sentiment. It is systems realism extended through time.

A society worthy of the future must ask whether its prosperity is borrowed or built. Borrowed prosperity consumes natural systems, inflates asset values, relies on household debt, underpays workers, neglects infrastructure, weakens public goods, and celebrates growth while fragility accumulates. Built prosperity invests in people, ecosystems, institutions, infrastructure, science, care, housing, and resilience. Borrowed prosperity feels abundant until the bill arrives. Built prosperity may require discipline, but it endures.

The distinction between borrowed and built prosperity is a useful final frame for the book. Inflation can reveal when supply systems and trust are strained. Debt can reveal when consumption or asset prices have been financed by future claims rather than productive capacity. Inequality can reveal when opportunity has been replaced by inheritance and compounding advantage. Housing scarcity can reveal when wealth accumulation has defeated shelter. Labor insecurity can reveal when profit has been built on weak bargaining power. Supply-chain fragility can reveal when cheapness has been built on the absence of buffers. Financial crises can reveal when returns have been built on leverage. Technological disruption can reveal when innovation has been built without shared governance. Climate change reveals when growth has been built on ecological debt.

Economic governance after equilibrium must shift society from borrowed prosperity to built prosperity. Built prosperity is not anti-growth. It is growth with foundations. It is productivity rooted in human capability. It is innovation linked to broad benefit. It is finance anchored in productive investment. It is housing as shelter before speculation. It is labor with dignity before cost. It is energy abundance without planetary destabilization. It is public policy designed for resilience. It is a democracy capable of correction.

This vision also requires a new language of freedom. Market ideology often defines freedom as choice within markets. Choice matters. Consumer choice, occupational choice, entrepreneurial choice, investment choice, and mobility are real freedoms. But choice without capacity is thin. A person choosing among unaffordable apartments is not meaningfully free in housing. A worker choosing between unsafe work and eviction is not meaningfully free in the labor market. A patient choosing between debt and untreated illness is not meaningfully free in healthcare. A student choosing between no degree and crushing debt is not meaningfully free in education. A community choosing between pollution and job loss is not meaningfully free in development.

Real freedom requires capability, security, voice, and alternatives. It requires public goods and fair markets. It requires protection from domination by employers, landlords, lenders, monopolies, platforms, and poverty. It requires ecological stability because there is no freedom in disaster. Economic governance after equilibrium should therefore be understood as freedom-building governance. It builds the conditions under which people can act, plan, create, care, dissent, move, belong, and flourish.

This is also a richer vision of responsibility. People should be responsible for their choices, but society must be responsible for the choice architecture it creates. It is unjust to demand responsibility from individuals while designing systems that make responsible action impossible or excessively costly. Telling families to save while rents consume income, telling workers to retrain while childcare is unaffordable, telling students to invest in education while debt is predatory, telling consumers to choose green while infrastructure is fossil-dependent, telling citizens to trust institutions while policy favors the powerful- these are not serious forms of responsibility. They are evasions.

A serious society asks what conditions make responsibility possible. It builds wages that allow saving, schools that develop talent, healthcare that protects mobility, housing that provides stability, transportation that connects opportunity, credit that supports rather than traps, technology that augments rather than manipulates, and climate policy that gives people real alternatives. Personal responsibility and social responsibility are not enemies. They are complements. Individuals can act responsibly when institutions support responsible action.

The same applies to firms. Businesses are essential creators of value. They innovate, employ, produce, invest, and organize. A healthy economy needs profitable firms. But firms also operate within public systems and create public consequences. They benefit from law, infrastructure, education, research, stability, and public rescue in crisis. They should therefore be expected to honor obligations to workers, consumers, communities, competitors, ecosystems, and democracy. Corporate responsibility cannot be reduced to voluntary philanthropy. It must be built into governance, law, markets, and accountability.

Shareholder value, when taken to an absolute, narrows the purpose of the firm. It encourages the firm to see wages, taxes, regulation, resilience, and environmental responsibility as costs to be minimized. But a firm is a social institution. It organizes human labor, uses public infrastructure, affects communities, shapes markets, and influences politics. Economic governance after equilibrium must recover the firm as a public actor, not in the sense that every firm is state-owned, but in the sense that corporate power carries social obligation.

The same is true of finance. Finance should serve the future by allocating capital to productive and socially useful purposes. When it becomes self-referential, extracting returns from leverage, speculation, fees, and asset inflation, it detaches from the real economy. The test of finance should not be only profitability. It should be about whether finance supports broad investment in innovation, housing, infrastructure, clean energy, small businesses, and resilience without creating systemic risk. Financial markets must be judged by the future they fund.

Technology must be judged similarly. A technology is not good merely because it is new, scalable, or profitable. It is good if it expands human capability, supports dignity, protects privacy, distributes benefits, strengthens knowledge, reduces harm, and respects democratic values. The governance of technology will be one of the central tasks of the coming century because technological feedback can transform society faster than law and culture can adapt. The lesson of this book is that scale changes moral responsibility. A small tool becomes a public concern when it becomes infrastructure.

Climate policy offers the most urgent example of post-equilibrium governance because ecological systems do not respond to ideology. The atmosphere does not care whether emissions were profitable. Oceans do not care whether the delay was politically convenient. Fires do not care whether markets priced risk correctly. Climate change is the great refutation of economics without biophysical humility. It forces the discipline to admit that some constraints are physical, not negotiable. It also offers an opportunity to rebuild prosperity on cleaner, fairer, more resilient foundations.

The work ahead is not only analytical. It is civic. Citizens must demand institutions capable of foresight. They must resist false simplicity. They must ask who benefits from narratives that deny complexity. They must judge leaders not only by promises, but by whether their policies alter harmful feedback loops. They must value prevention. They must support public capacity. They must insist that markets serve democratic ends. They must recognize that freedom, fairness, and resilience are mutually reinforcing.

There is a danger that complexity becomes overwhelming. The problems are interconnected, and the scale is large. But despair is not a serious response. Complexity does not mean everything is impossible. It means leverage points matter. A bank capital rule can reduce crisis risk. A zoning reform can unlock housing. A child allowance can reduce poverty and stress. A union law can strengthen worker voice. A clean energy standard can shift investment. A public health system can prevent catastrophe. A tax reform can reduce wealth concentration. A data portability rule can increase competition. A transmission line can unlock renewable power. A debt restructuring can restore possibility. A policy does not have to solve everything to change the trajectory.

The art is to identify interventions that change feedback. Some policies relieve suffering. Some change incentives. Some build capacity. Some redistribute power. Some create new institutions. Some prevent cascades. The best policies often do several at once. Affordable housing relieves rent burden, increases labor mobility, reduces homelessness, supports family stability, and weakens scarcity politics. Healthcare security protects health, reduces debt, improves labor mobility, and supports entrepreneurship. Clean energy investment reduces emissions, creates jobs, stabilizes energy costs, and improves air quality. Worker voice raises wages, improves dignity, strengthens democracy, and distributes productivity. Public education develops capability, reduces inequality, and supports innovation. These are systemic policies because they create positive feedback.

The conclusion of this book is therefore hopeful, but not naive. The same nonlinear dynamics that create crisis can create renewal. Feedback loops can reinforce both justice and injustice. Cumulative advantage can be democratized. Trust can be rebuilt through competent and fair institutions. Technology can broaden capability. Finance can fund transformation. Energy systems can become clean and abundant. Labor markets can provide dignity. Housing can become shelter again. Supply chains can become resilient. Public policy can learn. Democracy can govern complexity.

But none of this will happen automatically. There is no invisible hand that guarantees humane outcomes. There is no equilibrium toward justice. There is no natural tendency for concentrated power to dissolve itself. There is no market mechanism that ensures future generations are protected. There is no technological law that distributes gains fairly. There is no financial price that fully captures ecological loss. There is no shortcut around politics. The future must be designed, contested, built, corrected, and sustained.

Economic governance after equilibrium begins with the recognition that the economy is a moral system because it organizes human dependence. We depend on one another for food, shelter, work, care, credit, knowledge, energy, infrastructure, and trust. Markets coordinate some of this dependence. Governments structure it. Communities give it meaning. Ecosystems make it possible. When dependence is well organized, people experience it as freedom because institutions provide security, opportunity, and a voice. When dependence is organized poorly, people experience it as domination, precarity, debt, exclusion, and fear.

The purpose of economics should be to help societies organize dependence in ways that support human flourishing. That purpose is larger than efficiency, though efficiency matters. It is larger than growth, though growth can matter. It is larger than price stability, though price stability matters. It is larger than innovation, though innovation matters. The end is a society in which people can live with dignity, develop their capabilities, care for one another, participate in democracy, and pass on a livable world.

This is why the book's subtitle speaks of inequality, inflation, debt, markets, and crisis within a complexity economics inquiry. These are not separate problems. They are windows into the same reality: the economy is a dynamic system whose outcomes depend on feedback, power, institutions, and values. To understand any one problem well, we must understand its connections. To govern any one problem wisely, we must govern the system that sustains it.

The old equilibrium imagination gave economics a language of balance. The new complexity imagination must give economics a language of motion, fragility, adaptation, and responsibility. Balance is not enough. A society can be balanced by low levels of trust, high inequality, unaffordable housing, weak labor, concentrated finance, fragile supply chains, and rising ecological risk. Such a society is not healthy. It is merely temporarily organized around dysfunction. The goal is not equilibrium for its own sake. The goal is a just and resilient dynamic order.

A just and resilient order will never be final. Economic life will continue to change. New technologies will emerge. New crises will arrive. New conflicts will arise. New forms of power will develop. New ecological realities will press upon society. Governance after equilibrium is not a blueprint for permanent harmony. It is a method of democratic adaptation. It is the willingness to keep redesigning institutions in light of evidence, justice, and changing conditions.

This requires a civic virtue rarely celebrated in economic life: patience with complexity combined with urgency of action. We must be patient enough to understand systems and urgent enough to intervene before thresholds are crossed. We must be humble enough to revise and courageous enough to act. We must be realistic about incentives and uncompromising about dignity. We must be attentive to numbers and attentive to stories. We must be disciplined with resources and generous in building human capability. We must be open to innovation and alert to domination. We must respect markets and refuse to worship them.

The economy of the twenty-first century will test whether democracies can govern nonlinear systems without surrendering to authoritarian command or market fatalism. Authoritarianism promises control but suppresses voice, truth, and accountability. Market fatalism promises freedom but often abandons people to power they cannot contest. Democratic complexity governance offers a harder path: shared intelligence, contested values, institutional learning, public capacity, and moral responsibility. It is slower than command and more demanding than fatalism, but it is the only path worthy of free people.

The crises of our age are warnings. Inflation warns that price stability depends on systems of supply, trust, power, and policy. Debt warns that promises can become fragile. Inequality warns that advantage compounds unless institutions intervene. Housing warns that shelter cannot be left to the politics of scarcity. Labor warns that work without dignity destabilizes society. Supply chains warn that efficiency without buffers is brittle. Financial markets warn that belief, leverage, and liquidity can cascade. Technology warns that innovation without governance can concentrate power. Climate warns that the economy is embedded in the living Earth. Public policy warns that simple levers cannot govern complex systems.

The warning is severe, but it is not hopeless. Warnings are gifts if heeded. They tell us where systems are failing before failure becomes final. They give us the chance to change direction. The task now is to build an economics that can hear them.

The final claim of this book is simple: economic governance after equilibrium must be governance for resilience, justice, and human flourishing in a nonlinear world. It must be understood that systems amplify. It must protect those without buffers. It must discipline concentrated power. It must build public goods. It must align markets with moral purpose. It must respect ecological limits. It must strengthen democracy. It must learn continuously. It must act before the crisis hardens into collapse.

The end of simple economic explanations is not the end of economics. It is the beginning of economic maturity. It invites us to leave behind the comfort of mechanical metaphors and enter the harder, richer, more truthful world of living systems. In that world, nothing is isolated, nothing is purely technical, and nothing important is morally neutral. The economy is made and remade through choices, rules, expectations, institutions, and power. It can be redesigned.

A nonlinear world is dangerous because harm can compound. It is also hopeful because healing can compound. Trust can build trust. Fairness can build legitimacy. Public investment can build capability. Clean energy can build resilience. Worker voice can build democracy. Affordable housing can build stability. Financial discipline can build confidence. Technology, governed by people, can build shared intelligence. The future will be shaped by the loops we choose.

Equilibrium promised that the economy would find balance. Complexity teaches that balance is not given. It must be built, maintained, revised, and defended. The work of economics, then, is not to reassure us that the system will correct itself. It is to help us understand how systems move, how they fail, how they heal, and how they can be governed in service of life.

That is the task before us. That is the task of economic governance after equilibrium.

# REFERENCES

Arthur, W. Brian. *Complexity and the Economy*. Oxford: Oxford University Press, 2015.

Beinhocker, Eric D. *The Origin of Wealth: Evolution, Complexity, and the Radical Remaking of Economics*. Boston: Harvard Business School Press, 2006.

Delli Gatti, Domenico, Saul Desiderio, Edoardo Gaffeo, Pasquale Cirillo, and Mauro Gallegati. *Macroeconomics from the Bottom-Up*. Milan: Springer, 2011.

Farmer, J. Doyne. *Making Sense of Chaos: A Better Economics for a Better World.* New Haven, CT: Yale University Press, 2024.

Fisher, Irving. "The Debt-Deflation Theory of Great Depressions." *Econometrica* 1, no. 4 (1933): 337–357.

Haldane, Andrew G., and Robert M. May. "Systemic Risk in Banking Ecosystems." *Nature* 469, no. 7330 (2011): 351–355.

Kirman, Alan. *Complex Economics: Individual and Collective Rationality*. London: Routledge, 2010.

Minsky, Hyman P. *Stabilizing an Unstable Economy*. New York: McGraw-Hill, 2008.

Piketty, Thomas. *Capital in the Twenty-First Century*. Translated by Arthur Goldhammer. Cambridge, MA: Belknap Press of Harvard University Press, 2014.

Weber, Isabella M., and Evan Wasner. "Sellers' Inflation, Profits and Conflict: Why Can Large Firms Hike Prices in an Emergency?" *Review of Keynesian Economics* 11, no. 2 (2023): 183–213.

# About the Author

Lawrence R. Kunkel is a Game Theory and Complexity Economist. Kunkel's work embodies what might be called an interdisciplinary systems humanism: a fusion of complexity economics, political philosophy, social psychology, chaos theory, and ethical systems into a unified framework for understanding and improving human prosperity and freedom. Mr. Kunkel did his graduate work in the Division of Social Sciences at the University of Chicago (A.M., 1981), where he had matriculation privileges in the Graduate School of Economics, the Booth School of Business, the Law School, and the Committee on Social Thought. Mr. Kunkel served as the research assistant to George J. Stigler, the Charles R. Walgreen Distinguished Service Professor of Economics and the 1982 Nobel Laureate in Economics. He also studied under two other Nobel Prize Winners in Economics, Robert Lucas (1995) and Gary Becker (1992). Kunkel is the author of *The Moral Ecology of Collapse: Essays on Inequality, Complexity, and the Instability of Democratic Societies*, and *Democracy at the Edge of Chaos: Designing Institutions for Nonlinear Times.*